70104024

GENRE STUDIES AROUND THE GLOBE

BEYOND THE THREE TRADITIONS

Edited by

Natasha Artemeva and Aviva Freedman

Order this book online at www.trafford.com
or email orders@trafford.com

Most Trafford titles are also available at major online book retailers.

© Copyright 2015 Natasha Artemeva and Aviva Freedman.
All rights reserved. No part of this publication may be reproduced, stored in a retrieval
system, or transmitted, in any form or by any means, electronic, mechanical, photocopying,
recording, or otherwise, without the written prior permission of the author.

Print information available on the last page.

ISBN: 978-1-4907-6631-7 (sc)
ISBN: 978-1-4907-6633-1 (hc)
ISBN: 978-1-4907-6632-4 (e)

Library of Congress Control Number: 2015917436

Because of the dynamic nature of the Internet, any web addresses or links contained in
this book may have changed since publication and may no longer be valid. The views
expressed in this work are solely those of the author and do not necessarily reflect the
views of the publisher, and the publisher hereby disclaims any responsibility for them.

Any people depicted in stock imagery provided by Thinkstock are models,
and such images are being used for illustrative purposes only.
Certain stock imagery © Thinkstock.

Trafford rev. 03/04/2016

www.trafford.com

North America & international
toll-free: 1 888 232 4444 (USA & Canada)
fax: 812 355 4082

Remembering Pete Medway—colleague, teacher, friend

Chapter 1, "A text and its commentaies: Toward a reception history of 'Genre in three traditions' (Hyon, 1996)" by John Swales originally appeared in *Ibérica*, *24*, 103-116 (2012) by the European Association of Languages for Specific Purposes (AELFE). It is reproduced here by permission of the editor.

Chapter 2, "Critical reflections on genre analysis" by Vijay Bhatia originally appeared in *Ibérica*, *24*, 14-28 (2012) by the European Association of Languages for Specific Purposes (AELFE). It is reproduced here by permission of the editor.

Chapter 18, "The traps and trappings of genre theory" by Anne Freadman originally appeared in *Applied Linguistics*, *33*(5), 544-563 (2012) by Oxford University Press. It is reproduced here by permission of Oxford University Press.

Contents

Acknowledgements

This publication was supported through funding provided by the Social Sciences and Humanities Research Council (SSHRC) of Canada and by Carleton University, Ottawa, Canada. We would like to thank Janna Klostermann for her invaluable contribution to the preparation of this volume and Saira Fitzgerald for her editorial assistance.

Contributors

Natasha Artemeva is Associate Professor at Carleton University, Canada. She was a co-organizer of the international conference on genre studies "Genre 2012: Rethinking Genre 20 Years Later" (with Graham Smart and Jaffer Sheyholislami). She is a co-editor of *Rhetorical Genre Studies and Beyond* (with Aviva Freedman, 2006) and *Writing in Knowledge Societies* (with Doreen Starke-Meyerring, Anthony Paré, Miriam Horne, and Larissa Yousoubova, 2011). Her research interests lie in the areas of genre studies, theories of learning, and social theories of practice.

Anis Bawarshi is Professor of English at the University of Washington, USA. He is Co-Managing Editor of *Composition Forum*. His books include *Genre: An Introduction to History, Theory, Research, and Pedagogy* (with Mary Jo Reiff); *Genre and the Invention of the Writer*; *Scenes of Writing: Strategies for Composing with Genres* (with Amy Devitt and Mary Jo Reiff); and *Ecologies of Writing Programs* (coedited with Mary Jo Reiff, Michelle Ballif, and Christian Weisser). *Genre and the Performance of Publics* (coedited with Mary Jo Reiff) is forthcoming from Utah State UP.

Charles Bazerman, Professor of Education at the University of California Santa Barbara, USA, is Chair of the International Society for the Advancement of Writing Research. His books include *A Rhetoric of Literate Action*, *A Theory of Literate Action*, *The Languages of Edison's Light*, *Constructing Experience*, *Shaping Written Knowledge*, *The Informed Writer*, *The Handbook of Research on Writing*, *Traditions of Writing Research*, *Genre in a Changing World*, and *What Writing Does and How It Does It*.

Vijay Bhatia retired as Professor from the Department of English, City University of Hong Kong. His research interests include Critical Genre Analysis, academic and professional discourses; ESP and Professional Communication. Two of his monographs, *Analysing Genre: Language Use in Professional Settings* and *Worlds of Written Discourse: A Genre-based View*, are widely used in genre theory and practice. His third monograph on Critical Genre Analysis is to be published by Routledge in early 2016.

Vera Lúcia Lopes Cristovão is an Associate Professor and a member of the Language Studies Post-graduation Program at Londrina State University (UEL) in Brazil, the leader of the research group called Language and Education and a researcher for Brazilian National Council for Scientific and Technological Development (CNPq). Research interests: genres, writing studies, teacher education and ELT.

Amy J. Devitt, Professor of English and Chancellors Club Teaching Professor at the University of Kansas, USA, teaches courses in rhetoric and composition and English language studies and has administered the first-year writing and writing-across-the-curriculum programs. Her publications include over twenty articles and chapters and three books: *Writing Genres* (2004), *Scenes of Writing: Strategies for Composing with Genres* (with Anis Bawarshi and Mary Jo Reiff, 2003), and *Standardizing Written English: Diffusion in the Case of Scotland 1520-1659* (1989).

Jan Engberg is Professor of Knowledge Communication at the Department of Business Communication, School of Business and Social Sciences, at the University of Aarhus, Denmark. His research interests include the study of texts and genres in the academic field, cognitive aspects of domain specific discourse and the relations between specialised knowledge and text formulation as well as basic aspects of communication in domain-specific settings. Furthermore, he is co-editor of the international journal *Fachsprache* and member of the editorial or advisory boards of a substantial number of international scholarly journals.

Anne Freadman is Principal Professorial Fellow in French in the School of Languages and Linguistics, University of Melbourne, Australia. Over several decades, she has published many papers on genre, both descriptive and theoretical, and has applied the problematics of genre in such books as *The Machinery of Talk: Charles Peirce and the Sign Hypothesis* (Stanford UP, 2004), and *The livres-souvenirs of Colette: Genre and the Telling of Time* (Legenda, 2012). She is currently engaged on a book on diaries written by Jews under the Nazi occupation of France.

Aviva Freedman is Professor Emeritus in the School of Linguistics and Language Studies at Carleton University, Canada. Her scholarly career has been marked by an abiding interest in written language – its acquisition, development, and facilitation. In the late 80's, she seized on Miller's discussion of language as social action in response to Schutz' notion of socially constructed typified situations. Rhetorical Genre Studies consequently provided the context for her subsequent research and scholarship, which have issued in books, collections, essays, and research articles.

Janet Giltrow is Professor in the Department of English at the University of British Columbia, Canada. Taking rhetorical and linguistic approaches to discourse studies, she has published extensively on literary and non-literary stylistics; genre theory; ideologies of language; and academic writing, including two textbooks (*Academic Writing: Writing and Reading in the Disciplines*, 3rd ed. 2001; *Introduction to Academic Writing* 3rd ed. 2014). Her most recent publications include *Genres in the Internet*, ed. with D. Stein 2009, "Genre as Difference: the sociality of syntactic variation" (2010), "'Curious Gentlemen': The Hudson's Bay Company and the Royal Society, Business and Science in the Eighteenth Century" (2012), "The Pragmatics of Genre on the Internet" (2013).

Ann M. Johns, Professor Emerita, San Diego State University (USA) has been teaching academic reading and writing to, and conducting research on, first year university and secondary students for her entire professional life. Her publications include single-authored and edited books and more than 70 book chapters and articles on genre, teaching writing, and ESP, most of which involve novice or ESL/EFL students. She has also consulted and made conference presentations in 32 countries.

Martin Luginbühl is Full Professor for German Linguistics at the University of Neuchâtel, Switzerland. His current research focuses on media linguistics, genre studies, conversational analysis and language and culture. In 2014 he published the book *Medienkultur und Medienlinguistik* [*Media Culture and Media Linguistics*] (Peter Lang Publishers), a genre based comparison of the American "CBS Evening News" and the Swiss TV news show "Tagesschau" from the 1950s until today.

Carmen Daniela Maier, PhD, is Associate Professor and member of the Knowledge Communication Research Group and of the Center of Corporate Communication at the Department of Business Communication, School of Business and Social Sciences, Aarhus University, Denmark. Among her latest publications are the chapters "A multimodal analysis of the environment beat" in *Critical Multimodal Studies* (Routledge, 2013) and "Stretching the multimodal boundaries of professional communication" in *The Routledge Handbook of Language and Professional Communication* (Routledge, 2014). Together with Norris, she is the co-editor of *Interactions, Images and Texts: A Reader in Multimodality* (De Gruyter, 2014). Her research areas include multimodal discourse analysis, social semiotics, knowledge communication, environmental communication and corporate communication.

J. R. Martin is Professor of Linguistics at the University of Sydney, Australia. His research interests include systemic theory, functional grammar, discourse semantics, register, genre, multimodality and critical discourse analysis, focusing on English and Tagálog. Eight volumes of his collected papers (edited by Wang Zhenhua, Shanghai Jiao Tong University Press) have recently been published in China. Professor Martin was elected a fellow of the Australian Academy of the Humanities in 1998. In April 2014 Shanghai Jiao Tong University opened its Martin Centre for Appliable Linguistics.

Carolyn R. Miller is SAS Institute Distinguished Professor of Rhetoric and Technical Communication, Emerita, at North Carolina State

University, USA, where she taught from 1973 to 2015. She received her Ph.D. in Communication and Rhetoric from Rensselaer Polytechnic Institute, New York. Her professional service includes terms as president of the Rhetoric Society of America and editor of its journal, *Rhetoric Society Quarterly*. She is a Fellow of the Rhetoric Society of America and a Fellow of the Association of Teachers of Technical Writing.

Giovanni Parodi is presently Head of the Graduate School of Linguistics at Pontificia Universidad Católica de Valparaíso, Chile, and Editor in Chief of *Revista Signos. Estudios de Lingüística*. His fields of research are text linguistics, discourse psycholinguistics (reading comprehension and written production processes), and corpus linguistics. Currently he is conducting research in specialized academic/professional written discourse, discourse genres and multimodality. In his latest research line, he is using eye tracking technology. His publications include more than 60 articles in Spanish and English journals and several books (as author, editor and co-editor).

David Rose is Director of the Reading to Learn program, an international literacy program that trains teachers across school and university sectors, in Australia, Africa, Asia and western Europe (www.readingtolearn.com.au). He is an Honorary Associate of the University of Sydney, Australia. Dr Rose's research is focused on providing teachers with the tools to enable all students to read and write successfully. His work has been particularly concerned with Indigenous Australian communities, languages and education programs.

Natalia Rulyova is Lecturer in Russian in the Department of Modern Languages at the University of Birmingham, UK. She co-authored (with S. Hutchings) *Television and Culture in Putin's Russia: Remote Control* (London and New York: Routledge, 2009). She also co-edited (with B. Beumers and S. Hutchings, eds) *Globalisation, Freedom and the media after Communism: The past as future* (London and New York: Routledge), (with B. Beumers and S. Hutchings, eds) *The Post-Soviet Russian Media: Conflicting Signals* (London and New York: Routledge, 2009) and (with J.

Morris and V. Strukov, eds) Special Issue, *New Media in New Europe-Asia, Europe-Asia Studies* (Volume 64, Issue 8, 2012).

John M. Swales is Professor Emeritus of Linguistics at the University of Michigan, where he was also Director of the English Language Institute from 1985 to 2001. His books include *Genre Analysis: English in Academic and Research Settings* (Cambridge University Press, 1990), *Research Genres: Explorations and Applications* (Cambridge University Press, 2004), and his memoir *Incidents in an Educational Life* (University of Michigan Press, 2011). Although officially retired, he continues to serve on dissertation committees, undertake research projects, and write advanced EAP teaching materials.

Christine Tardy is an Associate Professor of English at the University of Arizona, USA, where she teaches courses in applied linguistics, TESOL, and writing studies. Her research focuses on genre theory and practice, second language writing, academic writing instruction, and the policies and politics of English. Her work appears in journals such as *English for Specific Purposes, Journal of Second Language Writing, Research in the Teaching of English,* and *Written Communication,* and numerous edited books.

Orlando Vian Jr is a Professor of English in the Department of Modern Foreign Languages and Literatures and a researcher in the Post-Graduate Program in Language Studies at the Universidade Federal do Rio Grande do Norte, Brazil, where he teaches courses in Applied Linguistics, ESP, Systemic Functional Linguistics and English language teacher education. His research interests include genre studies, English for Specific Purposes, English language teacher education and Systemic Functional Linguistics studies applied to Brazilian Portuguese.

Introduction

Everything is Illuminated, or Genre beyond the Three Traditions

Natasha Artemeva and Aviva Freedman

Carleton University (Canada)

Sometimes — if you're lucky and if the light is right — a new element/construct/concept is introduced into your field of vision, which suddenly alters the way everything else is, and can be, seen. For me, such a moment came when I serendipitously and almost simultaneously read Carolyn Miller's "Genre as Social Action" and heard Chuck Bazerman describe his research-in-progress at the 4C's[1].

To that point, Susanne Langer's insights about the incessant and powerful human drive to discover and create patterns out of ambient experience had shaped my thinking about composing and its teaching. Vygotksy's emphasis on the social had enriched this. But it was Miller and Bazerman who allowed me to see what I had been staring at for years without being able to formulate or articulate my emerging understanding. Their notion of genre clarified for me the many ways in which textual patternings (rhetorically and socially invented) interact dynamically with the social construal of situation-types (or humanly constructed experiential regularities).

Suddenly, everything was illuminated.

It gives me great pleasure to know that the insight that so captured my imagination and that of my colleague, Pete Medway, in the late 80's and early 90's, leading to our joint research and to the hosting of our conference here at Carleton, has been able to continue to fuel new research, new thinking, new directions.

Aviva Freedman (2012)

The framing quotation was written by one of the editors of this volume in anticipation of the conference, "Genre 2012: Rethinking genre twenty years later," [2] one of whose outcomes was the collection of essays that follows. The conference brought together scholars and researchers from a far wider range of international and disciplinary settings than had been assembled in North America before. The essays in this volume represent a range of contemporary perspectives on the notion of genre—not to speak of research into genres-in-action and theoretic reformulations as well as pedagogic reconceptualizations in the light of these understandings.

In 1996, Hyon published a much-cited article describing three major Anglophone traditions in genre studies: (a) English for Specific Purposes (ESP), (b) North American/New Rhetoric genre theory, more recently known as Rhetorical Genre Studies (RGS), and (c) the Sydney School of genre. For some time, Hyon's "three traditions" were considered a useful classification of contemporary approaches to genre studies (Hyland, 2003; Martin, this volume; Swales, this volume). However, in the past few years, some authors (e.g., Johns, 2011; Swales, 2009; Tardy, 2012) started to observe that the relationships among the traditions described by Hyon appeared to be in flux, with some traditions moving closer toward each other. This is not to say that distinctions among the genre traditions completely disappeared: as Hyland (2003) commented, the three approaches "clearly differ in the emphasis they give to text or context, the research methods they employ, and the types of pedagogies they encourage" (p. 22). Thus, for example, Martin (this volume) notes that SFL shares few commonalities with ESP and "fewer still with Rhetorical Genre Studies" (p.68). Nevertheless, as Swales (2009) put it, distinct traditions in genre studies, identified by Hyon, "coalesced somewhat, with the result that the divisions among the . . . traditions have become much less sharp" (p. 4). For example, a recent combination of ESP and RGS appears to be fruitful in genre research and pedagogy (cf. Artemeva & Myles, 2015; Johns, this volume; Tardy, 2012).

As well, it became clear that in addition to the three traditions described by Hyon, several other approaches to genre studies developed in different countries and in different languages (e.g., Bawarshi & Reiff, 2010; Bazerman, Bonini, & Figueiredo, 2009). For example, such approaches developed in South America in Spanish and Portuguese (see Bazerman et al, 2009; Cristovão, this volume; Motta-Roth & Heberle, 2015; Parodi, this volume; Vian Jr., this volume); in Europe in different languages, including English (see Cap & Okulska, 2013; Engberg & Maier, this volume; Luginbül, this volume; Rulyova, this volume), and in other parts of the world. What distinguished the more recently developed approaches from the three schools of genre identified by Hyon (1996) was the creative combination of theoretical perspectives they drew from (see Swales, this volume; Cristovão, this volume; Parodi, this volume; Vian Jr., this volume).

In other words, by the end of the first decade of the 21st century, the time was ripe for another North American scholarly gathering of the representatives of multiple genre traditions that would allow for a lively discussion of current trends in genre studies around the globe. The "Genre 2012" conference, co-organized by Natasha Artemeva, Graham Smart, and Jaffer Sheyholislami and held at Carleton University in Ottawa, Canada, provided a forum for such a discussion. The conference also marked the 20th anniversary of the international colloquium "Rethinking Genre," held at Carleton University in 1992. Two often cited collections edited by the colloquium co-organizers, Aviva Freedman and Peter Medway, *Genre and the New Rhetoric* and *Learning and Teaching Genre*, were published in 1994 as the outcome of the genre colloquium. Several genre conferences, held in Canada and in different parts of the world, followed, as did edited collections on genre studies (to name just a few, Artemeva & Freedman, 2006; Bazerman et al., 2009; Coe, Lingard & Teslenko, 2002).

Our volume continues the tradition of such publications and contributes to it by bringing under one cover genre research from different countries, languages, traditions, and approaches. Our objective in putting together this collection was to demonstrate current trends in international genre research and pedagogy.

In 2012, Tardy observed that regardless of the differences, all three Anglophone traditions in genre studies "define genre as social practice" (p. 167). All contributors to this volume appear to subscribe to this view; however, the approaches presented here vary "in the extent to which" they privilege "*practice . . . above text*" (Lillis & Scott, 2007, p. 10, emphasis in the original). Lillis and Scott warn us against too much reliance on "the 'textual bias' (Horner, 1999) – that is the treatment of language/writing as solely or primarily a linguistic object" (p. 10) (cf. Swales, this volume). This bias, they argue, may lead "to pedagogy and research" that take "text as the object of study which in turn leads to policy and pedagogical 'solutions' which are overwhelmingly textual in nature" (pp. 10-11). Alternatively, by seeing "genre as social practice" (Tardy, 2012, p. 167), educators and researchers alike move beyond perceiving recurrent patterns of discourse "as template-like structures that simply happen to look the way they do," which leads them to interpreting and treating genres as "products of the practices and values of a social group" (p. 167). This view of genre may result in very different policies and pedagogies.

Some of the approaches presented in this collection appear to fit in seamlessly into the three traditions, as established by Hyon (1996), some straddle the traditions, and some present other distinctive orientations, including combinations of several theoretical frameworks. The volume starts by discussing recent thinking developed within the three Anglophone schools of genre and within Brazilian and Chilean approaches. The first two chapters are by well-known ESP researchers, Swales and Bhatia. Both chapters are based on their "Genre 2012" presentations and reprinted from *Ibérica*, the journal published by European Association of Languages for Specific Purposes (AELFE), where they were published in 2012. In his chapter, Swales reflects on the role that Hyon's 1996 publication played in the development of perceptions of genre studies as a field and on the significance of her taxonomy of traditions for further developments in genre studies. In chapter 2, Bhatia discusses Language for Specific Purposes (LSP), a genre research tradition more linguistically encompassing than ESP, from which it originated. The chapter details such recent directions in LSP genre research as *critical genre analysis* and *interdiscursivity*, focusing on genres of legal discourse. In chapter 3, Martin makes an important contribution to the field of genre studies by describing in detail the original exigencies that led to the development of the Sydney School, as well as by pointing to the current directions of this genre studies tradition. In the chapter that follows, Bazerman presents a complex view of the place of genre in his social theory of literate action (2013) developed on the basis of of social sciences and RGS. Further, in chapter 5, Vian Jr. discusses a broad range of sources that Brazilian approaches to genre draw on, including, but not limited to, ideas proposed by Bakhtin (1981, 1986), RGS, the Sydney School, Socio-Discursive Interactionism (SDI), textual analysis, explicit genre pedagogy, and others. In the following chapter, Parodi presents a Chilean corpus-based approach to genre research, developed at the Pontifical Catholic University of Valparaiso, and demonstrates its application to the investigation of academic genres in different disciplines. In this approach, the social context is formally acknowledged, but not investigated in depth and the textual genre analysis used in the study includes both qualitative and quantitative components.

Chapters 7-9 are dedicated to questions that were raised by genre scholars in different years. For example, in her essay, Miller addresses the concepts of genre evolution, innovation, and function, and argues that perceiving genre as *functional* may help us better understand the processes of the emergence of new genres and genre change. Bawarshi, in chapter 8, continues the discussion by addressing and further developing Freadman's notion of uptake (1994, 2002, this volume), and by suggesting that in teaching, we need to focus not only on genres themselves but also on genre uptakes. Giltrow joins the conversation in chapter 9 with her proposal to combine pragmatics and RGS in our quest for meaning in human communication. She argues that RGS can make an important contribution to pragmatics in allowing us to see genre as a phenomenon of mutual consciousness of the interlocutors.

Chapters 10-12 are dedicated to research studies that focus on multimodal genres. Engberg and Maier combine several approaches to the study of multimodality and draw on such scholars as Kress, Jewett, Norris and others in their study of the new, multimodal, and not yet fully established ways of disseminating academic knowledge.

The chapter includes an analytical framework for the study of such emerging multimodal genres. In chapter 11, Luginbühl proposes a new, intermediate, level for genre analysis—the level of *genre profiles*, which he situates between the micro level of a single genre style and the macro level of cultural change. He applies his proposed approach to a longitudinal comparative genre analysis of two TV news shows, one developed and broadcast in the US and the other, in Switzerland. Rulyova follows this discussion of multimodal genres in chapter 12, wherein she draws on the work of Kress, Bakhtin, and ESP and RGS scholars in her investigation of social media identities as represented in a blog kept by a prominent critic and opponent of the Russian President.

Chapters 13-17 are dedicated to the issues of pedagogy. Thus, Rose presents a detailed step-by-step explanation of the application of Systemic-Functional Linguistics (SFL) and the work of the Sydney School to the development of genre pedagogy, known as the *Reading to Learn* program. Chapter 14, by Tardy, takes us from primary school classrooms to university courses in the USA and discusses an important issue of genre innovation. The question the chapter poses is "When are norm-departures judged as 'innovative'?" In other words, by drawing on the ESP and RGS literature, Tardy investigates, what actions make students' genre innovations acceptable and what do not. Johns's essay is also situated in the university classroom, in which first-year students who speak English as an additional language are confronted with new genres. Using insights from both the ESP and RGS genre traditions, Johns develops a pedagogical approach, which is based on students' prior knowledge of genres and on training students to become text and context researchers. In chapter 16, Devitt explores the ways in which theories developed within the three genre traditions have made genre-pedagogies more complex, and envisions future genre studies that include a mutually enriching interplay of theory, practice, and pedagogy. In the following chapter, Cristovão presents a detailed description of the pedagogical implementation of a Brazilian genre approach (see Vian Jr., this volume) to the teaching of genre to and learning of genres by secondary school students.

We chose to conclude the collection with a chapter by Freadman, which originally appeared in *Applied Linguistics*, *33*(5), 544-563 (2012). Freadman uses an example of a televisual political interview, a multimodal genre, in order once again to stress the importance of uptake for meaningful human communications (cf. Bawarshi, this volume; Devitt, this volume; Freadman, 1994, 2002). This chapter brings together in a discussion all the threads that run through the volume: genre conceptualization in different traditions, its theoretical underpinnings, and the pedagogical implications of genre studies; it also raises questions crucial for the future of the field. In other words, Freadman's chapter serves as a perfect conclusion to our volume.

The volume provides readers with a review of the three Anglophone traditions in genre studies and takes them beyond these traditions, to the approaches to genre studies that have developed in other national, linguistic, cultural, and disciplinary contexts. This collection is addressed to researchers, teachers, and students of genre who wish to familiarize themselves with recent developments in genre studies around the globe[3].

Natasha Artemeva and Aviva Freedman

Ottawa - Jerusalem

2013 - 2015

References

Artemeva, N. & Freedman, A. (2006). *Rhetorical Genre Studies and beyond*. Winnipeg, MB, Canada: Inkshed Publications.

Artemeva, N. & Myles, D. (2015). Perceptions of prior genre knowledge: A case of incipient biliterate writers in the EAP classroom. In N. Rulyova & G. Dowd, (Eds.). *Genre trajectories: identifying, mapping, projecting*. London & New York: Palgrave Macmillan.

Bawarshi, A. S., & Reiff, M. J. (2010). *Genre: An introduction to the history, theory, research, and pedagogy*. West Lafayette, IN: Parlor Press.

Bazerman, Charles. (2013). *A theory of literate action: Literate action Volume 2*. Perspectives on Writing. Fort Collins, Colorado: The WAC Clearinghouse and Parlor Press. Retrieved July 3, 2015 from http://wac.colostate.edu/books/literateaction/v2/

Bazerman, C., Bonini, A., & Figueiredo, D. (Eds.). (2009). *Genre in a changing world*. Perspectives on Writing. Fort Collins, Colorado: The WAC Clearinghouse and Parlor Press. Retrieved July 3, 2015 from http://wac.colostate.edu/books/genre/

Cap, P. & Okulska, U. (Eds.).(2013). *Analyzing genres in political communication: Theory and practice*. Amsterdam: John Benjamins.

Coe, R., Lingard, L. & Teslenko, T. (Eds.). (2002). *The rhetoric and ideology of genre*. Cresskill, NJ: Hampton.

Freadman, A. (1994). Anyone for tennis? In A. Freedman & P. Medway (Eds.), *Genre and the new rhetoric* (pp. 43-66). London, UK: Taylor and Francis. (Original work published 1987.)

Freadman, A. (2002). Uptake. In R. Coe, L. Lingard & T. Teslenko (Eds.), *The rhetoric and ideology of genre: Strategies for stability and change* (pp. 39-53). Creskill, NJ: Hampton Press.

Freedman, A. (2012). A welcome message from Aviva Freedman. *Genre 2012: Rethinking genre 20 years later. An international conference on genre studies*. Carleton University, Ottawa, On, Canada. Retrived July 3, 2015 from http://www3.carleton.ca/genre2012/

Freedman, A., & Medwey, P. (Eds.). (1994a). *Genre and the New Rhetoric*. Bristol, PA: Taylor & Francis.

Freedman, A. & Medway, P. (1994b). (Eds.) *Learning and teaching genre*. Portsmouth, NH: Boynton/Cook.

Hyland, K. (2003). Genre-based pedagogies: a social response to process. *Journal of Second Language Writing, 12,* 17–29

Hyon, S. (1996). Genre in three traditions: Implications for ESL. *TESOL Quarterly, 30,* 693-722.

Johns, A. M. (2011). The future of genre in L2 writing: Fundamental, but contested, instructional decisions. *Journal of Second Language Learning, 20*(1), 56-68.

Lillis, T. & M. Scott (2007). Defining academic literacies research: issues of epistemology, ideology and strategy. *Journal of Applied Linguistics, 4* (1), 5-32.

Motta-Roth, D. & Heberle, V. M. (2015). A short cartography of genre studies in Brazil. *Journal of English for Academic Purposes, 19,* 22-31. doi: 10.1016/j.jeap.2015.05.006

Swales, J. (2009). Worlds of genre--metaphors of genre. In C. Bazerman, A. Bonini, & D. Figueiredo (Eds.), *Genre in a changing world* (pp. 3-16). Fort Collins, CO: Parlor Press.

Tardy, C. (2012). A rhetorical genre theory perspective on L2 writing development. In R. Manchón, (Ed). *Trends in Applied Linguistics: L2 writing development: Multiple Perspectives.* (pp. 165-190). Berlin, DEU: Walter de Gruyter, ProQuest ebrary. Web. Retrieved 31 October 2014.

EndNotes

[1]   Conference on Colledge Composition and Communication (CCCC), http://
      www.ncte.org/cccc
[2]   Further referred to as "Genre 2012."
[3]   Throughout the volume, we have attempted to preserve authors' original
      spelling and punctuation, where possible.

Chapter 1

A Text and Its Commentaries: Toward a Reception History of "Genre in Three Traditions" (Hyon, 1996)[1]

John M. Swales

University of Michigan (USA)

More than a decade ago, Paul, Charney and Kendall (2001) made a case for giving more attention in rhetorical and discoursal studies of scholarly texts to what happens to those texts after they have appeared. They argue:

> To move beyond the moment, we need to find ways to gauge the effects of normal scientific texts on readers when they are first published, watch acceptance and rejection over time, and associate those effects reliably with rhetorical strategies in the texts. (2001, p. 374)

They claim that only in this way can we establish that writing, as well as methodology or findings, may play some part in its text's subsequent reception, whether that be apparent indifference, noisy controversy, or well-cited approval and adaptation. In consequence, we might imagine that a smooth, well-structured introduction would help garner citations, while another on a similar topic that is disjointed and hard-to-follow would be less successful. In fact, literary scholars had already been pointing out that texts may have both unexpected as well as expected uptakes; for example, Merleau-Ponty (1974) observed that the audiences at which writers aim are not pre-established, but are instead elicited by reactions to their written products. And here is Kermode (1985):

> Since we have no experience of a venerable text that ensures its own perpetuity, we may reasonably say that the medium in which it survives is commentary. All commentary on such texts varies from one generation to the next because it meets different needs. (p. 36)

Of course, certain well-known sayings, proverbs, lines of poetry, and key religious texts perpetuate themselves in oral telling and retellings, but for academic texts, we all depend on commentary, whether unsolicited or whether mediated by lists of required readings, or by reviews, or by recommendations from colleagues or mentors.

As it happens, in June 2012, Carleton University in Ottawa hosted a major conference entitled "Genre 2012: Rethinking genre 20 years later," a follow-up to a smaller gathering held in 1992 at the same venue and with a similar theme (Freedman & Medway, 1994). Not very long after the 1992 Carleton conference, Hyon published an article in *TESOL Quarterly* entitled "Genre in three traditions: Implications for ESL" (1996), that has become quite widely cited, accumulating over 300 hits on Google Scholar and over 50 citations in the Web of Science.[2] At the 2012 event, many of the leading figures in the development of studies of non-literary genres were present, including Martin for Systemic Functional Linguistics (SFL), Bhatia, Hyland and Johns for English for Specific Purposes (ESP), and Bazerman, Devitt and Miller for New Rhetoric Studies. So the purpose of this essay is to try and trace who has been citing the 1996 paper, and when and where, and then perhaps to attempt an answer to the question of why.

The 1996 Paper and Some Facts about its Origination

The published abstract will serve as an *aide-memoire* and summary of the paper (my emphases added):

> Within the last two decades, a number of researchers have been interested in genre as a tool for developing L1 and L2

writing instruction. Both genre and genre-based pedagogy, however, have been conceived of in distinct ways by researchers in different scholarly traditions and in different parts of the world, *making the genre literature a complicated body of literature to understand. The purpose of this article is to provide a map of current genre theories and teaching applications in three research areas* where genre scholarship has taken significantly different paths: a) English for Specific Purposes (ESP), North American New Rhetoric Studies, and c) Australian systemic functional linguistics. *The article compares definitions and analyses of genres within these three traditions* and examines their contexts, goals and instructional frameworks for genre-based pedagogy. The investigation reveals that ESP and Australian genre research provides ESL instructors with insights into the linguistic features of written texts as well as useful guidelines for presenting these features in classrooms. New Rhetoric scholarship, on the other hand, offers language teachers fuller perspectives on the institutional contexts around academic and professional genres and the functions genres serve within those settings. (Hyon, 1996, p. 693)

This then was the paper, which was loosely based on the first part of Hyon's PhD dissertation, for which I was the advisor, the second half being an EAP classroom experiment testing out a genre-based approach to academic reading. Some time in the early 1990s, we managed to get funding (the details now escape me) for Hyon to spend several months at the University of Sydney so that she could familiarize herself with the Australian approach to genre and genre-based pedagogy. Her original submission to *TESOL Quarterly* then was essentially a comparison between the ESP and SFL approaches, but one of the anonymous reviewers recommended that Hyon not go with a geographical binary, but rather with a three-part disciplinary framework, now to include New Rhetoric (or Rhetorical Genre Studies as it is now more commonly known).[3] I also asked Hyon by email for her reasons for submitting to *TESOL Quarterly*; she replied saying that she had three: *TESOL Quarterly* would have the widest audience; *TESOL Quarterly* had published little on genre approaches to ESL at that time; and "for me as a brand-new scholar, having an article published in *TESOL Quarterly* would be pretty special."

Possible Reasons for the Success of the 1996 Paper

Before we look at the citational record, it is worth stepping back and speculating as to which features of the paper might have led to its citational popularity. Here are five positive hypotheses for its success:

1. "Kairos or timeliness." In other words, "Genre in Three Traditions" came at the right moment; five years earlier, readers might have reacted with "What's this all about?", five years later the reaction might have been "Well, we know all this." As Freedman and Medway (1994) said at the time with reference to composition studies, "the word *genre* is on everybody's lips, from researchers and scholars to curriculum planners and teachers" (p. 1).

2. "A Review article." The paper provided a cognitive map of the world of non-literary genre studies and, in many fields, review articles tend to be highly cited. As Myers (1991) noted a review article "draws the reader into the writer's view of what has happened, and by ordering the recent past, suggests what can be done next" (p. 46).

3. "The magic number 3." It might be expected that the tripartitite division would appeal particularly to systemic-functional linguists and applied linguistics because of the Hallidayan penchant for dividing systems into three (that is, field/mode/tenor; idealtional/interpersonal/textual; three main types of appraisal, three main verb processes, etc.)

4. "ESL implications." Since it was published in *TESOL Quarterly*, it is possible that the more practical discussion toward the end of the paper would appeal to ESL teachers, materials writers and teacher educators.

5. "Quotable moments." The article had some memorable mini-texts or phrases that were frequently picked up later, such as Schryer's (1993) "Genres are stabilized for now," or even Swales' (1996) "occluded genres."

In addition, the article may have been cited because citing authors found that it did not represent their own understandings of the world of genre studies:

6. So those in ESP might argue, contra Hyon, that ESP approaches have, at least on occasion, questioned the prevailing academic ideologies;

7. Those in SFL might counter that there are advantages in conceiving of genre more broadly than in the other two traditions;

8. Those in Rhetorical Genre Studies might object that it is not true that their approach lacks any substantial instructional pedagogy;

9. And anybody might argue that Hyon's "map" exaggerates or minimizes differences among the three traditions.

Some Quantitative Data

Let us first consider how all the datable citations for Hyon (1996) in Google Scholar are distributed over time.

Table 1

Chronology of citations in Google Scholar

Period	No. of cites in Google Scholar
1996-1999	21
2000-2003	37
2004-2007	56
2008-2011	61

Although, at first sight, the numbers in Table 1 might seem to indicate that the 1996 article has become increasingly popular ever since its appearance, in reality they show only that Google Scholar's database has been continually expanding. At the least, however, the figures do confirm that the 1996 article was not a comet that blazed briefly across the scholarly sky and then fell into benighted obscurity; rather, it is probably cited today as much as it ever was.

The next question to ask is where it was cited, more particularly which journals carry the most citations. And here we need to remember that in our field Google Scholar will produce mostly book or dissertation citations, and Web of Science mostly journal citations.

Table 2

Citing journals (Google Scholar 79/301; Web of Science 45/51)

Journals	No. of cites in Google Scholar	Journals	No. of cites in Web of Science
English for Specific Purposes Journal	12	Journal of Second Language Writing	12
Journal of Second Language Writing	11	English for Specific Purposes Journal	11
TESOL Quarterly	4	TESOL Quarterly	4
Linguistics and Education	3	Applied Linguistics	2
TESL-EJ	3	Journal of Pragmatics	2
System	3	Modern Language Journal	2
Journal of English for Academic Purposes	3	Research in the Teaching of English	2

As can be seen in Table 2, in each case, the top three journals (*English for Specific Purposes*, *Journal of Second Language Writing* and *TESOL Quarterly*) all have an English-as-a-second language orientation, while those further down the lists cover a much wider area of applied language studies.

I then looked at the individual citing authors in the two databases and wherever possible assigned them to one of the three traditions. In some cases, this was relatively easy, such as placing Martin in Systemic Functional Linguistics, Berkenkotter in Rhetorical Genre Studies and Hyland in English for Specific Purposes; in others it was more difficult, either because I knew little or nothing about the author, or because a particular individual did not seem to "fit" into a particular tradition. Here are the findings:

Table 3

Presumed associates of each "tradition" in Google Scholar and Web of Science

Traditions	No. of cites in Google Scholar	No. of cites in Web of Science
English for Specific Purposes Journal	52	20
Systemic Functional Linguistics	11	11
Rhetorical Genre Studies	3	2

The Table 3 figures reinforce the previous ones; a preponderance of citations from the ESP "tradition," but with fairly substantial uptakes from the other two. These trends are further consolidated when we look at the more frequent individual citing authors such as, for English for Specific Purposes, Cheng, Martín-Martín, Hyland and Johns, for Systemic Functional Linguistics, Christie and Martin, and Berkenkotter for Rhetorical Genre Studies.

Selected Citational Details

Hyland (2004) divides citations into four categories: Block quotations, direct quotes, paraphrases and summaries. No block quotations from the 1996 paper were found, and very few direct quotes, the following example being one of a mere handful:

(1) Although Hyon (1996, p. 695) has pointed out that "... many ESP scholars have paid particular attention to detailing the formal characteristics of genres while focusing less on the specialized functions of texts and their surrounding social contexts," this sociocultural context has been addressed in more recent ESP genre-based work. (Flowerdew)[4]

This suggests then that the paper is not being cited for its memorable quotes (hypothesis 5). In contrast, most of the citations are parenthetical, often placing Hyon (1996) in a group along with others. The most common of these groupings is shown in the next example:

(2) When it comes to defining genres there is multiplicity of overlapping theories along with a range of competing terminologies (See Hyon, 1996, Johns, 2002). (Bruce)[5]

Given the frequent pairing of the 1996 paper with Johns' (2002) edited volume, *Genre in the Classroom: Multiple Perspectives*, it is worth looking at this book in more detail. There are nine citations of the 1996 paper in the collection, five of which are parenthetical, three by Johns herself in her introduction, and one each by Hyon (2002)[6] and Samraj (2002)[7] in their chapters. Three of the four remaining are these (my emphases):

(3) Yet, *as Hyon (1996) and others have noted*, there are considerable differences among theorists and practitioners about how genre should be described and what this means for the classroom. (Johns)

(4) As far as pedagogical application of the two approaches is concerned, *as Hyon (1996, p. 701) noted*, the focus of the Australian and ESP approach is ... (Flowerdew)

(5) *In her widely-quoted state-of-the-art article, Hyon (1996) distinguished* three "worlds" of genre scholarship ... (Flowerdew)

The last of these three is particularly interesting because it introduces the evaluative modifier "widely quoted". In fact, I found surprisingly few of these, noting in addition only three occurrences of "useful" and one of "influential." The remaining citation of the 1996 paper in the 2002 volume is quite long, but is worth quoting in full:

(6) Many of us working to develop genre-based language pedagogy in Australia have been quite surprised to lift our heads from day-to-day challenges of curriculum and syllabus design, materials development and classroom implementation to find that the diverse work we have been involved in for several years across many educational sectors and all states of the Commonwealth is now collectively known as the work of the "Sydney School" (Hyon, 1996). It is quite flattering in one sense to be seen as a force in the field deserving our own label, especially for those of us who live in Sydney, but there is also a danger that the label becomes as reductive of what we do pedagogically as it is of where we live geographically. (Feez)[8]

Apart from the wry and poignant voice of a rare practitioner, this commentary is notable for its criticism of the reductionist "Sydney School" label, a criticism reiterated by Martin at the Ottawa conference, who there argued that the SFL approach was not only a national movement in Australia, but also one with strong adherents internationally. As it happens, Hyon was not the originator of the term "Sydney School," even if her 1996 paper has inadvertently been largely responsible for its profusion.

Of the relatively few longer discussions of Hyon's (1996) paper, Benesch's (2001) treatment is largely descriptive, except for:

(7) That is, the primary goal is to help students fulfill the requirements of academic and professional settings so that

they can "succeed" (p. 700). (In Chap. 3, I discuss this goal as an ideological stance; for now, I accept Hyon's terms.)

Two others are Johns et al. (2006) and Swales (2009), both of whom question a simple tripartite division. Johns can serve as an illustration of this kind of problematization. Here is her opening sentence:

(8) The term *genre* has been interpreted in a variety of ways by experts from a number of traditions. Hyon in her 1996 *TESOL Quarterly* article, separated genre theorists and practitioners into three camps: ... (Johns et al.)[9]

And this is her opening to the Conclusion of the round table discussion:

(9) In the introduction to this paper, it was suggested that following Hyon (1996), genre theory and pedagogies might be divided into a few different camps and/or approaches; however, the situation is much more complex than that, as we have seen from the expert comments in this article. (Johns et al.)[10]

On the whole though, as Berkenkotter noted in a 2006 blog, Hyon's categories "have stuck," as can be seen from this recent and final citation:

(10) Hyon (1996) originally distilled, and more recently Tardy (2009) and Flowerdew and Wan (2010) and Bawarshi and Reiff (2010) have discussed current approaches to genre analysis as falling into three broad schools of thought. (Lockwood)[11]

Discussion

In this reception study of the 1996 paper, there have emerged few surprises. As in much of our field, we can see the regular accretion of citations over time – with under-recognized implications for the narrow citational windows used for measuring impact factors by the major databases. Further, most of these citations are parenthetical, with a decent minority integral, and including a small number of direct quotations, but no block quotes. Most citations are short, neutral and summative, with a few overtly positive and a very few demurring, as in the Feez quotation cited above (see example 6). Most are from within ESP, but there are also a good number of others from elsewhere, including such outliers as an article on musical genres from the *American Sociological Review*. In almost all cases, citers use just her family name, there being just four cases where "Hyon" is prefaced by "Sunny" – one in a Chinese paper, one from an article in *Computers and Composition*, and two from me in my 2009 chapter (belated recognition from the dissertation advisor?). All of the above findings are largely what we might expect from a well-cited but non-controversial article in applied language studies.

If, however, we probe into which aspects of the 1996 paper have been picked up in later commentaries, an interesting pattern does emerge. Most citations reference the opening pages of the Hyon article, with very few references to its closing ESL-implication pages, thus suggesting that hypothesis 4) is disconfirmed. Further, most of these citations occur in the opening pages of the citing works (articles, chapters, monographs, theses, etc). In effect, the 1996 paper is quoted for its map-making achievement, and its review of the "three traditions" is typically used by the citing works as a "framing device." In other words, Hyon's frame is reperformed again and again as a mechanism for structuring new introductory material, especially when the previous literature is being invoked and incorporated. This, then, is the principal legacy of the 1996 paper. As for the other hypotheses, there may well be a kairotic effect, although it has proved hard to trace and impossible to document. Hypothesis 3), the magic number three, is also unproven and was, in any case, not really meant to be taken seriously. Rather, Hyon (1996) has succeeded essentially because of its value as a review paper, and here it is worth quoting again Myers' (1991) conclusion that such an article, if well done, "draws the reader into the writer's view of what has happened, and by ordering the recent past, suggests what can be done next" (p. 46).

My own conclusion from attending the 2012 "Rethinking Genre" conference in Ottawa would be that the three traditions essentially survive, although with some attempts to find some middle ground along the three sides of the triangle. That said, in the limited space available, it is worth considering whether the invocation of "three schools" some 16 years after the appearance of the Hyon article does not represent a rather exclusionary conceptualization. There are, in fact, two further possible candidates: The Brazilian approach to genre (Vian, 2012) and the Academic Literacies movement, sometimes known as the "New London School." The former is known for its attempts to meld ESP-type and SFL-type genre analysis, along with a more critical approach (Critical Discourse Analysis), plus influence from Franco-Swiss Socio-discursive interactionism, as advocated by Bronckart and colleagues. As Bawarshi and Reiff (2010) have observed, the Brazilian synthesis suggests that rhetorical, linguistic and sociological approaches can be interconnected, with useful results of our understanding of genres and how they can be taught.

The other candidate is the Academic Literacies approach as represented by such people as Ivanič, Lillis and Street. This movement argues that ESP in particular has been excessively textual, rather than focusing on actual academic practices. Lillis and Scott (2007) argue:

> One important consequence of pre-identifying the "problem" as textual is that it leads to pedagogy and research that takes text as the object of study, which in turn leads to policy and pedagogical "solutions" which are overwhelmingly textual in nature. (pp. 10-11)

The other main focus of the New London School that differentiates it from ESP and perhaps SFL is that it tends to resist standard academic perceptions such as relative homogeneity of student populations, the relative stability of disciplines, or the power and authority of instructors. Members of the school claim that, as a result, ESP is too "accommodationist," thus suggesting some alignment with certain figures in the US-based Genre Studies movement.

It is now 20 years since the 1992 Genre conference and also now 20 years since the founding of the European Association of Languages for Specific Purposes (AELFE). Since the articles in *Ibérica*, the journal of the Association, have increasingly used the concept of genre as a guiding framework for subsequent linguistic and discoursal analysis, especially in this century, it is not hard to see that Hyon (1996) remains a useful heuristic for establishing that framework.

And a final thought would be whether a new form of genre-based pedagogy may not in the near future emerge in Spain given the current Spanish strength in studies of academic discourse, as represented by this very journal,[12] the ENEIDA project,[13] and volumes such as Pérez-Llantada's (2012) *Scientific Discourse and the Rhetoric of Globalization.*

References

Bawarshi, A. S., & Reiff, M. J. (2010). *Genre: An introduction to history, theory, research and pedagogy.* Anderson, SC: Parlor Press.

Benesch, S. (2001). *Critical English for academic purposes.* Mahwah, NJ: Lawrence Erlbaum.

Freedman, A., & Medway, P. (Eds.). (1994). *Learning and teaching genre.* Portsmouth, NH: Boynton/Cook.

Hyland, K. (2004). *Disciplinary discourses.* Ann Arbor, MI: University of Michigan Press.

Hyon, S. (1996). Genre in three traditions: Implications for ESL. *TESOL Quarterly, 30,* 693-722.

Johns, A. M. (Ed.). (2002). *Genre in the classroom: Multiple perspectives.* Mahwah, NJ: Lawrence Erlbaum.

Johns A., Bawarshi, A., Coe, R., Hyland, K., Paltridge, B., Rieff, M., & Tardy, C. (2006). Crossing the boundaries of genre studies: Commentaries by experts. *Journal of Second Language Writing, 15,* 234-249.

Kermode, F. (1985). *Forms of attention.* Chicago, IL: University of Chicago Press.

Leeder, C., & Swales, J. M. (2012). A reception study of articles published in *English for Specific Purposes* from 1990 to 1999. *English for Specific Purposes, 31,* 137-146.

Lillis, T., & Scott, M. (2007). Defining academic literacies research: Issues of epistemology, ideology and strategy. *Journal of Applied Linguistics, 4,* 5-32.

Merleau-Ponty, M. (1974). *The prose of the world.* London: Heinemann.

Myers, G. (1991). Stories and styles in two molecular biology review articles. In C. Bazerman & J. Paradis (Eds.), *Textual dynamics of the professions* (pp. 45-75). Madison, WI: University of Wisconsin Press.

Paul, D., Charney, D., & Kendall, A. (2001). Moving beyond the moment: Reception studies in the rhetoric of science. *Journal of Business and Technical Communication, 15,* 372-399.

Pérez-Llantada, C. (2012). *Scientific discourse and the rhetoric of globalization.* London: Continuum.

Schryer, C. F. (1993). Records as genre. *Written Communication, 10,* 200-234.

Swales, J. M. (1996). Occluded genres in the academy: The case of the submission letter. In E. Ventola & A. Mauranen (Eds.), *Academic writing: Intercultural and textual issues* (pp. 45-58). Amsterdam: John Benjamins.

Swales, J. M. (2009). Worlds of genre—metaphors of genre. In C. Bazerman, A. Bonini & D. Figueiredo (Eds.), *Genre in a changing world* (pp. 1-13). West Lafayette, IN: Parlor Press.

Vian, O. Jr. (2012, June). *Beyond the three traditions in genre studies: A Brazilian perspective.* Paper presented at Genre 2012—Rethinking Genre 20 Years Later. An International Conference on Genre Studies, Ottawa, Ontario.

EndNotes

[1] A spoken version of this study was presented at *Genre 2012 - Rethinking Genre 20 Years Later. An International Conference on Genre Studies*, Carleton University, Ottawa (26-29 June 2012). The chapter originally appeared in *Ibérica, 24,* 103-116 (2012) by the European Association of Languages for Specific Purposes (AELFE). It is reproduced here by permission of the editor.

[2] These in fact are higher numbers than the two most cited papers in *English for Specific Purposes* published from 1990 to 1999 (Leeder & Swales, 2012).

[3] Recently, Hyon revealed to me that this important – and very useful – anonymous reviewer was none other than Paltridge.

[4] Editors' note: (Flowerdew, 2005, p. 323). Flowerdew, L. (2005) An intergration of corpus-based and genre-based approaches to text analysis in EAP/ESP: Countering ctiticisms against corpus-based methodologies. *English for Specific Purposes 24,* 321-332.

[5] Editors' note: (Bruce, 2009, p. 106). Bruce, I. (2009). Results sections in sociology and organic chemistry articles: A genre analysis. *English for Specific Purposes 28* (2), 105-124.

[6] Editors' note: Hyon, S. (2002). Genre and ESL Reading: A classroom study. In A. Johns (Ed.). *Genre in the classroom: Multiple perspectives.* (pp. 121 -141). Mahwah, NJ: Lawrence Earbaum Associates.

[7] Editors' note: Samraj, B. (2002). Texts and contextual layers: Academic writing in content courses. In A. Johns (Ed.). *Genre in the classroom: Multiple perspectives.* (pp. 163-176). Mahwah, NJ: Lawrence Earlbaum Associates.

[8] Editors' note: (Feez, 2002, p. 44). Feez, S. (2002). Heritage and innovation in second language education. In A. Johns (Ed.). *Genre in the classroom: Multiple perspectives.* (pp.43-69). Mahwah, NJ: Lawrence Erlbaum Associates.

[9] Editors' note: p. 234.

[10] Editors' note: p. 247.

[11] Editors' note: (Lockwood, 2012, p. 16). Lockwood, J. (2012). Developing an English for specific purpose curriculum for Asian call centres: How theory can inform practice. *English for Specific Purposes 31,* 14-24.

[12] Editors' note: *Ibérica.*

[13] Editors' note: A Spanish project on Intercultural Studies for Academic Discourse led by Ana Moreno (see http://blogs.unileon.es/amoreno/?p=195).

Chapter 2

Critical Reflections on Genre Analysis[1]

Vijay K. Bhatia

City University of Hong Kong (China)

Prologue

I would like to reflect on my engagement with genre in three main episodes focusing on "genre analysis," "critical genre analysis" and "interdiscursivity," although there is also a preliminary episode that begins with my interest in and engagement with legal discourse. So my reflective narrative begins with legal discourse, which was my first interest. In fact, it was my involvement in legal discourse that brought me to genre analysis. Most of my work in law has focused on written discourse, in particular on legislation. What I have seen in the last four decades of my involvement in the analysis of legal genres is that although it is easy to criticize how parliamentary counsels draft legislation, it is very difficult to understand why it is written the way it is. There are issues of transparency, power, control, jurisdiction, and accessibility involved. Much of the literature on plain language law is biased toward an excessive concern for accessibility, often at the cost of other factors. One needs to consider other issues such as who is given the power to interpret the genre and who ultimately will be assigned control over its interpretation, and in what sort of jurisdiction and socio-political context. Once we consider all these issues, we realize that it is best to consider such genres on their own terms rather than imposing any single criterion to judge its construction, use and interpretation. So right from the beginning of my engagement with legal genres the question that has always been on mind, and to some extent it still does, is: "why do these and, for that matter, other professionals write the way they do?" The quest for the answer to this most important question led me to genre theory, as I know it even today. So let me reflect on my involvement and understanding of genre theory, with special emphasis on professional genres.

Episode One: Genre Analysis

Ever since the early conceptualisation of genre theory in the United Kingdom in 1980s I have been partly instrumental in developing it from a purely linguistic analysis of academic and professional genres to the analysis of professional practices and disciplinary cultures, thus integrating textual, strategic or socio-pragmatic, and other critical aspects of genre construction, interpretation, use, and exploitation in various professional contexts. What I would like to do in this narrative is to offer purely personal reflections on some of the critical developments in this theory in the last three decades. My own view of genre, as discussed in my 1993 book, *Analysing Genre: Language Use in Professional Contexts*, primarily as an instance of linguistic and rhetorical analysis, has developed into a more comprehensive multi-perspective and multidimensional view of genre analysis in my 2004 book on, *Worlds of Written Discourse: A Genre-Based View*. In its early form, genre theory was primarily concerned with the application of genre analysis to develop pedagogical solutions for ESP classrooms. For more than thirty years now it is still considered perhaps the most popular and useful tool to analyse academic and professional genres for ESP applications. Much of the credit for its exceptional achievement goes to the seminal works of Swales (1990, 2004) and Bhatia (1993) on the development of genre theory to analyse academic and professional genres, with an eye on applications to English for Specific Purposes (ESP), especially those used in research, legal, and business contexts. In my later work (Bhatia, 2004), which was an attempt to develop it further in order to understand the much more complex and dynamic real world of written discourse, my intention was to move away from pedagogic applications to ESP, firstly to focus on the world of professions, and secondly, to be able to see as much of the elephant as possible, as the saying goes, rather than only a part of it like the six blind men.

I believe that all frameworks of discourse and genre analysis offer useful insights about specific aspects of language use in typical contexts, but most of them, on their own, can offer only a partial view of complete genres, which are essentially multidimensional. Therefore, it is only by combining various perspectives and frameworks that one can have a more complete view of the elephant. Hence, there was a need to combine methodologies and devise multidimensional and multi-perspective frameworks. My attempt to propose a three-space model was an attempt in this direction (Bhatia, 2004).

In the context of this development, it is important to point out that in the early years of genre analysis, especially in the 1990s, there was relatively little direct discourse analytical work in the available literature published in other disciplinary fields; the situation however in the last few years changed considerably as many professions have made interesting claims about the study of organisations, professions and institutions based on evidence coming from different kinds of analyses of discourse, in particular Critical Discourse Analysis (CDA). There has been a substantial increase in research efforts to consider the contributions of discourse analytical studies in disciplinary fields such as law, medicine and healthcare, accounting and management, science and technology, where there is now a better understanding of the role of language not only in the construction and dissemination of disciplinary knowledge, but also in the conduct of professional practices (see for instance, Chiapello & Fairclough, 2002; Grant & Hardy, 2004; Grant, Hardy, Oswick & Putnam, 2004a, 2004b; Grant, Keenoy & Oswick, 2001; Mumby & Stohl, 1996). There is a significant recognition of the fact that many of these practices can be better understood and studied on the basis of communicative behaviour to achieve specific disciplinary and professional objectives rather than just on the basis of disciplinary theories. I initiated a project that investigated corporate disclosure practices through their typical communicative strategies of putting together a diverse range of discourses (accounting, financial, public relations, and legal) to promote their corporate image and interests, especially in times when they faced adverse corporate results, so as to control any drastic share price movement in the stock market. To my amazement, I discovered that it was not simply a matter of designing and constructing routine corporate documents, such as the Annual Corporate Reports, but was part of a strategically implemented corporate strategy to exploit interdiscursive space to achieve often complex and intricate corporate objectives through what I have referred to as "interdiscursivity" (Bhatia, 2010) to which I shall return in episode three.

This idea of studying professional practice through interdiscursive exploitation of linguistic and other semiotic resources within socio-pragmatic space was also the object of undertaking yet another project, in which I had collaboration from research teams from more than twenty countries consisting of lawyers and arbitrators, both from the academy as well as from the respective professions, and also discourse and genre analysts, which investigated the so-called "colonization" of arbitration practices by litigation processes and procedures (see Bhatia et al., 2003, 2008, 2009, 2010, 2012 & forthcoming). To give a brief background to this study let me point out that arbitration was originally proposed as an "alternative" to litigation in order to provide a flexible, economic, speedy, informal, and private process of resolving commercial disputes. Although arbitration awards, which are equivalent to court judgments in effect, are final and enforceable, parties at dispute often look for opportunities to go to the court when the outcome is not to their liking. To make it possible, they often choose legal experts as arbitrators and counsels, as they are likely to be more accomplished in looking for opportunities to challenge a particular award. This large-scale involvement of legal practitioners in arbitration practice leads to an increasing mixture of rule-related discourses as arbitration becomes, as it were, "colonized" by litigation practices, threatening to undermine the integrity of arbitration practice, and in the process thus compromising the spirit of arbitration as a non-legal practice. The evidence for all these studies referred to above came from the typical use of communicative behaviour, both spoken as well as written, of the participants and practitioners from different countries, disciplinary and professional practices and cultures, rather than just the disciplinary theories. So in the coming few years, we are more likely to find numbers of discourse-based studies being published in journals of these disciplines, such as management, medicine, arbitration, etc. The picture that emerges from our current understanding of the field indicates that in addition to ESP or more appropriately Language for Specific Purposes (LSP), discourse and genre analysis can contribute significantly to our understanding of organisational and institutional practices, in addition to its current applications to discursive and professional practices, in both academic as well as professional contexts. In fact, I would like to go further to suggest implications of current developments in genre theory for areas such as organisational communication, translation and interpretation, and document and information design. The emerging picture can be represented in Figure 1.

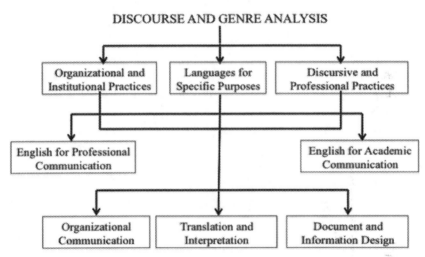

Figure 1. Discourse and genre analysis.

Emphasis in ESP-motivated Genre Analysis (GA) thus is on the production of meaning through the use of linguistic, rhetorical, and sometimes other semiotic resources, with some attention paid to the professional context it is situated in, and the communicative purposes it tends to serve; however, very little attention is generally paid to the way this production and communication of meaning is actually constrained and eventually realised, and in what ways this meaning is intended to be part of professional practices, in addition to what goes into its production, reception and consumption of knowledge so constructed. This emphasis on academic and professional practice in addition to discursive actions encourages an additional perspective to genre analysis, with a focus on what I would like to call "discursive performance," which extends the scope of analysis from genres as discursive products to professional practice that all discursive acts tend to accomplish. I have made an attempt to refer to this form of analysis as "critical genre analysis" (CGA) (see for details, Bhatia, 2008a, 2008b, 2010). Let me give more substance to what I mean by this.

Episode Two: Critical Genre Analysis

As briefly introduced here, Critical Genre Analysis (CGA) is an attempt to extend genre theory beyond the analyses of semiotic resources used in professional genres to understand and clarify professional practices or actions in typical academic and professional contexts. I would like to clarify that in spite of apparent similarities, CGA is meant to be different from Critical Discourse Analysis (CDA). CDA draws on the critical theory as cultural critique, and focuses on social relations of domination, typically grounded in class relations, including race and gender, specifically focusing on their oppressive sides. CDA thus tends to analyze social structures in such a way that they are viewed as invulnerable. It encourages recognition of domination without offering resources for action against such practices. Critical discourse analyses thus examine social structures and relations and analyze them in such a way that the analyses encourage the power and domination to disseminate oppressive actions in somewhat unequal social settings.

Critical Genre analysis, on the other hand, is a way of "demystifying" professional practice through the medium of genres. An interesting aspect of this analysis is that it focuses as much on generic artifacts, as on professional practices, as much on what is explicitly or implicitly said in genres, as on what is not said, as much on socially recognized communicative purposes, as on "private intentions" (Bhatia, 1995) that professional writers tend to express in order to understand professional practices or actions of the members of corporations, institutions and professional organizations. In CGA therefore no professional, institutional, or organizational practices are assumed but negotiated. They seem to be in a constant struggle between competing interests. CGA with its focus on practice considers individual members of professional organizations, though bound by their common goals and objectives, still having enough flexibility to incorporate "private intentions" within the concept of professionally shared values, genre conventions, and professional cultures. A notion of practice thus describes the relation between shared values and flexibility as dynamically complex, in that institutional and organizational ideologies, and constraints are often conventionalized and standardized, but not always static or inflexible. In professional communication, a theory of practice is a function of organizational and institutional structures as evident in the everyday activities of professionals, and conditions of production and reception are crucial. Besides, in professional communication in the age of computer-mediated communication, CGA also considers the overwhelming power and influence of technology in professional life. Thus professional practices give shape to actions in specific professional contexts, they get established so long as the members of the professional community continue to follow the conventions, which are shared by the members of a specific professional discourse community. CGA makes a commitment, not only to describe, but also to explain, clarify, and "demystify" professional practice. In this sense, CGA is not an initiative to change professional practices of individual disciplinary, institutional, and corporate communities, but to understand how professional writers use the language to achieve the objectives of their professions.

Episode Three: Interdiscursivity

One of the most important concepts that seem to be crucial to the study of professional genres and practices is what has been referred to as interdiscursivity (Bhatia, 2010). I have noticed that within the concept of genre and professional practice, one can see expert professional writers constantly operating within and across generic boundaries creating new but essentially related and/or hybrid (both mixed and embedded) forms to give expression to their "private intentions" within the socially accepted communicative practices and shared generic norms (Bhatia, 1995; Fairclough, 1995). Interdiscursivity is invariably across discursive events that may be genres, professional activities, or even more generally professional cultures. It is often based on shared generic or contextual characteristics across two or more discursive constructs and some understanding of these shared features is a necessary condition to an adequate understanding of the new construct. Interdiscursivity thus can be viewed as a function of "appropriation of generic resources" across three kinds of contextual and other text-external resources: genres, professional practices, and professional cultures.

From the point of view of genre theory, especially in the context of professional communication, it is necessary to distinguish appropriations across text-internal and text-external resources, the former often viewed as intertextuality, and the latter as interdiscursivity. Intertextuality operates within what we refer to as "textual space" and has been widely studied (Bakhtin, 1986; Fairclough, 1995; Foucault, 1981; Kristeva, 1980); however, a vast majority of appropriations often take place across text-external semiotic resources at other levels of professional, institutional and disciplinary discourses, such as genres, professional, institutional, and disciplinary practices, and professional, institutional and disciplinary cultures to meet socially shared professional, institutional, and disciplinary expectations and objectives, and sometimes to achieve "private intentions." These latter forms of appropriations that operate in what could be viewed as "socio-pragmatic space" are essentially interdiscursive in nature. It may be pointed out that often all these appropriations, whether text-internal or text-external, discursively operate simultaneously at all levels of discourse to realise the intended meaning, and have been widely used in the recontextualization, reframing, resemiotisation or reformulations of existing discourses and genres into novel or hybrid forms. In addition to this, appropriation of generic resources is also very common in various forms of hybrids, such as mixing, embedding and bending of genres (see for details Bhatia, 2004, 2008a, 2008b, 2010). The general picture representing interdiscursivity in genre theory can be summarised as follows in Figure 2.

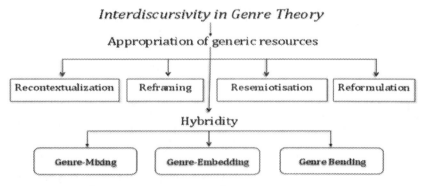

Figure 2. Interdiscursivity in genre theory.

I have already mentioned instances of interdiscursivity from at least two professional contexts to illustrate that it operates at all levels, generic, professional practice, and professional culture, but also to claim that it not only allows a more rigorous and comprehensive analysis of genres in and as professional practice, but at the same time, also encourages evidenced-based studies of professional and institutional practices and cultures through the genres they often use.

Epilogue

In this personal reflective narration of my engagement with genre analysis over more than three decades, I have made an attempt to account for the developments in genre theory right from its early conceptualisation in Swales (1981, 1990) and Bhatia (1993) through to its later developments as in Bhatia (2004, 2008a, 2008b, 2010). The account is significant in several respects. Firstly, it traces the development of genre theory from a predominantly lexico-grammatical and rhetorical analysis of genres towards a more interdiscursive and critical genre analysis and understanding of professional practice. It tends to offer a useful procedure for the study of professional practices, which otherwise are often discussed and explained through organizational, management, and other institutional theories (Boje, Oswick & Ford, 2004; Grant, Keenoy & Oswick, 2001; Hardy et al., 2004; Marshak et al., 2000; Oswick & Grant, 1997; Philips & Hardy, 2002). It thus presents a complementary methodological alternative in the form of genre-based investigations of professional, organizational and institutional practices. Secondly, it indicates a development of genre theory from a purely ESP or LSP pedagogic application to a more critical engagement leading to demystification of the realities of the professional world. Thirdly, it argues for a multidimensional and multi-perspective methodological framework to understand and analyse professional and academic genres, professional practices, and disciplinary and professional cultures as comprehensively as possible. At a more theoretical level, it thus creates a valuable research space for the development of a more comprehensive and delicate system of interdiscursivity in genre theory (Bhatia, 2010), which has not been sufficiently explored in the current literature on genre. More generally, it underpins the importance of a multidimensional and multi-perspective view of genre analysis, which, I believe, has tremendous potential for the future of genre studies. However, I must emphasize that this reflective account represents a subjective and very much personal and continual engagement with genre theory. I must close this critical account with the reminder that the story is not complete yet, and I am sure there will be much more to reflect on in the years to come.

References

Bakhtin, M. M. (1986). *Speech genres and other late essays*. Austin, TX: University of Texas Press.

Bhatia, V. K. (1993). *Analysing genre: Language use in professional settings*. London, UK: Longman.

Bhatia, V. K. (1995). Genre-mixing and in professional communication: The case of "private intentions" v. "socially recognised purposes." In P. Bruthiaux, T. Boswood & B. Bertha (Eds.), *Explorations in English for professional communication* (pp. 1-19). Hong Kong: City University of Hong Kong.

Bhatia, V. K. (2004). *Worlds of written discourse: A genre-based view*. London: Continuum International.

Bhatia, V. K. (2008a). Genre analysis, ESP and professional practice. *English for Specific Purposes, 27*, 161-174.

Bhatia, V. K. (2008b). Towards critical genre analysis. In V. K. Bhatia, J. Flowerdew & R. Jones (Eds.), *Advances in discourse studies* (pp. 166-177). London, UK: Routledge.

Bhatia, V. K. (2010). Interdiscursivity in professional communication. *Discourse and Communication, 21*(1), 32-50.

Bhatia, V. K., Candlin, C. N., & Gotti, M. (Eds.). (2003). *Arbitration in Europe: Legal discourse in a multilingual and multicultural context*. Bern: Peter Lang.

Bhatia, V. K., Candlin, C. N., & Engberg, J. (Eds.). (2008). *Legal discourse across cultures and systems*. Hong Kong: Hong Kong University Press.

Bhatia, V. K., Candlin, C. N., & Evengilisti, P. (Eds.). (2009). *Legal discourse in multicultural contexts*. Bern: Peter Lang.

Bhatia V. K., Candlin, C. N., & Gotti, M. (Eds.). (2010). *The discourses of dispute resolution*. Bern: Peter Lang.

Bhatia V. K., Candlin, C. N., & Gotti, M. (Eds.). (2012). *Arbitration practice and discourse: Issues, challenges and prospects*. London, UK: Ashgate Publishing Group.

Bhatia, V. K., & Garzone, G. (2012). *Discourse analysis of arbitration awards*. Newcastle upon Tyne: Cambridge Scholars Publication.

Boje, D., Oswick, C., & Ford, J. (Eds.). (2004). Language and organization: The doing of discourse. *Academy of Management Review, 29*(4), 571-577.

Chiapello, E., & Fairclough, N. (2002). Understanding the new management ideology: A transdisciplinary contribution from critical discourse analysis and new sociology of capitalism. *Discourse & Society, 13*(2), 185-208.

Fairclough, N. (1995). *Critical Discourse Analysis.* London: Longman.

Foucault, M. (1981). *The archaeology of knowledge.* New York: Pantheon Books.

Grant, D., & Hardy, C. (2004). Introduction: Struggles with organizational discourse. *Organization Studies, 25*(1), 5-13.

Grant, D., Hardy, C., Oswick, C., & Putman, L. L. (Eds.). (2004a). *The Sage handbook of organizational discourse.* London, UK: Sage.

Grant, D., Harvey, C., Oswick, C., & Putnam, L. L. (2004b). Introduction: Organizational discourse, exploring the field. In D. Grant et al. (Eds.), *The Sage handbook of organizational discourse* (pp. 1-36). London, UK: Sage.

Grant, D., Keenoy, T., & Oswick, C. (2001). Organizational discourse: Key contributions and challenges. *International Studies of Management and Organization, 31*, 5-24.

Hardy, C., Grant, D.; Keenoy, T., Oswick, C., & Philips, N. (Eds.). (2004). Organizational discourse [Special issue]. *Organizational Studies, 25*(1).

Kristeva J. (1980). Word, dialogue and novel. In J. Kristeva (Ed.), *Desire in language* (pp. 64-91). Oxford: Blackwell.

Marshak, R. J., Keenoy, T., Oswick, C., & Grant, D. (2000). From outer words to inner worlds. *The Journal of Applied Behavioral Science, 36*(2), 245-258.

Mumby, D. K., & Stohl, C. (1991). Power and discourse in organizational studies: Absence and the dialectic of control. *Discourse and Society, 2*, 313-332.

Mumby, D.K. & Stohl, C. (1996): Disciplining organizational communication studies *Management Communication Quarterly,* 10.1 (50-73).

Oswick, C., Grant, D. (1997): Organizational metaphors: ways of thinking or sources of emptiness, in Glinka, B., and Hensel, P. (Eds.), *The space report, special issue of Master of Business Administration.* Warsaw: The Academy of Entrepreneurship and Management.

Philips, N., & Hardy, C. (2002). *Discourse analysis: Investigating processes of social construction.* Thousand Oaks: Sage Publications.

Swales, J. M. (1981). *Aspects of Article Introductions.* Aston ESP Research Report, LSU. Birmingham, UK: The University of Aston in Birmingham.

Swales, J. M. (1990). *Genre analysisa: English in academic and research settings.* Cambridge, UK: Cambridge University Press.

Swales, J. M., (2004). *Research Genres: Explorations and Applications.* Cambridge, UK: Cambridge University Press.

EndNotes

[1] A spoken version of this study was presented at *Genre 2012 - Rethinking Genre 20 Years Later. An International Conference on Genre Studies*, Carleton University, Ottawa (26-29 June 2012). The chapter originally appeared in *Ibérica, 24,* 14-28 (2012) by the European Association of Languages for Specific Purposes (AELFE). It is reproduced here by permission of the editor.

Chapter 3

One of Three Traditions: Genre, Functional Linguistics, and the "Sydney School"

J. R. Martin

University of Sydney (Australia)
Martin Centre for Appliable Linguistics, Shanghai
Jiao Tong University (China)

Mythology

As we all know intellectual history, like all history, is formed in an interested way, by its composers, about their object of study. And it may involve various phrases of reification. For example, the literacy programs with which I have been involved now for over three decades (Rose, this volume; Rose & Martin, 2012) were initially christened in passing by Green and Lee (1994):

> Our investigations and arguments are situated in part within the context of, and in response to, a major recent intervention into writing pedagogy in Australia, based on the systemic-functional linguistics of Michael Halliday, who until recently was Professor of Linguistics at the University of Sydney. This work, which for the sake of economy we shall refer to here in terms of the "Sydney School" has been organized around a particular linguistic understanding of the concept of "genre"... (p. 208)

Alongside Richardson (1994), Green and Lee had been commissioned to write an article dealing with genre-based literacy pedagogy in Australia—articles published in one of the two volumes of papers on genre arising out of the 1992 "Rethinking Genre" conference held at Carleton University in Ottawa (Freedman & Medway 1994a, b). These three authors had not in fact attended the conference, at which no representatives of the "Sydney School" were present. And no proponents of "Sydney School" literacy programs, nor experts in the Systemic Functional Linguistics (hereafter SFL) underpinning these programs, were included in either volume.[1] Writing in the companion 1994b volume to the one christening the Australian work, the editors certify the "Sydney School" appellation and situate this genre movement as an educational linguistics initiative:

> ...the parallel genre project that has developed from quite different sources in Australia. Sometimes referred to as the *"Sydney School"* [emphasis added] after its main institutional base in the University of Sydney's Department of Linguistics, formerly headed by M A K Halliday, the Australian genre movement is an educational application of the systemic functional linguistics of Halliday and his followers... (Freedman & Medway, 1994a, p. 9)

Not all names stick, but this one was soon to be canonised in Hyon (1996), where the Australian work is placed as one among three traditions—alongside what she refers to as the English for specific purposes (hereafter ESP) and North American New Rhetoric studies (hereafter referred to as Rhetorical genre studies, RGS for short); Hyon reinforces the conflation of SFL genre theory (Martin & Rose, 2008) with "Sydney School" genre-based literacy programs (Rose & Martin, 2012) and their focus on primary and secondary education, and non-professional workplace texts:

> ...Martin and his systemic colleagues have defined genres as staged, goal-oriented social processes... In analysing these social processes, Australian genre scholars have differed from both ESP and New Rhetoric researchers in their focus on primary and secondary school genres and non-professional

workplace texts rather than on university and professional writing. (Hyon, 1996, p. 697)

Genre-based pedagogy in Australia has raised the concerns of some North American scholars, who are wary of the explicit style of teaching promoted by the *Sydney School* [emphasis added] (Freedman, 1994). (Hyon, 1996, p. 711)

By Johns (2002), this canon is used to organise a well-known book on classroom applications of genre theory (with direct representation from the "Sydney School"):

Part I The Sydney School

Part II Related Approaches

Part III English for Specific Purposes

Part V The New Rhetoric

And Bawarshi and Reiff's (2010) introduction to genre history, theory, research and pedagogy, confirms a further generation of scholars in this history:

Led by the work of J. R. Martin and supported by scholarship in the field of education linguistics in Australia, Systemic Functional approaches to genre arose in part in response to concerns over the efficacy of student-centered, process-based literacy teaching, with its emphasis on "learning through doing. (p. 32)

Sydney School [emphasis added] approach—A pedagogical approach to genre that emerged in response to an Australian national curriculum aimed at K-12 students. (p. 218)

Fortunately, by 2012 at the "Genre 2012—Rethinking Genre Twenty Years Later" conference in Ottawa, the Sydney School was well represented, as keynote and special session speakers (myself and Rose) and as presenters in parallel sessions (several students and colleagues). This meeting confronted Australians first hand with the

taken for granted nature of the history I've sketched out above—
naturalised a little further as the idea our genre theory grew out of
our literacy interventions in primary schools as part of a response to
the hegemony of process writing in Australia.

For the record, the University of Sydney research group[2]
developing studies of register and genre from circa 1980 to 1985
included Plum, who worked on a variety of spoken genres elicited
from dog breeders (Plum, 1998), Ventola, who studied Finnish
migrants' interactions with Australian staff in post office and travel
agency service encounters (Ventola, 1987), Eggins, who examined
dinner table conversations among her housemates and friends
(Eggins & Slade, 1997), Rothery, who was interested in doctor/
patient consultations as well as primary school writing (Rothery,
1996), and myself, a would-be critical linguist, who was working on
environmental and administrative discourse (Martin, 1985a, 1986a,
1986b). This work is consolidated in Martin (1992) and extended in
Christie and Martin (1997); for a comprehensive updated introduction
see Martin and Rose (2008); for seminal papers see Martin (2012b,
2012c). Unfortunately, Freedman and Medway (1994a, 1994b) refer
to none of the foundational SFL work published by 1994 in their
introductions, although they do cite critiques of Sydney School
interventions by Green and Lee (1994), Luke (1996)[3] and Threadgold
(1988) and the debates in Reid (1987). Similarly Hyon (1996) makes no
reference to the SFL work by Ventola (1987) or Martin (1992), and as
far as anyone can recall, she didn't in fact meet with Martin when
doing fieldwork in Australia in 1994. Martin (1984) is in fact the
seminal article popularising this SFL work for an education audience
(also not referenced by Freedman & Medway, nor Hyon).

Accordingly in section 2 below I try to clarify the way in which
genre is modelled in SFL, and then move on to deal with two key
issues arising from the 2012 Ottawa conference here (namely context
and change) in sections 3 and 4 respectively. For further discussion of
the development of genre theory in Australia see Martin (1999a, 2001,
2014a, 2014b).

Modelling Genre in SFL

First stratification. In SFL, co-tangential circles of increasing
diameter are used to model levels of abstraction in language

(Figure 1). SFL is distinctive among functional theories in working with a stratified content plane, with two levels, lexicogrammar and discourse semantics, both configured as resources for making meaning in discourse. The special responsibility of lexicogrammar is words and structures—meanings made through clauses in other words; the special responsibility of discourse semantics is text structure—meaning beyond the clause (including cohesive relations of various kinds, turn-taking structure and so on). The strata are related through the concept of metaredundancy, with discourse semantics an emergently complex pattern of lexicogrammatical patterns, and lexicogrammar an emergently complex pattern of phonological ones (Lemke, 1995).

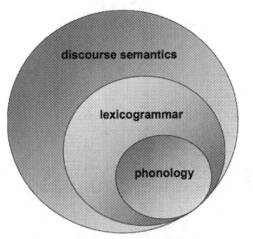

Figure 1. SFL's stratified model of language[4]. Reprinted from "Systemic typology and topology," by J.R. Martin and C. Mathiessen, 1991, in F. Christie (Ed.), *Literacy in Social Processes: Papers from the inaugural Australian Systemic Linguistics Conference, held at Deakin University, January 1990.* (pp. 345-383). Darwin: Centre for Studies in Language in Education, Northern Territory University. Reprinted with permission.

SFL is also distinctive among functional theories in modelling context as an additional stratum of meaning (akin to Hjelmslev's notion of a connotative semiotic); Halliday's perspective on this is outlined in Figure 2 (e.g., Matthiessen & Halliday, 2009), where context is used as the cover term for field, tenor and mode. This orientation to context was influenced by Firth's (1957) notion of meaning as function in context, which was in turn influenced by Malinowski's context of situation (1923) and context of culture (1935).

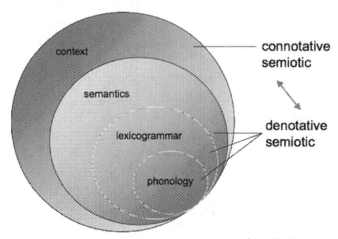

Figure 2. Context as a higher stratum of meaning (a Hallidayan perspective).

Early in the 1980s, Martin and his students proposed stratifying the context plane, as register and genre (with register adopted as the cover term for field, tenor and mode). This means that genre is a pattern of register patterns, just as register (field, tenor and mode) are patterns of discourse semantics patterns, and so on until the least abstract stratum, phonology[5], is reached (Figure 3).

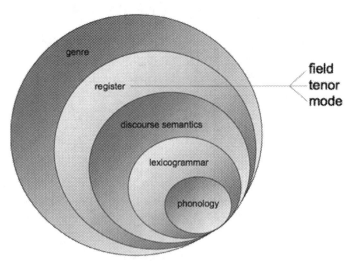

Figure 3. Context as higher strata of meaning (a Martinian perspective).

Technically speaking then a genre can be defined as a recurrent configuration of meaning, selecting appropriate field, tenor and mode variables and staging them as unfolding phases of meaningful discourse. This of course was far more than we could explain to the teachers we began working with in the 1980s, in a nation where progressive educators had systematically removed all knowledge about language (KAL) from the curriculum (on the specious grounds that it was useless and harmful—useless because it supposedly didn't help students learn to read or write and harmful because it took time away from student-centred learning[6]). We were faced with the challenge of re-introducing KAL, and decided to begin not with grammar but with genre. Accordingly in our practice, we re-articulated SFL's more technical understanding of genre (with which I began this paragraph) in terms of seeing genre in educational contexts as "a staged, goal-oriented social process"— staged because it usually takes us more than one phase of discourse to achieve our purpose, goal-oriented because we feel a sense of frustration and interruption if we don't negotiate our way through the structure of the genre, and social because we undertake genres interactively with others. This proved a workable characterisation of genre for our initial school interventions. This transfer selectively recontextualises one aspect of the theory it is drawing upon, in the interests of practice—a perfectly natural development. But when the recontextualisation into practice is mis/taken for the theory itself, as I am arguing has been the case with "Sydney School" practice and SFL theory, confusion naturally abounds.

Modelling Context

As noted above SFL has a distinctive perspective on context, which it models as either one or two higher strata of meaning. This perspective was imaged through co-tangential circles above, thereby encoding the notions of metaredundancy (i.e., pattern of patterns) and emergent complexity. This perspective can be referred to as supervenient. It contrasts with a more pervasive orientation to context in pragmatics and discourse analysis which sees context as extra-linguistic—as the sensory and/or conceptual environment in which language is embedded. This orientation can be referred to as circumvenient, and imaged as concentric circles. The complementarity is outlined in Figure 4 below.

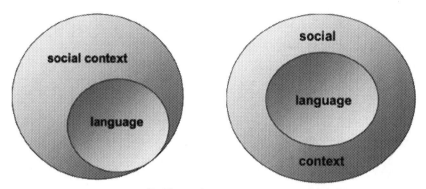

Figure 4. Supervenient (left) and circumvenient (right) perspectives on language and context. Reprinted from "Modelling context: matter as meaning," by J. R. Martin, 2013, in C. Gouveia & M. Alexandre (Eds.), *Languages, metalanguages, modalities, cultures: Functional and socio-discursive perspectives.* (pp. 10-64). Lisbon: BonD & ILTEC. Reprinted with permission.

As explored in Martin (2013) the supervenience project is an audacious one, but one which SFL has been pursuing now for more than six decades by way of construing language, register and genre as systems of meaning. From this work we might highlight phonology (Halliday & Greaves, 2008), lexicogrammar (Halliday & Matthiessen, 2004), discourse semantics (Martin 1992; Martin & Rose 2003/2007), register (Martin, 1992; Christie & Martin, 1997), genre (Martin & Rose, 2008) and language typology (Caffarel et al., 2004); for recent developments see Bednarek & Martin (2010), Hasan et al. (2005, 2007), Halliday and Webster (2009), Matthiessen (2007, 2010), Webster (2008, 2015); for key terms see Matthiessen et al (2010). For the supervenience project to succeed it is of course necessary to model the various modalities of communication that accompany language in the instantiation of a genre. Accordingly SFL has pushed on, as "systemic functional semiotics" one might say, to model image, sculpture, architecture, sound, gesture, facial expression, and activity itself as semiotic systems in similar terms (for recent developments see Dreyfus et al., 2011; Kress & van Leeuwen, 1996/2006; Martinec, 2005; O'Toole, 1994/2011; Painter et al., 2013; Unsworth, 2001; van Leeuwen, 1999, 2011). So what is treated as extra-linguistic in the circumvenience model is construed as semiotic and incorporated into a now multimodal supervenience perspective on the realisation of genre—along the lines of that imaged as Figure 5.

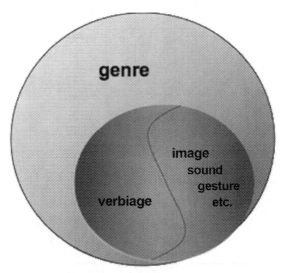

Figure 5. The inter-modal realisation of genre (across denotative semiotics). Reprinted from "Modelling context: matter as meaning" by J. R. Martin, 2013, in C. Gouveia & M. Alexandre (Eds.), *Languages, metalanguages, modalities, cultures: functional and socio-discursive perspectives.* (pp. 10-64). Lisbon: BonD & ILTEC. Reprinted with permission.

In Hjelmslev's terms, SFL thus models context in two ways—(i) by construing register and genre as connotative semiotics (i.e., higher levels of meaning) and (ii) by construing the communication systems (including activity) which function alongside language as parallel denotative semiotics (i.e., the attendant modalities of meaning in Figure 5 above). So the conception of genre as recurrent configurations of meanings introduced above has to be understood in relation to this work as recurrent configurations of multimodal meanings, and genre has the job not only of coordinating field, tenor and mode and their realisations across strata, but the instantiation[7] of meaning across semiotic systems as well. If this seems too ambitious a project, then the following anecdote from Halliday might help set the tone. Halliday was a PhD student at the time and had been to a series of three lectures by Hjelmslev at the School of

Oriental and African Studies (SOAS) in London, where the famous Dane spoke on the semiotics of traffic lights (cf. Hjelmslev, 1947). Halliday was one of the postgraduate students who were privileged to be invited to afternoon tea in the Senior Common Room to meet the visiting professor. There he overheard the following repartee:

> Firth: The trouble with you, Louis, is that you are too stratospheric.
>
> Hjelmslev: No, John. You are stratospheric. I have no ceiling.
>
> (Halliday, 2002, p. 118)

With ancestors like these, SFL's concern with modelling context as semiosis is unsurprising.

The "Sydney School" is sometimes criticised for talking a lot about context but not doing anything about it. I hope this brief excursion into SFL theoretical architecture helps to clarify the picture. Figure 3 is in fact suggesting that a culture can be conceived as a system of genres (coordinating a system of field, tenor and mode variations and their realisations in language); Figure 5 adds to this the idea that relevant extra-linguistic context can be brought into the picture as denotative semiotic systems. This is of course hard to see if the "Sydney School" educational practice is mistaken for SFL theory, and if there is an over-reliance on secondary accounts such as Richardson (1994) or Hyon (1996), whose references stop in 1994 before the flowering of work in multimodal discourse analysis inspired by O'Toole (1994) and Kress and van Leeuwen (1996). So the issue is not whether SFL models context or not, but how SFL's construal of context as meaning compares with alternative perspectives.

Crucial here is SFL's commitment to a relational theory of meaning, evolving as it does out of the theoretical legacy of Saussure (1916) and Hjelmslev (1961). This stems from Saussure's concept of the sign, which he saw as the inextricable bonding of signifié and significant (Figure 6). For him, the sign is analogous to a piece of paper, with one side signifié and the other signifiant. Signifié and significant in other words have no significance apart from their bonding with one another.

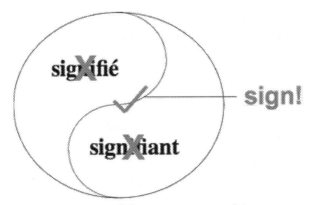

Figure 6. Saussure's concept of the sign. Reprinted from *Systemic Functional Grammar: A next step into the theory - axial relations,* by J. R. Martin, 2013, (Chinese translation and extensions by Wang Pin & Zhu Yongsheng). Beijing: Higher Education Press. Reprinted with permission.

Saussure's conception of the sign contrasts sharply with our common sense understanding, which sees a sign as standing for a concept (or referring to an aspect of the material world). This alternative perspective is outlined in Figure 7 below, using a supervenience diagram to model the relation of a symbol to a concept—exemplified with the image we conventionally view as standing for peace. This is the understanding of signs that most of us operate with in everyday life, and which from Saussure's perspective utterly confounds our understanding of language and semiosis.

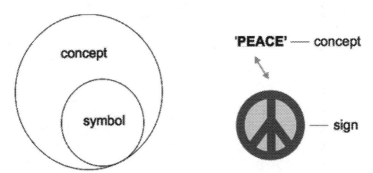

Figure 7. Common sense understanding of the sign.

Hjelmslev was one of the key linguists to develop Saussure's insights. As noted above, he used the example of traffic lights to illustrate another of Saussure's key ideas, namely the idea that the meaning of a sign is its relation to other signs. As Saussure explained, in language there are nothing but differences; there are no positive terms. A simple semiotic system of this kind is outlined as Figure 8 below. Signs are positioned there as bonds of traffic flow with colour; the meaning of each such sign is its relation to other signs in the system—technically its valeur. The system imparts a specific order to an otherwise amorphous physical reality (i.e., the continuum of perceivable hues in the spectrum of light and the "bumper first" chaos one experiences in countries where a system of this kind is either absent or ignored). Language, Saussure argued, is a system of signs.

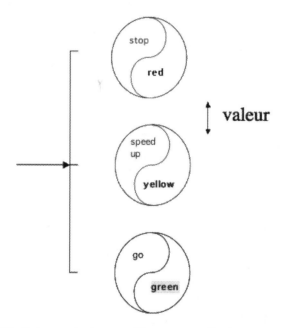

Figure 8. Traffic light semiosis as an illustration of valeur.

Hjelsmlev takes the further steps of demonstrating that language is not a simple system of signs (like traffic lights, human protolanguage or animal communication), but a stratified system of signs. He referred to these as content form and expression form, which he opposed to content substance and expression substance—where substance refers to the amorphous conceptual and physical reality unformed by semiosis. This perspective is modelled as a supervenience hierarchy in Figure 9 below (using the SFL's terms for the two levels of abstraction, alongside Hjelmslev's complementarity).

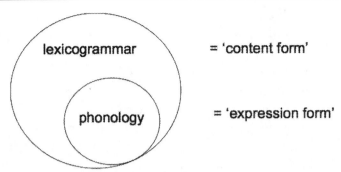

Figure 9. Language as a stratified system of signs. Reprinted from "Systemic typology and topology," by J.R. Martin and C. Mathiessen, 1991, in F. Christie (Ed.), *Literacy in Social Processes: Papers from the inaugural Australian Systemic Linguistics Conference*, held at Deakin University, January 1990. (pp. 345-383). Darwin: Centre for Studies in Language in Education, Northern Territory University. Reprinted with permission.

Note that Hjelmslev is not challenging the inextricable bonding of signifié and signifiant proposed by Saussure. Rather he is pointing out that the bonding of signifié with signifiant is so complex that a stratified account of the relations involved is required. Language in other words is the network of relations that bonds signifié and signifiant. Drawing on another of Saussure's analogies, we can say that the sign is like a coin—its value is its relation to other coins of different denominations and linguists work in the very highly differentiated space between heads and tails—researching not physical or biological, but semiotic, reality.

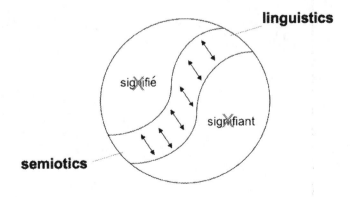

Figure 10. The focus on linguistic and semiotic research.

As noted above SFL builds on this conception of language by developing stratified content (Figure 1 above) and context (Figure 3 above) planes. Critically, in doing so SFL adopts a relational perspective on meaning, elaborated by Halliday and his colleagues out of the insights of Saussure, Hjelmslev and Firth. Thus in SFL meaning has to do with valeur—the place of any unit in the stratified network of relations bonding signifié with signifiant. This approach contrasts with representational theories of meaning, whereby signs refer to objects in the real world and/or concepts in the mind.

Why is this important? What then in this framework is the meaning of genre? Since SFL adopts a relational theory of meaning, the meaning of a genre is it valeur. As Saussure, Hjelmslev and Firth stressed, in order to effectively explore valeur we have to consider both system and structure (paradigmatic and syntagmatic relations in Hjelmslev's terms). And following Halliday, SFL privileges system, taking structure as the manifestation of systemic valeur. Consider the following account of a minor offence involving a teenager who has swapped his mobile phone for a stolen one and has got caught in possession of the stolen goods. The genre at stake here is a member of the story family (Martin & Rose, 2008, Chapter 2)—technically a kind of recount. It begins with an element of structure shared across this family, termed Orientation (following Labov & Waletzky, 1967). The function of the Orientation is to set the story in time and place and introduce the main characters. This is followed by the Record of events, in which what happens unfolds chronologically in a matter of fact way, with nothing flagged through evaluation as remarkable. The story concludes with a Re-orientation, which closes this story-telling phase of whatever else is going on and makes room for additional elements of structure or perhaps another genre.

Text 1:

[1] Orientation

Yeah, I was, I was walking to a mate's house.

Record of events

This guy just came up to me

and goes "Do you want to buy a phone?"

and I go "No".

and I go "Do you want to swap?"

[inaudible] want to swap with my phone

and he looked at my phone

and he goes "Yeah"

and we swap

and I went and stayed at my mate's house

and when it came to night time I was going back home,

and he was walking, was walking up the road

and the police just came and got us.

Re-orientation

That's it.

In this case we are in fact in a Youth Justice Conference, a form of diversionary justice practiced in New South Wales, Australia. The Convenor of the conference has invited this recount as part of the obligatory testimony phase of the conference macro-genre; but she is unsatisfied with it is two respects. For one thing, she wants more detail, which she prompts in an Extension stage.

[1 continued] **Extension**

Convenor: And then what happened? They came and got you. They found the phone. What did they say to you?

- Young Person (YP): They go that this phone was stolen

Convenor: OK. What did you say?

- YP: I go, you know, I swapped it. Yeah, they just took took me.

Convenor: Took you where?

- YP: Police station

Convenor: And who did they ring when they brought you to the police station?

- YP: My dad.

And for another she wants the young person to evaluate what went on, which she elicits in an Interpretation stage:

[1 continued] **Interpretation**

Convenor: And what did dad say when he got here?

- YP: He (was) just asking why am I here? And the police told him.

Convenor : And was he happy? Did he say anything to you?

- YP: Don't go anywhere.

Convenor: As is when you get home you've got to stay home? Do you think your father was disappointed in you?

- YP: Yep.

...

Convenor: Do you think you deserved the lecture? Why did you deserve the lecture?

- YP: Because I did something wrong.

...

Convenor: Do you think that mum and dad were disappointed in you? Were you disappointed in yourself? Or Not? Or you don't care?

- YP: Yeah.

Convenor: Yeah or you don't care?

- YP: Disappointed in myself.

This then opens up the possibility of further evaluation by the Victim or Victim's representative if present, or the Convenor, on their behalf if not. Keep in mind here that we are just beginning to probe the valeur of this story at the stratum of genre. If we were writing a monograph instead of a paper, we could push on to explore its field (including both the conferencing and the misdemeanour), its tenor (the power and solidarity relations involved) and its mode (phases of dialogue punctuated with the reconstruction of past experience and later on with proposals for the future); and then we would push on to consider how discourse semantic systems construe field, enact tenor and compose mode; and how lexicogrammatical systems realise the discourse semantic ones; and how phonological and gestural systems realise the lexicogrammatical ones; and how space grammar (seating, ambience etc.) configures the meaning of the text alongside linguistic and paralinguistic resources. There's a large SFL toolkit available here, one which keeps expanding with each generation of research. In relation to this toolkit we are of course just providing a glimpse of the genre here; for further coverage of this forensic linguistics project see Martin (2012f).

Taking the structure reviewed above into account, and its recurrence across the conferences we observed and analysed, we decided to name this member of the story family a commissioned recount. It differs from personal recounts in not having the ongoing prosody of evaluation we find in the recounts of everyday life we exchange to sustain our solidary relations with family and close friends who are interested in the ordinary things we do and how we feel about them. Negotiating intimacy depends on sharing attitudes to the details of day-to-day life. Here on the other hand we encounter Young Persons who enact a small target persona, providing as little detail as possible in a "bald-on-record" recount. Details and evaluation have to be extracted by the Convenor.

These observations, and the detailed analyses across strata they gloss over, put us in a position to begin to formalise, at the level of genre, the meaning of a commissioned recount (i.e., its valeur). We can approach this typologically or topologically. Typologically, we are interested in categorical distinctions based on privileged demarcating criteria; topologically we are interested in graded categories based on privileged scaled criteria. The simplest form of typological analysis is the list, such as the outline of certain member of the story genre family and their structure in Table 1 below. The table names the genres, specifies their nuclear staging and characterises the way their events unfold in relation to evaluation; for details of the work on which this is based see Martin (1992), Eggins and Slade (1997), Martin and Plum (1997), Plum (1998), Martin and Rose (2008).

Table 1

Selected story genres (their structure, event profile and evaluation)

genre (and nuclear staging)	events	reaction ('evaluation')
recount Record of Events	unproblematic	*running commentary*
anecdote Remarkable Event ^ Reaction	unexpected disruption	*emotional empathy*
exemplum Incident ^ Interpretation[8]	noteworthy incident	*moral judgement*
observation Event description ^ Comment	significant event	*appreciate value*
narrative (Labov) Complication ^ Evaluation ^ Resolution	problem ^ solution	*build^release tension*
gossip, news story, thematic ... **narrative** etc.		...

Optional stages shared across members of the story family (e.g., Abstract, Orientation, Coda) have not been included above. While the influence of Labov and Waletzky (1967) is reflected in some of the labelling, note that this research challenges (i) the idea that there is one story genre structure (based on Labov & Waletzky's narrative of personal experience), (ii) the idea that any text which unfolds chronologically is a story (cf. for example Coffin, 2006, on history genres or Martin & Rose, 2008, on procedures and explanations) and (iii) the idea that almost anything at all can be talked about as narrative as in some of the humanities discourse influenced by continental critical theory (cf. Martin, 2008, for discussion). I should also note here that research into the family of story genres is a far from completed project, and reflects at this stage a bias towards the spoken story genres exchanged in interviews and conversation—based on the gaze of Eggins, Plum, Slade and our more recent restorative justice research (see however Rose, 2006, 2011 on the continuities between spoken and written story genres).

Figure 11 below classifies commissioned recounts in relation to our current understanding of the valeur of key story genres. The network begins with time structured stories (as opposed to western broad-sheet news stories which no longer unfold chronologically), and divides them into those in which events unfold as expected and those which involve surprise. Expectant stories (the recounts) are then split into those with an ongoing prosodic evaluation of events as they unfold and the commissioned recount which has no evaluation until it is extracted by the Convenor after the events have been told. There is obviously a great deal more to say about this network and the recurrent configurations of meaning on which it is based, which I cannot possibly do justice to here. The main point the network at this stage is simply to illustrate how SFL approaches the meaning of a commissioned recount typologically at the level of genre.

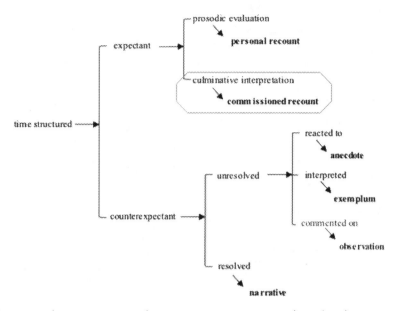

Figure 11. The commissioned recount as a story genre (typology).

Figure 12 below exemplifies the complementary topological perspective on genre relations. Topological representation involves setting up two or more clined axes which allow units to be positioned as more or less like one another with respect to the dimensions selected (Martin & Matthiessen, 1991). In Figure 12 for example the vertical axis scales genres according to the degree to which evaluation is localised culminatively towards the end of the genre or diffused prosodically as the text unfolds; the horizontal axis grades genres according to the degree to which the evaluation of the story is inscribed by the narrator or prescribed by the interlocutor hearing or reading the story. The topology thus construes a semantic space in which we can position genres. Accordingly in relation to Figure 12 we can informally position anecdotes, exemplums and observations in the upper left part of the topology with the narrator's point concentrated towards the end. Narrative and recount fall into the lower left quadrant, since their narrator's evaluation is more diffusely realised, more so in personal recounts than in narratives. The lower right-hand quadrant includes the implicitly moralising thematic narratives which are interpreted after being told by literary critics and apprentice critics in secondary school and university literature classrooms (Rothery & Stenglin, 1997). Our commissioned recount is then positioned in then upper right-hand quadrant, since its point is prescribed by the Convenor after its Record of Events and Extension stages. Depending on the criteria involved and our ability to quantify measures, units can be formally rather than informally positioned along such clines. Topological analysis is especially useful for positioning specific instances of a genre as more or less prototypical; this is important for considering genres from a dynamic perspective, as they evolve in culture, and for formative assessment purposes, as they develop in the repertoire of apprentice speakers and writers.

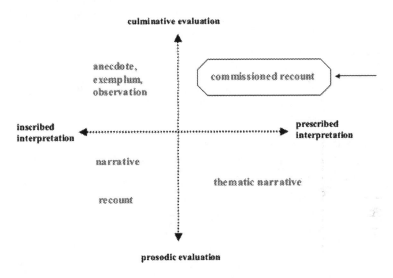

Figure 12. The commissioned recount as a story genre (topology).

The "Sydney School" is sometimes criticised for studying the form of genres rather than their meaning (and this invites a further step of dismissal whereby studying form is stigmatised as a focus on genre conventions). I hope that this excursion into SFL's theoretical lineage helps to clear up this confusion. It is quite true, in Saussure and Hjelmslev's terms, that SFL studies form. But this means that it studies form not substance; it doesn't mean that it studies form not meaning—since form and meaning are not dualised in this Firthian tradition. On the contrary, it is precisely by formalising language and context as a network of relations that SFL operationalises its relational theory of meaning. Figures 11 and 12 for example are designed to display the valeur of genre, just as system networks across strata, metafunctions and ranks are deployed to model language and context as systems of difference—and thereby model language, register and genre as resources for meaning. So the issue is not whether SFL studies form instead of meaning, but rather how SFL's relational theory of meaning compares with alternative representational perspectives. What for example does a cognitive perspective which treats genres as artefacts of individual speakers' intentions tell us that a relational perspective on meaning does not? What does an ethnographic perspective add to our understanding of genre, foregrounding as it often does the idea that the meaning of a genre is not in the text but in its context and that we therefore need involve ourselves as participant observers to know what is going on? What can cognitive and ethnographic perspectives find out by asking speakers what they mean when enacting one or another genre? How might the results of these inquiries be suitably presented to linguists such as myself who are trained by American structuralists (Gleason and Samarin) not to believe anything a native speaker says about their language? How might the results of such inquiries be effectively presented to social realist sociologists who can't see any "-graphy" in ethnography[9] which has departed so far from Malinowski's practice that an alternative spelling is perhaps required—ethNOgraphy they might jibe (cf. Bernstein, 1996/2000, p. 170).

Modelling Change

In Section 4 above I concentrated on SFL's relational theory of meaning and its model of context as strata of meaning (register and genre). Before concluding I will touch briefly on the issue of semiotic change, around which once again there has been considerable confusion as far as criticism of "Sydney School" genre theory has been concerned. Once again we need to go back to basics, and look carefully at SFL's orientation to genesis in relation to semiotic systems. The first thing we need to do is distinguish three key perspectives on time—logogenesis, ontogenesis and phylogenesis (e.g., Halliday & Matthiessen, 1999). Logogenesis refers to a time frame commensurate with the unfolding of a text. Ontogenesis refers to the development of an individual's semiotic repertoire. Phylogenesis refers to the evolution of the reservoir of meanings resourcing a culture. As Halliday & Matthiessen (1999, pp. 17-18) explain, as far as semogenesis concerned, phylogenesis provides the environment for ontogenesis, which provides the environment for logogenesis— just as logogenesis provides the material for ontogenesis which in turn provides the material for phylogenesis (Figure 13 below). All of the strata introduced above can be explored from the perspective of each time frame. And all time frames can be explored from both a synoptic and a dynamic perspective (cf. Martin, 1985b; Ventola, 1987; on exchange and genre structure).

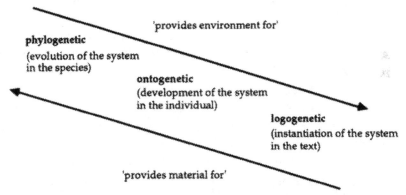

Figure 13. Semogenetic time frames. Reprinted from Halliday, M. A. K. & Matthiessen, C. M. I. M. (1999). *Construing experience through language: A language-based approach to cognition.* (p. 18). London: Cassell. Bloomsbury. Reprinted with permission.

SFL is well known for its concern with logogenesis, *Cohesion in English* (Halliday & Hasan, 1976) and *English Text* (Martin, 1992) being the landmark discourse analysis resources. Overwhelmingly, synoptic accounts of genre structure, cohesive ties and discourse structure are provided (e.g., Table 1 above) since the development of animated visualisations capable of dynamically modelling text as it unfolds is still in its infancy. Zappavigna et al. (2010) and Zappavigna (2012) provide a glimpse of what might be developed over the next generation. Linguistics is lagging behind the physical and biological sciences in this regard.

As far as ontogenesis is concerned, Halliday (1975) and Painter (1984, 1998) are the main sources for work on language development in the home from birth to school. Christie and Derewianka (2008) and Christie (2012) explore the development of writing in primary and secondary education. These studies all adopt the strategy of providing synoptic snapshots of the resources available at different stages of development (e.g., every six weeks for Halliday, 1975, and Painter, 1984). A complementary dynamic perspective on emergent complexity as systems develop across strata and metafunctions awaits development.

As far as phylogenesisis concerned the best-known work in SFL concerns the evolution of scientific discourse in English (Halliday, 2004). Wignell (2007) complements this with his study of the evolution of social science. Once again these histories monitor evolution by providing synoptic snapshots of relevant language resources at different stages of evolution. Theoretically, the main paper on language in relation to the evolution of human consciousness is Halliday (1994), which interfaces SFL with the neo-Darwinian neurobiology of Edelman (e.g., Edelman, 1992).

It is in the context of this perspective on semogenesis that Martin (1985a, 1986b) proposes his left/right protagonist/antagonist model for considering genre in relation to environmental issues. Iedema et al. (1994) focus on the evolution of the 20th century English broadsheet news story out of 19th century recounts, including a social semiotic analysis of the factors at play in the re-shaping of this genre. Veel (1998) and Martin (2002) consider the effect of ecological and environmental discourse on science and physical geography writing in secondary school (its "greening" as it were). And the entire "Sydney School" project has been designed to promote ontogenetic language change—namely the expansion of students' genre repertoires in schooling (Rose, this volume; Rose & Martin, 2012).

More recently, in our restorative justice research (Martin, 2012f), we noted with interest the apparent evolution of the commissioned recount out of the personal recount genre, with its bald-on-record Record of Events, optional Extension and evaluation extracting Interpretation. A full range of field, tenor and mode factors are arguably responsible for this re-negotiation of the genre (e.g., the formal institutionalised legal field, the polarised tenor relations among interlocutors and the turn-controlled face-to-face multi-party mode). Based on the closely related field, tenor and mode variables at play we might predict that a comparable genre would emerge in the testimony tabled in truth and reconciliation hearings.

Looking beyond the Testimony step, we also noted the apparent evolution of the macro-genre designed for the training of Youth Justice Conferencing Convenors. Conferencing is in fact the third phase of a staged response to adolescent offenders legislated in the New South Wales Young Offenders Act. The initial phase involves an on the spot warning by police. For more serious or subsequent offences police may require the offender and a support person to attend a meeting at the police station where they are formally cautioned. For more serious or subsequent offences still a conference may be recommended, in which the Young Person admits to his misdemeanour, discusses it with the Victim or Victim's representative, hopefully apologises for his behaviour and agrees to some form of reparation by way of community service. Alternatively the Young Person appears before a magistrate in court and runs the risk of juvenile detention and a criminal record (Figure 14).

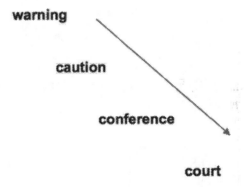

Figure 14. New South Wales Young Offenders Act staged response to offences.

Youth Justice Conferences are regularly attended by the arresting Police Officer and a Police Liaison Officer. One of their jobs for which they are trained is in fact to deliver the caution in the second phase of the responses outlined in Figure 14. Although conference designers made no provision in their outline of proceedings for a lengthy monologic intervention by Police Officers, we found that in many conferences Police Officers did so intervene, delivering what looked to us like the kind of thing they might have said at the police station in the caution phase (i.e., a future oriented warning about what will happen if the

Young Person does not reform; Martin, 2012f). So in practice, within just a few years of its implementation, the macro-genre[10] evolved to the point where we feel reasonably confident about including this elemental genre in its structure; the Caution step is positioned between the Rejoinder and Outcome plan phases in Figure 15 below.

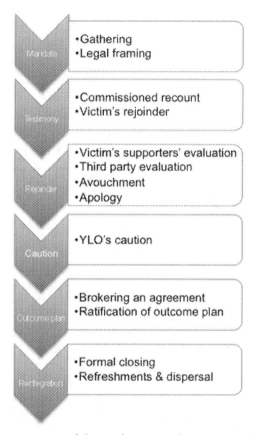

Figure 15. The current state of the evolving Youth Justice Conference macro-genre. Reprinted from "Beyond redemption: Choice and consequence in Youth Justice conferencing," by J. R. Martin and M. Zappavigna, 2014, in Fang Yan & J. Webster (Eds.), *Developing Systemic Functional Linguistics: Theory and application.* (pp. 18-47). London: Equinox. Reprinted with permission.

The "Sydney School" is sometimes criticised for having a fossilised notion of genre that does not acknowledge change, a critique based on the canonical models of genres used to initiate the apprenticeship of novice writers in school. This critique confuses SFL with prescriptive "school grammar" traditions that invoke grammatical rules to discourage the intrusion of spoken language and non-standard dialects into classroom discourse, whereas SFL describes language as a flexible evolving resource for meaning. "Sydney School" research has described the genres that students typically read and write in school, and designed a metalanguage for discussing them. Its critics appear to have confused these descriptions with the prescriptions of the school grammarians they (or perhaps their parents) grew up with.

Once again I hope that this excursion into the SFL theory informing "Sydney School" practice helps to clarify this confusion. Genres, like all linguistic and semiotic resources involve semogenesis, across logogenetic, ontogenetic and phylogenetic time frames. Importantly, all of the systems involved are metastable—invested with a finely tuned balance of inertia and change. The issue is not whether SFL engages with language change or not, but rather how it models change. The real challenge for SFL is how to move beyond synoptic snapshots of different "état de langue" and dynamically model the interacting factors which precipitate and discourage genesis. Zappavigna (2012) provides an illuminating study of this tension in her study of the emergent social networking mode Twitter.

Confusion about semogenesis can lead to highly charged debates in which concerns with creativity and power are brought into play. Teaching students to master genres is sometimes argued to be ontogenetically impossible, once genres are recontextualised from their deployment in communities of practice outside school into the classroom. Alternatively, if mentoring mastery of genres is admitted as possible, then it is argued that it is in any case ontogenetically undesirable, because it stifles the innovative discourse students would otherwise be producing. And it is further suggested that even if mastery is possible, it is ontogenetically and phylogenetically pointless, because mastering a genre does not confer power on an individual or redistribute power in society—since power has to do with "social" factors above and beyond language use. I've addressed these issues with counter-examples elsewhere (e.g., Martin, 1997, 1999c 2002; Martin & Matthiessen, 2014), often drawing on Bakhtin's observation that creativity depends on mastery of the genre (Bakhtin, 1986, p. 80) and pointing out the sublime hypocrisy of scholars who tell us not to teach the very discourses whose authority they are deploying to critique us (cf. Christie, 2010). Let me try again here.

Consider Text 2 below, jointly constructed by Australian Aboriginal students in a university preparation course. It discusses their growing awareness of the importance of education for Indigenous people.

Text 2:

[2] As a child I did not yearn for knowledge. I was learning from the adventures of life. I learnt how to ride a bike in the backstreets of Redfern, how to catch crayfish with a stick down at the riverbank, how to make chewing gum from tar off the road, and how to play football with my cousins and friends. As long as I listened to my elders and respected them, I learnt everything I needed to know.

It was only when I started school, and I had to learn a new set of rules, that I felt frightened and ignorant.

From my first day at school I wanted to learn simple things, everyday things like how to make friends, win fights, but stay out of trouble. Later, growing up as a teenager in high school, I longed for more important things, to succeed at schoolwork, to be treated equally, to go to parties and eventually leave school and get a job.

But then it dawned on me that not only I needed an education, but my family also needed a role model. I discovered that it was not just my confidence and opportunities that were limited, but the future prospects of my people.

That is when I decided to go to university, when the desire for my education became the greater desire for the education of my people. It was this urge to fulfil my potential, to live my life with confidence and respect, that gave me a goal in life, that transformed an intimidated person into a confident one, that drove an idle person to become a hard worker, that turned a lazy person into a motivated student, that forced someone who felt like a failure to become a success.

Education is indispensable; failure in school closes down opportunities in life; until the schools learn to educate our children, life will be a struggle for our people.

Before I proceed further can I ask you to stop for a moment and reflect on how you read this autobiographical recount. Do you have a sense that the indigenous students involved are stifled or enabled by the genre? Do you think they feel more or less confident about their writing than before undertaking the task? Do you view this as a step towards independent tertiary sector writing in another field in a comparable genre, or a straight-jacket locking them in? Do you feel it is naïve or prescient to suggest that writing of this kind might help prepare such students for their tertiary studies? Do you consider success in university empowering or depowering for students of this kind? Are you prepared to answer any of these questions on the basis of this text alone? Would interviewing these students or their teacher provide you with the information you need to answer these questions, or just give you more data to analyse and consider? What other texts would you need to bring to bear? How many more? How analysed?

Resuming then—following Coffin (2006) we can treat Text 2 as an autobiographical recount, for which she uses a generalised staging structure closely related to our work on Text 1 above (Orientation, Record of Events, Re-Orientation). The text begins with an Orientation stage, positioning its narrator as growing up in Redfern, a well-known Indigenous community in Sydney, Australia (the reference to elders confirms the indigenous ethnic origin of the writers). The Record of Events[11] then unfolds through three sectors of schooling (primary, secondary and tertiary) with each sector giving rise to a growing awareness of the importance of education for Indigenous people.

[2'] Orientation

As a child I did not yearn for knowledge. I was learning from the adventures of life. I learnt how to ride a bike in the backstreets of Redfern, how to catch crayfish with a stick down at the riverbank, how to make chewing gum from tar off the road, and how to play football with my cousins and friends. As long as I listened to my elders and respected them, I learnt everything I needed to know.

Record of Events

It was only when I started school, and I had to learn a new set of rules, that I felt frightened and ignorant.

From my first day at school I wanted to learn simple things, everyday things like how to make friends, win fights, but stay out of trouble. Later, growing up as a teenager in high school, I longed for more important things, to succeed at schoolwork, to be treated equally, to go to parties and eventually leave school and get a job.

But then it dawned on me that not only I needed an education, but my family also needed a role model. I discovered that it was not just my confidence and opportunities that were limited, but the future prospects of my people.

That is when I decided to go to university, when the desire for my education became the greater desire for the education of my people. It was this urge to fulfil my potential, to live my life with confidence and respect, that gave me a goal in life, that transformed an intimidated person into a confident one, that drove an idle person to become a hard worker, that turned a lazy person into a motivated student, that forced someone who felt like a failure to become a success.

Education is indispensable; failure in school closes down opportunities in life; until the schools learn to educate our children, life will be a struggle for our people.

This jointly constructed text was produced (Rose, 2011) in the Joint Rewriting step of Rose's Reading to Learn teaching/learning pedagogy (cycle 2 in Figure 16 below). Christie (2002) describes such classroom pedagogies as curriculum genres. In the Reading to Learn curriculum genre (Rose & Martin, 2012), cycle 1 (Preparing for Reading, Joint Construction and Individual Construction) has a focus on recognising and using the organisation of the whole text, including its stages and phases (for phases see Rose, 2006; Martin & Rose, 2008). The focus of cycle 2 (Detailed Reading, Joint Rewriting and Individual Rewriting) is on recognising and appropriating the patterns of language within and between sentences. Cycle 3 provides opportunities to focus on grammatical structure and graphology.

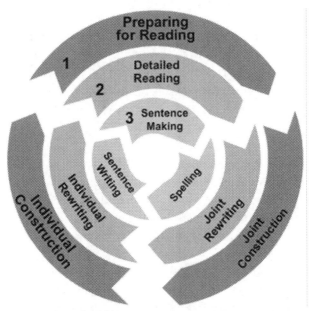

Figure 16. Rose's Reading to Learn teaching/learning cycles. Reproduced from *Reading to Learn: Accelerating learning and closing the gap. Teacher training books and DVDs*, by D. Rose, 2015, Sydney: Reading to Learn. Reproduced with permission.

The basic rule of thumb in genre based pedagogy is not to ask students to write before first making clear through models the genre they are expected to write, and also involving them in jointly constructing a text in the same genre (which functions as a further model). The model used by Rose for Text 2 above is extracted from the summative autobiographical recount of Nelson Mandela's life at the end of his autobiography (analysed in some detail in Martin, 1999b; Martin & Rose, 2003/2007; for discussion of this and related history genres see Martin and Rose (2008, Chapter 3). In the Preparing for Reading step of cycle 1, the text was first briefly discussed with the class, including its field and the sequence in which it unfolds. The text was next read aloud with the class, and then discussed in more depth. Instead of proceeding directly to Joint Construction of an autobiographical text with a different field, further layers of support were provided for these students through Detailed Reading—with a focus on Mandela's language choices in each paragraph and sentence. This decision was motivated on the one hand by the serious literacy problems ongoingly experienced by most students in this class, and the complexity and richness of Mandela's writing on the other. In this case, Rose particularly wanted to focus on the resources Mandela uses to engage us with the processes of his inner life and the effects of is desire for freedom (bold face in Text 3[12] below) and the rhetoric of negation and concession that he deploys to negotiate the expectations of readers (underlined in Text 3 below).

Text 3:

[3] I was <u>not</u> born with a **hunger** to be free. I was born free—free in every way that I **could know**. Free to run in the fields near my mother's hut, free to swim in the clear stream that ran through my village, free to roast mealies under the stars and ride the broad backs of slow-moving bulls. As long as I obeyed my father and abided by the customs of my tribe, I was <u>not troubled</u> by the laws of man or God.

It was <u>only</u> when I **began to learn** that my boyhood freedom was an illusion, when I **discovered** as a young man that my freedom had <u>already</u> been taken from me, that I began to **hunger** for it.

At first, as a student, I **wanted** freedom <u>only</u> for myself, the transitory freedoms of being able to stay out at night, read what I **pleased** and go where I **chose**. Later, as a young man in Johannesburg, I **yearned** for the basic and honourable freedoms of achieving my potential, of earning my keep, of marrying and having a family—the freedom <u>not to be</u> obstructed in a lawful life.

But then I slowly saw that not only was I <u>not</u> free, <u>but</u> my brothers and sisters were <u>not</u> free.

I saw that it was not just my freedom that was curtailed, <u>but</u> the freedom of everyone who looked like I did.

That is when I joined the African National Congress, and that is when the **hunger** for my own freedom became the **greater hunger** for the freedom of my people. It was this **desire** for the freedom of my people to live their lives with dignity and self-respect that **animated** my life, that **transformed** a frightened young man into a bold one, that **drove** a law-abiding attorney to become a criminal, that **turned** a family-loving husband into a man without a home, that **forced** a life-loving man to live like a monk. I am <u>no more</u> virtuous or self-sacrificing than the next man, <u>but</u> I **found** that I could <u>not even</u> **enjoy** the poor and limited freedoms I was allowed when I **knew** my people were <u>not free</u>.

Freedom is <u>indivisible</u>; the chains on any one of my people were the chains on all of them, the chains on all of my people were the chains on me.

Rose was also concerned to draw students' attention to the way in which Mandela continually elaborates his meanings, particularly through parallel grammatical structures. The elaborations highlighted in Detailed Reading as the class works through the text sentence by sentence are outlined below. During Detailed Reading students identify and highlight these patterns on their own copy of the text with the teacher's guidance, discussing their significance as they go, in terms of both the field and the author's language choices.

born free

= free in every way that I could know.

= Free to run in the fields near my mother's hut,

free to swim in the clear stream that ran through my village,

free to roast mealies under the stars

and ride the broad backs of slow-moving bulls.

my boyhood freedom was an illusion,

= my freedom had already been taken from me

freedom only for myself,

= transitory freedoms

> = stay out at night,
>
> read what I pleased
>
> and go where I chose.

basic and honourable freedoms

> = achieving my potential,
>
> earning my keep,
>
> marrying and having a family

= the freedom not to be obstructed in a lawful life.

desire for the freedom of my people... animated my life,

> > = that transformed a frightened young man into a bold one,
> >
> > that drove a law-abiding attorney to become a criminal,
> >
> > that turned a family-loving husband into a man without a home,
> >
> > that forced a life-loving man to live like a monk.

Freedom is indivisible;

> = the chains on any one of my people
>
> were the chains on all of them,
>
> = the chains on all of my people
>
> were the chains on me.

Detailed Reading is typically followed by Joint Rewriting, in which students practise the language patterns drawn to their attention in Detailed Reading. The function of Joint Rewriting is to practise the art of appropriating language resources from accomplished authors into one's own repertoire, a skill normally acquired tacitly by a few privileged students but brought to consciousness here. As both Detailed Reading and Joint Rewriting can be very time consuming, they are typically practised only on short passages.

In contrast, Joint Construction is a curriculum genre designed in genre writing pedagogy to appropriate the overall structure of genre models to construct new texts (Rothery, 1996), without appropriating the model's language patterns in detail. In Rose's refinement of Joint Construction, the model text is projected for all to see, its structure is reviewed (stage by stage and phase by phase), and each stage and phase is labelled on the model and on students' copies. The teacher then guides the students as they build up a new field, making notes on a class board. Once key features of the new field have been assembled, the new text is written on the board, as students take turns to scribe the wordings suggested by the class (with the teacher guiding this process as needed).

In this particular lesson, Detailed Reading was applied to Mandela's whole text, so Joint Construction of Mandela's overall text structure was combined with Joint Rewriting of his detailed language choices. The technique in this case involved the teacher pointing out Mandela's language choices in each sentence of the model text, and the class then choosing comparable patterns for the new field. Through Detailed Reading, all students already had a strong control of these language patterns, so applying them to a new field was comparatively easy to do. The result of this exercise was Text 2 above, subsequent to which the students practised the same task individually, using the same text structure and language patterns in new fields of their own choice.

Now that I have revealed the scaffolding[13] responsible for the indigenous voice manifested in Text 2, it might be useful to return to the questions I asked immediately after introducing the text and ask how its origins in a genre-based literacy program affect the way you value this piece of writing. Is the scaffolding enabling or stifling creativity?[14] Is the scaffolding empowering students or not? I imagine that for some of you your answer to these questions has as much to do with your predispositions toward a visible pedagogy as with the ontogenesis a pedagogy of this kind manages to achieve. How can we rise above axiological predispositions of this kind—in the interests of our students?

Dialogue

At the 2012 genre conference in Ottawa concerns were raised about the lack of dialogue between the "Sydney School" and the ESP and Rhetorical Genre Studies (RGS) traditions. Reviewing the construal of "Sydney School" work by scholars in the latter two traditions following on from the 1992 Ottawa genre conference I have emphasised the importance of distinguishing between theories (like SFL) and derived practices (like those of the "Sydney School"). And I have tried to clarify the SFL approach to context and semogenesis informing "Sydney School" action research. This dialectic of theory and practice has been an important one as far as the evolution of SFL has been concerned, and I do not want to downplay its significance— for the development of genre theory in SFL (Martin & Rose, 2008), or appraisal (Martin & White, 2005), or work on multimodality (Painter et al., 2013). But SFL as a functional linguistic theory is not the same thing as its selective recontextualisation in "Sydney School" practice. And if we want to foster dialogue amongst the "three traditions" and beyond it is important to be clear about when we are talking about theory and when we are talking about practice informed by theory.

In Ottawa I also emphasised the importance of access to data as far as dialogue is concerned. There is a good deal of overlapping terminology across the three traditions, which from a linguistic perspective makes it essential that examples of the discourse being interpreted as genre be tabled in presentations and publications. I appreciate that this can be awkward, when scholars are dealing with long texts—too long for a handout, and too long for display on a Power Point slide. But Web 2 affords various ways in which this limitation can be overcome and we need to exploit them more carefully in future in the interests of a more engaging dialogue.

Another problem that was aired in Ottawa was the excluding technicality of the functional linguistic tradition. I wasn't quick enough on my feet when this problem was raised to caution participants about the apparent transparency of RGS discourse.

Looking over the work of my educational linguistics colleagues over the years as they try and apprentice students into humanities discourse of this kind it is clear that they are engaged in a daunting task. Both the ESP and RGS traditions have their own distinctive patterns of argumentation, their own field-specific axiologies, their own sophisticated ways of texturing written discourse, their own favoured inter-texts and references, their own specialised use of what look like everyday words—generally composed in highly cultivated modes of literary expression. Speaking as a linguist, I see the mastery of discourse of this kind as a far more challenging task than learning the selectively recontextualised SFL technicality of the "Sydney School"—especially when our teacher/linguists have now spent so many productive decades directly confronting this issue (cf. Rose & Martin, 2012, Chapter 4). Has the apparent transparency of ESP and RGS discourse occluded the gaze of ESP and RGS scholars as far as the challenge of the cultivated texture of their own discourse is concerned?

What all this amounts to saying is that there is inevitably a degree of incommensurability in the discourses of different theories and practices. SFL, ESP and RGS are very different kinds of knowledge structure, as explored in Christie (2008), Hood (2011), and Martin (2012a). My experience over four decades of work in clinical, educational and forensic linguistics is that real engagement with another discipline depends on having a common problem to solve, and a shared politics driving us towards a solution to that problem. Without this impetus it is hard to make the time for learning enough of another theory to converse productively. SFL scholars like myself have worked intensively with sociologists over the decades on various issues, and I can certainly attest to the challenge of learning to read, appreciate, and raid another knowledge structure (for constructive dialogue amongst SFL and social realist scholars see Christie, 1999; Christie & Martin, 2007; Christie & Maton, 2011; Hasan, 2009; Maton et al., 2015; for my thoughts on interdisciplinary dialogue see Martin, 2011). As Maton and I have been exploring recently, dialogue is facilitated by specific family resemblances between theories. For SFL linguistics and social realist sociology these include (i) depth ontology (for example the stratification hierarchy introduced in section 2 above, (ii) relational thinking (for example, SFL's approach to language and context as a network of relationships) and (iii) accountability (i.e., the ability of a theory to put its theory at risk in relation to data as opposed to producing another reading of say Shakespeare). SFL shares fewer family resemblances of this order with ESP and fewer still with Rhetorical Genre Studies.

There is more to say than my word count permits. Let me close with this. In Ottawa more than one reference was made to the well-worn metaphor[15] "If all you have is a hammer, everything looks like a nail." This usefully draws attention to the amount of work done by a concept like genre across the three traditions. In SFL it is one part of an extravagant toolkit, one which has evolved to provide an ever richer account of social semiosis (which is arguably the most complex phenomenon to have evolved on our planet, evolving as it has out of biological phenomena, which have in turn evolved out of physical ones). Genre, it appears to me, does more work in the less extravagant ESP tool bag, and more work still in the far less technical discourse of RGS. What then is the nature of the nail that RGS, or ESP, or SFL hits? To explore this we need more meetings, and it would be wonderful not have to wait another 20 years!

References

Bakhtin, M. M. (1986). The problem of speech genres. In C. Emerson & M. Holquist (Eds.), V. W. McGee (Trans.), *Speech genres and other late essays* (pp. 60-102). Austin, TX: University of Texas Press.

Bawarshi, A. S., & Reiff, M. J. (2010). *Genre: an introduction to history, theory, research, and pedagogy.* West Lafayette, IN: Parlor Press/WAC Clearinghouse.

Bednarek, M., & Martin, J. R. (Eds.). (2010) *New discourse on language: Functional perspectives on multimodality, identity and affiliation.* London: Continuum.

Bernstein, B. (2000). *Pedagogy, symbolic control and identity: Theory, research, critique* (Rev. ed.). London: Taylor & Francis. (Original work published 1996)

Caffarel, A., Martin, J. R., & Matthiessen, C. M. I. M. (Eds.). (2004). *Language typology: A functional perspective.* Amsterdam: John Benjamins.

Christie, F. (Ed.). (1999). *Pedagogy and the shaping of consciousness: Linguistic and social processes.* London: Cassell.

Christie, F. (2002). *Classroom discourse analysis.* London: Continuum.

Christie, F. (2008). Genres and institutions: Functional perspectives on educational discourse. In M. Martin-Jones, A. M. de Mejia, & N. H. Hornberger (Eds.), *Encyclopedia of language and education* (2nd ed.), *Vol. 3: Discourse and education* (pp. 29-40). New York: Springer.

Christie, F. (2010). The "grammar wars" in Australia. In T. Locke (Ed.), *Knowledge about language in the English/literacy classroom* (pp. 55–72), London: Routledge/Taylor and Francis.

Christie, F. (2012). *Language education throughout the school years: A functional perspective.* Malden, MA: Wiley-Blackwell.

Christie, F., & Derewianka, B. (2008). *School discourse.* London: Continuum.

Christie, F., & Martin, J. R. (Eds.). (1997). *Genre and institutions: Social processes in the workplace and school.* London: Cassell.

Christie, F., & Martin, J. R. (Eds.) (2007). *Language, knowledge and pedagogy: Functional linguistic and sociological perspectives.* London: Cassell.

Christie, F., & Maton, K. (Eds.). (2011). *Disciplinarity: functional linguistic and sociological perspectives*. London: Continuum.

Coe, R., Lingard, L., & Teslenko, T. (2002a). Genre as action, strategy and *differeance*: An introduction. In Coe et al., (Eds.), *The rhetoric and ideology of genre* (pp. 1-10). Cresskill, NJ: Hampton Press.

Coffin, C. (2006). *Historical discourse: The language of time, cause and evaluation*. London; Continuum.

Dreyfus, S., Hood, S., & Stenglin, M. (Eds.). (2011). *Semiotic margins: Reclaiming meaning*. London: Continuum.

Edelman, G. (1992). *Bright air, brilliant fire: On the matter of the mind*. New York: Basic Books.

Eggins, S., & Slade, D. (1997). *Analysing casual conversation*. London: Cassel (republished Equinox, 2006).

Firth, J. R. (1957). *Papers in Linguistics 1934-1951*. Oxford: Oxford University Press.

Freedman, A. (1994). "Do as I say": the relationship between teaching and learning new genres. In A. Freedman & P. Medway (Eds.), *Genre and the new rhetoric* (pp. 191-210). London: Taylor & Francis.

Freedman, A., & Medway, P. (Eds.). (1994a). *Learning and teaching genre*. Portsmouth, NH: Boynton/Cook.

Freedman, A., & Medway, P. (Eds.). (1994b). *Genre and the new rhetoric*. London: Taylor & Francis.

Geertz, C. (1974). From the native's point of view: On the nature of anthropological understanding. *Bulletin of the American Academy of Arts and Sciences, 28*(1), 26-45.

Green, B., & Lee, A. (1994). Writing geography lessons: Literacy, identity and schooling. In A. Freedman & P. Medway (Eds.), *Learning and teaching genre* (pp. 207-224). Portsmouth, NH: Boynton/Cook.

Halliday, M. A. K. (1975). *Learning how to mean: Explorations in the development of language*. London: Edward Arnold.

Halliday, M. A. K. (1994). On language in relation to the evolution of human consciousness. In S. Allen (Ed.), *Of thoughts and words: The relation between language and mind* (pp. 45-84). London: Imperial College Press.

Halliday, M. A. K. (2002). M. A. K. Halliday. In K. Brown & V. Law (Eds.), *Linguistics in Britain: Personal histories* (pp. 116-126). London: Publications of the Philological Society.

Halliday, M. A. K. (2004). *The language of science*. London: Continuum.

Halliday, M. A. K., & Greaves, W. S. (2008). *Intonation in the grammar of English.* London: Equinox.

Halliday, M. A. K., & Hasan, R. (1976). *Coheson in English.* London: Longman.

Halliday, M. A. K., & Matthiessen, C. M. I. M. (1999). *Construing experience through language: A language-based approach to cognition.* London: Cassell. (reprinted by Equinox 2004)

Halliday, M. A. K., & Matthiessen, C. M. I. M. (2004). *An introduction to functional grammar* (3rd ed.). London: Arnold.

Halliday, M. A. K., & Webster, J. (Eds.). (2009). *Continuum companion to systemic functional linguistics.* London: Continuum.

Hasan, R. (2009). *Semantic variation: The Collected Works of Ruqaiya Hasan Vol. 2.* London: Equinox.

Hasan, R., Matthiessen, C. M. I. M., & Webster, J. (Eds.). (2005). *Continuing discourse on language: A functional perspective* (Vol. 1). London: Equinox.

Hasan, R., Matthiessen, C. M. I. M., & Webster, J. (Eds.). (2007). *Continuing discourse on language: A functional perspective* (Vol. 2). London: Equinox.

Hjelmslev, L. (1947). Structural analysis of language. *Studia Linguistica, 1,* 69-78.

Hjelmslev, L. (1961). *Prolegomena to a theory of language.* Madison, Wisconsin: University of Wisconsin Press.

Hood, S. (2011). Does it matter what genre means?: Analysing introductions to research articles within different traditions. *Journal of University of Science and Technology Beijing, 27*(2), 8-16.

Hyon, S. (1996). Genre in three traditions: Implications for ESL. *TESOL Quarterly, 30* (4), 693-722.

Iedema, R., Feez S., & White, P. (1994). *Media literacy (Write it right literacy in industry research project - Stage 2).* Sydney: Metropolitan East Disadvantaged Schools Program.

Johns, A. M. (Ed.). (2002). *Genre in the classroom: Applying theory and research to practice.* Mahwah, NJ: Lawrence Erlbaum.

Kress, G., & van Leeuwen, T. (2006). *Reading images: The grammar of visual design* (2nd ed.). London: Routledge. (Original work published 1996)

Labov, W., & Waletzky, J. (1967). Narrative analysis. In J. Helm (Ed.), *Essays on the verbal and visual arts,* (Proceedings of the 1966 Spring

Meeting of the American Ethnological Society, pp. 12-44). Seattle: University of Washington Press.

Lemke, J. L. (1995). *Textual politics: Discourse and social dynamics.* London: Taylor & Francis.

Locke, T. (Ed.). (2010). *Beyond the grammar wars: A resource for teachers and students on developing language knowledge in the English/literacy classroom.* London: Routledge.

Luke, A. (1996). Genres of power? Literacy education and the production of capital. In R. Hasan & G. Williams (Eds.), *Literacy in society* (pp. 308-338). London: Longman.

Malinowski, B. (1923). The problem of meaning in primitive languages. In C. K. Ogden & I. A. Richards, *The meaning of meaning* (pp. 296-336). New York: Harcourt Brace & World.

Malinowski, B. (1935). *Coral gardens and their magic.* London: Allen & Unwin.

Martin, J. R. (1984). Language, register and genre. In F. Christie (Ed.), *Deakin university children course reader* (pp. 21-30). Geelong: Deakin University Press.

Martin, J. R. (1985a). *Factual writing: Exploring and challenging social reality.* Geelong: Deakin University Press.

Martin, J. R. (1985b). Process and text: Two aspects of human semiosis. In J. D. Benson & W. S. Greaves (Eds.), *Systemic perspectives on discourse: Selected theoretical papers from the 9th International Systemic Workshop* (pp. 44-70). Norwood, NJ: Ablex.

Martin, J. R. (1986a). Intervening in the process of writing development. In C. Painter & J. R. Martin (Eds.), *Writing to mean: Teaching genres across the curriculum* (pp. 11-43). Applied Linguistics Association of Australia.

Martin, J. R. (1986b). Grammaticalising ecology: The politics of baby seals and kangaroos. In T. Threadgold, E. A. Grosz, G. Kress & M. A. K. Halliday (Eds.), *Semiotics, ideology, language* (pp. 225-268). Sydney: Sydney Association for Studies in Society and Culture.

Martin, J. R. (1992). *English text: System and structure.* Amsterdam: John Benjamins.

Martin, J. R. (1994). Macro-genres: The ecology of the page. *Network, 21*, 29-52.

Martin, J. R. (1995). Text and clause: Fractal resonance. *Text, 15*(1), 5-42.

Martin, J. R. (1997). Analysing genre: Functional parameters. In F. Christie & J. R. Martin (Eds.), *Genre and institutions: Social processes in the workplace and school* (pp. 3-39). London: Cassell.

Martin, J. R. (1999a). Modelling context: The crooked path of progress in contextual linguistics (Sydney SFL). In M. Ghadessy (Ed.), *Text and context in functional linguistics* (pp. 25-61). Amsterdam: John Benjamins.

Martin, J. R. (1999b). Grace: The logogenesis of freedom. *Discourse Studies, 1*(1), 31-58.

Martin, J. R. (1999c). Mentoring semogenesis: "Genre-based" literacy pedagogy. In F. Christie (Ed.), *Pedagogy and the shaping of consciousness: Linguistic and social processes* (pp. 123-155). London: Cassell.

Martin, J. R. (2001). A context for genre: Modelling social processes in functional linguistics. In J. Devilliers & R. Stainton (Eds.), *Communication in linguistics: Papers in honour of Michael Gregory, Theoria Series 10* (pp. 287-328). Toronto: GREF.

Martin, J. R. (2002). From little things big things grow: Ecogenesis in school geography. In Coe et al., (Eds.), *The rhetoric and ideology of genre* (pp. 243-271). Cresskill, NJ: Hampton Press.

Martin, J. R. (2008). Negotiating values: Narrative and exposition. *Journal of Bioethical Inquiry, 5*(1), 41-55.

Martin, J. R. (2010a). *Systemic functional linguistics theory: Collected works of J R Martin Vol. 1.* Shanghai: Shanghai Jiao Tong University Press.

Martin, J. R. (2010b). *Discourse semantics: Collected works of J R Martin Vol. 2.* Shanghai: Shanghai Jiao Tong University Press.

Martin, J. R. (2011). Bridging troubled waters: Interdisciplinarity and what makes it stick. In F. Christie & K. Maton (Eds.), *Disciplinarity: Functional linguistic and sociological perspectives* (pp. 35-61). London: Continuum.

Martin, J. R. (2012a). Writing and genre studies. In C. A. Chapelle (Ed.), *The encyclopedia of applied linguistics* (pp. 411-420). Oxford: Wiley-Blackwell.

Martin, J. R. (2012b). *Genre studies: Collected works of J. R. Martin. Vol. 3.* Shanghai: Shanghai Jiao Tong University Press.

Martin, J. R. (2012c). *Register studies: Collected works of J. R. Martin. Vol. 4.* Shanghai: Shanghai Jiao Tong University Press.

Martin, J. R. (2012d). *Critical discourse analysis/Positive discourse analysis: Collected works of J. R. Martin. Vol. 6.* Shanghai: Shanghai Jiao Tong University Press.

Martin, J. R. (2012e). *Language in education: Collected works of J. R. Martin. Vol. 7.* Shanghai: Shanghai Jiao Tong University Press.

Martin, J. R. (2012f). *Forensic linguistics: Collected works of J. R. Martin. Vol. 8.* Shanghai: Shanghai Jiao Tong University Press.

Martin, J. R. (2013). Modelling context: matter as meaning. In C. Gouveia & M. Alexandre (Eds.), *Languages, metalanguages, modalities, cultures: functional and socio-discursive perspectives.* Lisbon: BonD & ILTEC. 10-64.

Martin, J. R. (2014a). Looking out: Functional linguistics and genre. *Linguistics and the Human Sciences* 9(3), 303-317.

Martin, J. R. (2014b). Evolving systemic functional linguistics: Beyond the clause. *Functional Linguistics, 1*(3). Retrieved from http://www.functionallinguistics.com/content/pdf/2196-419X-1-3.pdf

Martin, J. R., & Matthiessen, C. M. I. M. (1991). Systemic typology and topology. In F. Christie (Ed.), *Literacy in social processes: Papers from the inaugural Australian systemic linguistics conference, held at Deakin University, January 1990* (pp. 345-383). Darwin: Centre for Studies in Language in Education, Northern Territory University.

Martin, J. R., & Matthiessen, C. M. I. M. (2014). Modelling and mentoring: Teaching and learning from home through school. In L. Barrat & A. Mahboob (Eds.), *Englishes in multilingual contexts: Language variation and education* (pp. 137-163). London: Springer.

Martin, J. R., & Plum, G. (1997). Construing experience: Some story genres. *Journal of Narrative and Life History, 7,* 1-4.

Martin, J. R., & Rose, D. (2007). *Working with discourse: Meaning beyond the clause* (2nd ed.). London: Continuum. (Original work published 2003)

Martin, J. R., & Rose, D. (2008). *Genre relations: Mapping culture.* London: Equinox.

Martin, J. R., & Rose, D. (2012). Genres and text: Living in the real world *Indonesian Journal of Systemic Functional Linguistics, 1*(1), 1-21.

Martin, J. R., & Veel, R. (Eds.). (1998). *Reading science: Critical and functional perspectives on discourses of science.* London: Routledge.

Martin, J. R., & White, P. R. R. (2005). *The language of evaluation: Appraisal in English.* London: Palgrave.

Martinec, R. (2005). Topics in multimodality. In Hasan et al. (Eds.), *Continuing discourse on language: A functional perspective* (Vol. 1, pp. 157-181). London: Equinox.

Maton, K., Hood, S., & Shay, S. (Eds.). (2015). *Knowledge-building: Educational studies in legitimation code theory.* London: Routledge.

Matthiessen, C. M. I. M. (2007). The "architecture" of language according to systemic functional theory: Developments since the 1970s. In R. Hasan, C. M. I. M. Matthiessen & J. Webster (Eds.), *Continuing discourse on language: A functional perspective* (Vol. 2, pp. 505-562). London: Equinox.

Matthiessen, C. M. I. M. (2010). Systemic functional linguistics developing. *Annual Review of Functional Linguistics 2* (pp. 8-63). Beijing: Higher Education Press.

Matthiessen, C. M. I. M., & Halliday, M. A. K. (2009). *Systemic functional grammar: A first step into the theory.* Beijing: Higher Education Press.

Matthiessen, C. M. I. M., Teruya, K., & Lam, M. (2010). *Key terms in systemic functional linguistics.* London: Continuum.

McCormack, R. (2014). Reading Mandela: Genre pedagogy versus ancient rhetoric. *Linguistics and the Human Sciences, 9*(2), 177-200.

O'Toole, M. (2011). *The language of displayed art* (2nd ed.). London: Leicester University Press. (Original work published 1994)

Painter, C. (1984). *Into the mother tongue.* London: Pinter.

Painter, C. (1998). *Learning through language in early childhood.* London: Cassell.

Painter, C., Martin, J. R., & Unsworth, L. (2013). *Reading visual narratives: Image analysis in children's picture books.* London: Equinox.

Plum, G. (1998). *Text and contextual conditioning in spoken English: A genre-based approach* (Monographs in Systemic Linguistics, no. 10). Nottingham: University of Nottingham.

Reid, I. (1987). (Ed.). *The place of genre in learning.* Geelong: Centre for Studies in Literary Education, Deakin University.

Richardson, P. (1994). Language as personal resource and as social construct: Competing views of literacy pedagogy in Australia. In A. Freedman & P. Medway (Eds.), *Learning and teaching genre* (pp. 117-142). Portsmouth, NH: Boynton/Cook.

Richardson, P. (2004). Literacy, genre studies and pedagogy. In W. Sawyer & E. Gold (Eds.), *Reviewing English in the 21st century* (pp. 119-128). Melbourne: Phoenix Education.

Rose, D. (2006). Reading genre: A new wave of analysis. *Linguistics and the Human Sciences, 2*(2) 185–204.

Rose, D. (2011). Learning in linguistic contexts: Integrating SFL theory with literacy teaching. In F. Yan, H. Guowen, Z. Yongsheng, Z. Delu & Y. Xinzhang (Eds.), *Studies in functional linguistics and discourse analysis III* (pp. 222-240). Beijing: Higher Education Press.

Rose, D., & Martin, J. R. (2012). *Learning to write, reading to learn: Genre, knowledge and pedagogy in the Sydney School.* London: Equinox.

Rothery, J. (1996). Making changes: Developing an educational linguistics. In R. Hasan & G. Williams (Eds.), *Literacy in society* (pp. 86-123). London: Longman.

Rothery, J., & Stenglin, M. (1997). Entertaining and instructing: Exploring experience through story. In F. Christie & J. R. Martin (Eds.), *Genre and institutions: Social processes in the workplace and school* (pp. 231-263). London: Cassell.

Saussure, F. (1966). *Course in general linguistics.* New York: McGraw-Hill. (Original work published 1916)

Smart, G. (2012). Discourse-oriented ethnography. In J. P. Gee & M. Handford (Eds.), *The Routledge handbook of discourse analysis* (pp. 147-159). New York: Routledge.

Threadgold, T. (1988). The genre debate. *Southern Review, 21*(3), 315-330.

Unsworth, L. (2001). *Teaching multiliteracies across the curriculum: Changing contexts of text and image in classroom practice.* Buckingham: Open University Press.

van Leeuwen, T. (1999). *Speech, music, sound.* London: Macmillan.

van Leeuwen, T. (2011). *The language of colour: An introduction.* London: Routledge.

Veel, R. (1998). The greening of school science: Ecogenesis in secondary classrooms. In J. R. Martin & R. Veel (Eds.), *Reading science: Critical and functional perspectives on discourses of science* (pp. 114-151). London: Routledge.

Ventola, E. (1987). *The structure of social interaction.* London: Pinter.

Webster, J. (Ed.). (2008). *Meaning in context: Strategies for implementing intelligent applications of language studies.* London: Continuum.

Webster, J. (Ed.). (2015). *The Bloomsbury Companion to M. A. K. Halliday.* London: Bloomsbury.

Wignell, P. (2007). *On the discourse of social science.* Darwin: Charles Darwin University Press.

Zappavigna, M. (2012). *Discourse of twitter and social media: How we use language to create affiliation on the web.* London: Continuum.

Zappavigna, M., Dwyer, P., & Martin, J. R. (2010). Visualising appraisal prosody. In A. Mahboob & N. Knight (Eds.), *Appliable linguistics* (pp. 150-167). London: Continuum.

EndNotes

[1] Editors' Note: We are certain that our colleague Peter Medway would
have joined us in expressing our regret that Martin and his colleagues
were not invited to the 1992 conference, some 23 years ago. We meant no
disrespect. In fact, we were unaware of his work, and that of the SFL group
at the University of Sydney, at the time that the invitations were sent out.
One goal of that conference was to bring together scholars from a wide
range of disciplines, all of whose focus was genre studies, and most of
whom were not fully aware of each others' work. We approached scholars
working in the fields of rhetoric, applied language studies, literary studies,
composition theory, communications, and pedagogy, etc. in each of those
areas. At the same time, we tried to get international representation:
we succeeded in bringing together scholars from Great Britain, from
the Unites States, from Canada, and from Australia. In fact, several
Australians were present; it was through their discussion of the work
being undertaken in Sydney that we became aware of that enterprise.
Accordingly, the article by Paul Richardson, in the *Learning and Teaching
Genre* (1994) volume, devotes almost 20 pages to that work, including quite
detailed exposition of Jim Martin's work.

[2] According to Ventola (1987), this group included Suzanne Eggins, Chris
Nesbitt, Guenter Plum, Cate Poynton, Lynn Poulton, Joan Rothery, Anne
Thwaite, Eija Ventola, and myself.

[3] Cited as Luke (1994) in Freedman & Medway (1994b, p. 19), presumably
based on a pre-publication draft, since the paper did not actually appear
until 1996.

[4] I am referring just to phonology here to simplify the presentation; the
least abstract stratum for writing is of course graphology, and for signing,
gesture.

[5] Locke (2010) updates this enduring contestation, shrouded as it ever is by
the fogs of war; this book has a refreshingly international perspective.

[6] A discussion of the cline of instantiation (system to instance relations)
in relation to the hierarchy of stratification (supervenience) is beyond
the scope of this paper; see Bednarek & Martin (2010), Matthiessen and
Halliday (2009) for discussion.

[7] Smart (2012) usefully clarifies and exemplifies Geertz's (1974) dialectic
of "experience-near concepts" and "experience-distant concepts"
underpinning the kind of interpretive ethnography that has the potential
to enrich our understanding of genre.

[8] For genre and macro-genre see Martin (1994, 1995, 1997), Martin and
Rose (2008, 2012); basically the idea is that an elemental genre (such as
a commissioned recount) is to a macro-genre as a clause is to a clause

complex (Halliday & Matthiessen, 2004).

9   Rose (2011) offers a more detailed analysis of stages and phases in this text, and begins his Record of Events stage *From my first day at school...*

10   The analyses displayed here are from Rose (2011).

11   My thanks to David Rose for his careful editing of my recount of his practice here.

12   Those of you concerned with playful deployments of genre might enjoy reading McCormack (2014), which presents a play involving an imaginary debate between myself and the Roman rhetorician Quintilian about the most effective analysis of the original Mandela text.

13   Wiki attributes the metaphor to either Kaplan or Maslow as follows:
The first recorded statement of the concept was Abraham Kaplan's, in 1964: "I call it *the law of the instrument,* and it may be formulated as follows: Give a small boy a hammer, and he will find that everything he encounters needs pounding."
Maslow's hammer, popularly phrased as "if all you have is a hammer, everything looks like a nail" and variants thereof, is from Abraham Maslow's *The Psychology of Science,* published in 1966. (http://en.wikipedia.org/wiki/Law_of_the_instrument)

14   Figures 1, 2, 3, and 9 in this chapter use this motif.

15   The label for this evaluative stage in the exemplum genre is the same as the one we introduced above for the extracted evaluation in commissioned recounts. In principle this re-deployment of labels for nuclear stages in different genres should be avoided; but it has been hard to find enough appropriate distinctive terms—and the moralistic attitudes featuring in the commissioned recount's extracted evaluation are in fact comparable to those found in the Interpretation of exemplums.

Chapter 4

A Genre Based Theory of Literate Action

Charles Bazerman

University of California, Santa Barbara (USA)

Genre, like amazing grace, came on me when I was lost—lost as I tried to find conceptual clarity in the details and variety of scientific writing. I entered into an empirical study of scientific writing because in the 1960s and 1970s those in writing and rhetoric, as well as most academics and educators, were treating all non-fiction, certainly all academic writing, as a single type— an undifferentiated category, just better or worse, and written according to standards of grammatical correctness or literary elegance. The more I looked at scientific writing, and more broadly academic writing, the more variety I found, the more dimensions of variation, the more invention, the more situations and meanings, the more historical change. All my stereotypes of scientific writing had gotten disrupted in the complexity of social studies of science (under the kind guidance of Robert Merton, the founder of the field, see Merton, 1938 & 1973) as I began to see writing as social communication, within academic groupings with varying epistemic projects. My first published study, "What Written Knowledge Does," was highly hedged to indicate that I was not claiming typicality or generality for the three examples I analyzed in depth—but presented them only as spots on a geography yet to be defined (first presented in 1979 and published as Bazerman, 1981). When I met Miller at the 1979 convention of the Conference on College Composition and Communication in Minneapolis and heard the ideas about genre she was developing for the theory section of her dissertation (later to become Miller, 1984), I found a way to bring order to the social and textual complexity I was finding. In particular, with her connecting the rhetorical tradition of genre studies with the phenomenological concept of typified action, as understood by participants, I saw a way to see how social processes could produce patterned textual practices through communicative processes of co-alignment of individual perspectives.

Of course, in a way genre was already there in the inquiry, for rhetoricians talking about scientific writing as a single thing were using a type which they then tried to subsume into the forensic, deliberative, and epideictic types of classical rhetoric, seeing little difference between Greek oral deliberation in the agora and published science. Teachers of technical writing also had their generalized types, largely based on textual characteristics. These broad types missed the specifics that most practitioners of academic genres knew when they wrote and could report, if you could talk to them in a way that evoked practice talk, rather than evaluative talk which relied on the familiar analytical terms of their education concerning grammar, standardized form, and the like.

That disjunction between evaluative and practice types suggests several of the things we have since learned about genre. Genre can exist at different levels of specificity and on different principles, depending on the sophistication of the user, but also the situations and purposes for which types are invoked. Genre identification results from a process of recognition and use, rather than an inherent feature of language or texts—a process in languaging and reflection on language, not purely in the language object itself. Genre is a matter of perception. Practitioners make distinctions that are not always organized in theory. People can over time, with greater experience, make different and more refined distinctions among texts, as well as see different patterns of similarity.

In my literary days (my 1971 doctoral dissertation was on poetry occasioned by the death of Queen Elizabeth I and the accession of King James I) I had gotten some sense of the variation and differentiation of genre, following patterns of social organization and social events. The Latin schoolmasters wrote in certain styles and genres and the London guildsman in others; those mourning the loss of a queen in genres different than those seeking a position from the new king. Though I had a sense of social and activity distribution of genres, I could not link literary and social theory, nor could I apply my insights to scientific writing. But then Miller indicated how phenomenology and typification could bridge rhetorical theory and social theory. I began to see genre and typification everywhere. This mind altering condition was indeed hallucinogenic for me (and I have seen it in others) in tempting the belief that one could create a stable taxonomy of genre types. Yet the more I looked at the historical and social transformations of genre, the more it became evident that only ethno-taxonomies (that is, the types invoked by practitioners in practice) are theoretically sustainable, and these ethno-taxonomies are only quasi-stable, held together only as long as dynamics, regulations, social forces, and rhetorical situations supported shared social understandings.

The world became even more hallucinogenic as I saw the communicative world as one of processes, with forms coming in and out of the mist. This means that it is hard to know how writers were able to frame comments and elaborate thoughts to be intelligible and effective—unless they make assumptions and followed patterns. Similarly readers need to be able to make assumptions about the writers' intentions embodied in texts. To make their way in this world and assert their presence, needs, and interests, people have to rely on models, precedents, and simplified rules. In this way we create cloud clusters of ideas, knowledge, and activity that are as transient as our thoughts, but held together contingently by co-orientation to signs evoking enough common understanding for immediate practical purposes. Inscribed signs endure and travel more than spoken, but also present more difficulties in creating co-alignment and reasonably shared mutual understanding. People contingently structure these cloud clusters through networks and regulations of texts—forming the basis of modern institutions within information and knowledge societies. But these networks and regulations are more fragile than we imagine, as they are only maintained insofar as people keep them alive through repeated use and alignment to them. Indeed in this moment of digital transformation our networks, regulations, and orientations are now up for readjustment as our technologies of information are changing although the underlying social and cognitive processes are the same. It is just the transient configurations are coming together and crystallizing under different conditions with different temporary and mutable stabilizing forces. Any long-lasting configuration needs lots of social and psychological energy to keep it in the air and keep it quasi-stable, although that constant infusion of energy can bring with it new interests and vectors, moving the genres in new directions.

Yet even as I became aware of the fragility and transience of generic appearances, I began to see the tremendous power of the typification processes and the specific role of written genres in forming our modern way of life and our modern systems of knowledge. I saw this within the historical and social research I was doing on the experimental article, and other scientific genres; in Edison's insertion of electric technology within our economic, social, cultural and material lives; in numerous cases in the history of environmental science and environmentalism; and in other sites of empirical work I have engaged and continue to engage in. I also saw this in the practical work of orienting writing students to the worlds they were writing for. On the theoretical plane I saw this as I attempted to make sense of the particulars I found. I had been sketching out this theoretical picture at the edges of the empirical work: in passages in articles, in latter chapters of historical books (Bazerman, 1988, 1999), in introductions to collections (Bazerman & Paradis, 1991), and in articles that promised fuller exposition (Bazerman, 2000). Now I have finally published a two volume theoretical work (Bazerman, 2013a, 2013b). One volume presents a practical theory of rhetoric—that is a picture of writing that helps us engage in writing and make strategic choices. The other volume presents an account of humans as writing creatures, the challenges they must confront, the resources they harness, and the consequences for engaging in these odd practices of leaving little bits of ink or electrons on various media for others to find and make sense of. The remainder of this chapter summarizes those volumes in two ways. First I will give a narrative account of how the theory grows out of genre, and then I will give a more structured introduction based on the tables of contents of the two volumes.

The theory realized in both volumes is multidisciplinary, grounded in intersecting theoretical lines of several traditions in contemporary social science. The theory, nonetheless, has genre and typification near its center, for genre and typification create a conjunction where numerous theories operating in different spheres can meet. The connection between rhetorical force and social typification opened up ways to think systematically about social action, and how participants perceive action—as indicated in the Miller 1984's title of "Genre as Social Action." Actually I had written an earlier chapter "Scientific Writing as a Social Act" for a collection edited by Miller and others (Bazerman, 1983). In that chapter, I summarized various social theories of science and considered what their consequences for writing would be, but that article came to no solid conclusion. After seeing an early version of Miller's paper, and with typification in hand, I could see how those theories (many of them having a base in phenomenology) aligned with scientific texts and text production. Further Mertonian functional structural sociology places at the heart of social structure the perception of social actors about structured choices within their perceived fields of social action (Stinchcombe, 1975). Putting perceived structured choices together with genre and typification, I could see how social structures arose and ramified through perceptual processes. The mechanisms of social reproduction through local action have been more recently elaborated by the structurationism of Giddens (1984) and Bourdieu's theories of practice, habitus, and social field (1977, 1990). Merton, however, got to these ideas more through pragmatism than phenomenology. Merton's sources connected with much of contemporary American social science which had its roots in pragmatism, mediated by such early figures as George Herbert Mead with his ideas of the social formation of the self arising out of the need to communicate and perceptions of how others saw us and understood us (Mead, 1934). Methodologically these dual sources of phenomenology and pragmatist sociology place genre research well within the tradition of sociological ethnography. Sociological ethnography in turn lies behind much of organizational theory that attends to perspectives of participants. Research in technical and business communication had already been going in that direction, but genre then provided an important link in how texts and textual practices become organized in social settings to carry out actions. The researchers who then brought genre and typification into understanding technical and organizational writing (such as Van Nostrand, 1997; Dias et al 1999; Winsor, 2003; and Smart, 2006) were building on already prepared ground.

These researchers implicitly drew on organizational ethnography and technical writing research (going back at least to Odell and Goswami, 1985), but were more explicitly drawing on another resource which genre theory opened up—Vygotskian activity theory. This is a resource of interest to all in language studies because, like Mead's theories, it links the learning of language to cognitive development and development of personality—but provides more specific and detailed mechanisms and evidence than provided by Mead. I had encountered Vygotsky earlier in thinking about the effects of writing education, but when I saw the social typifications of genre in terms of Vygotskian cultural tools, the implications became apparent. Learning to use a genre would direct cognitive activity and development. This early insight drove my development of genre theory, seeing the linkage between learning academic genres and developing disciplinary ways of thought. More recently, I have started an empirical program to demonstrate the cognitive developmental effects of learning specialized genres (Bazerman 2009; Bazerman, Simon, & Pieng, 2014; Bazerman, Simon, Ewing, & Pieng, 2013).

During the mid-1980s, Vygotskian developmental theory allowed me to find an alternative answer to the epistemological problem that was behind the conflicts that became known as the science wars—how mere words and symbols passed among chatting humans could capture anything about the ambient world outside the minds of individuals and societies. Vygotsky demonstrated in a number of studies working with young children how language was learned dynamically in the course of material activity and was thus deeply saturated with our experience of the world (Vygotsky, 1978, 1986). Scientific language and genres, further, were learned within rigorous material practices of experimentation and evidence gathering. In *Shaping Written Knowledge* (Bazerman, 1988), I elaborated this position in the theoretical chapter "How language does the work of science."

The Vygotskian path leads as well to activity theory resting on the fundamental notion of both the individual and society engaged in complex activities, which required the assembly of functional systems (either internally for the individual or externally for the society). The external aspect of functional activity systems was elaborated by Leont'ev (1978) and then Engestrom (1987), who addressed organizational issues, with a particular focus on how tools, rules, resources, and division of labor were organized among participants for the production of the object—as embodied in Engestrom's now famous heuristic triangles. Russell (1997) and Spinuzzi (2003) have begun to elaborate the potential of activity systems for writing, and have been followed up by many others.

The internal aspect of functional activity systems looking into the neuropsychological organization of individuals was pursued by Vygotsky's other major protégé and collaborator, Luria. Luria (1961, 1969, 1970, 1972, 1976, 1979) investigated the internal cognitive formation of functional systems and their disruption, including brain function and disruption—providing some of the important insights now driving cognitive neuroscience). Issues of internal cognitive functional systems are of immense importance to understanding writing, and tread some of the same ground as Flower and Hayes (1981), but with a more variable, situational, sociocultural, and personal developmental approach. The potential of this line of activity theory for understanding cognition in writing has been little explored.

Together both lines of the Vygostkian model of internal and external activity provide means for considering the interaction of individual and group activity systems, and provide potential for understanding the social formation of cognition. Vygotsky himself focused most directly on how interpersonally experienced signs and symbols became internalized to form tools for thinking, perception, and self-regulation. This process gives us a way to understand specialized modes of thought developed through participation in socially organized activities. That is, thinking like a lawyer or a chemist comes from participating in the activities of a lawyer or a chemist and communicating with legal and chemistry peers in professional activity settings. As one of the key devices for organizing concepts and activities in distinctive social systems, genre itself becomes one of the ways that organizes language experience and becomes part of cognitive resources of the individual. These cognitive resources then are also at hand as one externalizes internal thoughts in new circumstances to form new statements—and these formulations emerge as genre-formed utterances, though each new instantiation potentially changes the genre. Thus we come to speak our thoughts in genres, and learn from each other in genres, even as we change genres in each new use.

The social landscape of genres and the range of thoughts expressed and expressible are constantly transformed through new utterances, but with continuity of typifications of evolving domains. In the genres and their circulation we find the mechanisms of socially distributed thoughts, which each individual makes sense of and incorporates in the self, and each self contributes to the public resources and vitality. This vision incorporates Volosinov's (1973) and Bakhtin's (1981, 1986) views about social speech and ideology (along with Volosinov's comments about internal cognition formed by language that are slightly earlier than Vygotsky's, but not nearly as developed).

The intersection of Vygotsky, Volosinov, and Bakhtin over genre also brings with it intertextuality and the chronotope, where intertextuality represents our reliance on each other's words as structured through the repertoire and stance of the genres of each activity system or social domain (Devitt, 1991 and Berkenkotter et al., 1991 were among the earlier explorers of this dimension within contemporary genre theory). The explicit social marking of intertextuality makes evident why citation studies have been as powerful as they have been in mapping scientific work and why the number crunching, network mapping of scientometrics holds such fascination, even though the tools it has developed do not yet capture the full richness of the ways in which texts represent each other and form and re-form social stories and relationships of communal action (Koschnick, 2013).

The chronotope (Bakhtin, 1981) provides us a way of analyzing the world and actions represented in each of the genres and thus expressible within each domain (Schryer, 2002 was a pioneer in exploring the potential of chronotope for genre theory). Together chronotope and intertextuality provide tools for understanding the social and material worlds indexed and activated within genres and their associated activity systems. The conjunction of intertextuality and chronotope within activity-directed genred utterances helps us confront the issue of what knowledge is, of what use it is, how it is formed, and how it is maintained within the social groupings that attend to and align with various genres. The indexicality of intertextuality and chronotope also provides ways of understanding how texts become meaningful to groups and create degrees of alignment among participants—without relying on unsustainable assumptions on one side about meaning being solidly fixed and immanent in the text or on the other side about inherent understanding of abstract meanings. While study of the symbol system can tell us many things about the symbol system and how we have come to order it in conformity with our needs and capacities, study of the symbol system alone does not get us to meaning, unless we assume that meaning is immanent in the words. Further, meaning as a construct of minds in isolation makes communication of meaning equally problematic, at least since the time of Locke, unless one assumes great similarity of minds and experiences. Rather the approach that comes from genre as typification finds meaning only in attributions people make, and the puzzle is to understand how people come to make close-enough attributions to signs to make the symbol system function for coordinating social life and work. The mechanisms of participating in typified, genred worlds provides ways for people to develop sufficient coalignment and common resources for organizing their minds in ways that make them better able to understand each other.

Co-orientation towards genred written texts can bootstrap larger, increasingly organized groupings of people across time and space, sharing common knowledge, activity orientations, and regulations, forming institutions of modernity. Goody (1986) in his book *The Logic of Writing and the Organization of Society*, began to articulate how writing transformed society, but if we add genre theory in all the complexity and dimensionality I have been sketching out, we can see more concretely how the circulation of texts creates common commitments, cognitive horizons, material relations, and ongoing activity—such that people live their lives with reference to and engaged within social entities that stretch across space and time, and are not just caught up in the people and objects in their immediate sight and hearing (Bazerman, 2006). Writing provides mid-level mechanisms to link micro and macro-sociology. Writing's extension of social action from the local to the distant makes clear why learning to write is so important for participation in the major institutions of modernity, and why increases of domain specific writing skills bring empowerment in those domains. Conversely, lack of skill means disempowerment and marginality.

I have gestured at a lot of ground in this essay, tying together over forty years of loose strings with the strings increasingly tangled and intertwined. I have told the story as a synthetic narrative of making connections. The two volume work ties together these strings more tightly with more theoretical coherence. The second volume, in particular, presents the various sources and connective reasoning of the theory. The first part of this volume presents a view of what it means to be human and the role of symbolic communication in the formation of socially active selves. I look at three major lines of social scientific thinking of the last century (with earlier roots) as I mentioned above—Vygotsky (with Leont'ev and Luria extensions), Schutz (1967) and the sociological phenomenologists, and the pragmatists with a special focus on Dewey (1910, 1947), Mead (1934), and Sullivan (1953). Given the social communicative formation of active social selves, the second part of the volume examines the orders we have made through our symbolic interaction: social, interactional, linguistic, utterance, meaning, and the world indexed through meanings. I end with a consideration of the spot these orders put us on as writers.

The first volume, based on the view of our place in the communicative world set out in the second volume, then provides a practical view of what it means to be a writer and how we might think of our writing tasks. It is meant to inform practice, to provide us a way of perceiving the structure of choices in front of us. That is, it provides a way of strategically reflecting on our situation to help us in our choice making. Rather than taking the fundamental problem of rhetoric to be persuasion in high stakes oral platform oratory within a set of taken for granted social institutions, this rhetorical theory takes as its fundamental problem literate action— making ourselves understood and interactionally effective at a distance. The problem of communicating at a distance presents us with the puzzle of locating our communication in a recognizable site of social interaction, despite our text traveling through time and space. Genre and all the typifications that go with it provide the solution to this puzzle—by creating a shared space of mutual alignment for interaction, and invoking the larger activity systems the genre is recognizably part of. The consequent problems are how one acts within that space to bring about change, and how one's text emerges to take its place within the social world of intertexts, thereby changing the communicative landscape by performing social speech acts and creating social facts. Thus the rhetoric includes an account of individual and social processes of text production as well as processes of social uptake and transformation. Meaning only emerges within those social and individual processes by which we make, understand, and act on meaning. This rhetoric has implications for how we teach writing so students can better understand what they can accomplish through writing and how.

The two volumes attempt to understand why and how we carry off the bizarre magic of communication at a distance, mediated by marks on a page or screen. They do so on the basis of contemporary social and psychological theory, grounded in empirical investigations of writing. In so doing, they aim to help us understand the consequences of our choices, and thus should help us choose with an expanded sense of our options. Only time and social processes will tell whether I have hit a useful mark.

References

Bakhtin, M. M. (1981). *The dialogic imagination.* Austin: University of Texas Press.

Bakhtin, M. M. (1986). The problem of speech genres. In C. Emerson & M. Holquist (Eds.), *Speech genres and other late essays* (pp. 60-102). Austin: University of Texas Press.

Bazerman, C. (1981). What written knowledge does: Three examples of academic discourse. *Philosophy of the Social Sciences, 11*(3), 361-88.

Bazerman, C. (1983). Scientific writing as a social act: A review of the literature of the sociology of science. In R. Anderson, R. J. Brockmann & C. Miller (Eds.), *New Essays in Technical Writing and Communication* (pp. 156-184). Farmingdale: Baywood.

Bazerman, C. (1988). *Shaping written knowledge: The genre and activity of the experimental article in science.* Madison: University of Wisconsin Press.

Bazerman, C. (1999). *The languages of Edison's light.* Cambridge: MIT Press.

Bazerman, C. (2000). A rhetoric for literate society: The tension between expanding practices and restricted theories. In M. Goggin (Ed.), *Inventing a discipline* (pp. 5-28). Urbana IL: NCTE.

Bazerman, C. (2006). The writing of social organization and the literate situating of cognition: Extending Goody's social implications of writing. In D. Olson and M. Cole (Eds.), *Technology, literacy and the evolution of society: Implications of the work of Jack Goody* (pp. 215-240). Mahwah, NJ: Erlbaum.

Bazerman, C. (2009). Genre and cognitive development. In C. Bazerman, A. Bonini, D. Figueiredo (Eds.), *Genre in a changing world* (pp. 279-294). Fort Collins, CO: Parlor Press and WAC Clearinghouse.

Bazerman, C. (2013a). *Rhetoric of literate action.* Fort Collins, CO: Parlor Press and WAC Clearinghouse.

Bazerman, C. (2013b). *Theory of literate action.* Fort Collins, CO: Parlor Press and WAC Clearinghouse.

Bazerman, C. & Paradis, J. (1991). Introduction. In C. Bazerman & J. Paradis (Eds.), *Textual dynamics of the professions: Historical and contemporary studies of writing in professional communities* (pp. 3-10). Madison: University of Wisconsin Press.

Bazerman, C., Simon, K, & Pieng, P. (2014). Writing about reading to advance thinking: A study in situated cognitive development. (pp. 249-276). In G. Rijlaarsdam, P. D., Klein, P. Boscolo, L. C. Kirkpatrick, & C. Gelati (Eds.), *Studies in Writing: Writing as a learning activity, 28.* Leiden: Brill. DOI: 10.1163/9789004265011_012

Bazerman, C., Simon, K., Ewing, P., & Pieng, P. (2013). Domain-specific cognitive development through writing tasks in a teacher education program. *Pragmatics and Cognition,* 21(3), 530-551. DOI 10.1075/pc.21.3.07baz

Berkenkotter, C., Huckin, T., & Ackerman, J. (1991). Social context and socially constructed texts: The initiation of a graduate student into a writing research community. In C. Bazerman & J. Paradis (Eds.), *Textual dynamics of the professions* (pp. 191-215). Madison: University of Wisconsin Press.

Bourdieu, P. (1977). *Outline of a theory of practice.* Cambridge: Cambridge University Press.

Bourdieu, P. (1990). *The logic of practice.* Stanford, CA: Stanford University Press.

Devitt, A. (1991). Intertextuality in tax accounting: Generic, referential, and functional. In C. Bazerman & J. Paradis (Eds.), *Textual dynamics of the professions* (pp. 336-380). Madison: University of Wisconsin Press.

Dewey, J. (1910). *How we think.* Boston: D. C. Heath.

Dewey, J. (1947). *Experience and education.* New York: Macmillan.

Dias, P., Pare, A., Freedman, A., & Medway, P. (1999). *Worlds apart: Acting and writing in academic and workplace contexts.* Mahwah, NJ: Erlbaum.

Engeström, Y. (1987). *Learning by expanding: An activity-theoretical approach to developmental research.* Helsinki: Orienta-Konsultit.

Flower, L., & Hayes, J. R. (1981). A cognitive process theory of writing. *College Composition and Communication,* 32(4), 365-87.

Giddens, A. (1984). *The constitution of society.* Berkeley: University of California Press.

Goody, J. (1986). *The logic of writing and the organization of society.* Cambridge: Cambridge University Press.

Leont'ev, A. N. (1978). *Activity, consciousness, and personality.* Englewood Cliffs, NJ: Prentice-Hall.

Luria, A. R. (1961). *The role of speech in the regulation of normal and abnormal behavior.* New York: Pergamon.

Luria, A. R. (1969). Speech development and the formation of mental processes. In M. Cole & I. Maltzman (Eds.), *A handbook of contemporary soviet psychology* (pp. 121-162). New York: Basic Books.

Luria, A. R. (1970). The functional organization of the brain. *Scientific American, 222*(3), 66-78.

Luria, A. R. (1972). *The man with a shattered world.* Cambridge, MA: Harvard University Press.

Luria, A. R. (1976). *Cognitive development: Its cultural and social foundations.* Cambridge, MA: Harvard University Press.

Luria, A. R. (1979). *The making of mind: A personal account of Soviet psychology.* Cambridge, MA: Harvard University Press.

Mead, G. H. (1934). *Mind, self, and society.* Chicago: University of Chicago Press.

Merton, R. (1938). Science, technology and society in seventeenth century England. *Osiris, 4*(2), pp. 360–632. Bruges: St. Catherine Press.

Merton, R. (1973). *The sociology of science.* Chicago: University of Chicago Press.

Miller, C. (1984). Genre as social action. *Quarterly Journal of Speech, 70,* 151-67.

Odell, L., & Goswami, D. (Eds.) (1985). *Writing in nonacademic settings.* New York: Guilford Press.

Russell, D. (1997). Rethinking genre in school and society: An activity theory analysis. *Written Communication, 14*(4), 504-554.

Koschnick, D. (2013). Tracking our writing theorists through citations. Doctoral Dissertation. Gevirtz Graduate School of Education. University of California Santa Barbara.

Schryer, C. (2002). Strategies for stability and change. In R. Coe & T. Teslenko (Eds.), *The rhetoric and ideology of genre* (pp. 73-102). New York: Hampton Press.

Schutz, A. (1967). *The problem of social reality.* The Hague: Martinus Nijhoff,

Smart, G. (2006). *Writing the economy: Activity, genre, and technology in the world of banking.* London: Equinox.

Spinuzzi, C. (2003). *Tracing genres through organizations: A sociocultural approach to information design.* Cambridge, MA: MIT Press.

Stinchcombe, A. L. (1975). Merton's theory of social structure. In L. Coser (Ed.), *The idea of social structure* (pp. 11-34). New York: Harcourt Brace Jovanovich.

Sullivan, H. S. (1953). *The interpersonal theory of psychiatry.* New York: Norton.

Van Nostrand, A. D. (1997). *Fundable knowledge.* Mahwah, NJ: Erlbaum.

Volosinov, V. N. (1973). *Marxism and the philosophy of language.* Cambridge, MA: Harvard University Press.

Vygotsky, L. S. (1978). *Mind in society: The development of higher psychological processes.* Cambridge, MA: Harvard University Press.

Vygotsky, L. S. (1986). *Thought and language* (Alex Kozulin, Trans.). Cambridge, MA: MIT Press.

Winsor, D. (2003). *Writing power: An ethnographic study of writing in an engineering center.* Albany: SUNY Press.

Chapter 5

Beyond the Three Traditions in Genre Studies: A Brazilian Perspective

Orlando Vian Jr.

Federal University of Rio Grande do Norte (Brazil)

Chaos breaks across the lines that separate scientific disciplines. Because it is a science of the global nature of systems, it has brought together thinkers from fields that had been widely separated.

John Gleick (1987, p. 5)

My aim in this chapter is to discuss, from a bird's eye view, aspects of what has been referred to as a Brazilian perspective on genre studies—a fairly reductionist categorization, since we are looking at a very complex phenomenon and through a lens incapable of taking into account all of its angles. It is impossible for a single approach to attend to all of the multifaceted linguistic, sociological, cultural and rhetorical aspects involved in genres, let alone describe all of their features. Therefore, I argue, from the outset, that it is impossible to speak of a "Brazilian approach" to genre studies as a uniform tradition, a closed, encapsulated system of its own. I align myself with scholars such as Bawarshi and Reiff (2010) and Swales (2012), who suggest that text/discourse[1] and genre research in Brazil encompasses, among others, the different aspects relating to genres, listed above. I also advocate for understanding Brazilian genre studies from the perspective of complexity theory (Larsen-Freeman, 1997, 2002, 2011, 2013; Larsen-Freeman & Cameron 2008; Morin, 2011).

This chapter will start by examining the international development of genre studies and classificatory frameworks and then move to the Brazilian context. From there, I will briefly summarize the Bakhtinian tradition and the theory of Socio-Discursive Interactionism (SDI). I will conclude by positioning genres as complex phenomena, and by highlighting the need for critical, complex and ecological approaches to genre studies.

The Emergence of Genre Studies

With the publication of Swales' seminal work in 1981, genre studies was brought into the field of Linguistics and Applied Linguistics. His work was followed closely by Miller's (1984) study on genre as social action, Kress' (1989) work on linguistic processes as sociocultural processes, and Martin's (1985/1989) research on writing in schools. Since its emergence in 1981, Anglophone genre studies has focused on three different areas (Hyon, 1996; Johns, 2002; Paltridge, 2001): (1) Australian Sydney School (based on Systemic Functional Linguistics, SFL), (2) English for Specific Purposes (ESP), and (3) Rhetorical Genre Studies (RGS) (also known aa North American New Rhetoric studies and New Rhetoric genre theory), as identified in Hyon's (1996) article. As Paltridge (2001) points out, "there are a number of ways in which these approaches to the descriptions of genres overlap, and ways in which they are quite different from each other" (p. 12).

Classifying Genre Studies

In the past decade or so, we have seen many publications focusing on the so-called three Anglophone traditions in genre studies (Hyon, 1996). Swales (2012) indicates that for over three decades, these "three traditions essentially survive, although with some attempts to find some middle ground along the three sides of the triangle" (p. 112). Swales further points to two likely candidates for this middle ground, as alternatives for genre studies among the several existing genre theories: the Brazilian approach to genre discussed in this chapter (also see Bawarshi & Reiff, 2010; Cristovão, this volume) and the approach proposed by the New London Group (1996). According to Swales, the Brazilian approach attempts to combine the ESP- and SFL-types of genre analysis with a more critical approach, Critical

Discourse Analysis (CDA), and with influences from Franco-Swiss Socio-Discursive Interactionism (SDI) as advocated by Jean-Paul Bronckart and colleagues (e.g., Bronckart, 2013). As Bawarshi and Reiff (2010) have observed, the Brazilian approach brings together rhetorical, linguistic and sociological approaches to genre (p. 112).

While Swales (2012) offers an overarching view of the Brazilian approach, my own inquiry is grounded in an understanding of Brazilian post-colonial reality (García Canclini, 1995) seen in the context of genre studies, with particular attention paid to the ways in which the complexity theory, also known as Complex Sciences (Ellis &Larsen-Freeman, 2009; Larsen-Freeman & Cameron, 2008; Morin, 2011) have impacted the discipline. García Canclini (1995) argues that post-colonial Latin American cultures are hybrid in the sense that they bridge traditional Latin American ways with modern international advancements. Hybridity is a useful concept to help us understand the efforts of Brazilian genre researchers to transform theoretical concepts into teaching tools and, in turn, respond to the contextual and pedagogical needs of the post-colonial reality.

The Emergence of Genre Studies in Brazil

Genre studies has been a growing discipline in Brazil since the mid-1990s. In this context, and in order to meet the needs of language teaching, teacher education, and curriculum design/material production at all school levels and in varied language teaching contexts, a dialogue among the various theories developed. The National Curriculum Parameters (*Parâmetros Curriculares Nacionais,* PCN) issued by the Brazilian Ministry of Education (Brasil Secretaria da Educação Fundamental, 1997) aimed to set the guidelines for teaching elementary, middle, and high school levels.

The PCN parameters for both mother tongue and foreign language teaching indicate that pedagogical and educational practices should be genre-based. Although the PCN text does not explicitly refer to a specific genre theory, a Bakhtinian view seems to be implicit in the PCN document. Further, the PCN introduces genres as the focus of classroom practices (e.g., reading, listening, speaking and writing), and texts as units of such practices. Other initiatives have taken a similar approach. Introduced in 2006, the National Curricular Orientations for High School (*Orientações Curriculares Nacionais para o Ensino Médio*, OCEM) reinforced the role of genres as a pedagogical resource for the Brazilian educational system. The document[2] (Brasil Secretaria De Educação Básica, 2006) reads:

> The main objective of teaching is a set of processes of making meaning of texts, which are the concrete material of discursive genres. (p. 36).

Following the publication of the PCN, genre studies research proliferated in a variety of research centers in the five regions of Brazil.

Another clear example of the emergence of genre studies in Brazil was the creation of the Symposium on Genre Studies in 2003 (*Simpósio sobre Gêneros Textuais*, SIGET). Providing a forum for the intellectual exchange in contemporary genre research, the SIGET conference has become increasingly popular, and, after its fourth edition, has moved to hosting international scholars. SIGET provides researchers with the opportunity to discuss theoretical and methodological issues among themselves and with invited guest speakers from different genre traditions and different countries. Contributing to the development of genre studies in Brazil, the Textual/Discursive Genres research group (*Gêneros Textuais/ Discursivos*) was created within the National Association of Research and Graduate Programs in Letters and Linguistics (*Associação Nacional de Pesquisa e Pós-Graduação em Letras e Linguística*, ANPOLL) in 2009. The research group holds seminars and meetings to exchange research, present ongoing studies, and plan materials for language teaching and research publications (e.g., Meurer, Bonini & Motta-Roth, 2005; Nascimento & Rojo, 2014).

Altogether, there has been a dramatic increase in scholarship on genre studies in Brazil. For example, the number of genre studies presentations increased from 45 (mini-courses, round tables, panels) at the SIGET V genre conference in 2009 (Borges, 2009) to 578 at the SIGET VI conference in 2011, and the diversity of the conference events increased. Similarly, a growing number of recent publications (e.g., Dias & Dell'Ísola, 2012; Nascimento & Rojo, 2014) is indicative of the growing prominence of genre studies in Brazil.

Notable Research

Meurer and Marcuschi are two pioneering genre studies scholars in Brazil, who are committed to building bridges between theoretical frameworks and encouraging a critical view of genre studies. Meurer (2002, 2006) investigates genres and their use in English Language teaching while Marcuschi's (2009) contribution primarily aims at mother tongue (Portuguese) teaching. Meurer (2002) proposes a critical view of genre studies:

> Describing and explaining genres in relation to representations, social relations and identities embedded in them may serve to show that in speech, and through it, individuals produce, reproduce, or challenge structures and social practices which they are part of. A critical approach of this kind may help to understand that representing the world in a certain way constructs and interprets texts, showing that certain relationships and identities are forms of ideology. (p. 28)

Here Meurer illustrates how the production of genres is linked to the production of social structures in which they are embedded. Echoing this focus on the social, Meurer and Motta-Roth (2002) state:

> We study genres in order to understand more clearly what happens when we use language to interact in social groups, once we perform actions in society through stable processes of writing/reading and speaking/listening, incorporating stable forms of utterances. (p. 12)

Drawing from Bakhtin (1986), Meurer and Motta-Roth positioned genre as "a recurrent communication event in which a determined human activity, involving roles and social relations, is mediated by language" (2002, p. 11), showing the relevance and importance of Bakhtin's thought to genre studies in Brazil.

Classifying Genre Studies in Brazil

Given the plethora of studies in genre in Brazil, and the dichotomy between genre and discourse, much attention has been paid to classifying Brazilian genre studies. Rojo (2005), Marcuschi (2008), Motta-Roth (2005), along with Pereira and Rodrigues (2009), have introduced classificatory frameworks (as follows). Rojo (2005) distinguishes between research on discursive and textual genres. According to Rojo (2005), discursive genre studies focus on the situations wherein utterances (chains of spoken or written language) or texts (coherent stretches of language) are produced as embedded in their socio-historical contexts while textual genre studies focus on the description of textual features (p. 185). Examining the trends in genre studies in Brazil, Marcuschi (2008) identifies four streams, including studies based on: (a) the Bakhtinian tradition; (b) Swalesian genre analysis propositions; (c) Systemic Functional Linguistics; and (d) varied influences from different scholars (e.g., Bakhtin, Adam, Bronckart), including North-American scholars (e.g., Bazerman, Miller), and scholars representing critical literacy perspective (e.g., Kress, Fairclough). In the previously mentioned 2005 collection, Meurer, Bonini and Motta-Roth grouped Brazilian genre studies under three categories (see Table 1).

Table 1

Approaches to genre studies (Meurer, Bonini, & Motta-Roth, 2005)

Socio-semiotic	Socio-rhetoric	Socio-discursive
Hasan	Swales	Bakhtin
Martin	Bazerman	Adam
Fowler	Miller	Bronckart
Kress		Maingueneau
Fairclough		

Four years later, Pereira and Rodrigues (2009), after having analyzed different theoretical and methodological approaches, grouped genre studies according to six categories (see Table 2).

Table 2

Schools of genre studies according to Pereira and Rodrigues (2009)

Socio-semiotic	Socio-rhetoric	Socio-discursive interactionist	Semio-discursive	Socio-cognitivist	Dialogic
Halliday	Swales	Bronckart	Charaudeau	Koch	Bakhtin
Hasan	Bazerman	Schneuwly	Maingueneau	Marcuschi	
Eggins	Freedman	Dolz			
Thompson	Miller				

These different attempts to classify directions in Brazilian genre studies indicate that there is not a single "Brazilian" way of looking at genre.

The Bakhtinian Tradition and its Influence on Genre Studies in Brazil

Bakhtinian theory has been widely embraced across Brazil, and Bakhtin's view of genres as "relatively stable types of utterances" (1986, p. 60) is commonly used by Brazilian researchers both directly by those who explicitly accept it and indirectly by those who have integrated this concept with other theoretical perspectives. I start this section by introducing Bakhtin's and his circle's work, and then move to exploring how it has influenced theories of genre in Brazil.

In his seminal essay, "The problem of speech genres" (1986), Bakhtin expands the understanding of genre, emphasizing the role and place of genres in the social sphere, in the "real utterances of others" (p. 62). In *Problems of Dostoevsky's Poetics* (1984), he points out that language studies (focusing on linguistics) and discourse studies (focusing on metalinguistics) should not mix, since they have distinct theoretical objectives. In *Marxism and Philosophy of Language* (1973), Voloshinov, a member of Bakhtin's circle, argues for using a sociological method to study language. He analyzes types of verbal interactions, articulates their conditions of production, and analyzes their linguistic forms. In turn, he considers both the broader social context and the specific context of the production of utterances and the linguistic forms.

There has been a strong Bakhtinian tradition in Brazilian literary studies, which is often attributed to the influential work of Professor Boris Schnaiderman, who taught at the University of São Paulo where he introduced a course on Russian Language and Literature. Following Schnaiderman's work, studies of the Bakhtinian tradition have spread throughout Brazil, which was evidenced by the re-translation of numerous Russian texts including those of Dostoyevsky, Bakhtin and his circle. There has also been an increase in Bakhtinian literary studies, which has carried over to Linguistics and Applied Linguistics and has helped to cultivate a Brazilian field of study known as Dialogic Discourse Analysis. Bakhtin's influence on Brazilian genre studies is also evidenced by the publication of two volumes on key concepts in Bakhtinian theory (Brait, 2005, 2006), and the launching of the *Bakhtiniana—Revista de Estudos do Discurso*, a bilingual journal on Bakhtinian studies. Marcuschi (2009) argues that Bakhtin is an author who "represents a kind of theoretical common sense in relation to the conception of language" (p. 152) in genre studies across the country.

Bakhtinian views serve as the foundation for the Socio-Discursive Interactionism theoretical framework (Bronckart, 1999, p. 141), one of the most influential epistemological frameworks in the field of genre studies in Brazil. SDI was developed by Dolz and Schneuwly (1998) at the University of Geneva; it uses social interactionism and integrates research conducted by Vygotsky, Mead, Dewey, Wallon and others (Bronckart, 2013, p. 65) in order to analyze pedagogical interventions in language teaching, known in Brazil as *didactic sequences* and *language didactics* (see Cristovão, this volume). Within a classroom project, didactic sequences are understood as systematically organized classroom language activities (Dolz & Scheneuly, 1998). Within the SDI approach, genre is viewed as a meditational tool. The unit of analysis in the SDI approach includes (1) the verbal activity (i.e., a psychological unit); (2) the text (i.e., a communicative unit); and (3) the text genre (i.e., a praxeological unit). SDI is well-known in Brazil for its methodological concern for teaching languages and texts. It was, for the most part, initially concerned with mother tongue teaching only, and, later, with foreign language teaching. Cristovão and Nascimento (2005) point out that this approach focuses on the integration of psycho-social and linguistic/discursive teaching parameters as a way of examining how language use is connected with the social contexts in which it is produced (p. 37). SDI has had a strong impact on Brazilian educational contexts.

Bakhtin's influence on genre studies in Brazil is also evidenced by the number of studies drawing on his theories. For example, Gomes-Santos's (2003) analysis of articles on genre research published in Brazilian journals of language and linguistics shows that 77 out of 133 studies reviewed by the author included Bakhtinian views in their theoretical frameworks (Table 3).

Table 3

A summary of theoretical frameworks used in journal publications on genre studies (adapted from Gomes-Santos [2003])

Theoretical framework	Number of articles
Textual linguistics and/or conversation analysis	31
Bakhtin, Geneve Group and/or other authors	26
Bakhtin and other authors	28
Anglophone studies (Fairclough, Swales, Bathia, etc.) and Brazilian authors using similar theories	20
Bakhtin and French discourse analysis	12
Bakhtin and anglophone genre studies	7
Bakhtin and studies in textual linguistics	4
Geneve group and/or other authors	3
French school of discourse analysis and other discursive studies	2
TOTAL	133

As we can see from Table 3, Brazilian genre research commonly draws on Bakhtin's theory.

Critical, Complex and Ecological Approaches to Genre Studies

In addition to the various approaches to genre theory, including the Bakhtinian and SDI approaches presented in this chapter, a critical view of genre has recently been proposed in Brazil. I join the advocates of this critical view, which encompasses the understanding that texts belong to one or more genres and genres constitute social relations. Taking into account the historical development of Brazilian genre studies and drawing on the work of Meuer (2000, 2004, 2006) and Freire's (1992) concept of critical capacity as the "perception of the relationships between text and context" (p. 11), Motta-Roth (2008) suggests that critical genre analysis allows for (a) the description of a communicative action to be realized in a text representing a genre; (b) the identification of the linguistic items realizing these acts, which refer to a context of situation/culture as used in the SFL-based genre and register analysis (Halliday & Hasan, 1989); and (c) the interpretation of discourses permeating the text and constituting relations/tensions in a given discursive event. These three points indicate the need for a more open view of genres, that does not simply focus on the linguistic realizations of a text belonging to a specific genre, but that critically examines the complex ways that genres constitute social relations.

As I mentioned in the introduction, when we discuss traditions in genre studies, we are dealing with a very complex phenomenon. While Hyon's (1996) seminal article and her tripartite classification for genre studies was an early attempt to classify theories of genre, my own account presented in this chapter has highlighted the need for a more nuanced, complex understanding of the existing approaches to the study of genre. Much scholarship, some of which has been mentioned in this chapter, has been excluded from recent Anglophone attempts to classify theories of genre. For example, French textual linguistic perspectives of the kind proposed by Adam (2011) and his colleagues are not often mentioned in genre studies in English. Another perspective in genre studies that has not been considered in English publications is the socio-cognitive approach, which is also based on textual linguistics (Koch, 2005, 2006; Koch & Cunha Lima, 2004) and which views genres as interrelated with human social and cognitive competences. Further, another recent non-English trend in genre studies, currently circulating throughout Brazil but still restricted to only a few research centers, is the perspective on discursive traditions (Kabatek, 2005, 2006), which relates aspects of textual linguistics and grammaticalization to linguistic change (Castilho, 2006). As studies advance, new possibilities open up and new approaches to the study of genre develop.

In the context of the changes in the area of genre studies, Prior (2009) argues that contemporary North-American and Australian

> genre analysts have been moving from a focus on genres as isolated phenomena to a recognition of how specific types of texts are formed within, infused by, and constitutive of *systems of genres*. Genres have been described in terms of *chains* (Swales, 2004; Fairclough, 2004); *colonies* (Bhatia, 2002); *repertoires* (Devitt, 2004); *sets and systems* (Bazerman, 2004; Devitt, 1991) and *ecologies* (Spinuzzi, 2004). (pp. 277-283, emphasis in the original)

This change of focus from genre as an isolated phenomenon to genres that are a part of systems recognizes the intricacies involved in genres and genre interactions. In turn, this recognition demands a complex perspective that accounts for the overlapping and interfacing ways of understanding genre.

As mentioned above, within the Brazilian context, the notion of hybridity is useful for making sense of the ways studies of genres interface and overlap. Brazilian studies of genre blend a myriad of theories from distinct languages and different perspectives. While post-colonial cultures have typically been the beneficiaries of ready-made collections—artistic, cultural, religious, political— from hegemonic nations, it is now time for post-colonial cultures to *decollect* (García Canclini, 1995) the received collections and reformulate them according to their own socio-cultural variables and needs. Resisting ready-made understandings and over-simplification, current scholarship needs to honour multiple, non-fixed, and dynamic ways of understanding.

Complexity theory can also contribute to studies of genre. Due to the complex nature of genre studies, the change in the perspectives on theoretical and methodological approaches to genre studies might be facilitated through reliance on the science of complexity. Morin (2011) introduces a two-fold understanding of complexity:

> At first glance, complexity is a tissue (*complexus*: what is woven together) of inseparably linked heterogeneous constituents: it puts forth the paradox of the one and the many. Secondly, complexity is effectively the fabric of happenings, actions, interactions, feedbacks, determinations, accidents, which constitute our phenomenic world. (p. 13)

Taking into consideration this duality proposed by Morin, we should then take an interdisciplinary, ecological approach to genres, considering how their different features are interconnected (see discussions of a rhizome in Bawarshi, this volume; Deleuze & Guattari, 1987).

Bringing the idea of complexity to Applied Linguistics, Larsen-Freeman and Cameron (2008) point out that complexity theory "aims to account for how the integrating parts of a complex system give rise to the system's collective behavior and how such a system simultaneously interacts with its environment" (p. 1). Further, in their research, Larsen-Freeman and Cameron (2008) present five key features of complex systems: heterogeneity of elements or agents, dynamics, non-linearity, openness, and adaptation (p. 36). Engaging with complexity theory, scholars should examine genre not only for its linguistic features, but also for complex, interconnected features (e.g., cultural, sociological, individual, psychological, political, philosophical, anthropological). While much work is being done to integrate notions of complexity in the study of genre, Waldrop (1992) warns, "complexity research is trying to grapple with questions that defy all the conventional categories" (p. 9). As he puts it, understandings of complexity are "new and wide-ranging" and "nobody knows quite how to define . . . [complexity], or even where. . . [its] boundaries lie" (1992, p. 9).

Given that recent genre research has focused on systems, chains, colonies, repertoires, ecologies, families of genres (Prior, 2009), an ecological and rhizomatic view (cf. Bawarshi, this volume) is also required. Deleuze and Guattari (1987) view rhizomes as "ceaselessly established connections between semiotic chains, organizations of power, and circumstances relative to the arts, sciences, and social struggles" (p. 7). They point out that a rhizome has no beginning or end, "it is always in the middle, between things, interbeing, *intermezzo*" (p. 25, italics in the original). Similarly, in this chapter I suggest, as I did in the past (Vian Jr., 2003), that we look at genre as a rhizome (cf. Bawarshi, this volume), especially when examining the relationship between genres and their contexts of production). Drawing on complexity theory (Larsen-Freeman & Cameron, 2008; Morin, 2005), I argue that the rhizome is a suitable metaphor for understanding genres and their dynamic, heterogeneous, non-linear, open, and adaptive nature.

Viewing genre as a complex phenomenon, it is also important to consider knowledge from an ecological perspective, in which social, philosophical, neurological, cognitive, anthropological, historical, and several other different aspects of knowledge should be taken into account. Almeida (2010), while discussing scientific knowledge and traditional knowledge, argues:

> An ecology of knowledge, that is, an operation of thought that takes into account the chain of multiple correlations, determinations, approximations and also distinct patterns of self-organization of phenomena, is configured as one of the meta-principles for internal communication of scientific knowledge and these [meta-principles] with other forms of knowledge. (p. 151)

As genres emerge from different social practices, a complex, ecological view is necessary for a better understanding of the phenomenon of genre.

Final Remarks

Research in Linguistics and in Applied Linguistics in Brazil has seen an increasing interest in the concept of genre. In this chapter, I have demonstrated how genre has become a concept of paramount importance in language teaching (following the publication of the Brazilian National Curriculum Parameters in 1998 and the OCEM in 2006). In this chapter, I have traced developments within the complex research field and in the complex notion of genre. I have also surveyed Brazilian genre research, including different theories, different research paths and different dialogues, while promoting dialoguing and positioning Brazil as a hybrid, post-colonial context.

Throughout this analysis, I have highlighted local researchers' continued engagement with researchers and theories from all over the world and in a diversity of languages. Weaving together the work of Brazilian researchers—locally and globally—I have introduced an understanding of genre that differs from Hyon's (1996) somewhat limited view of the traditions in genre theory. I have detailed how, in Brazil, theories of genre have developed from local researchers' extensive international engagements, particularly with French,

Russian, and German theories. Liberating genre theory from the Anglophone focus of Hyon's (1996) research, I have positioned the Brazilian approach, if we are to use this term, as an undoubtedly ecological, hybrid, post-colonial, complex and rhizomatic perspective, in which text-context-language are interconnected.

I should finally mention that I am aware of the limitations and biases presented in this chapter, which are the result of my own particular experience with genre theories and research. Nonetheless, I believe that confronting different opinions and exchanging experiences is a sound way of enriching the field and showing what is happening beyond the three traditions, outside Anglophone circles. My hope is that this chapter offers a more nuanced, hybrid, and complex understanding of genre.

References

Adam, J-M. (2011). *A linguística textual: Introdução à análise textual dos discursos* [Textual linguistics: An introduction to textual analysis of discourses]. São Paulo: Cortez Editora.

Almeida, M. C. (2010). *Complexidade, saberes científicos e saberes da tradição* [Complexity, scientific knowledge and traditional knowledge]. São Paulo: Livraria da Física Editora.

Bakhtin, M. M. (1984). *Problems of Dostoevsky's poetics*. Minneapolis: University of Minnesota Press.

Bakhtin, M. M. (1996). The problem of speech genres. In C. Emerson & M. Holquist (Eds.), *Speech genres & other late essays* (pp. 60-102). Austin, TX: University of Texas Press.

Bawarshi, A. S., & Reiff, M. J. (2010). *Genre: An introduction to history, theory, research, and pedagogy*. West Lafayette, IN: Parlor Press and WAC Clearinghouse.

Borges, F. G. B. (2012). Os gêneros textuais em cena: uma análise crítica de duas concepções de gêneros textuais e sua aceitabilidade na educação no Brasil [Textual genres on stage: A critical analysis of two textual genre conceptions and their acceptability in education in Brazil]. *Revista Brasileira de Linguística Aplicada, 12*(1), 119-140.

Brait, B. (2005). *Bakhtin: conceitos-chave* [Bakhtin: key concepts]. São Paulo: Editora Contexto.

Brait, B. (2006). *Bakhtin: outros conceitos-chave.* [Bakhtin: Other key concepts]. São Paulo: Editora Contexto.

da Brasil Secretaria Da Educação Fundamental. (1997). *Parâmetros Curriculares Nacionais: Introdução aos Parâmetros Curriculares Nacionais* [National Curricular Parameters: Introduction to the National Curricular Parameters]. Brasília: Ministério da Educação. Retrieved from http://mecsrv04.mec.gov.br/sef/estrut2/pcn/pdf/livro01.pdf.

Brasil Secretaria da Educação Básica. (2006). *Orientações curriculares para o ensino médio- Linguagens, códigos e suas tecnologias* [National Curricular Orientations for High School. Languages, codes and their technologies]. (Vol. 1). Brasília: Ministério da Educação.

Retrieved from http://portal.mec.gov.br/seb/arquivos/pdf/ book_volume_01_internet.pdf.

Bronckart, J-P. (1999). *Atividades de linguagem, textos e discursos – Por um interacionismo sócio-discursivo* [Language activities, texts and discourses for a social-discursive interactionism]. São Paulo: Educ.

Bronckart, J-P. (2013). The language system at the heart of the systems that make up the human being. In C. A. M. Gouveia & M. F. Alexandre (Eds.), *Languages, metalanguages, modalities, cultures: Functional and socio-discursive perspectives* (pp. 65-84). Lisbon: BonD & ILTEC.

Castilho, A. T. (2006). Proposta funcionalista de mudança linguística. Os processos de lexicalização, semanticização, discursivização na constituição das línguas. [Functional proposal of linguistic change. Lexical, semantic, and discursive processes in the structure of languages]. In Lobo, T.; Ribeiro, I.; Carneiro, Z. & Almeida, N. (Orgs.). *Para a história do português brasileiro: novos dados, novas análises*. [For a history of Brazilian Portuguese VI: New data, new analyses]. Salvador: EDUFBA.

Deleuze, G., & Guattari, F. (1987). *A thousand plateaus: Capitalism and schizophrenia* (Brian Massumi, Trans.). Minneapolis, MN: University of Minnesota Press.

Dias, R., & Dell'Ísola, R. L. P. (2012). *Gêneros textuais: Teoria e prática de ensino em LE* [Textual genres: Theory and practice in Foreign Language Teaching]. Campinas: Mercado de Letras.

Dolz, J.; Schneuwly, B. (1998). *Pour un enseignement de l'oral.* [Teaching the spoken language]. Paris : ESF Éditeur.

Ellis, N., & Larsen-Freeman, D. (2009). *Language as a complex adaptive system.* Ann Arbor, MI: Wiley-Blacwell/Language Learning Research Club, Univeristy of Michigan.

Freire, P. (1992). *Pedagogia do oprimido* [Pedagogy of the oppressed]. São Paulo: Paz e Terra.

García Canclini, N. (1995). *Hybrid cultures: Strategies for entering and leaving modernity.* Minneapolis, MN: University of Minnesota Press.

Gleick, J. (1987). *Chaos: Making a new science.* London: Penguin Books.

Gomes-Santos, S. N. (2003). A linguística textual na reflexão sobre o conceito de gênero [Textual linguistics in the reflection on the concept of genre]. *Cadernos de Estudos Linguísticos, 44,* 315-323.

Halliday, M.A.K. & Hasan, R. (1989). *Language, context and text: Aspects of language in a socio-semiotic perspective.* Oxford: Oxford University Press.

Hyon, S. (1996). Genre in three traditions: Implications for ESL. *TESOL Quarterly, 30*(4), 693-722.

Johns, A. M. (2002). *Genre in the classroom: Multiple perspectives.* Mahwah, NJ: Lawrence Erlbaum.

Kabatek, J. (2005). Sobre a historicidade de textos. [About the historicity of texts]. In *Linha d'água.* 17. São Paulo: USP/APLL.

Kabatek, J. (2006). Tradições discursivas e mudança lingüística. [Discursvie traditions and linguistic change]. In Lobo, T.; Ribeiro, I.; Carneiro, Z. & Almeida, N. (Orgs.). *Para a Historia do Português Brasileiro VI* [For a history of Brazilian Portuguese VI: New data, new analyses]. Salvador: EDUFBA.

Koch, I. G. V. (2005). *O texto e a construção dos sentidos* [Text and meaning construal]. (8th ed.). São Paulo: Contexto.

Koch, I. G. V. (2006). *A inter-ação pela linguagem* [Inter-action through language]. (8th ed.). São Paulo: Contexto.

Koch, I. G. V., & Cunha-Lima, M. L. (2004). Do cognitivismo ao sociocognitivismo. [From cognitivism to socio-cognitivism]. In F. Mussalim & A. C. Bentes (Eds.), *Introdução à lingüística: Fundamentos epistemológicos.* [An introduction to linguistics: Epistemological foundations] (pp. 251-300). São Paulo: Cortez.

Kress, G. (1989). *Linguistic processes in sociocultural practice.* Oxford: Oxford University Press.

Larsen-Freeman, D. (1997). Chaos/Complexity science and second language acquisition. *Applied Linguistics, 18* (2), 141-165.

Larsen-Freeman, D. (2002). Language acquisition and language use from a chaos/complexity theory perspective. In C. Kramsch (Ed.), *Language acquisition and language socialization* (pp. 33-46). London: Continuum.

Larsen-Freeman, D. (2011). Complex dynamic systems: A new transdisciplinary theme for applied linguistics? *Language Teaching, 45*(2), 202-214.

Larsen-Freeman, D. (2013). Introduction: complexity theory—a new way to think. *Revista Brasileira de Linguistica Aplicada.* Special issue on Complexity Studies in *Applied Linguistics, 13*(2), 369-373.

Larsen-Freeman, D., & Cameron, L. (2008). *Complex systems and applied linguistics.* Oxford: Oxford University Press.

Marcuschi, L. A. (2009). *Produção textual, análise de gêneros e compreensão.* [Textual production, genre analysis and comprehension]. (3rd ed.). São Paulo: Parábola Editorial.

Martin, J. R. (1989). *Factual Writing: Exploring and challenging social reality*. Geelong, Vic.: Deakin University Press (Original work published 1985 by Oxford University Press)

Meurer, J. L. (2000). O conhecimento de gêneros textuais e a formação do profissional da linguagem [Textual genre knowledge and the education of the language professional]. In M. B. M. Fortkamp & L. M. B. Tomitch (Orgs.) *Aspectos da Lingüística Aplicada: estudos em homenagem ao Professor Hilário Inácio Bohn* [Aspects of Applied Linguistics: Studies in honor of professor Hilário Inácio Bohn]. Florianópolis: Insular: 149-166.

Meurer, J. L. (2002). Uma dimensão crítica do estudo de gêneros textuais. [A critical dimension in textual genre study]. In J. L.Meurer & D. Motta-Roth (Eds.), *Gêneros textuais e práticas discursivas: Subsídios para o ensino da linguagem*. [Textual genres and discursive practices: Subsidies for language teaching] (pp. 17-29). Bauru: Edusc.

Meurer, J. L. (2004). Ampliando a noção de contexto na lingüística sistêmico-funcional e na análise crítica do discurso [Amplifying the notion of context in systemic functional linguistics and in critical discourse analysis]. *Linguagem em (Dis)curso, 4.* Special issue, 133-157.

Meurer, J. L. (2006). Integrando estudos de gêneros textuais ao contexto da cultura. [Integrating textual genre studies in the context of culture]. In A. M. Karwoski, B. Gaydecka & K. S. Brito (Orgs.). *Gêneros textuais: reflexões e ensino (2a. ed.) revista e aumentada*. [Textual genres: Reflections and teaching (2nd edition revised and expanded]. Rio de Janeiro: Lucerna: 165-185.

Meurer, J. L., & Motta-Roth, D. (2002). *Gêneros textuais e práticas discursivas: Subsídios para o ensino da linguagem* [Textual genres and discursive practices: Subsidies for language teaching]. Bauru: Edusc.

Meurer, J. L., Bonini, A., & Motta-Roth, D. (Eds). (2005). *Gêneros: teorias, métodos, debates* [Genres: Theories, methods, debates]. São Paulo: Parábola.

Miller, C. (1984). Genre as social action. *Quarterly Journal of Speech, 70,* 151-167.

Morin, E. (2011). *Introdução ao pensamento complexo* [Introduction to complex thinking] 4th edition. Porto Alegre: Editora Sulina.

Motta-Roth, D. (2008). Análise crítica de gêneros: contribuições para o ensino e a pesquisa de linguagem [Critical genre analysis: contributions to teaching and language research]. *Revista D.E.L.T.A.*, vol. 24, no. 2, 341-383.

Pereira, R. A., & Rodrigues, R. H. (2009). Perspectivas atuais sobre gêneros do discurso no campo da lingüística. [Current perspectives on speech genres in the field of linguistics]. *Revista Letra Magna, 11*, 1-18.

Paltridge, B. (2001). *Genre and the language learning classroom.* Ann Arbor, MI: University of Michigan Press.

Prior, P. (2009). From speech genres to mediated multimodal genre systems: Bakhtin, Voloshinov, and the question of writing. In C. Bazerman, A. Bonini & D. Figueiredo (Eds.), *Genres in a changing world* (pp. 17-34). Fort Collins, CO: The WAC Clearinghouse,

Rojo, R. H. R. (2005). Gêneros do discurso e gêneros textuais: questões teóricas e aplicadas [Textual genres and discursive genres: Theoretical and applied issues]. In J.L. Meurer, A. Bonini & D. Motta-Roth (Eds.), *Gêneros: teorias, métodos, debates* [Genres: theories, methods, debates]. (pp. 184-207). São Paulo: Parábola.

Swales, J. (1981). *Aspects of article introductions.* Birmingham, UK: Language Studies Unit, University of Aston.

Swales, J. M. (2012). A text and its commentaries: Toward a reception history of "Genre in three traditions" (Hyon, 1996*). Ibérica, 24*, 103-116.

The New London Group.(1996). "A pedagogy of Multiliteracies: Designing social futures", *Harvard Educational Review, 66* (1), 60-92.

Vian Jr., O. (2013). Rhizome, language-games and Systemic Functional Linguistics: ontogenetic dialogues. In C. A. M. Gouveia & M. F.Alexandre (Eds.), *Languages, metalanguages, modalities, cultures: Functional and socio-discursive perspectives* (pp. 85-98). Lisbon: BonD & ILTEC.

Volosinov, V. N. (1973). *Marxism and the philosophy of language.* New York: Seminar Press.

Waldrop, M. M. (1992). *Complexity: The emerging science at the edge of order and chaos.* New York, NY: Simon & Schuster.

EndNotes

[1]   A distinction is usually made in Brazil between textual and discursive
       genres as it will be developed in the following item.
[2]   All translations are the author's.

Chapter 6

A Genre-Based Study Across the Discourses of Undergraduate and Graduate Disciplines: Written Language Use in University Settings[1]

Giovanni Parodi

Pontificia Universidad Católica de Valparaíso (Chile)

The question of how written genres vary across disciplines in different languages has received a good deal of interest in the last two decades, particularly in the case of empirical research conducted in the Spanish language (e.g., Burdiles, 2012; Cubo de Severino, Lacon & Puiatti, 2012; Jarpa, 2012; Martínez, 2012; Parodi, 2010a, 2014). This empirical research has contributed to the description of both academic and professional communication processes and has become the source for designing reading and writing genre-based programs for native speakers of Spanish (e.g., Arnoux, 2002, 2009; Castañeda & Henao, 1995; Marinkovich, Peronard & Parodi, 2006; Parodi, 2010a; Peronard, Gómez, Parodi, Núñez & González, 1998; Resnik & Valente, 2009). While we have devoted the last few years to examining and accounting for specialized genres employed in vocational, or secondary level, education (Parodi, 2005) and at the undergraduate level (e.g., Ibáñez, 2010; Parodi, 2010a), only recently have we turned our attention to graduate contexts, particularly at the doctoral level (e.g., Martínez, 2012; Parodi, 2010b).

In this chapter, we aim to identify, describe, and quantitatively assess the academic genres found in a corpus of 3,272 texts that graduate and undergraduate university students are assigned to read in order to access specialized information across seven disciplines: Biotechnology, Chemistry, Economics, History, Linguistics, Literature and Physics. In this chapter, we review literature on academic discourse and written genres, and describe the corpus and the methods employed. We present the results of the study and discuss them, including in the discussion a comparative analysis of the frequency of occurrence of all genres identified across disciplines. In the conclusion we discuss the contribution of the study into our understanding of disciplinary academic discourses and the implications of the study for future research.

Academic Discourse and University Genres

In the first half of the 20th century, as noted by Parodi (2003), more attention was paid to the development of theoretical approaches and models of reading comprehension processes, than to the study of writing. In contrast, with the emergence of such fields of study as Genre Studies, Writing across the Curriculum and Writing in the Disciplines (e.g., Bazerman & Russell, 1995; Bhatia, 1993, 2004, 2012a, 2012b; Freedman & Medway, 1994; Miller, 1984; Russell, 2002), the second half of the 20th century and the beginning of the 21st century have witnessed a significant increase in the studies focusing on academic writing (e.g., Arnoux, 2009; Bazerman, 1994, 2012; Bazerman, Krut, Lunsford, McLeod, Null, Rogers & Stansell, 2009; Marinkovich, Morán & Benítez, 1997). A large number of academic and professional specialized writing programs have recently been created. With this shift in focus, genre researchers have been paying more attention to disciplinary writing. Among the studies of disciplinary writing, many identify and describe disciplinary genres, mostly in English as a first and as a foreign language, and, more recently, in Spanish as a first language. Genre-based studies of the comprehension processes in reading have become less common.

In response to this apparent imbalance in genre research in reading and writing, our research focuses on academic discourses in university settings and on genres that are read in this context. We are interested in genres that circulate at the undergraduate and graduate levels of university education. As Figure 1 shows, we understand that there is a wide variety of genres that readers go through during their academic and professional training. The exploration of the diversity of these discourses from a disciplinary literacy perspective, in terms of both comprehension and production processes, is at the centre of our study. Figure 1 shows that academic university discourse exists in a discourse context in which readers encounter genres which stem from other discursive realms, not all of them produced originally in an academic environment. Based on the study of undergraduate genres from the PUCV-2010 Corpus, Parodi (2010c) proposed that academic discourse could be seen as a *miscellaneous*[2] *discourse*, composed of different genres, not only coming from academic settings but also from those that are professional or scientific, thus constituting a heterogeneous configuration.

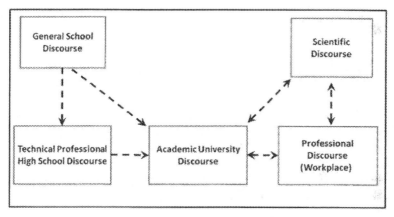

Figure 1. Academic and professional contexts and genres (Parodi, 2010c).

Genre itself is a highly contested notion, sometimes contrasted and sometimes used synonymously with other related terms such as text type, superstructure, and register (e.g., Biber, 1988; Martin, 1992; Paltridge, 2002; van Dijk, 1977). If we consider all possible theoretical alternatives, the concept of genre may appear elusive; however, the rich discussions of varying approaches to genre open many possibilities regarding how to study discourse genres (e.g., Bazerman, 1994, 2012; Bhatia, 2004, 2012a & b; Freedman & Medway, 1994; Hyon, 1996; Martin, 2012; Martin & Rose, 2008; Miller, 1984, 2012; Parodi, 2010a; Swales, 1990, 2004, 2012). The existing approaches to genre and schools of thought differ in terms of the emphasis given to the "predictability and dynamism of the genre's formal features, or the importance given to the wider social context" (Handford, 2010, p.258). Notwithstanding, Swales (2009, 2012) detects a tendency towards the unification of genre approaches, and proposes that some theoretical underpinnings may be closer to schools of thought that in the past could have been perceived as oppositional. In the same vein, Bhatia (2004) advances a definition of genre that highlights related concepts and prioritizes conventions, disciplinarity, and linguistic and discursive forms:

> Genre essentially refers to language use in a conventionalised communicative setting in order to give expression to a specific set of communicative goals of a disciplinary or social institution, which give rise to stable structural forms by imposing constrains on the use of lexicogrammatical as well as discoursal resources. (p.23)

Complementing Swales' and Bhatia's approaches, and for the purposes of this study, we follow Parodi's (2010c) multidimensional conception of discourse genre, which highlights the interactions between the linguistic, social, and cognitive dimensions of discourse. Figure 2 illustrates such interactions.

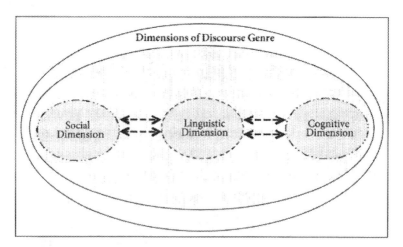

Figure 2. An interactive and three-dimensional conception of genre (Parodi, 2010e).

According to Parodi's (2010e) three-dimensional conception of genre, genres are complex entities that capture the communicative purposes of speakers and writers in contextual, cognitively situated interactions by means of concrete texts that materialize meanings in construction. The linguistic dimension plays, then, a fundamental role linking the contextual and the cognitive dimensions. Parodi also adds that the discourse entities called genres operate in specific social situations, achieving a certain stability, due to their eminently cognitive nature, and are stored in the memory of speakers/listeners and readers/writers. Parodi also proposes that, in the case of academic discourse, academic texts collected in a corpus represent specific instances of social interaction and that their study allows for the identification of their typical lexical and grammatical features. Moreover, the classification of texts according to genres facilitates the observation of patterns in the linguistic cartography of a specific genre (Halliday & Matthiessen, 2006; Hasan, 1996; Matthiessen, 1995). In this study, we claim that genres have a linguistic dimension, which is recognizable like a cartographic map or an organizational pattern, which becomes a concrete manifestation of a more abstract entity. This cartography, which includes not only the patterns of lexicogrammatical features (Parodi, 2005) but also the functional and rhetorical organization of texts in terms of, for instance, macro-moves and moves (Burdiles, 2012; Ibáñez, 2010; Martínez, 2012; Parodi, 2010e; Swales, 1990, 2004), becomes a key component for the understanding of disciplinary literacies in academic settings.

In sum, the principles underlying Parodi's (2010e) conceptual proposal may be summarized as a few core ideas: (a) genres are articulated in a dynamic and complex manner and have cognitive, linguistic, and social dimensions; (b) the relation among these three dimensions is not symmetrical, but rather an interaction in a dialectal cycle in which the possible differences appear only to some degree, since these dialectical interaction processes are inseparable; (c) most essentially, genres are cognitive constructs; (d) the context is "out there", but the context is mainly considered as a cognitive artifact in this genre perspective; (e) genres are acquired socio-constructively, which means that the process of construction occurs through situated and distributed cognition (van Dijk, 2008; van Dijk & Kintsch, 1983; Virtanen, 2004) in a varying range of settings; and (f) genres may be acquired through formal and informal environments, but academic literacy (reading and writing) in academic and professional domains is an educational tool that may help to facilitate the processes of genre construction.

In university settings genres have shown interesting diversity across disciplines. First, some of them are created specifically for university contexts while others are imported from more prototypically professional or scientific realms (Bolívar & Parodi, 2015; Parodi, 2010b, 2014). Second, some genres display didactic or informative recursive patterns while others contain specialized and dense prose. Third, some genres are read as a point of access to disciplinary information and are rarely written in a university context. Likewise, recent research in this field has observed that prototypical genres, such as, for example, the Critical Review and the Research Article, written in graduate and undergraduate university settings, are also relevant to professional scientific work (Parodi, 2010a; Jarpa, 2012).

Corpus Compilation and Methods:
The PUCV-2010 Corpus and the PUCV-UCSC-2013 Corpus

The PUCV-2010 Corpus is a collection of written texts that serve as required and complementary readings for students from six PhD programs in the Social Sciences and Humanities (SS&H) and Basic Sciences. The corpus consists of the texts used in 12 PhD programs (two per discipline) taught at six Chilean universities. The texts were selected by analyzing core and elective courses in each PhD program, except for the materials included in the PhD thesis. Table 1 shows the six disciplines included in the PUCV-2010 Corpus.

Table 1

Disciplines contained in the PUCV-2010 Corpus

Field	Discipline
Social Sciences & Humanities (SS&H)	History
	Linguistics
	Literature

Basic Sciences	Biotechnology
	Physics
	Chemistry

The disciplines presented in Table 1 were selected in order to obtain a range of possible variations in written documents from different doctoral programs. We aimed at collecting a diversified corpus of studies in order to detect variation across genres and disciplinary domains along several lines of research. Table 2 provides detailed information on the texts compiled in the corpus.

Table 2

Number of texts contained in the PUCV-2010 Corpus

Area and discipline		Number of texts per discipline	Total number of texts per area
Social Sciences & Humanities	History	592	2,603 (82.7%)
	Linguistics	1,065	
	Literature	946	
Basic Sciences	Biotechnology	227	544 (17.3%)
	Physics	181	
	Chemistry	136	
Total		3,147 (100%)	

As shown in Table 2, the PUCV-2010 corpus is not only one of the most extended academic corpora available today in the world, but it is also one of the most diverse. We are not aware of any other corpus, in any language or languages, compiled following our criteria and principles, that is, consisting of the texts that are actually read by doctoral students and that reflects the academic discourse of six disciplines. The procedures followed to compile the corpus are summarized in Table 3.

Following the same compilation protocol, we collected the PUCV-UCSC-2013 corpus in the discipline of Economics in two university undergraduate programs, and also compiled all texts students were given as part of the academic curriculum in Commercial Engineering and Accounting. The eight steps described in Table 3 were followed and we arrived at total of 124 texts. So, the total number of texts in both corpora under study in this research is 3,271.

Table 3

Corpus compilation procedures

Step	Associated Procedure
1	Organization of a database containing full detailed information of the programs' curricula (including the required and optional course descriptions).
2	Organization of a database containing all the required and complementary bibliographic references included in the course descriptions.
3	Elaboration of a survey submitted to professors of all programs, including a request for complementary course reading materials not included in the course descriptions that were given to the students to read.
4	Collection of complementary course reading materials, including handouts, didactic guides, digital files and photocopied documents.
5	Internet search to find material already available in digital format, in order to reduce digitization time.
6	Collection of print texts from libraries and professors' offices.
7	Process of photocopying each text in order to create a print-format data base for future reference.
8	Training of research assistants to compile and scan all texts in order to have a complete digital database of all the texts included in the corpus.

Methods

The present study follows the approach developed by Parodi, Ibáñez, and Venegas (2010) to identify genres based on a corpus of texts. The approach is based on five fundamental criteria: (a) the communicative macro-purpose, (b) the discourse organization mode, (c) the relationship between the participants, (d) the ideal context of circulation, where the texts were actually produced; and (e) the modality. Parodi et al. (2010) introduced an integrative approach to criteria and variables that combined deductive and inductive methods. This means that in their work they operationalized conceptual categories that come from a combination of sources: (a) the theoretical framework, (b) the researchers' prior knowledge and (c) the empirical data that stem from the text, in a rather "corpus-driven approach". Therefore, in our case the combination of methods is the most important issue, in order to achieve the best and most accurate distinction among genres within a corpus.

The five criteria were operationalized in a set of variables (for details, see Parodi et al. 2010). These variables were analyzed in the texts under the principle of "predominance" of one variable over another. This means that, from our multidimensional perspective, we are aware that genres are neither homogeneous nor stable units. Several communicative macro-purposes coexist within each genre and the modes of discursive organization vary. We have also kept in mind the precaution that a key difficulty in genre analysis is the lack of consensus on criteria and category names, as Gardner and Nesi (2013) pointed out (cf. Graves, Hyland, & Samuels, 2010; Zhu, 2004), when classifying into genre families an English corpus of 2,858 texts, written for assessment purposes by undergraduate and graduate university students from more than thirty academic disciplines. Thus, texts in different contexts may be classified into genre families differently. It is not easy, in Ganobcsik-Williams's (2004) words, to know what differences, if any, exist between a "research term paper" and a "scholarly article," for example, or between a "book review" and a "book report."

Results and Discussion

Genre Identification: PUCV-2010 Corpus

In this section, we present the 30 genres that emerged from the analysis of the first corpus conducted by our research team, following the matrix proposed by Parodi et al. (2010). This analysis was conducted on the entire PUCV-2010 Corpus, that is, on the 3,147 texts collected from the six disciplines at the doctoral level. Table 4 summarizes the results.

The empirical findings of the first study reflect a wide range of genres. In general, efforts were made to identify the least number of genres possible, avoiding unnecessary nomenclature proliferation and sub-specification.

Table 4

Genres identified in the PUCV-2010 Corpus

PUCV-2010 Genres and Associated Codes					
1	Anthology	ANT	16	Manifest	MAF
2	Atlas	ATL	17	Novel	NOV
3	Bibliographic Reference	BR	18	Opinion Article	OA
4	Biography	BIO	19	Poem	POE
5	Museum Guide	MG	20	Proceedings	PRO
6	Complete Works	CW	21	Report	RE
7	Dictionary	DC	22	Research Article	RA
8	Didactic Guide	DG	23	Review	REV
9	Disciplinary Text	DT	24	Scientific Note	SN
10	Dramatic Works	DW	25	Scientific Report	SR
11	Editorial	EDI	26	Textbook	TB
12	Epistolary	EPI	27	Story	ST
13	Errata	ERR	28	Technical Note	TN
14	Gospel	GO	29	Thank-you Speech	TUS
15	Graphical Abstract Index	GAI	30	Thesis	THE

As previously stated, we are aware of the difficulties in assigning one particular text to a genre category, as Ganobcsik-Williams (2004) and Gardner and Nasi (2013) pointed out. Consequently, keeping this idea in mind, genres were named following simple tagging rules, attempting, most of the time, to express their most common usage. When possible, we maintained the genre names used in previous studies (e.g., Gardner & Nasi, 2013; Martin & Rose, 2008; Parodi, 2004, 2009, 2010a; Parodi & Gramajo, 2007; Swales, 1990, 2004), especially in the cases of strong agreement, such as Atlas, Biography, Proceedings, Research Article, Textbook, and Thesis (see Appendix for examples of genre definitions). In the case of relatively new genres, we decided to name them according to the traditions in each discourse community or by the names identified in the texts themselves (as for example, Graphical Abstract Index, Technical Note, and Dictionary). The genres that have a strong tradition in some disciplines but do not regularly receive a clear and straightforward name were identified following our previous proposition and definition (Parodi et al., 2010). This is the case with the so called Disciplinary Text (DT), a genre very commonly employed in Social Sciences and Humanities (Parodi, 2009, 2010a), but not easily identifiable under one traditional name or a label with wide and validated recognition. Parodi et al. (2010) define it in this way:

> Disciplinary Text: The communicative macro-purpose of this discourse genre is to persuade readers of one or more subject matters of a particular discipline. Ideally, the context of circulation is the scientific field [or scholarly field, more broadly], and the relationship between the participants is between an expert writer and an expert reader. Preferably, an argumentative mode of discourse organization is used. Multimodal resources are also employed. (p. 50)

The DT is typically a specialized book covering one or several connected topics, which may be an edited collection or a single- or co-authored volume. Most of the time, the DT consists of a theoretical discussion (which may or may not include examples) or the presentation and argumentation of one theory, representing the ideas or the approach of one scholar or a school of thought. In Linguistics, for example, the genre of the DT includes most books written by, for example, Chomsky, Halliday, and Benveniste. In the last two or three decades, the DT genre has evolved to include empirical data, but normally combined with deep theoretical discussions. As part of this evolution, the texts in this genre have become more multimodal. New multisemiotic resources and complex

artifacts such as tables, graphs, and figures are now being employed
to construct meanings (for a detailed analysis and description of this
genre, see Ibáñez, 2010).

Quantitative Results

Interestingly, the number of genres identified in this first study
(30) is higher than the previously identified number in studies
conducted on Spanish corpora (e.g., PUCV-2003 Corpus and PUCV-
2006 Corpus, see Parodi, 2004, 2009, 2010a, or Parodi & Gramajo,
2007 for details). This could tentatively be explained by the fact
that it was the first time that genres at the doctoral level and in
the six disciplines were examined. These two variables, the level of
education and the discipline, together may explain why more genres
were identified. Then, the texts of the corpus classified by genre were
further analyzed quantitatively in order to determine the frequency
of their occurrence. Figure 3 shows the percentages of the occurrence
of each genre within the corpus.

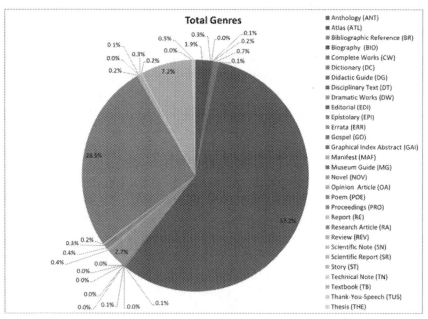

Figure 3. General quantification of the genres identified in the PUCV-2010
Corpus.

The percentages presented in Figure 3 provide information about the academic corpus and the identified genres. Despite the ample heterogeneity of discursive genres found in this academic corpus of texts collected from the six disciplines, it is evident that the discourse mechanisms most commonly used to communicate specialized knowledge at the PhD level do not vary significantly. Only two genres stand out: the Disciplinary Text (DT), with the highest occurrence of 57%, and the Research Article (RA) with a 26% occurrence. The third most common genre is the Textbook (TB), with only 7% (see Table 4).

The Novel and the Anthology are the final two genres that represent relatively high percentages of occurrence, in the fourth and fifth place with 3% and 2%, respectively. It is worth noting the important presence of these two genres of a clearly literary nature as part of the academic discourse at the doctoral level. Their possible function within the corpus will be discussed in more detail later in the chapter. The other 25 genres identified in the PUCV-2010 Corpus do not occur in more than 1% of the texts in the corpus, with the absolute numbers very close to zero. This indicates that the majority of these genres occur only in a few instances in the corpus of 3,147 texts. The figures indicate that the academic discourse in the disciplines under study is constructed by a limited range of generic resources. Most of the texts in the corpus belong to a very limited range of discursive formats, apparently, very idiosyncratic and easily recognizable: the DT, the RA, and the TB. In other words, the findings reported here show that specialized knowledge across the six disciplines is built and transmitted mainly, through clearly defined genres that focus on three types of discourse interactions:

a) Elaboration of theory, conceptual reflection, theoretical and methodological discussions, reporting of empirical findings, as in the Disciplinary Text;

b) Communication of research results and empirical findings, as in the Research Article; and

c) Communication and teaching of theoretical and applied concepts, modeling of procedures, introduction of problems and their solutions, as in the Textbook.

Figure 4 presents the total number of texts from each of the six disciplines under study.

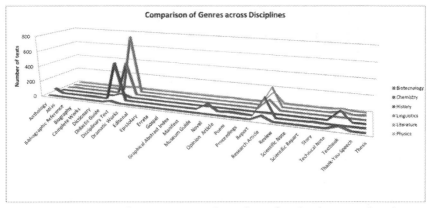

Figure 4. Occurrence of genres across disciplines (in absolute numbers).

Figure 4 presents the data that confirm the wide generic variation, but limited diversity of fundamental and prototypical discourse mechanisms, in disciplinary academic discourse. Thus, we highlight that DT is quite an important genre in the academic discourse of the disciplines under study, as the absolute figures in Figure 4 show (more than 700 texts in Linguistics, about 600 in Literature, and more than 400 in History). This shows that the DT is a fundamental genre in the transmission of specialized information and becomes an indispensable medium that enables the construction of disciplinary knowledge in the three SS&H disciplines at the doctoral level. Likewise, the singular role of DT in the SS&H disciplines corresponds to the findings reported by Parodi (2010d) based on a corpus of undergraduate university texts in the disciplines of Psychology and Social Work. As already noted, the DT genre is characterized by the elaboration, presentation, and discussion of theories; to a lesser degree, the DT also gives space to the communication of empirical research findings. The most prototypical focus of the DT is theoretical argumentation, not necessarily supported by empirical data, in which one theory is described and, sometimes, competing and alternative theories are also explained and discussed.

On the other hand, the percentages in Figure 4 also reveal that the RA and the TB are genres that occur in the academic discourse of several disciplines under study. Although absolute figures show their less frequent occurrence in comparison to the DT, the number of texts that belong to these genres are quite high and add up to between 100 and 200 texts in some cases.

Genre Identification: PUCV-UCSC-2013 Corpus

Following the corpora analysis, we proceeded to study the PUCV-UCSC-2013 Corpus of the texts collected from the discipline of Economics at the undergraduate level. The genre identification, based on 125 texts, is presented in Table 5.

Table 5

Genres identified in the PUCV-UCSC-2013 Corpus of Economics texts

PUCV-UCSC-2013 Genres		
1	Didactic Guide	DG
2	Exercise Guide	EG
3	Report	RE
4	Research Article	RA
5	Textbook	TB

This comparatively small corpus of undergraduate academic university discourse in Economics is relevant to our research for two main reasons: first, because it offers a complementary direction for the research in a new discipline not previously studied in Spanish from the genre identification perspective; second, because there is no agreement on the discursive nature of Economics in terms of whether its language is closer to that of the discourses of Social Sciences and Humanities, or that of Basic Sciences (Henderson, Dudley-Evans & Backhouse, 1993; Klamer, 1990; Kuhn, 1970; McCloskey, 1983, 1985, 1994; Mosini, 2011). This interesting issue is studied here in terms of the written discourse genres that represent the disciplinary discourse in Economics.

The data presented in Table 5 include five identified genres. Three of these are of a pedagogic nature (DG, EG, and TB) and clearly reveal the academic focus of the writer as a teacher responsible for choosing genres that support the construction of specialized disciplinary knowledge. In these three genres the roles played by the writer and reader show the prominence given to the interaction between the participants, particularly to the way the writer/teacher guides the reader as a student by providing a cartography of the disciplinary knowledge organized carefully, step by step. In these genres the information is organized in separate units and presented gradually, employing a variety of didactic resources (Bondi, 1996a & b; Klamer, 1990; Parodi, 2010c & d). The other two genres in Table 5 (RA and RE) are closer to workplace interactions and show the need for establishing links with the future professional discourse environment that the students may encounter in the future. In RA and RE, disciplinary knowledge is not organized with the pedagogical purpose of teaching new concepts, but rather with the purpose to communicate contemporary scientific information. In what follows, we offer the results of a step-by-step analysis of the texts in each of the seven disciplines, which was conducted to examine the genres and their frequency of occurrences.

Discourse Genres across Seven Disciplines

First, we present the results for the academic discourse of the three disciplines in basic sciences: Chemistry, Physics and Biotechnology.

Chemistry. Figure 5 shows absolute numbers of genres found in the discipline of Chemistry.

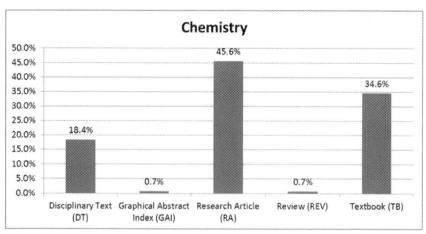

Figure 5. Genres in Chemistry.

As Figure 5 indicates, five genres emerged from the analysis of the 136 texts in Chemistry. In order of occurrence they are: RA, TB, DT, SRE, and IRG. It is evident that RA, TB, and DT are the most prototypical and fundamental genres in the discipline while the other two genres are far less frequent (0.7%) and play a rather marginal role. It is interesting that highly specialized informative resources, such as RA and DT, are involved in the transmission of knowledge together with other means of a more educational and instructional function (TB), which applies informative and reformulation strategies. Regarding the latter genre, Parodi (2010e) described its main function in disciplines such as Industrial Chemistry and Construction Engineering in the teaching of concepts and procedures by means of exemplification and problem solving in highly illustrative formats. The data collected at the doctoral level and presented here point towards the combination of genres and a trend towards higher specialization.

Physics. Figure 6 shows absolute numbers of genres found in the discipline of Physics.

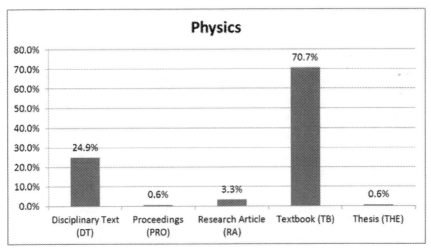

Figure 6. Genres in Physics.

Similar to Chemistry, Figure 6 shows that five genres were identified in the 181 texts that constitute the Physics corpus. The three most frequently occurring genres in Physics were TB (70.7%), DT (24.9%), and RA (3.3%). The occurrence frequency of the other two genres, Proceedings and Thesis, barely reached 0.6%. The relationship between the participants in these genres can be defined as between experts, just as in the RA and the DT. However, it is the Textbook genre that stands out as the prevalent discourse tool used to access the disciplinary content in Physics, through which educational strategies are deployed such as the definition of specialized concepts, exemplification, classification, and presentation of problems with their corresponding solutions and modeling. In this genre, the type of the relationship highlighted is between an expert and a non-expert. This means that 70.7% of the texts from the discipline of Physics belong to a genre that provides a framework that progressively scaffolds access to information and enables the construction of disciplinary knowledge in a very didactic manner, and with an aim to instruct the audience under training.

Biotechnology. Figure 7 demonstrates the 14 genres present in the disciplinary discourse of Biotechnology.

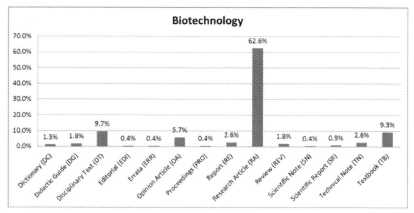

Figure 7. Genres in Biotechnology.

Just as Figure 7 indicates, the number of genres in the academic discourse of Biotechnology is considerably higher than that in the other two disciplines in basic sciences. Despite the greater diversity of genres identified in the corpus of 227 texts in this discipline, as compared to Chemistry and Physics, there are three genres that occur most frequently in all three disciplines: the RA (62.6%), the DT (9.7%), and the TB (9.3%). The other 11 genres have a low frequency of occurrence. Unlike in the disciplinary discourse of Physics, the hierarchical order of these three genres as discursive pedagogical devices in Biotechnology is different. In this case, the RA is the most relevant genre, the one that presumably gives access to information and scaffolds the construction of specialized knowledge within the discipline. As is well known, this genre circulates information among experts, communicates state-of-the-art knowledge and disseminates scientific findings of a theoretical and empirical nature. The communicative macro-purpose of the genre is to persuade the audience by means of diverse argumentative strategies. The DT is the second specialized genre that also establishes an expert-to-expert relationship between the writer and the reader.

As for the TB, it also holds an important place in the discourse of Biotechnology, although it ranks third in terms of the frequency of occurrence (9.3%). This analysis demonstrates that in Biotechnology, different genres of different didactic degree are combined for the purpose of reaching semi-specialized audiences. The heterogeneity of genres in the discourse of this discipline is characterized by genres such as the Editorial, the Technical Note, the Report, the Review, the Didactic Guide, and the Dictionary. All of these genres have a frequency of occurrence of more than 1%. The wide diversity of genres in Biotechnology (14 in total) makes this discipline, as we discuss below, the second most heterogeneous in the PUCV-2010 Corpus.

Figures 8, 9 and 10 present the genres identified in the three SS&H disciplines: Linguistics, History, and Literature. First of all, we will review the genres found in the academic discourse of Linguistics.

Linguistics. Figure 8 shows genres found in the discipline of Linguistics.

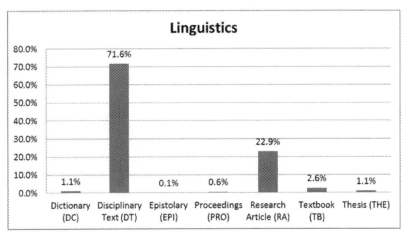

Figure 8. Genres in Linguistics

The analysis of the 1,065 texts in the corpus of texts for doctoral training in Linguistics resulted in the identification of seven genres (Figure 8). From these seven genres, only two have a high frequency of occurrence: the DT (71.6%) and the RA (22.9%). Both genres are prototypical of the transmission of the highly specialized knowledge. The low frequency of occurrence of the TB genre (2.6%), unlike in the disciplinary discourses in Basic Sciences, indicates that it is not a prototypical discourse mechanism in this field. Previous studies conducted on the PUCV-2006 Corpus have already highlighted this difference between academic discourse in undergraduate SS&H and Basic Sciences and Engineering programs (Parodi, 2010d, Ibáñez, 2010). The empirical data presented in this chapter show that this difference is also found in the academic discourses at the doctoral level. The DT is as relevant in SS&H as TB is in Basic Science. Likewise, although with a less frequent occurrence rate, the RA becomes the second most important genre in the discourse of doctoral training in Linguistics. Clearly, in this discipline, knowledge is transmitted through books, followed in percentage of the occurrence frequency by research articles published in scientific journals, both in paper and electronic formats.

History. Figure 9 shows a wide variety of genres found in the academic discourse of doctoral training in History. 13 genres have been identified, with the DT accounting for the 71.6% of the total genre frequency of occurrence.

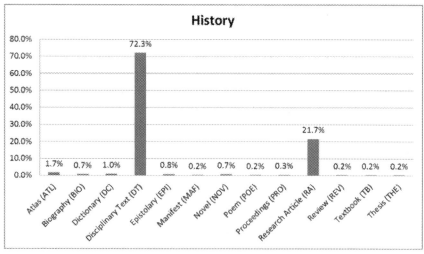

Figure 9. Genres in History

As Figure 9 demonstrates, out of the 13 genres found in the 502 texts collected from this discipline, only two have a high frequency of occurrence: the DT (72.3%) and the RA (21.7%). From the remaining 11 genres, only two have a frequency of occurrence above 1%: the Atlas and the Dictionary.

Although an important generic variation is found in the academic discourse of doctoral studies in History, its generic composition in terms of the frequency of occurrence is very similar to that observed in Linguistics, except for a considerably more limited heterogeneity. Likewise, the academic discourses of Linguistics and History reveal that both disciplines share similar discourse devices used to access disciplinary information. This finding notwithstanding, it is necessary to conduct a more detailed study of the texts that constitute these common disciplinary genres. The mere categorization within a genre does not necessarily mean that such texts are structured identically or that the functional and rhetorical organization plays the same role in both disciplines. In this regard, Parodi (2010d) and Ibáñez (2010) showed through an analysis of rhetorical moves that the structures of the TB and DT genres vary across disciplines, especially in the SS&H and Basic Science.

In the discipline of History, the genres identified as Epistolary[3], Novel, and Poem are also worth mentioning. The presence of these genres tells us of two possible types of discourse within the History corpus: the genres that serve as the source of information or content to be studied, and other genres that are based in part on the contributions of source genres and serve the purpose of presenting analyses of the source genres. This distinction reflects the double discursive nature of the discipline.

Literature. Finally, we present the analysis of the 946 texts that comprised the corpus compiled in the discipline of Literature, in which 15 genres were identified (Figure 10).

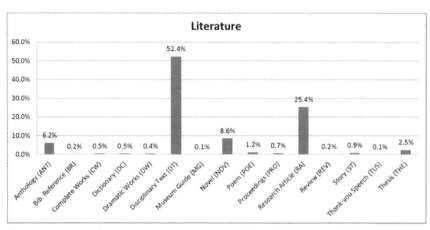

Figure 10. Genres in Literature

The study of this disciplinary corpus revealed that the academic discourse in Literature has the highest generic variation. In terms of the frequency of occurrence, and similar to the findings in Linguistics and History, two genres emerged as occurring most frequently: the Disciplinary Text (52.4%) and the Research Article (25.4%). This finding adds to the previously obtained evidence that the discourses of the three SS&H disciplines share, as a common characteristic, the high specialization of the texts and the use of genres characterized by the expert-to-expert relationship between the writer and the reader. As seen from the data (Figure 10), the Literature academic discourse at the PhD level does not contain any occurrences of the genres of a pedagogical nature or those that display didactic strategies directed towards teaching and guiding the reader/student. No instances of the Textbook or Didactic Guide genres were found in the discourse of this discipline. Similarly, the frequency of occurrence of the Textbook or Didactic Guide genres in the academic discourses of History and Linguistics are either very low or non-existent.

Among the genres in the Literature corpus, we identified literary genres such as the Anthology, Novel and Story, which are significantly different from the Disciplinary Text and the Research Article. In order to further explore these distinctions, we reclassified the texts from this discipline as those that belong to either literary or non-literary genres. Figure11 shows the percentage of the frequency of occurrence of these two genre categories.

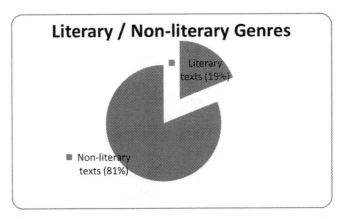

Figure 11. Total percentage of texts in literary and non-literary genre categories in Literature.

As Figure 11 shows, 19% of genres in the discipline of Literature are identified as literary. This means that 19% of the genres in the academic discourse in the doctoral programs in Literature constitute the matter or focus of study and research. 81% of genres identified in this disciplinary corpus are non-literary. These genres present descriptions and discussions of, or reflections on, theories, models or, concepts, and analyze texts that belong to genres classified as literary. This distinction appears quite revealing since it illustrates a particular feature of the specialized academic discourse in Literature, in which two types of genres are clearly set apart. The generic constitution of the corpus in Literature reveals a special feature, which was also found in the History corpus but to a lesser extent. Thus, among the identified genres, there are those used to communicate the results of reflective and analytical activities (e.g., the Disciplinary Text, the Research Article, the Thesis, the Review) applied to other genres (the Novel, the Poem, the Story, the Complete Works, etc.), or the "raw" material from which the other genres emerge. To further explore this finding we recalculated the frequency of occurrence of the identified genres, but this time as part of literary or non-literary macro-genres.

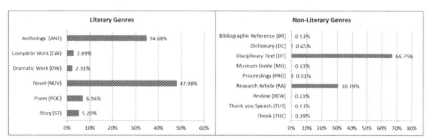

Figure 12. Comparison of the frequency of occurrence of literary and non-literary genres.

As Figure 12 demonstrates, the Novel (47.98%) and the Anthology (34.68%) are the most frequently found literary genres in the corpus, followed by the Poem and the Story. This means that, at the doctoral level, narrative genres are preferred as objects of study and analysis, followed by poetry. The analytical work and research in Literature are carried out mainly through the Disciplinary Text (66.75%) and the Research Article (30.79%). Both genres are characterized by a high degree of specialization and limited techniques of dissemination to less specialized audiences. Other non-literary genres identified in this corpus show a very low frequency of occurrence, in which only one, Proceedings, reaches 1%, and it shares the feature of high specialization with the DT and the TB.

Economics. In addition, and as part of the second study, 125 texts collected from two undergraduate programs in Economics, were analyzed and, as noted above, five genres were identified. The distribution of the frequency of occurrence is discussed in detail below.

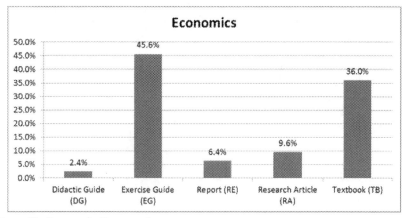

Figure 13. Genres in Economics.

As Figure 13 indicates, out of the five genres identified in the 125 texts collected from Economics at the undergraduate level, only two are characterized by a high frequency of occurrences: the Exercise Guide (EG) (45.6%) and the Textbook (36%). Each of the remaining three genres have the frequency of occurrence below 10%: the Research Article (9.6%), the Report (6.4%) and the Didactic Guide (2.4%). This relative generic variation found in the academic discourse of Economics and the understanding that the pedagogical genres (the EG and the TB) are found to have the highest frequency of occurrence, represent novel findings distinct from the findings of previous studies of the undergraduate genres in academic discourses of social sciences and humanities (Bondi, 1996a & b; Henderson, Dudley-Evans & Backhouse, 1993; Klamer, 1990; Parodi, 2010a, 2011a, 2014). The findings are novel and distinct in that genres of the discipline of Economics now appear closer to the discourses of the Basic Science disciplines rather than to the SS&H disciplinary discourses. The academic discourses of Linguistics, Literature, History, Psychology, and Social Work have displayed a considerable variety of genres, while the academic discourse of Economics appears to be characterized by a comparatively lower heterogeneity, which again makes it more similar to the discourses of most Basic Science disciplines.

This finding contributes to genre studies and research on disciplinarity. It also indicates that not all academic discourses use similar language resources to support knowledge construction and that genres across one disciplinary domain are not as homogeneous as may be expected, even if they belong to SS&H. The new results open the opportunities for a detailed analysis of the academic discourse in Economics, for example, the analyses that Parodi and Burdiles (2013) and Parodi, Boudon and Julio (2014) are now conducting on textbooks and some other genres.

The Venn diagram in Figure 14 illustrates the distribution of the 31 discourse genres identified in the academic discourses of seven disciplines in the study of the PUCV-2010 and PUCV-UCSC-2013 corpora and highlights those that are shared by two or more disciplines and those that belong exclusively to one specialized domain. Based on these data, the RA stands out as the only genre that occurs in every one of the seven disciplines in the combined corpus. This finding shows that research articles published in disciplinary journals, both in paper and electronic formats, constitute a genre that serves as the most common means of distributing and communicating disciplinary knowledge. This finding also shows that in the seven disciplines, regardless of the generic variation, specialized knowledge is partially communicated through a relatively common discourse resource. This suggests that both writers and readers from the SS&H and Basic Science undergraduate and doctoral programs construct and employ genres that share similar discourse organization when they want to communicate theories and empirical findings.

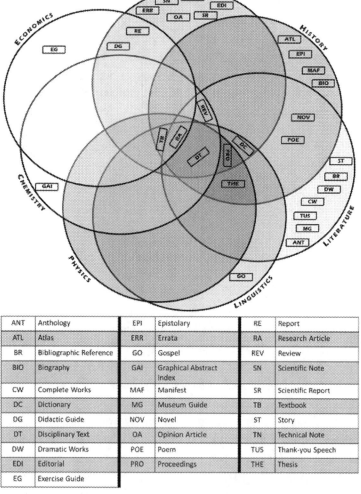

ANT	Anthology	EPI	Epistolary	RE	Report
ATL	Atlas	ERR	Errata	RA	Research Article
BR	Bibliographic Reference	GO	Gospel	REV	Review
BIO	Biography	GAI	Graphical Abstract Index	SN	Scientific Note
CW	Complete Works	MAF	Manifest	SR	Scientific Report
DC	Dictionary	MG	Museum Guide	TB	Textbook
DG	Didactic Guide	NOV	Novel	ST	Story
DT	Disciplinary Text	OA	Opinion Article	TN	Technical Note
DW	Dramatic Works	POE	Poem	TUS	Thank-you Speech
EDI	Editorial	PRO	Proceedings	THE	Thesis
EG	Exercise Guide				

Figure 14. Intersection of genres across the seven disciplines (combining PUCV-2010 Corpus and PUCV-UCSC-2013 Corpus).

It is worth noting that the academic discourse of Physics analyzed in this study does not contain any prototypical genres that are exclusive to the discipline. From the five genres identified in the discourse of this discipline, all are shared with three, four, five or seven other disciplines. The discourses of each discipline from among Linguistics, Economics, and Chemistry were found to possess at least one exclusive genre. Figure 14 also shows that the discourses of Biotechnology (eight genres), Literature (seven genres), and History (four genres) have an important number of idiosyncratic genres, although many of them do not have a high frequency of occurrence. Based on the data collected, Figure 15 shows the distribution of the disciplinary academic discourse genres from the least diverse to the most diverse.

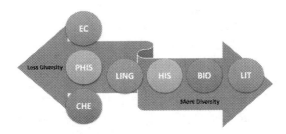

Figure 15. Diversity continuum of genres across disciplines.

As Figure 15 demonstrates, the academic discourses in Economics, Physics, and Chemistry have the least diversity in genre (five genres each), while Literature discourse is the most diverse (15 genres), followed by the academic discourse in Biotechnology (14 genres). History follows with 13 different genres. Linguistics is located in the centre of this continuum with a total of seven genres. This analysis shows that there are no clear-cut differences in the generic variation in the academic discourses of the SS&H and Basic Science disciplines. While the academic discourse in Linguistics is closer to the one in Economics, Physics, and Chemistry in terms of generic variation, the discourse in Biotechnology is as varied as are the specialized discourses of History and Literature. The genre diversity in the undergraduate discourse in Economics reveals interesting features in terms of genre diversity, which make it closer to the Basic Science discourse; in other words, the important presence of textbooks and exercise guides indicates that this discipline constructs knowledge in the ways similar to Chemistry and Physics, rather than in the ways typical of SS&H discourses--that is, different from the ways of the discourses of Psychology and Social Work discourse (Bondi, 1996a, b; Parodi, 2010c, 2011a, 2014). What the previous research and present study have demonstrated is that the Disciplinary Text is the most common genre used in knowledge construction in the SS&H university discourses, while the Textbook is the most relevant genre in the Basic Science university discourses. This is why the findings concerning Economics discourse are so revealing. Besides, they are compatible with McCloskey's (1983, 1985, 1994), Klamer's (1990), and Balak's (2006) observations that economists themselves prefer to view the discourse of Economics as objective and scientific, and thus being closer to the Physics, Chemistry, and Biology discourses.

Examining the data provided in Figure 15 in detail, it is worth restating that the disciplinary discourse of Literature is the only one that presents two macro-genres: literary and non-literary. Although these macro-genres are also present in the academic discourse of History at the doctoral level, they are not used in the same way as in Literature. In this regard, it could be possible to consider the genres in the literary macro-genre as non-specialized. In many cases, as Parodi (2005) points out, texts belonging to this literary macro-genre show prototypical features (e.g., first and third person singular and plural pronouns, second person singular pronouns, periphrastic forms of future tense, imperfect tense, and time and negation adverbs). These lexicogrammatical features have been associated with a lower degree of complexity and informational density, typical of literary oral and written texts and more distant from specialized technical texts (Parodi, 2005).

Conclusions

This chapter has identified and documented 31 discourse genres as they appear in a corpus of 3,272 texts from academic discourses in seven disciplines (Biotechnology, Chemistry, Economics, History, Linguistics, Literature, and Physics). The marked differences in the findings point to major variations in the way academic discourses are constructed through genres across these disciplines. However, the calculation of the frequency of occurrence of texts pertaining to each genre indicates that only a few prototypical genres of academic and disciplinary discourse at undergraduate and graduate levels occur with high frequency. The most frequent and fundamental genres from a quantitative perspective are: Disciplinary Text, Research Article, Textbook, and Exercise Guide. As follows from the analysis conducted from a cross-disciplinary perspective, the Research Article is identified as the only genre that is present in the discourses of all the seven disciplines.

The findings of the present study both complement and extend the results obtained by Parodi (2010a). They do not follow the previously identified, more traditional generic distinction between the academic discourses of SS&H and BS, in which the Disciplinary Text was found to be the most prototypical of SS&H, and the Textbook the most prototypical of Basic Science. The finding of the present study that the most prototypical genre of the discourse of Economics is the TB calls for a deeper analysis necessary to establish whether the discourses of Economics discourse are more similar to the discourses of SS&H, as it has been assumed, or to the discourses of Basic Science. Another important finding is the double articulation of genres observed in Literature and History. The study has shown that the discourses of Literature and History include literary and non-literary macro-genres, with non-literary macro-genres addressing the study and analysis of non-literary macro-genres. This findings indicates the primarily discursive nature of research in Literature and History, as compared to a more experimental approach in the other disciplines analyzed. The study also indicates that the identified genres are not entirely homogenous and demonstrates that they may possess idiosyncratic and prototypical features according to their discipline of origin; that is, while the study identified four genres (the TB, RA, DT and EG) that act as important discourse mechanisms across the disciplines, these genres may differ in their rhetorical move organization or demonstrate variation in terms of the predominance of a more theoretical or a more empirical approach. Parodi (2010d, 2011a), Ibáñez (2010), and Martínez (2012) have shown that Textbooks, Disciplinary Texts and Doctoral Theses, respectively, show idiosyncratic features across disciplines; Burdiles (2012) studied a genre that showed a finer, subdiscipline variation (the Clinical Case in Medicine). The two corpora investigated in this chapter need to be studied further to identify such variations.

From the perspective of language classroom practice, a deeper understanding of how written language functions in specialized genres across disciplines should help to design reading and writing tasks to enable university students to become familiar with the discursive tools that promote access to the information and scaffold knowledge construction. Developing reading and writing strategies in specialized university contexts is a fundamental step to become an active member of a discourse community and to be part of a disciplinary environment. In this regard, the data contributed by this study opens doors for further studies. The findings of the present study pave the way for planning and creating the "reading and writing across disciplines" programs based on the perspective in which psycholinguistics is informed by corpus linguistics (Parodi, 2011c).

References

Arnoux, E. (2002). *La lectura y la escritura en la universidad* [Reading and writing in university]. Buenos Aires, AR: Eudeba.

Arnoux, E. (Ed.). (2009). *Escritura y producción de conocimiento en las carreras de postgrado* [Writing and knowledge production in graduate courses]. Buenos Aires, AR: Arcos.

Balak, B. (2006). *McCloskey's rhetoric: Discourse ethics and economics.* London, UK: Routledge.

Bawarshi, A. & Reiff, M. (2010). *Genre: An introduction to history, theory, research, and pedagogy.* West Lafayette, IN: Parlor Press.

Bazerman, C. (1994). *The informed writer: Using sources in the disciplines.* New York, NY: HMH.

Bazerman, C. (June, 2012). *A genre based theory of literate action.* Keynote speech presented at the International Conference Genre 2012: Rethinking Genre 20 Years Later, Ottawa, Ontario, Canada.

Bazerman, C., Bonini, A. & Figueiredo, D. (Eds.) (2009). *Genre in a changing world: Perspectives on writing.* West Lafayette, IN: Parlor Press.

Bazerman, C., Krut, R., Lunsford, K., McLeod, S., Null, S., Rogers, P. & Stansell, A. (2009). *Traditions of writing research.* London, UK: Routledge.

Bazerman, C.& Russell, D. (Eds.) (1995). *Landmark essays on writing across the curriculum.* London, UK: Routledge.

Bazerman, C.& Wiener, H. (2009). *Writing skills handbook.* 5th edition. Boston, MA: Cengage Publishing.

Bhatia, V. (1993). *Analysing genre: Language use in professional settings.* London, UK: Longman.

Bhatia, V. (2004). *Worlds of written discourse: A genre based view.* New York; London: Continuun.

Bhatia, V. (2012a, June). *Critical genre analysis.* Keynote speech presented at the International Conference Genre 2012: Rethinking Genre 20 Years Later, Ottawa, Ontario, Canada.

Bhatia, V. (2012b). Critical reflexions on genre analysis. *Ibérica, 24,* 17-28.

Biber, D. (1988). *Variation across speech and writing.* Cambridge, UK: Cambridge University Press.

Bolívar, A. & Parodi, G. (2015). Academic and professional discourse. In M. Lacorte (Ed.), *The routledge handbook of hispanic applied linguistics* (pp. 459-476). New York, NY: Routledge.

Bondi, M. (1996a). World of fact and world of hypothesis in Economics textbooks. In V. N. Zamagni (Ed.), *Annale 1994/1995* (pp. 341-354). Università degli Studi di Bologna, Facoltà di Economia, Sede di Forlì. Cesena, IT: Società Editrice.

Bondi, M. (1996b). Language variations across genres: Quantifiers and worlds of reference in (and around) economics textbooks. *Anglais de Specialité, 2,* 24-47.

Burdiles, G. (2012). *Descripción de la organización retórica del género Caso Clínico de la medicina a partir del Corpus CCM-2009* [Description of the rhetorical organization of general clinical case in Medecine on the basis of the CCM-2009 corpus] (Unpublished doctoral dissertation). Pontificia Universidad Católica de Valparaíso, Valparaíso, Chile.

Castañeda. L. & Henao, J. (1995). *La lectura en la universidad* [Reading in university]. Medellín, Colombia: Universidad de Antioquía.

Cubo de Severino, L., Lacon, N., & Puiatti, H. (Eds.). (2012). *Escribir una tesis: Manual de estrategias de producción* [Write a thesis: Production strategies manual]. Córdoba, Spain: Comunicarte.

Freedman, A. & Medway, P. (Eds.). (1994). *Genre and the New Rhetoric.* London, UK: Taylor & Francis.

Ganobcsik-Williams, L. (2004). *A report on the teaching of academic writing in UK higher education.* London, UK: Royal Literary Fund.

Gardner, S. & Nesi, H. (2013). A classification of genre families in university writing. *Applied Linguistics, 34*(1), 25-52.

Graves, R., Hyland, T. & Samuels, B. (2010). Undergraduate writing assignments: An analysis of syllabi at one Canadian college. *Written Communication, 27*(3), 293-317.

Halliday, M. & Matthiessen, C. (2006). *Construing experience through meaning: A language-based approach to cognition.* London, UK: Continuum.

Handford, M. (2010). What can a corpus tell us about specialist genres? In A. O'Keeffe & M. McCarthy (Eds.), *The Routledge handbook of corpus Linguistics* (pp. 255-269). London, UK: Routledge.

Hasan, R. (1996). The nursery tale as a genre. In C. Cloran, D. Butt & G. Williams (Eds.), *Ways of saying: Ways of meaning: Selected paper* (pp. 156-187). London, UK: Cassell.

Henderson, W., Dudley-Evans, A., & Backhouse, R. (Eds.). (1993). *Economics as language*. London, UK: Routledge.

Hyon, S. (1996). Genre in three traditions: Implications for ESL. *TESOL Quarterly, 30*(4), 693-722.

Ibáñez, R. (2010). Disciplinary text genre as a means for accessing disciplinary knowledge: A study from genre analysis perspective. In G. Parodi (Ed.), *Academic and professional genres in Spanish* (pp. 219-246). Amsterdam, NL: John Benjamins.

Jarpa, M. (2012). *Macrogénero académico evaluativo: Descripción retórica-estructural en la comunidad de aprendizaje de Postgrado en Biotecnología* [Evaluative academic macrogenre: Rhetorical and structural description in a graduate apprenticeship community in Biotechnology] (Unpublished doctoral dissertation). Pontificia Universidad Católica de Valparaíso, Chile.

Klamer, A. (1990). The textbook presentation of economics discourse. In W. Samuels (Ed.), *Economics as discourse* (pp. 129-154). London, UK: Kluwer.

Kuhn, T. (1970). *The structure of scientific revolutions*. Chicago, IL: University of Chicago Press.

Marinkovich, J., Morán, P., & Benítez, R. (1997). *La enseñanza de la escritura en el aula: Una metodología interdisciplinaria* [Teaching writing in the classroom: Interdisciplinary methodology]. Valparaíso, Chile: Imprenta Carroza.

Marinkovich, J., Peronard, M. & Parodi, G. (2006). *LECTES: Programa de lectura y escritura* [LECTES: A program for teacing reading and writing]. Valparaíso, Chile: EUV.

Martin, J. (1992). *English text. System and structure*. Philadelphia, PA: John Benjamins.

Martin, J. (2012, June). *Genre, identity, and restorative justice: Rule and role in youth justice conference*. Keynote speech presented at the International Conference Genre 2012: Rethinking Genre 20 Years Later, Ottawa, Ontario, Canada.

Martin, J. & Rose, D. (2008). *Genre relations: Mapping culture*. London, UK: Equinox.

Martínez, J.D. (2012). *Descripción y variación retórico-funcional del género Tesis Doctoral: Un análisis desde dos disciplinas y dos comunidades discursivas a partir del Corpus Te DiCE-2010* [Rhetorical and functional description and variation of the PHD thesis: an analysis from two disciplines and two discourse communities on the TeDiCE-2010 Corpus] (Unpublished doctoral dissertation). Pontificia Universidad Católica de Valparaíso, Chile.

Matthiessen, C. (1995). *Lexicogrammatical cartography: English systems.* Tokyo, JP: International Language Sciences Publishers

McCloskey, D. (1983). The rhetoric of economics. *Journal of Economic Literature, 31*(2), 482-504.

McCloskey, D. (1985). *The rhetoric of economics.* Madison, WI: University of Wisconsin Press.

McCloskey, D. (1994). *Knowledge and persuasion in economics.* Cambridge, UK: Cambridge University Press.

Miller, C. (1984). Genre as social action. *Quarterly Journal of Speech, 70,* 151-167.

Miller, C. (2012, June). *Do genres evolve?* Keynote speech presented at the international conference Genre 2012: Rethinking Genre 20 Years Later, Ottawa, Ontario.

Mosini, V. (2011). *Reassessing the paradigm of economics: Bringing positive economics back into the normative framework.* London, UK: Routledge.

Paltridge, B. (2002). Genre, text type, and the English for academic purposes. In A. Johns (Ed.), *Genre in the classroom* (pp. 73-90). Mahwah, NL: Erlbaum.

Parodi, G. (2003). *Relaciones entre lectura y escritura* [Reading and writing connections].Valparaíso, CL: EUV.

Parodi, G. (2004). Textos de especialidad y comunidades discursivas técnico-profesionales: Una aproximación basada en corpus computarizado [Specialty texts and technical-professional discourse communities: A computerized corpus approach]. *Revista Estudios Filológicos, 39,* 7-36.

Parodi, G. (2005). Lingüística de corpus y análisis multidimensional: Exploración de la variación en el Corpus PUCV-2003 [Corpus linguistics and multidimentional analysis: Exploration of the variation across the PUCV-2003 Corpus]. In G. Parodi (Ed.), *Discurso especializado e instituciones formadoras* [Specialized discourse and educational institutions] (pp. 83-126). Valparaíso, CL: EUV.

Parodi, G. (2009). El Corpus Académico y profesional del Español PUCV-2006: Semejanzas y diferencias entre los géneros académicos y profesionales [The academic and professional corpus of Spanish PUCV-2006: Similarities and differences amiong academic and professional genres]. *Revista Estudios Filológicos, 44,* 123-147.

Parodi, G. (Ed.). (2010a). *Academic and professional genres in Spanish.* Amsterdam, NL: John Benjamins Pub. Co.

Parodi, G. (2010b). Multisemiosis y lingüística de corpus: Artefactos (multi)semióticos en los textos de seis disciplinas en el Corpus PUCV-2010 [Multisemiotics and corpus linguistics: Multisemiotic artifacts in the texts of six disciplines in the PUCV-2010 corpus]. *Revista de Lingüística Teórica y Aplicada (RLA), 48,* 233-270.

Parodi, G. (2010c). University academic genres: A miscellaneous discourse. In G. Parodi (Ed.), *Academic and professional genres in Spanish* (pp. 83-100). Amsterdam, NL: John Benjamins Pub. Co.

Parodi, G. (2010d). Written discourse genres: Towards an integral conception from a sociocognitive perspective. In G. Parodi (Ed.), *Academic and professional genres in Spanish* (pp. 17-36). Amsterdam, NL: John Benjamins Pub. Co.

Parodi, G. (2010e). The textbook genre and its rhetorical organisation across four scientific disciplines: Between abstraction and concreteness. In G. Parodi (Ed.), *Academic and professional genres in Spanish* (pp. 171-188). Amsterdam, NL: John Benjamins Pub. Co.

Parodi, G. (2011a). The rhetorical organisation of the textbook genre across disciplines: A "colony-in-loops"? *Discourse Studies, 12*(1), 195-222.

Parodi, G. (2011b). La teoría de la comunicabilidad: Notas para una concepción integral de la comprensión de textos escritos [The communicability theory: Notes for an integral conception of written texts comprehension]. *Revista Signos. Estudios de Lingüística, 44*(76), 145-167.

Parodi, G. (2014). Genre organisation in specialised discourse: Disciplinary variation across university textbooks. *Discourse Studies, 16*(1), 65-87.

Parodi, G., Boudon, E. & Julio, C. (2014). La organización retórica del género Manual de Economía: Un discurso en tránsito disciplinar [The rhetorical organization of the textbook in economics: A discourse in transit]. *Revista de Lingüística Teórica y Aplicada (RLA), 52*(2), 133-163.

Parodi, G. & Burdiles, G. (2013, November). *El pronombre ELLO como mecanismo encapsulador en el discurso académico de la Economía: función gramatical y referencia textual* [Pronoun ELLO as an encapsulator mechanism in the academic discourse of economics:

Functional and textual reference]. Paper presented at the Annual Meeting of the Sociedad Chilena de Lingüística (SOCHIL). Concepción, Chile.

Parodi, G. & Gramajo, A. (2007). Technical-professional discourses: Specialized and dissemination text types. In G. Parodi (Ed.), *Working with Spanish corpora* (pp. 145-172). London, UK: Continuum.

Parodi, G., Ibáñez, R. & Venegas, R. (2010). Discourse genres in PUCV-2006 academic and professional corpus of Spanish: Criteria, definitions, and examples. In G. Parodi (Ed.), *Academic and professional genres in Spanish* (pp. 37-64). Amsterdam, NL: John Benjamins.

Peronard, M., Gómez, L., Parodi, G., Núñez, P. & González, J. (1998). *Programa LyC: Leer y comprender* [LandC Program: Reading and comprehension]. Santiago, CL: Editorial Andrés Bello.

Resnik, G. & Valente, E. (2009). *La Lectura y la escritura en el trabajo de taller: Aspectos metodológicos* [Reading and writing in workshop study: Methodological aspects]. Buenos Aires, AR: Universidad Nacional General Sarmiento.

Russell, D. (2002). *Writing in the academic disciplines: A curricular history.* Carbondale, IL: Southern Illinois University Press.

Swales, J. (1990). *Genre analysis.English in academic and research settings.* Cambridge, UK: Cambridge University Press.

Swales, J. (2004). *Research genres: Exploration and applications.* Cambridge, UK: Cambridge University Press.

Swales, J. (2009). Worlds of genre - Metaphors of genre. In C. Bazerman, A. Bonini & D. Figueiredo (Eds.), *Genre in a changing world* (pp. 3-16). Fort Collins, CO: The WAC Clearing House & Parlor Press.

Swales, J. (2012, June). *Texts and commentaries: Toward a reception study of "Genre Tradition" (Hyon, 1996).* Keynote speech presented at the international conference Genre 2012: Rethinking Genre 20 Years Later, Ottawa, Ontario.

van Dijk, T. (1977). *Text and context: Explorations in the semantics and pragmatics of discourse.* New York; London: Longman

van Dijk, T. (2008). *Discourse and context. A sociocognitive approach.* Cambridge, UK: Cambridge University Press.

van Dijk, T. & Kintsch, W. (1983). *Strategies of discourse comprehension.* New York, NY: Academic Press.

Virtanen, T. (Ed.). (2004). *Approaches to cognition through text and doscourse.* Berlin, DE: Mouton de Gruyter.

Zhu, W. (2004). Writing in business courses: an analysis of assignments types, their characteristics, and the required skills. *English for Specific Purposes, 1*(2), 11-135.

Appendix

Definitions of Research Article and Textbook (Parodi et al., 2010)

Research Article (RA): Discourse genre whose communicative macro-purpose is to persuade its audience about a given point of view, either by means of a review of the theoretical framework or the reporting of results of an empirical study. Ideally, its circulation context is the scientific setting and the relationship between the participants is between expert writer and expert reader. Preferably, discourse is organized in a pre-eminently argumentative mode and it incorporates multimodal resources.
Textbook (TB): Discourse genre whose communicative macro-purpose is to instruct students about concepts and/or procedures in a specialized topic. Ideally, its circulation context is the educational setting and the relationship between the participants is between expert writer and non-specialist readers. Preferably, discourse is organized in a descriptive mode and it integrates multimodal resources.

EndNotes

1   This research was funded by FONDECYT Projects 1130033 and 1090030.
2   The term miscellaneous is used in the sense of heterogeneous.
3   In this analysis, the term 'Epistolary' refers to a collection of letters.

Chapter 7

Genre Change and Evolution

Carolyn R. Miller

North Carolina State University (USA)

Upon those that step into the same rivers ever-newer
waters flow . . .

—Heraclitus (DK22B12)

Prologue

Heraclitus supposedly said that everything is in flux, that you
can't step into the same river twice. Known to us now only from
second-hand sources and anecdotes, he reportedly suffered from
melancholia and died of dropsy in an unsuccessful attempt at
self-treatment in a dung-heap. He was called "obscure" by his
contemporaries and "the weeping philosopher" by the Romans,
and he might well have wept had he foreseen the ridicule to which
his thought about change would be subjected by successors. Plato
and Aristotle accused him of denying the law of non-contradiction,
claiming the identity of opposites, and positing that everything that
is the same is actually different. Even today, philosophers disagree on
how to interpret his cryptic statement about the river. Did he mean
that it is and is not the same river? Or did he mean, as some have
suggested, that "rivers can stay the same over time even though,
or indeed because, the waters change," that is, that the stability
of larger structures is made possible by the fact that constituent
elements within them change (Graham, 2005, §3). Similarly, granting

the difficulties of reconstructing Heraclitean thought but also granting some subtlety to the opposition of sameness and difference, others suggest that "the unity of the river as a whole is dependent upon the regularity of the flux of its constituent waters"; "a complex whole ... might remain 'the same' while its constituent parts are for ever changing" (Kirk, Raven, & Schofield, 1983, p. 197).

It has become less difficult for us now to accept the notion that everything is indeed in constant flux, at both the microscopic and the cosmic levels: we know about the expanding universe, the undulations of lightwaves, Brownian motion, electron spin, sliding tectonic plates, the erosion of canyons and uplifting of mountains, the origin and extinction of species. But my premise is that in the 21st century, we still struggle to understand sameness and difference, stability and change, tradition and innovation in the world of human experience. Genre studies are part of this struggle.

Evolutionary Thought in Genre Studies

There seems to be no question that we are in a period of dramatic genre change: new forms and capabilities develop every day, with incessant claims in web news and blogs that this or that is a "new genre" demanding our attention. Anyone who searches Google or Lexis-Nexis will find numerous such claims in mainstream media, promotional material, and user-generated internet content, including genres such as aristocrunk, steampunk, torture porn, haul videos, lolcats, fan-fic, kiddie noir, chillwave, mockumentary, and dirtbag sitcom. It's dizzying. We seem to need genres to help us make sense of this blooming, buzzing confusion, genres to help locate ourselves in the "mayhem and trivia" of this mediated socio-cultural world (Heffernan, 2009).

In trying to understand the process of genre change and the emergence of what seem to be "new genres" in both new and old media, we have come to rely heavily on the concept of "evolution." This is a term that, in English, at least, is usually associated with biological change and diversity, so we might ask whether it is appropriate to use it in talking about social and discursive change. What work does it do and what work does it keep us from doing? When we adopt the language of evolution, what do we import to our conceptualization of genres, of large-scale rhetorical action, and of the rhetorical organization of culture? As Berkenkotter (2007) has already asked, "how literally—or heuristically—should we take the concept of 'genre evolution'?" (p. 178).

The language of "evolution" pervades recent genre scholarship, not only in rhetorical studies (Bazerman, 1984, p. 191; Berkenkotter & Huckin, 1993, pp. 481–482; Jamieson, 1973, p. 168, 1975, p. 406; Miller, 1984, p. 163) and linguistics (Ayers, 2008, p. 39; Herring, Scheidt, Bonus, & Wright, 2005, p. 144; Hyland, 2002, p. 115; Skulstad, 2005, p. 72) but also in literary studies (Dimock, 2007, p. 1384; Fowler, 1971, p. 206; Javitch, 1998, p. 169) and media studies (film and television) (Altman, 1999, p. 70; Feuer, 1992, p. 151; Mittell, 2001, p. 11), as well as in information sciences and new media studies (Clark, Ruthven, & Holt, 2009, p. 2; Kanaris & Stamatatos, 2009, p. 500; Liestøl, 2006, p. 266; Paolillo, Warren, & Kunz, 2011, p. 277). In fact, we don't seem to have any other language for describing how genres change over time.[1] The language of evolution (including related biological metaphors, such as "chromosome," "ancestry," and "genealogy") invokes an analogy between cultural change and organic or biological change over time. What this analogy provides genre studies is a model that includes both diachronic change and synchronic variation. With diachronic change, we take note of relatedness, that is, an explanation of continuity through inheritance or influence over time. With synchronic variation, we take note of alternate forms and "family resemblances," of co-existing difference and similarity in varying degrees. Both dimensions contribute to the explanation of adaptation or "fitness," the apparent result of a competitive process by which variations are selected and preserved over time, producing (incremental) change. "Fitness," interestingly, is a term of art in both evolutionary and rhetorical theory: Darwin came to use Spencer's phrase "survival of the fittest" as a synonym for "natural selection,"[2] and rhetoricians have adopted Bitzer's (1968) expression "fitting response" as discourse that is adapted to its situation; we also have the related ancient concept of *decorum*. Schryer's (1993) description of genres as collections of variable features that are "stabilized-enough" or "stabilized-for-now" captures this process well, and could as well be applied to organic species as to discourse genres.

If we look into the history of these ideas, we can see "evolution" not as a mere metaphor or handy analogy for the process of genre change but as a set of ideas that has been as central to thinking about cultural change as about biological change. What is of particular interest is that the attempts to understand change and variation in the biological world and in the human world arose at about the same time and informed each other. Scholarship on the history of evolutionary thought is voluminous, and I can't possibly treat it in adequate detail here, but in order to summarize a very long and complex story, I'll begin with a sketch of the sources of Darwin's insights into the origin of species and then move to an equally sketchy account of the inquiry into linguistic and literary diversity. I'll then consider two specific issues where genre theory might learn from the discussions in biology: these issues concern taxonomy and teleology.

Evolutionary Thought in Biological Sciences

Versions of evolution predate Darwin by nearly a century, arising during the transition of the Enlightenment into Romanticism, informing inquiry into both the natural world and the history of language, with these two threads intertwined from the beginning. In examining the sources of Darwin's insights into the origin of species alongside the inquiry into linguistic and literary diversity, what we see, in both cases, is a very long and difficult process that involved a fundamental transformation of thinking from essentialism to what the great 20th century evolutionary biologist Mayr (1982) calls "population thinking" (pp. 45–46). I believe these two kinds of thinking are both alive in genre studies today.

Essentialism is represented well by Plato's theory of forms: the fixed, unchanging, and distinct *eide* or essences that exist independent of the phenomenal world, which is merely their imperfect manifestation. From the perspective of the *eide*, variations are uninteresting, merely signs of the imperfection of the empirical world. According to Mayr (1982), essentialism "dominated the thinking of the western world" to an extent that is now difficult for us to comprehend (p. 38). Population thinking, in contrast, which Mayr calls "a peculiarly biological concept, alien to the thinking of the physical scientist" (p. 487), takes the unique individual as the starting point for analysis, not the type, valuing diversity and variation rather than stable abstractions. It is more empirical and inductive, less mathematical and abstract. "By introducing population thinking," says Mayr, "Darwin produced one of the most fundamental revolutions in biological thinking" (p. 487).

Evolutionary thinking in biology is rooted in Enlightenment efforts to understand the natural world. Natural philosophers like Linnaeus, Buffon, LaMettrie, Lamarck, Diderot, Cuvier, and others including Darwin's own grandfather, Erasmus (Bowler, 1989), struggled to understand the grand harmonious plan assumed both by natural theologists and by rational mechanists to be ordering the universe. Linnaeus's decades-long labor to create a taxonomy of the natural world is one of the most important and earliest of these efforts. Linnaeus aimed to represent the rational plan of divine creation within his classification system, an ambition revealed in the title of his first work: *Systema Naturae,* published in 1735. He began with 18th century assumptions: that species were invariant, that the relationships among them would reflect a single orderly system, and that this system would be a linear hierarchy, commonly represented as a tower, or ladder, the *scala naturae,* or "great chain of being," with nature arranged in order of perfection, or complexity, connecting the divine through the angelic and then the human to the animal, plant, and inanimate levels of existence (Bowler, 1989, p. 59; see also Dennett, 1995, p. 64 ff.; Mayr, 1982, p. 201). As he worked, however, Linnaeus came to realize that the burgeoning natural world could not be represented well by a single linear system, that species were not immutable, and that similar species might be related to each other, probably by hybridizing (Bowler, 1989). According to a 1957 study by the then-president of the Swedish Linnaean Society, "It is quite incontestable that Linnaeus in the 1750's had once for all given up his thesis of the absolute fixity of species. The most impressive evidence . . . is that . . . he removed the statement *nullae species novae* [there are no new species] from the preface of the 12th edition of the *Systema Naturae* [1766] and crossed out the words *Natura non facit saltus* [nature does not make leaps] in his own copy of the *Philosophia botanica* [1751]" (Hofsten, 1957, p. 85).

Meanwhile in France, the *philosophes* were creating a "new, completely materialistic worldview" that included the first modern evolutionary theories that were also antiteleological (Reiss, 2009, p. 60). The multi-volumed *Natural History* published by Georges-Louis Leclerc, Comte de Buffon, initiated what became the collective project of comparative anatomy; significantly, his fourth volume (published in 1753) included sections on the horse and the ass that used anatomical homologies to speculate on the relatedness not only of these two domestic animals but of all vertebrates (Reiss, 2009, p. 68). Somewhat later, Cuvier followed his own earlier work on comparative anatomy with a 1796 publication on fossil elephants, the new world mastodon and the Siberian mammoth, comparing them to living African and Indian elephants and claiming them as four distinct species, with the fossil species apparently extinct; his subsequent 1812 four-volume work on fossil studies is now regarded as the "founding document of vertebrate paleontology" (Reiss, 2009, p. 90). In Reiss's summary, "[t]he problem that the natural world presented to Cuvier at the end of the eighteenth century was the problem of the diversity of biological form, in its broadest aspect. This problem was not just . . . how best to classify forms—that is, how to find the most *natural* system of classification (whatever that might mean)—but also how to *interpret* the system achieved" (pp. 98-99). These problems—finding a basis for classification and understanding what it means—should sound familiar to genre theorists.

The evidence that piled up inductively in the great collections of the naturalists—Linnaeus's in Uppsala and the royal collections in Paris with which Buffon and Cuvier both worked—weakened belief in linear, hierarchical systems like the *scala naturae* and convictions about the fixity of species. It became possible to conceive of nature as a creative power and creation as an open-ended process (Bowler, 1989, p. 77). In a world where the evidence for organic change had become undeniable, Darwin's explanatory project, according to Dennett (1995), was two-fold: to demonstrate that modern species had descended from earlier ones and to show how this could be so, that is, to find a mechanism for descent with modification (p. 39). His solution, combining both diachronic and synchronic dimensions, involved random variation of features within a breeding population, continuity or inheritability of variations, overproduction of offspring, and "natural selection" produced by competition for survival (that is, survival of the fittest).[3]

In the long process of developing his explanation, Darwin occasionally represented the diachronic and synchronic dimensions of the problem together as a tree diagram. His first such representation appears in a notebook in 1837, where he is clearly thinking through lines of descent with variation; Bowler (1989) tells us that Darwin came early to the view that evolution is a branching process, exemplified in the conditions of geographic isolation he observed in the Galápagos Islands, and that in 1837 he began exploring the idea that ordinary variation is the key to long-term organic change (p. 170). The *Origin* included just one diagram, that of a generalized tree to hypothesize descent with modification and differential survival (Darwin, 1859, pp. 116–117).[4] As he came to understand the role of competition and the likelihood of extinction, Darwin also came to accept that a materialist, rather than theological, explanation was needed, that the designs of a Creator were neither necessary nor relevant to the process of organic change (Bowler, 1989, pp. 168–170). So natural theology is replaced by a natural mechanics; the notion of the species as a fixed type is replaced by the population of variants, and the linear hierarchy of the great chain of being is replaced by the figure of the branching tree.[5]

Evolutionary Thought in the Human Sciences

Darwin's project became thinkable not only as a result of Enlightenment rational empiricism and mechanistic materialism, but also because of the intellectual countercurrent of European Romanticism. Romanticism challenged the power of stable classifications and hierarchical relations to account for the world, offering instead developmental views of history (which became in some hands teleological, a theme that has troubled evolutionary thinking ever since) (Bowler, 1989; Reiss, 2009). In addition, an analogy between the human world and the organic world was made explicit in much Romantic thought, well before Darwin, taking form particularly in discussions of the history of language and the history of literature.

In the 18th century, linguists had studied language in order to understand "the mechanism of the mind," but in the 19th century, according to Culler (1986) they turned to the study of linguistic forms, "whose resemblances and historical links with other forms must be demonstrated" (p. 71). Historical linguistics was born, assisted in part by religious interest in discovering the "*lingua Adamica*," the original tongue. Europeans exploring what is now India had noticed similarities between Sanskrit and the ancient European languages, Greek and Latin; such observations led to proposals in the latter half of the 18th century that these ancient languages had a common source and that Germanic and Celtic languages might also be related in a larger Indo-European family of languages (Hoenigswald, 1962). The developments in comparative anatomy inspired some of this work. As Schlegel, the German poet and literary critic, said in 1808: "That decisive factor which will clear up everything is . . . comparative grammar, which will give us altogether new insights into the genealogy of languages, in a manner similar to that in which comparative anatomy has shed light on higher natural history" (cited in Hoenigswald, 1962, p. 1). Darwin himself in the first edition of the *Origin* made a brief but explicit connection between biological change and language change by proposing that the "pedigree of mankind" could illuminate the classification and relationships of languages, both living and extinct (1859, p. 422).

A central figure in the development of historical linguistics was August Schleicher (1821–1868). Schleicher developed a scientific view of language, with no need for theological axioms, arguing as early as 1848 that language has to be regarded as a natural organism because languages can be classified into genera, species, and subspecies (Maher, 1966, p. 4), terms that he borrowed from the Linnaean classifications of a century earlier (Richards, 2002, p. 26). Perhaps his most lasting contribution was *Stammbaumtheorie*, family-tree theory, which introduced tree-diagrams to show groups of related languages. In his systematic study of European languages published in 1850, Schleicher described language development as an evolutionary process, "spoke of the Indo-European languages in terms of family relationships" (Koerner, 1972, pp. 260-262), and proposed that their developmental history could be represented as a *Stammbaum*, a stem-tree (Richards, 2002, p. 34). In 1853, he published the first such diagram and by 1860, before he read Darwin, was using them frequently (Richards, 2002, p. 34).[6] There is speculation that Schleicher developed his approach to language not directly from biological scientists, but rather from his education as a classical philologist, trained to create manuscript stemmata according to the doctrine of shared errors (Hoenigswald, 1962, p. 8). His teacher, Ritschl, worked also on human genealogy (Maher, 1966, p. 8), so the family tree may be the most direct model for this form of representation that proved useful in both biological and humanistic inquiry (Maher, 1966, p. 8).

Linguistics was not the only human science in which an evolutionary model took hold. In literature as well, the evidence of diversity and change became difficult to ignore: the novel, after all, just didn't fit into the essentialist triad of epic, drama, and lyric attributed to Aristotle and Horace and enshrined in literary neoclassicism.[7] Neoclassical poetics, operating under the same 18th century assumptions that Linnaeus struggled with (the invariance of species and the orderly hierarchy of the their relationships), is known for its prescriptive rules, invoked, says Duff (2009), to both modernize and scientize the literary enterprise (p. 34). In Dubrow's (1982) summary, "What engage[s] [neoclassical critics] above all . . . is repeating and refining the rules for each genre and testing particular works against those norms. They also return frequently to the problem of the hierarchy of genres, sometimes accepting and sometimes challenging Aristotle's pronouncement about the supremacy of tragedy" (p. 70). As the rules were drawn from a narrow selection of poetic productions (primarily the genres of classical antiquity) but assumed to be "timelessly immutable," they provoked heated discussion about the value of such works as medieval romances, Renaissance tragicomedies, and the novel (Fowler, 1982, pp. 27–28). A statement by Baillie (1747) illustrates the dual emphasis on essentialism and rules:

> The genuine work therefore of criticism is to define the limits of each kind of writing, and to prescribe their proper distinctions. Without this there can be no legitimate performance, which is the just conformity to the laws or rules of that manner of writing in which the piece is designed. But the manner must be defined before the rules can be established; and we must know, for example, what history is before we can know how it differs from novel and romance, and before we can judge how it ought to be conducted. (p. 87)

The obsession with order and rules, which extended beyond literature to architecture, music, and painting, has been attributed to "a profound fear of disorder in the individual psyche and the body politic" (Dubrow, 1982, p. 71) and characterized as a "reaction to the chaos and fanaticism of the 1640s and 1650s" (Duff, 2009, p. 37). Such fears provoked what Toulmin (1990) has characterized as a "Quest for Certainty" in the early 17th century (p. 36). This somewhat desperate quest, he says, provoked a transformation in philosophy in which "general principles were in, particular cases were out[;] . . . the permanent was in, the transitory was out" (pp. 32, 34). We can see in this quest a hospitable environment for the essentialism of neoclassical genre theory and resistance to thinking about variation and change. The neo-classical genre system also served multiple social needs: for aspiring poets, increasingly influential critics, publishers and booksellers, librarians, teachers, and ordinary readers, the system provided convenience, familiarity, and structures of recognition (Duff, 2009, p. 39).

However, the 18th century was more than a reaction to the 17th. By the middle of the century, according to Wellek (1963), "biological and sociological speculation . . . stimulated analogous thinking about literature" (p. 38). And the authority of classical models was tested by what Prince (2003) calls "specifically modern factors":

> The rise of unsanctioned literary kinds (such as the novel) and an audience that favored them; the tendency of female authors to inhabit both new and old genres in decidedly different ways . . .; the hunger for printed material of all kinds; the competition between writers of high and low culture; the efficacy of pamphlets, reviews, broadsides, and occasional and periodical essays in shaping debates about culture; the influence of middle-class morality upon drama—these factors and many others destabilized the received authority of neoclassical genres while keeping attention focused on genre. (p. 455)

Attention to the historical and contingent nature of the cultural categories that we call genres helped launch the movement that became literary Romanticism and became characteristic of it. Duff (2009) calls attention to a number of developments that illustrate the newly fluid role that genre played, noting, for example, that in multiple published collections of poetry, "the use of generic terms with adjectival qualifiers [such as 'elegaic sonnet,' 'pathetic ballad,' sentimental pastoral'] . . . increased markedly in the late eighteenth century" (p. 51). Such genre-mixing became an overt critical ideal (p. 165), with Schlegel declaring that "the romantic imperative demands the mixing of all genres" (quoted in Duff, 2009, p. 162). The very title of Wordsworth's revolutionary *Lyrical Ballads* is a case in point, mixing the classical lyric with the popular ballad. Duff also points to the interest in marginalized genres and folk or "primitive" literature as evidence of this new turn in genre theory. Romanticists associated with the "primitivist" movement, presuming an authenticity in early civilizations, used a "stemmatic" method similar to that of the historical linguists to trace related forms back to an "ur-genre" (Rajan quoted in Duff, 2009, pp. 173–174). Duff (2000) calls Romanticism's abandonment of aesthetic fixity "a remarkable episode in the history of ideas," pointing out that "an effort of imagination is required to recall a time when it was believed that genres were static, universal categories whose character did not alter across time" (p. 4). In an interesting parallel, Dennett (1995) notes that:

> We post-Darwinians are so used to thinking in historical terms about the development of life forms that it takes a special effort to remind ourselves that in Darwin's day species of organisms were deemed to be as timeless as the perfect triangles and circles of Euclidean geometry. (p. 36)

After Darwin, as evolutionary thinking percolated through the later 19th century, it was applied to literature in France by Ferdinand Brunetière and in England by John Addington Symonds (who was influenced by Spencer) (Conley, 1986, p. 72, n. 72; Fishelov, 1993, p. 22); it was applied to technology by Karl Marx and Samuel Butler; and it continued to influence the study of language until the early decades of the 20th century, when Saussure persuaded linguists to set aside diachronic concerns (as they were already abandoning biological metaphors) and treat language as a synchronic system (Culler, 1986, p. 82). Saussure refocused linguistics, ushering in a period when language and literary studies took such a distinct lack of interest in evolution that in 1956, Wellek (1963) could claim that "Fifty and sixty years ago the concept of evolution dominated literary history; today . . . it seems to have disappeared almost completely" (p. 37).

As Fishelov (1993) shows, much of the literary dissatisfaction with evolutionary theory derived from its false application or from mistaken understandings (particularly with regard to determinism, a topic I take up below). As interest in evolutionary thinking declined, so also did interest in genre, in part because of the continuing Romanticist opposition to convention and commitment to radical creativity (Duff, 2000, pp. 3-5), and in both literature and linguistics genre study fell out of favor through much of the 20th century.

I think there's an interesting and complex story yet to be told about the revitalization of an evolutionary genre theory in the decades after Wellek made his statement. I don't know that story yet, but I suspect it will involve a number of currents in the human sciences, such as, from cognitive psychology, Gestalt theory, schema theory, and category theory; from sociology, theories of typification and structuration; from philosophy, Langer's interests in "pattern," and possibly ordinary-language philosophy; and will include tributaries such as Kuhn's (1970) notion of "paradigm" and in social psychology and media research, "frame theory."

The parallel story to be told is that of the evolutionary model and its continuing appeal to historians aiming to illuminate cultural and intellectual change. Kuhn (1970), for example, though his model of scientific change is usually cast in quite different terms (those of political revolutions), invokes the analogy with biological evolution at several points in his argument, noting that the process he has been describing is "the selection by conflict within the scientific community of the fittest way to practice future science" and even invoking the model of a tree: "Imagine an evolutionary tree representing the development of the modern scientific specialties from their common origins in, say, primitive natural philosophy and the crafts" (pp. 172, 205). Other philosophers and historians of science have made evolution their central explanatory model. One prominent effort is Toulmin's (1972) examination of conceptual change within what he called "rational enterprises" or intellectual disciplines, not on the grounds of a direct analogy between biology ("natural selection") and disciplines ("rational selection") but by positing "a more general form of historical explanation" of which both are examples (p. 135); this "general form" is in essence identical to Dennett's (1995) "abstract" model of evolution, "the differential survival of [variable] replicating entities," as Dawkins put it, which is independent of any particular substrate or form of expression (cited in Dennett, 1995, p. 343). Another effort of this kind is Hull's (1988) "evolutionary account of the interrelationships between social and conceptual development in science" presented with a great deal of attention to Darwinian and post-Darwinian evolutionary biology (p. 12).[8]

But now I'd like to turn from this historical sketch to consider two specific areas in which genre theorists might learn from the extensive and concerted efforts by biological scientists to conceptualize evolution. I'll focus on two issues central to the development of evolutionary theory: taxonomy and teleology.

Taxonomy

The problem of taxonomy is represented by the tree diagrams used in both biology and historical linguistics. What kinds of relationships are being mapped? What is the unit of analysis? Under essentialism, the unit was the fixed species, and affinities and similarities are the relationships. The whole taxonomy aimed to represent "the plan of creation of the designer of the world" (Mayr, 1982, p. 148). Such taxonomies assisted in naming and identification, and thus, in appreciating the complexity and beauty of creation. Essentialism precluded the notion that species themselves could change, or "transmute." Classification of these fixed entities was achieved by "downward division" based on Aristotelian logic, with the assumption that this "natural" structure would reflect the "order and logic in the created world" (Mayr, 1982, pp. 159, 199). Thus, one begins with easily recognizable and widely accepted categories—such as trees, shrubs, and herbs—and divides each of these into subordinate classes of plants on the basis of "differentiae" that allegedly represent the "true essences of these organisms" (Mayr, 1982, p. 160) (see Figure 1).

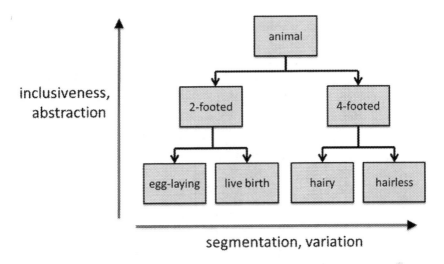

inclusiveness, abstraction

segmentation, variation

Figure 1. Downward classification, based on Mayr (1982).

The problem is that there was little agreement about these differentiae, about which similarities and differences are "essential." For example, in the animal kingdom, it made a great deal of difference whether one chose as the first differentia whether the animal had blood or not, whether it was hairy or hairless, or whether it was two-footed or four-footed (Mayr, 1982, p. 161). And as for plants, according to Mayr (1982), "no two botanists of the 17th century arrived at the same classification" (p. 207). It slowly became clear that the *scala naturae* and the assumptions of a fixed and manageable number of species would never be adequate to the complexity and multiplicity of the natural world.

The developing taxonomic chaos contributed to the weakening of essentialism and led to a slow and almost imperceptible transformation of taxonomic theory in the century after the publication of the 10th edition of Linnaeus's *Systema Naturae* in 1758. The alternative approach that developed—upward, or compositional, classification—was inductive and empirical, driven by the interest in diversity that Linnaeus's work had stimulated and the continual discovery and description of new species. Upward classification begins with the observation and cataloguing of variation and diversity, and the grouping of organisms by multiple features, rather than one (see Figure 2). This is what Mayr (1982) calls "population thinking" (pp. 45–46).

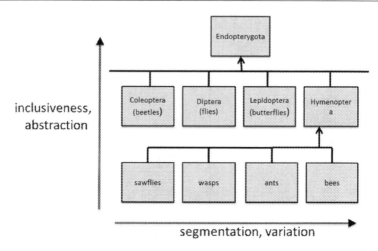

Figure 2. Upward classification, based on Mayr (1982); the vertical scale is later recognized as representing descent, rather than classificatory inclusiveness.

In upward classification, what is being classified are not species, but individuals, specimens: the species is not the starting assumption but rather the hypothesis that needs to be discovered or demonstrated. The essentialist approach to species presumed that all members of a species share the same essence, that each species is distinct from all others, that each is constant over time, and that the variation of members from the essence is limited (p. 260). The population thinker recognizes both variation and continuities across individuals, and the species concept becomes notoriously difficult to pin down. Dennett (1995) notes that Darwin declined to provide a definition of species, holding that it was more prudent to consider it a term of convenience rather than one of principle (pp. 44–45); he adds that "More than a century after Darwin, there are still serious debates among biologists . . . about how to define *species*" (p. 95). Similarly, Mayr (1982) claims that "There is probably no other concept in biology that has remained so consistently controversial as the species concept" (p. 251).

All of this sounds to me a lot like our discussions about how to define and recognize a genre. We have our essentialists and our population thinkers. Among the essentialists we might number Aristotle, Northrop Frye, and certain linguists and literary scholars. These theorists base their definitions on a posited essence—a theory of communication that maps formal possibilities, or fundamental features or capabilities of language. Among the population thinkers we could include ethnographers and applied linguists, like Schryer and Swales, who gather large numbers of specimens and examine them for similarities of social or linguistic features, developing categories inductively. These researchers help us to catalogue the amazing diversity of human communicative activity and the ways it interacts with social and technological change.

But there is another kind of thinking that can shed light on genres, a line of reasoning that is neither fully essentialist nor empirical, but perhaps is something of both. And to understand this third kind of thinking, we have to go back to the concept at the heart of the matter, the species, the genre—the type. For the corpus linguists or the population biologists, the type represents the collection of specimens: on the shelf, in the drawer, distributed across the environment. It's a description of an empirical multiplicity. For the essentialists, whether biological or discursive, the type represents a fundamental capability or possibility, given the conditions of existence. But what we have learned from phenomenological sociology and from cognitive psychology is that types can also be thought of as social agreements, shared recognitions, about what is worth noticing in the world: what recurs and what signifies. The type represents what we agree has happened and what we expect may happen. This is what we might call a nominalist approach to the problem, which makes the type neither a collection nor an essence but literally a "name," or rather, what is invoked by the fact of our naming something, a shared "concept."[9]

I have elsewhere suggested that genres may be found where we have names for types of discourse, that is, for shared expectations about what constellation of discourse features will achieve which social action: "the 'de facto' genres, the types we have names for in everyday language, tell us something theoretically important about discourse" (Miller, 1984, p. 155). This hunch is borne out by Rosch's (1978) work in cognitive psychology on categorization and concept prototypes,[10] which shows that "categories are generally designated by names," that is, we name groups of objects in our world that we consider to be "equivalent" in some useful way, according to the principles of cognitive economy and social perception (p. 6). Moreover, categorization, like evolution, involves both vertical and horizontal dimensions (see Figure 3).

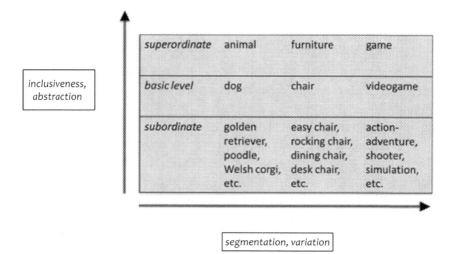

Figure 3. Levels of conceptual categories and their dimensions, reflecting Rosch (1978).

On the vertical dimension, the most common and useful names indicate what Rosch calls "basic categories," which indicate the most inclusive, or abstract, level that also recognizes what she calls "natural discontinuities" in perception (p. 6). The basic level designates categories that are relatively easy for us to discriminate from background variation and relatively important for us to interact with and talk about. Members of superordinate categories share fewer attributes and are thus less useful for ordinary purposes; members of subordinate categories share more attributes and are thus more difficult to discriminate. The psychological research focuses on objects in the world such as dogs and cats, chairs and tables, but it seems reasonable to suppose that the same principles could be at work with discursive objects such as sonnets and eulogies, blogs and videogames. Researchers have shown that "knowledge is mainly organized at the basic level" by testing for how many attributes people can list at different levels of abstraction (for example, furniture, chair, easy chair), which categories children learn first, and at which level people can form mental images (Lakoff, 1987, pp. 46–487). Rosch (1978) cites corroborating work showing that "basic-level categories are most often coded by single signs": for example, ethnobotanists can show this for plant names in various cultures, and others have confirmed this pattern with sign language (p. 10).

On the horizontal dimension, our categories divide the world into repeatable units, to which we refer when we use names like "dog," "table," "news report," "novel," "blog," and "tweet." According to Rosch (1978), these "basic cuts in categorization are made at . . . discontinuities" between "information-rich bundles of perceptual and functional attributes" (pp. 5-6). Thus, "the division of the world into categories is not arbitrary" but rather is based on "the correlational structure of the environment" (Rosch & Mervis, 1975, p. 602). Categories both reflect and constitute the perceived structure of the social world, much like Schutz's types (1970). Because perceptions change over time with new conditions and new capabilities and may differ between social groups, category systems may not be stable or consistent. If perceived discontinuities are relatively stable, however, the categories may come to seem like "natural kinds," with essences, criterial features that discriminate the dog from the cat, the chair from the table. But just as evolutionary biologists have had difficulties identifying species, cognitive psychologists have demonstrated that our everyday categories are similarly difficult to square with an essentialist approach. Like species, our categories do not have clear boundaries; they change over time and across locations and groups; they do not produce logical taxonomies based on consistent criteria (Lakoff, 1987, p. 187 ff.). Genres, as Devitt (2000) notes in discussing recent literary approaches, are systems of contrasts, existing in relation to each other (p. 200).

Conceptual categories, like biological species, are better understood through Wittgenstein's notion of family resemblances[11] than through essences or logical criteria (Rosch, 1978; Rosch & Mervis, 1975). This means, first, that we don't need criteria in order to judge how well a specimen fits a category, and second, that specimens within a category do not necessarily all share any common feature but that each shares at least one feature with another specimen. Within a family, some members will have similar noses, perhaps many will have similar skin and hair coloring, and some will have similar body types. Some may share many features with other members, and some may share only one feature with only a few others. And all, as a "population," share fewer features with members of other families. A category is a loose cluster with perhaps questionable instances on the margins and some instances that seem fairly "central" or most representative of the concept. These central specimens are "prototypes" that are most easily identified. Rosch's (1975) research shows that specimens that function as prototypes are "those which bear the greatest family resemblance to other members of their own category and have the least overlap with other categories" (pp. 598-599).

On the horizontal dimension, then, the category-type (the species, or the genre) is always going to be a bit fuzzy, although the relevant test is of social utility. On the vertical dimension, there are two possible scales: one is level of abstraction, which is characteristic of essentialist, top-down category formation, as practiced by Linnaeus and by virtually every biologist before Darwin; the other is diachronic, showing shared ancestry, relationships of replication over time, and discerned by bottom-up empirical inquiry. Biological thought has completely rejected levels of abstraction for the diachronic relationship of common ancestry, because this is the scale that explains evolution in both dimensions, change over time and the existence of synchronic categories—species and variations. Rosch's aforementioned research on cognitive category formation works with the scale of abstraction, focusing on the levels at which our perceptual discriminations are functional. I would submit that genre theory needs to take both scales into account, because our shared recognitions are based both on agreements about what level of discrimination is functional and on shared experience with antecedent genres.

The implications for genre theory are that the categories of rhetorical interaction that genres represent are indeed sociocognitive entities: they are neither essentialist-objective "natural kinds" nor fully empirical-materialist corpora. They are, rather, social concepts on a "basic" cognitive level that correspond with the experiential history and functional needs of the community that posits them. They help us carve meaningful units out of the blur of artifacts and stimuli that surround us. And they are capable of changing over time because they are constituted not by any essential features but by shared recognitions. If we want to understand why a combination of features occurs as it does, then the genealogy is helpful; but if we simply want to write a good blog, or teach about blogging, then we need to attend to the range of variation of features that are recognizable, functional, and fitting.

Teleology

Darwin's notebooks show that as early as the late 1830s, he had pretty much abandoned the widely accepted assumptions of natural theology that the adaptations of organisms to their environments are the result of design and that design requires a Designer (Bowler, 1989, p. 169). These assumptions have proven quite resilient, however, and we are still having Victorian-like discussions about creationism (or intelligent design), even to judge only by the titles of the several recent books written to refute it—Dawkins's *The Blind Watchmaker*, Reiss's *Not by Design: Retiring Darwin's Watchmaker*, and Dennett's own book. Darwin's "dangerous idea,"[12] in Dennett's (1995) formulation, is exactly this, that over time a mindless algorithm can produce the effects of design, that "the various processes of natural selection, in spite of their underlying mindlessness, are powerful enough to have done all the design work that is manifest in the [natural] world" (p. 60), that "the biosphere is . . . the outcome of nothing but a cascade of algorithmic processes feeding on chance" (p. 59). However, the language that Darwin (1859) chose to express his central idea, "natural selection," with its intimations of choice and agency, embeds constant reminders of a Designer. Given the strength and pervasiveness of natural theology in Darwin's time, his well documented rhetorical caginess about how to introduce the ideas that he well knew were dangerous (see, for example, Campbell, 1987), and his own occasional ambivalence, he has a very hard time not treating natural selection as an agent, as in this well known passage: "It may be said that natural selection is daily and hourly scrutinising, throughout the world, every variation, even the slightest; rejecting that which is bad, preserving and adding up all that is good; silently and insensibly working, whenever and wherever opportunity offers, at the improvement of each organic being in relation to its organic and inorganic conditions of life" (p. 84). Darwin himself apparently conceded that "natural selection" was "a bad term" (cited in Dennett, 1995, p. 73).

If evolution is a general model of historical explanation that applies to cultural change as well as to biological change, must we also relinquish teleology, let go of the fourth and final cause? Is cultural evolution also a mindless algorithm? Or, since we think of ourselves as purposeful beings, and we interpret others as seeking goals, do we need a teleological model of change, different from that of the biologists? These questions highlight the relationship between genres and their users and environments of use. And although few might be tempted to posit a divine Discourse Designer, we do need to consider the issue of individual and systemic discursive agency. For the present, I would like to dramatize the issue by contrasting Swales's focus on communicative purpose with my own focus on rhetorical exigence, as this is a difference of long standing and one that points up some interesting problems in characterizing the pragmatic dimensions of discourse.

In 1990, Swales presented a "working definition" of genre that offered "communicative purpose" as a "privileged criterion" for identifying the members of a genre (p. 58). At the time, and in subsequent work, he recognized some complications of this approach, for example, that purpose is not always legible from a communicative event (either by an analyst or by a participant), and that purpose may be multiple, conflicted, unrealized, layered, implicit, ineffable, insincere, and so on (Askehave & Swales, 2001; Swales, 1990)— qualities that are not helpful in a "privileged criterion." These recognitions led him, not to turn elsewhere for a central criterion but rather to recommend how the analyst can approach the problem of identifying purpose more responsibly: "it is sensible to abandon social purpose as an immediate or quick method for sorting discourses into generic categories, while retaining it as a valuable long-term outcome of analysis" (Swales, 2004, p. 72; see also Askehave & Swales, 2001). This central criterion, however, remains somewhat mysterious: it seems to be centered on the communicator, the "user" or perhaps "animator" of the genre, though it is necessarily social and thus cannot be the same as the private intentions of individuals. Swales (2004) also uses some alternative expressions, equating purpose at one point with "function" and elsewhere with "use-value" (pp. 69, 99). Nevertheless, inferring from our everyday understanding of purpose, we might say that purpose is the aspect of communication that drives towards a goal beyond the communication event itself: an end for which communication is the means; a state or situation, if achieved, that is outside of and beyond and, usually, subsequent to discourse. The goal *pulls* the speaker or writer and the text and the audience toward itself, and purpose links us to the goal *avant la letter*; it is anticipatory (see Figure 4).

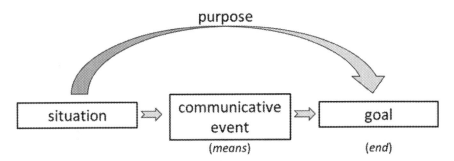

Figure 4. Components of communicative situation and directionality of communicative purpose, reflecting Swales (1990).

My own focus has been not on purpose but on exigence, and the associated term "motive." These may be just as mysterious as "purpose" (perhaps more so), but I think they are different in significant and useful ways. I learned the word "exigence" from Bitzer, and while I think there are lots of problems with Bitzer's formulation, it remains useful, especially when complexed with Burke's notion of "motive" (1969). Bitzer (1968) defines exigence as "an imperfection marked by urgency . . . a defect, an obstacle, something waiting to be done, a thing which is other than it should be" (p. 6). It is not a goal toward which one aims but a problem away from which one needs to move: it motivates action, pushing us from behind, so to speak. A "motive" is what "moves" us. The recurrent exigence of a genre is a matter not of material forces but of shared social recognitions, or what I have called "an objectified social need" (Miller, 1984, p. 157).

Both purpose and exigence are ways of addressing the question "why?" but they provide different kinds of answers. *Purpose* poses the question from an *actor's* point of view: why are you doing this? what is your aim or goal? It is teleological, implying a movement *toward*, inviting assumptions about progress, improvement, perfection, and hierarchy, all of which have become suspect in evolutionary biology but remain tempting prospects for human culture. In contrast, *exigence*, or what we might more generally term *function*, poses the question from a *system's* point of view: why does this happen? what does it achieve not only for any actors or agents involved but also for the stability and viability of the rest of the system? It implies a movement *away from*, invoking assumptions about instabilities and perturbations but also about continuity and endurance (see Figure 5).

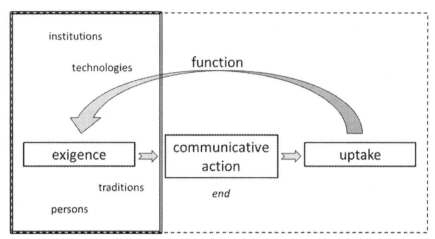

Figure 5. Components of communicative situation and directionality of communicative function, reflecting Miller (1984).

In *purpose*, we see the potential for change and innovation; in *function*, we see the forces of stabilization and adaptation. My contention then is that *function* is specifically useful for thinking about genre because it requires us to consider recurrence, repetition, reproduction, whereas *purpose* turns our attention toward the individual, the singularity, the nonce event. If we say that a genre is functional, then we look to how it satisfies recurrent, "generic" needs within a system; if we say that a genre serves purposes, we're no longer looking at the system or at the genre but rather at texts, at persons, at specific communicative events, and we have to explain replication in terms of multiple, individual, strategic actions.

I do not mean to suggest that genres don't allow for innovation but rather that they require us to account for innovation within a context of imperfect replication and incomplete stabilization, and I think this is exactly what the evolutionary model emphasizes. In biology, some innovations (most, in fact) are non-functional and many are destructive. Non-functional innovations may be replicated, may acquire function and become favored, or may be rapidly eliminated because the organisms carrying them cannot reproduce. But they are always being judged by the system, by the interactions between the organism and its environment. So evolutionary thinking turns our attention not only to recurrence but also to the ecological system, the environment, in which both innovation and recurrence have meaning and are judged. If we adopt the minimal model of evolutionary change and posit that genres change by "the differential survival of [variable] replicating entities," (Dawkins, cited in Dennett, 1995, p. 343), then any genre acquires recognition as a genre in virtue of its having survived, that is, having been replicated sufficiently. And survival value of a genre means that there are social recognitions, practical accomplishments, and satisfactions in it as a form of social action. This, again, means that the genre is *functional*. But at the same time, survival through replication also means that the genre has changed, since replication is never duplication, and since even the fact of replication changes the significance of its force and patterns.

We might see here some similarity to Fishelov's (1993) notion of "generic productivity," which he offers as the "hallmark" of survival, rather than looking for survival in reception (p. 37). As Fishelov puts it, a genre is productive when it "plays an active role on the literary scene," that is, when "the works of a genre serve as a 'stimulus' for the production of other texts that are perceived as 'belonging' to this genre" (pp. 38-39). Genre productivity is a useful notion, but with two caveats. First, productivity can take forms other than the production of new texts by other rhetors: a genre is productive also when it is recognized and responded to, when it is "replicated" in the minds of others. Thus, even a genre with very few instantiating texts can be productive and thus survive. The second caveat is to Fishelov's dismissal of reception as a marker of evolutionary survival, a dismissal that goes along with his focus on "texts" rather than on communicative action (and which I attribute to his training as a literary rather than rhetorical scholar). In cultural evolution, production and reception are interdependent markers of "survival." As Fishelov himself notes, the relationship between production and reception is "dialectical" (p. 36); that is, adaptation works both ways: production adapts to the environment (in both its specific and systemic dimensions), and the receptive system is reshaped by the ongoing actions of its constituents. Genres, I would suggest, are particularly useful ways of thinking about cultural change over time in this respect: because they are vehicles of cultural reproduction, they require us to look at both production and reception, to both particular purposes (and how these are made recognizable to others within a system of multiple constraints) and systemic functions.

I want to suggest, then, that thinking in terms of *function* can help us understand genre change *because* of its focus on recurrence and the genre system as a whole, and that the general model of evolution can be productive in this regard. But we shouldn't push the analogy too far, beyond the minimal model.[13] Evolutionary biologists tell us that the only "purposes" that genes or organisms have is to replicate themselves: this is their teleology. In genre theory, we must be able to take into account the experiential fact that we are purposeful beings in quite other (or perhaps I should say "additional") ways, and our understandings of genre change must be able to take into account the role of singularities, of the determined or inspired or disruptive individual and of unprecedented and surprising situations, for these are the sources of variation, subject to selection pressures that include not only cultural conventions, conditions, and values but also the purposes of others. My point is that to make these specifically relevant to genre theory, we must look at them under the aspect of the recurrent and the systemic. The challenge for genre studies—in rhetorical genre studies particularly—is to attend in both directions appropriately, both toward *purpose* and toward *function*. We must study the variety of influences on historical change and thus the multiple factors that an evolutionary theory must acknowledge. When do the efforts and intentions of individual agents make a difference? When do institutions, financial and market forces, systems and structures, the weight of tradition have effects? What kind of influences does technology wield?

In conclusion, I don't want to be understood as suggesting that our understanding of cultural change must borrow from biology. Rather, I'm suggesting that evolution is a model of change more general than either biology or language, one that applies equally but differently to both. And I'm not advocating that we become taxonomists of genre, or that we must draw family trees of the genres we teach or study, or that we abandon the notion of purpose or intention in understanding our socio-discursive environment. I do want to urge that we be conscious of the assumptions we make about essences and antecedents, of how and why we identify something as a genre; that we be alert to the differences between classification by abstraction and classification by descent; that we distinguish between purpose and function and their implications for personal agency vs. systemic and situational pressures. We have much learn about the process of genre change and the emergence of new genres, and we need all the tools we can find. I hope that this look at evolutionary theory can be useful in that effort.

References

Altman, R. (1999). *Film/genre*. London: British Film Institute.

Arthur, W. B. (2009). *The nature of technology: What it is and how it evolves.* New York: Free Press.

Askehave, I., & Swales, J. M. (2001). Genre identification and communicative purpose: A problem and a possible solution. *Applied Linguistics, 22*(2), 195–212.

Ayers, G. (2008). The evolutionary nature of genre: An investigation of the short texts accompanying research articles in the scientific journal *Nature. English for Specific Purposes, 27*, 22–41.

Baillie, J. (1747). An essay on the sublime. In A. Ashfield & P. de Bolla (Eds.), *The sublime: A reader in British eighteenth-century aesthetic theory* (pp. 87–100). Cambridge: Cambridge University Press.

Bazerman, C. (1984). Modern evolution of the experimental report in physics: Spectroscopic articles in physical review, 1893–1980. *Social Studies of Science, 14*(2), 163–196.

Berkenkotter, C. (2007). Genre evolution? The case for a historical perspective. In V. K. Bhatia, J. Flowerdew & R. Jones (Eds.), *Advances in discourse studies* (pp. 178–191). London: Routledge.

Berkenkotter, C., & Huckin, T. N. (1993). Rethinking genre from a sociocognitive perspective. *Written Communication, 10*(4), 475–509.

Biletzki, A., & Matar, A. (2009). Ludwig Wittgenstein. *Stanford Encyclopedia of Philosophy*. Retrieved from http://plato.stanford.edu/entries/wittgenstein/

Bitzer, L. F. (1968). The rhetorical situation. *Philosophy and Rhetoric, 1*, 1–14.

Bowler, P. J. (1989). *Evolution: The history of an idea* (Revised ed.). Berkeley, CA: University of California Press.

Burke, K. (1969). *A grammar of motives*. Berkeley: University of California Press.

Campbell, J. A. (1987). Charles Darwin: Rhetorician of science. In J. Nelson, A. Megill & D. McCloskey (Eds.), *The rhetoric of the human sciences: Language and argument in scholarship and public affairs* (pp. 69–86). Madison: University of Wisconsin Press.

Clark, M., Ruthven, I., & Holt, P. O. B. (2009). The evolution of genre in Wikipedia. *Journal for Language Technology and Computational Linguistics, 24*(1), 1–22.

Conley, T. (1986). The linnaean blues: Thoughts on the genre approach. In H. W. Simons & A. A. Aghazarian (Eds.), *Form, genre, and the study of political discourse* (pp. 59–78). Columbia, SC: University of South Carolina Press.

Culler, J. (1986). *Ferdinand de Saussure.* Ithaca, NY: Cornell University Press.

Darwin, C. (1859). *On the origin of species by means of natural selection, or the preservation of favoured races in the struggle for life.* [J. van Wyhe & S. Asscher (Eds.)]. Retrieved from http://darwin-online.org.uk/content/frameset?itemID=F373&viewtype=side&pageseq=1

Darwin, C. (1868). *The variation of animals and plants under domestication.* Retrieved from http://darwin-online.org.uk/content/frameset?pageseq=1&itemID=F878.1&viewtype=text

Dennett, D. C. (1995). *Darwin's dangerous idea: Evolution and the meanings of life.* New York: Simon & Schuster.

Devitt, A. J. (2000). Integrating rhetorical and literary theories of genre. *College English, 62*(6), 696–718.

Dimock, W. C. (2007). Introduction: Genres as fields of knowledge. *Publications of the Modern Language Association, 122*(5), 1377–1388.

Dubrow, H. (1982). *Genre.* London: Methuen.

Duff, D. (2009). *Romanticism and the uses of genre.* Oxford: Oxford University Press.

Duff, D. (Ed.). (2000). *Modern genre theory.* New York: Pearson Education.

Feuer, J. (1992). Genre study and television. In R. C. Allen (Ed.), *Channels of discourse, reassembled: Television and contemporary criticism* (2nd ed., pp. 138–160). Chapel Hill, NC: University of North Carolina Press.

Fishelov, D. (1993). *Metaphors of genre.* University Park, PA: Penn State University Press.

Fowler, A. (1971). The life and death of literary forms. *New Literary History, 2*(2), 199–206.

Fowler, A. (1982). *Kinds of literature: An introduction to the theory of genres and modes.* Cambridge, MA: Harvard University Press.

Genette, G. (1992). *The architext: An introduction.* Berkeley, CA: University of California Press.

Gould, S. J. (1977). *Ever since Darwin: Reflections in natural history.* New York: W. W. Norton & Co.

Graham, D. W. (2005). Heraclitus. *Internet Encyclopedia of Philosophy.* Retrieved from http://www.iep.utm.edu/heraclit/

Gross, A. (2007). Darwin's diagram: Scientific visions and scientific visuals. In K. S. Fleckenstein, S. Hum & L. T. Calendrillo (Eds.), *Ways of seeing, ways of speaking: The integration of rhetoric and vision in constructing the real* (pp. 52–80). West Lafayette, IN: Parlor Press.

Gross, A. G., Harmon, J. E., & Reidy, M. (2002). *Communicating science: The scientific article from the 17th century to the present.* New York: Oxford University Press.

Heffernan, V. (2009). Uploading the avant-garde. *New York Times Magazine.* Retrieved from http://www.nytimes.com/2009/09/06/magazine/06FOB-medium-t.html

Herring, S. C., Scheidt, L. A., Bonus, S., & Wright, E. (2005). Weblogs as a bridging genre. *Information, Technology & People, 18*(2), 142–171.

Hoenigswald, H. M. (1962). On the history of the comparative method. *Anthropological Linguistics, 5*(1), 1–11.

Hofsten, N. v. (1957). Linnaeus's conception of nature. *Kungl. Vetenskaps-Societetens Årsbok*, 65–101.

Hull, D. L. (1988). *Science as a process: An evolutionary account of the social and conceptual development of science.* Chicago: University of Chicago Press.

Hyland, K. (2002). Genre: Language, context, and literacy. *Annual Review of Applied Linguistics, 22*, 113–135.

Jamieson, K. M. (1975). Antecedent genre as rhetorical constraint. *Quarterly Journal of Speech, 61*, 406–415.

Jamieson, K. M. H. (1973). Generic constraints and the rhetorical situation. *Philosophy and Rhetoric, 6*(3), 162–170.

Javitch, D. (1998). The emergence of poetic genre theory in the sixteenth century. *Modern Language Quarterly: A Journal of Literary History, 59*(2), 139-169.

Kanaris, I., & Stamatatos, E. (2009). Learning to recognize webpage genres. *Information Processing and Management, 45*, 499–512.

Kirk, G. S., Raven, J. E., & Schofield, M. (1983). *The presocratic philosophers: A critical history with a selection of texts* (2nd ed.). Cambridge: Cambridge University Press.

Koerner, E. F. K. (1972). Towards a historiography of linguistics: 19th and 20th century paradigms. *Anthropological Linguistics, 14*(7), 255–280.

Kuhn, T. S. (1970). *The structure of scientific revolutions* (2nd ed.). Chicago: University of Chicago Press.

Lakoff, G. (1987). *Women, fire, and dangerous things: What categories reveal about the human mind.* Chicago: University of Chicago Press.

Liestøl, G. (2006). Conducting genre convergence for learning. *International Journal of Continuing Engineering Education and Lifelong Learning, 16*(3/4), 255–270.

Maher, J. P. (1966). More on the history of the comparative method: The tradition of Darwinism in August Schleicher's work. *Anthropological Linguistics, 8*(3, Part II), 1–12.

Margolis, E., & Laurence, S. (2011). Concepts. In E. N. Zalta (Ed.), *Stanford encyclopedia of philosophy.* Retrieved from. http://plato. stanford.edu/archives/fall2012/entries/concepts/).

Mayr, E. (1982). *The growth of biological thought: Diversity, evolution, and inheritance.* Cambridge, MA: Belknap Press.

Miller, C. R. (1984). Genre as social action. *Quarterly Journal of Speech, 70*(2), 151–176.

Mittell, J. (2001). A cultural approach to television genre theory. *Cinema Journal, 40*(3), 3–24.

O'Hara, R. J. (1988). Homage to Clio, or, toward an historical philosophy for evolutionary biology. *Systematic Zoology, 37*(2), 144–155.

Paolillo, J. C., Warren, J., & Kunz, B. (2011). Genre emergence in amateur flash. In A. Mehler, S. Sharoff & M. Santini (Eds.), *Genres on the web: Computational models and empirical studies* (Vol. 42, pp. 277–302). Dordrecht: Springer.

Prince, M. B. (2003). Mauvais genres. *New Literary History, 34*(3), 453–479.

Reiss, J. O. (2009). *Not by design: Retiring Darwin's watchmaker.* Berkeley, CA: University of California Press.

Richards, R. J. (2002). The linguistic creation of man: Charles Darwin, August Schleicher, Ernst Haeckel, and the missing link in nineteenth-century evolutionary history. In M. Dörries (Ed.), *Experimenting in tongues: Studies in science and language* (pp. 21–48). Stanford, CA: Stanford University Press.

Rosch, E. (1978). Principles of categorization. *Cognition and categorization* (pp. 27–48). Hillsdale, NJ: Lawrence Erlbaum Associates.

Rosch, E., & Mervis, C. B. (1975). Family resemblances: Studies in the internal structure of categories. *Cognitive Psychology, 7*, 573–605.

Schryer, C. F. (1993). Records as genre. *Written Communication, 10*, 200–234.

Schutz, A. (1970). *On phenomenology and social relations: Selected writings.* Chicago: University of Chicago Press.

Skulstad, A. S. (2005). The use of metadiscourse in introductory sections of a new genre. *International Journal of Applied Linguistics, 15*(1), 71–86.

Swales, J. M. (1990). *Genre analysis: English in academic and research settings.* Cambridge: Cambridge University Press.

Swales, J. M. (2004). *Research genres: Explorations and applications.* Cambridge: Cambridge University Press.

Toulmin, S. (1972). *Human understanding: The collective use and evolution of concepts.* Princeton: Princeton University Press.

Toulmin, S. (1990). *Cosmopolis: The hidden agenda of modernity.* Chicago: University of Chicago Press.

Wellek, R. (1963). The concept of evolution in literary history. In S. G. Nichols (Ed.), *Concepts of criticism* (pp. 37–53). New Haven: Yale University Press.

Wells, S. (2014). Genres as species and spaces: Literary and rhetorical genre in *The Anatomy of Melancholy. Philosophy & Rhetoric, 47*(2), 113–136.

EndNotes

[1]   Berkenkotter (2007) suggests that Kuhn's revolutionary model of paradigm shifts is more descriptive, at least for the psychiatric case study. And an important new study by Wells (2014) offers a spatial or geographic metaphoric system for understanding genres, finding it especially useful for mixed or doubtful texts such as Burton's *Anatomy of Melancholy* (1857).

[2]   Though it does not appear in the first edition of *Origin*, Darwin adopted it and attributed it to Spencer in his 1868 work, *The Variation of Animals and Plants under Domestication*: "This preservation, during the battle for life, of varieties which possess any advantage in structure, constitution, or instinct, I have called Natural Selection; and Mr. Herbert Spencer has well expressed the same idea by the Survival of the Fittest" (p. 6).

[3]   See Dennett's (1995) basic model of evolution ("maximally abstract") (p. 343) and Gould's (1977) similar summary (p. 11).

[4]   The sketch from Darwin's notebook can be viewed in an online exhibition at the American Museum of Natural History (http://www.amnh.org/exhibitions/past-exhibitions/darwin/the-idea-takes-shape/i-think). Gross (2007) discusses the rhetorical-conceptual function of the diagram published in the *Origin*.

[5]   The importance of the tree figure has been emphasized in O'Hara's (1988) discussion of "tree thinking," after Mayr's "population thinking"; tree thinking changes questions of state to questions of change (p. 151).

[6]   The diagram is reproduced in Richards (2002, p. 35). Whether or not Schleicher held an evolutionary view of the human species before Darwin's *Origin* (a matter of some speculation), he clearly had such a view after reading it in German translation (pp. 31, 37). In fact, he argued in an 1863 commentary on the *Origin* that the historical study of languages could help substantiate hypotheses about organic evolution: in particular that linguistics provided evidence about competition, extinction, and increasing complexity and more generally that the processes of language descent and human descent were virtually identical, that language and mind had evolved together. Schleicher also pointed out that the tree-diagram in the *Origin* was hypothetical, whereas his own diagrams were empirical (p. 27).

[7]   Genette (1992) has made clear just how mistaken this attribution is.

[8]   Hull's model was adopted by Gross and his colleagues to explain the genre of the scientific research article (Gross, Harmon, & Reidy, 2002). Arthur (2009) has applied a modified version of evolution to technological change.

[9]   Mayr (1982) suggests that medieval nominalism influenced early empiricists such as Francis Bacon and might have been an anticipation of population thinking (pp. 308–309).

10   See the connection between categories and concepts in Margolis & Laurence (2011).

11   For a brief explanation of the point in Wittgenstein, see Biletzki & Matar (2009).

12   Also, in Dennett's (1995) opinion, "the single best idea anyone has ever had" (p. 21).

13   To my mind, meme theory, suggested by Richard Dawkins as a way of thinking about cultural change in evolutionary terms, does push the analogy too far, looking for analogues of the mechanisms of reproduction and selection. But this is a topic for another occasion.

Chapter 8

Accounting for Genre Performances: Why Uptake Matters

Anis Bawarshi

University of Washington (USA)

A couple of years ago, I was invited to give a lecture on genre, for which I submitted the following abstract:

Over the past 20 years, scholarship in rhetorical genre studies has contributed a great deal to our understanding of how genres mediate social activities, providing insight into how systems of related genres coordinate ways of knowing and doing within recurring situations. From this scholarship has emerged a view of genres as both social (typified, recognizable, and consequential ways of organizing texts, activities, and social reality) and cognitive phenomena (involved phenomenologically in how we recognize, encounter, and make sense of situations). Yet genre research has not accounted as fully for what Anne Freadman (1994) has called genre uptake—the taking up or performance of genres in moments of interaction and innovation. Genre uptake is informed by genre knowledge but also by one's sense of self, one's memory of prior uptakes, as well as by other affective, embodied, and material factors that make uptakes, while to some extent habitual, also momentary and unpredictable. A focus on uptake allows us to account more fully for the dynamics of agency and the contingent, impromptu, multi-directional performances of genre—and their implications for genre research and teaching.

A week later, I received a poster announcing my lecture. The poster contained a series of variously sized boxes, some of which were shaded and contained relevant information about the lecture: title, my name, date and time, location, and brief version of my abstract. In between these shaded boxes were unshaded ones, some blank and some containing outlines of human figures engaged in various acts of pushing against and bouncing within the boxes. Here, I thought, is genre uptake in action. Not only does the poster take up my abstract in another genre, and in so doing continue the process of genre coordination that would eventually bring me and others to the lecture, but the poster itself performs a representation of uptake. I was amused by the human figures performing acts of uptake within genre constraints, especially the way these uptake performances depict individuals pushing against genre boundaries and performing gymnastic-like improvisations within them. I was also taken by the short squiggly lines around the figures, denoting points and degrees of energy that propel uptake performances. While I expected a poster uptake of my abstract and title, I did not expect *this* uptake. What happens in the uptakes between genres, such as between an abstract and its uptake poster, is the subject of this chapter.

What happens in-between genres has not been studied or understood as much as it needs to be in Rhetorical Genre Studies, in my view. More attention has been paid to genres themselves: as social artifacts that can tell us things about how and why individuals perform typified actions in certain situations; about how genres mediate social actions and function as sites of power; about how the explicit teaching of genre conventions can help students gain access to various systems of activity; about how genres relate to one another in the coordination of social activities; about how genres help construct and reproduce the situations that call for them. Genre scholarship has taught us a great deal about the ways that genres help us define and make sense of recurring situations while providing the typified rhetorical and linguistic means for acting in these situations. As Bazerman (1997) has famously described:

> Genres are not just forms. Genres are forms of life, ways
> of being. They are frames for social action. They are
> environments for learning. They are locations within which
> meaning is constructed. Genres shape the thoughts we form
> and the communications by which we interact. Genres are
> the familiar places we go to create intelligible communicative
> action with each other and the guideposts we use to explore
> the unfamiliar. (p. 19)

As these metaphors suggest, genres have become understood as symbolic interconnected worlds we inhabit for the construction and exchange of meanings and actions: habitats for and habits of perceiving and acting. Genres help us recognize situations as requiring certain responses and help provide the typified rhetorical and linguistic strategies we use to act within them.

From this understanding, genre scholars have developed several useful metaphors to describe how related genres enable their users to perform social actions over time, including genre chains (Swales, 2004), genre sets (Devitt, 1991), genre systems (Bazerman, 1994), genre repertoires (Orlikowski & Yates, 1994), genre colonies (Bhatia, 2002), and genre ecologies (Spinuzzi & Zachry, 2000). These metaphors have enabled genre researchers to describe various micro and macro levels of genre relations as well as the social interactions, the distribution of cognition, and the social construction of space-time that genres help coordinate within contexts of activity. But they also risk objectifying genres. Genres, it must be remembered, are not ontological, although our ways of talking about them often makes it seem as if they are. Genres rather are typifications, potentialities, performance cues—what Bazerman (2004) has called "social recognition phenomena" and what Beebee (1994) has called "use-values" that orient our apprehension and exchange of texts. So while we know a lot more about what genres are and how genres relate to one another in complex ways, we do not know as much about the complex performances that take place in-between and around genres. By drawing our attention to the extra-textual factors that inform genre performances, uptake challenges us to consider history, materiality, embodiment, improvisations, emotion, and other *agentive* factors that genre studies has tended to overlook in its focus on genres as objects, artifacts, sites, and meditational tools. As Freadman (2012) recently put it:

> No genre can do more than predict the kind of uptake that would make it happy, and no speaker or writer can completely secure an uptake. This is partly because no discursive event is a pure example of any genre, and partly because of the unpredictable historical complexity of its moment and its ongoing action. We cannot . . . reflect productively on uptake outside of discussions of genre, nor is it productive to theorize the action of genres without uptake. Genre is destabilized by uptake even as it asserts its power. (p. 560)

This is why uptake matters; uptake is relevant to the study and teaching of genre performance, maintenance, and change *and* uptake compels us to pay attention to the historical-material conditions that shape genre performances.

Following Freadman (1994, 2002), genre scholars have described uptake as the taking up or contextualized performance of genres in moments of interaction (see, for example, Bastian, 2015; Bawarshi, 2008; Dryer, 2008; Emmons, 2009; Kill, 2006; Rounsaville, 2012; Seidel, 2007). Uptake is the result of genre action (for example, the conference proposal is the uptake of the call for papers). At the same time, uptake is a situated cognitive and social transaction that enables genre action (for example, the recognition that certain genres are connected to other genres in certain ways, at certain times, etc.). Uptake, then, as a *relational* sense, is a vital part of genre knowledge, but because it takes place within a complex scene of agency, it also exceeds genre knowledge and may not always or often be textually visible. That is, while genre uptake is informed by genre knowledge, it is also informed by one's sense of self, one's memory of prior uptakes, the timing and stakes of a discursive event and its participants (Freadman, 2012), as well as by other affective and material factors that make uptakes, while to some extent habitual, also momentary, unpredictable, and subject to relations of power. Because uptake is at once the result of and the hidden dimension of genre knowledge, a focus on genre uptake, I argue, allows us to account for the dynamics of agency, thereby attending to the complex, contingent, multi-directional performances of genre in real time and space.

Situating Uptake

Within speech act theory, uptake traditionally refers to how an illocutionary act (saying, for example, "it is hot in here" with the intention of getting someone to cool the room) gets taken up as a perlocutionary effect (someone subsequently opening a window) under certain conditions. The important thing to note in this commonly used example is how a perlocutionary effect involves the embodiment of an illocutionary act—there is a body in motion and time that takes up an utterance, and that uptake is subject to a complex set of conditions that inform its movement. Such embodiment and emplacement are crucial to uptake.

In her groundbreaking and influential work, Freadman (2002) applies uptake to genre theory, arguing that genres are defined in part by the uptakes they condition and secure within social activities. Uptake helps us understand how systematic, normalized relations between genres coordinate complex forms of social action—how and why and when genres get taken up in certain ways and not others, and what gets done and not done as a result.

As Freadman (2002; this volume) is careful to note, however, uptake does not depend on causation but on *selection*. Uptake, she explains, "selects, defines, or represents its object . . . This is the hidden dimension of the long, ramified, intertextual memory of uptake: the object is taken from a set of possibilities" (p. 48). We note here how uptake involves agency. But it is not a directly causal form of agency. Rather, Freadman tells us, uptakes have memories, which means they are informed by learned inclinations and embodied dispositions, attachments to prior successes and failures, one's sense of authority and cultural capital, one's perceived sense of stakes, motivation, and task relevance, as well as other affective factors and historical-material influences, such as access to certain tools.

As such, how we take up a genre is guided by our genre knowledge, but it is not limited to it. This is why genre knowledge alone is not enough to account for genre performance, and why we need to examine the complex factors that are at play within uptake's scene of agency. This is what I think Freadman means in her brilliant definition of uptake as "the bidirectional relation that holds" between genres (p. 40). The key word, as I understand it, is "holds," which suggests a relational force that informs, legitimizes, and results in certain actions.

There is a risk, however, despite Freadman's warning, in conceptualizing genre uptake too much in terms of causation, as in a call for papers leads to a proposal, or an assignment prompt gets taken up as a student paper which gets taken up in teacher feedback, etc. As Clay Spinuzzi (2003) has argued, the metaphors genre scholars have used to describe genre relations have tended to rely on such sequential uptakes at the risk of overlooking the more complex, impromptu relations and uptakes that animate genre performances within activity systems. In response, Spinuzzi and Zachry (2000) have suggested the metaphor of "genre ecology" to describe the contingent and less sequenced relationships among genres within and between networks of activity. In his study of a telecommunications company, for instance, Spinuzzi (2008) observed that it does not operate in a modular, hierarchical way, but much more in a heterogeneous, multiply-layered way that involves "assemblages of human and nonhumans." Within these assemblages, "links are made across and among [people, artifacts, and practices] in fairly unpredictable ways" (p. 7).

To think of genres in ecological ways, Spinuzzi (2004) argues, also means paying attention not only to the official genres within an actor-network but also to "the informal, unofficial assemblages of genres that we often bring to bear on our work" (p. 3). These are in part what Swales (1996) has called "occluded genres" that operate behind the scenes and play crucial mediating roles within genre networks. But, as Spinuzzi describes, they also include objects like planning talk, notes, annotational genres, marginal notes, which are more idiosyncratic and improvisational. Likewise, Prior (2009) has recently argued that we need to pay attention to "mediated multimodal genre systems" (p. 18) that include written and visually inscribed genres as well as oral and embodied genres. In describing genre networks as assemblages—as multi-dimensional, interdependent, less clearly demarcated, and dynamically agentive— Spinuzzi and Prior have begun to conceptualize genre networks and performances in post-humanistic ways.

In referring to genre systems as ecological, I am mindful of recent concerns raised by Applegarth (2012) about the ways biological metaphors naturalize genre relations and change while overlooking, as Applegarth puts it, that "genres are the product of power-inflected historical choices, and that the limitations and pressures that shape them are human constructions" (p. 457). On the other hand, there is also a risk, I think, in too strong an anthropological perspective, which can overlook spatial (see Dryer 2008; Reiff 2011) and materialist perspectives on agency and their implications for how we account for uptakes.

Work in materiality has expanded in the last decade to include not only Marxist historical materialism but also what Coole and Frost (2010) call "new materialisms" (p. 2). Historical materialism focuses on economic structures of power—on relations of production and commodification. While historical materialism is anthropological in its focus on human labor, use and exchange value, and so on (Coole & Frost, 2010), new materialisms take a posthumanist approach to materiality by acknowledging matter itself as agentive and vital (what Bennett [2010] has called "vibrant matter" [p. viii]). In so doing, they challenge a view of matter as inert, dependent on external causalities, and ontologically distinct from self-conscious, autonomous human agents. Such reorientations toward matter "compel us to think of causation in far more complex terms; to recognize that phenomena are caught in a multitude of interlocking systems and forces and to consider anew the location and nature of capacities for agency" (p. 9). Paying attention to uptake allows us to examine causation in this more complex way and to recognize the interlocking systems and forces at play in performances of genre.

Deleuze and Guattari's (1987) work offers an intriguing metaphor for describing the dynamic, interconnected webs and multi-directional movements of genre uptakes. Deleuze and Guattari's most basic distinction is between a tree and a rhizome (although they acknowledge that there are tree-like rhizomes and rhizome-like trees, such as the banyan tree). A tree represents the image of singularity and self-containment, even when clustered in a forest. Even though a tree's roots spread out below ground, they are still all connected to the *one* tree: they form a singular hierarchy that flows from roots to branches. For Deleuze and Guattari, trees represent hierarchies and binary systems.

According to Deleuze and Guattari (1987), "tree logic" (p. 12) is the dominant symbol of reality for much of the world, especially the West: from linguistics to psychoanalysis to genealogy to theology to feudalism and class structures. What they call an arborescent model of thought permeates our lives: we think in terms of family trees and genealogies; we have the Chomskian linguistic tree structure, which begins at point "S" and proceeds by dichotomy; our computer files are arranged in tree-like structures; psychoanalysis, with its search for root causes, attempts to impose tree logic on the unconscious.

In challenging this arborescent model of thought, Deleuze and Guattari (1987) were in search of a way of accounting for multiplicity that is not subject to principles of unity, binary logics, or interiority. For this, they proposed the concept of *rhizomes*. The Oxford English Dictionary (2010) defines a rhizome as "an elongated, usually horizontal, subterranean stem which sends out roots and leafy shoots at intervals along its length" ("Rhizome"). Examples of rhizomes include: ginger, irises, crab grass, potato plants, yams. A simplified schematic of a rhizome can be seen in Figure 1.

Figure 1. Rhizome (From *Pest Notes: Green Kyllinga* by K. Ling (University of California Division of Agriculture and Natural Resources Publication 7459). Reprinted with permission from the UC Statewide IPM Programpublic domain).

Rhizomes offer a different way of thinking about the world, one that is anti-hierarchical and characterized by interconnection, heterogeneity, and multiplicity. Unlike a tree root, a rhizome is an underground, lateral network of stems that has no unique, singular origin. By its very nature, a rhizome is an assemblage of lines and directions. As Deleuze and Guattari (1987) explain, "any point in a rhizome can be connected to anything other, and must be. This is very different from the tree or root, which plots a point, fixes an order. . . .There are no points or positions in a rhizome, such as those found in a structure, tree, or root. There are only lines" (pp. 7-8).

Instead of points and positions, beginnings and endings, a rhizome is made up of multiple entry points and connects any point to any other point, like an underground burrow. As Deleuze and Guattari (1987) write, a rhizome "is composed not of units but of dimensions, or rather directions in motion. It has neither beginning nor end, but always a middle from which it grows and which it overspills" (p. 21). This state of always-being-in-the-middle (in between things, "of comings and goings") is crucial to an understanding of rhizomes, because it puts the focus on lines of connectivity and lines of motion rather than on points, positions, or objects. Every rhizome, according to Deleuze and Guattari, is made up of lines of territorialization which organize it and locate it (territorialize it), as well as lines of deterritorialization (or lines of flight) from which it flows and expands.

Within a rhizome, tubers, such as potatoes, are accumulations that store energy. But these accumulations are not what define the rhizome; what characterizes a rhizome are the lines and directions in motion. A rhizome, according to Deluze and Guattari, is the embodiment of intensities, emergences, and desire uncontained by predetermined structures or pre-established paths. But what does this all mean for uptake, agency, and genre performances?

To a certain extent, I would argue that genre studies has already been thinking about genre relations in rhizomatic ways, from Schryer's (1994) research on veterinary school genres to Paré's (2000) research on hospital social workers and their rhizomatic network of interdependencies. Russell (1997, 2010), in particular, has turned to research in phenomenology and activity systems theory to describe how networks of related, sometimes conflicting genres coordinate and enable individuals to carry out consequential actions within and between systems of activity. In Russell's (1997) example of an intermediate cell biology course, for instance, the course texts link the activity system, through research articles, to other biology research activity systems, which, through research grants, links cell biology to funding agencies, pharmaceutical companies, and so on. Russell (2010), following Engeström, Engeström, and Kärkkäinen (1995) describes these relations as "polycontextual," which allows us to recognize genre relations in fairly rhizomatic ways, as they emerge in and across multiple contexts.

Yet, I think Deleuze and Guattari's (1987) work on rhizomes invites us to push things further. As mentioned earlier, what interests Deleuze and Guattari most about rhizomes are the lines of movement, the directions in motion. They are interested in what they call "volatile junctures: the point of application of a force moving through a space at a given velocity in a given direction" (Massumi, 1987, p. xiii). In short, they offer us a means through which to think in more dynamic ways about agency, performance, and the scene of uptake. In the schematic of a rhizome reproduced earlier, one could argue that the stems that grow out of the ground are the genres—the socially recognizable, namable, analyzable objects that have defined social functions. But uptakes are the lines of motion that connect genres. Remember that Freadman (2002) defines uptake as "the bidirectional relation that holds" between genres (p. 40). Thinking of uptake in rhizomatic ways allows us to understand causation in more complex, less predictable ways, and to recognize the interlocking systems and forces at play in performances of genre. It also invites us to look not just at genres as artifacts but also at the performative spaces between them.

One of the reasons Deleuze and Guattari (1987) are interested in rhizomes is because of their "transformational operations" (p. 15). Here, too, thinking of genre uptakes in rhizomatic ways invites us to pay attention to improvisational uptakes, uptakes that do not follow pre-established channels. Along these lines, Schryer (2011) has recently described the need to analyze texts as "fleeting performances that pull together strategies from a repertoire of available but also evolving strategies" (p. 46). There is an interesting connection here to uptake memory. Deleuze and Guattari argue that while long term memory can be arborescent (ordered and hierarchized like a tree), short term memory is more rhizomatic:

more discontinuous, improvisational, nomadic. Thinking of genres as rhizomes invites us, then, to focus not only on what Freadman (2002) has called the "long, ramified, intertextual memory of uptake" (p. 48), but also the short, nomadic, more materially inflected memories that also inform how we encounter and take up genres in less predictable, perhaps more resistant ways. Returning to Spinuzzi's (2000) observation about how a genre ecology connects human and non-human, thinking about genre uptakes in rhizomatic ways also allows us to pay attention to genre performances as embodied and emotioned. As Emmons (2009) has described in her work with genre and depression, "language manifests itself within the body via a series of intergeneric translations": from consultation to symptoms to diagnosis to prescription to medication to ingestion (p. 136). Rhetorical Genre Studies, in particular, has tended to privilege the socially defined nature of recurrence over the materiality of situation (Bleich, 2001). A materialist approach to genre uptake examines not only situated, typified cognition, but also how forms of cognition become "sedimented at a corporeal level where they are repeated as habits ... lodged in bodily memory" (Coole & Frost, 2010, p. 34) and inflected as such.

We see an example of this in the work that Jarratt, Mack, Sartor, and Watson (2007) have done with knowledge transfer. In examining how students encounter writing tasks and draw on prior knowledge, Jarratt and her colleagues identify the important role "pedagogical memory" plays in students' ability to recollect and make connections (or not) between new writing tasks and prior writing instruction. In one memorable case, Jarratt et al. describe a student who recalls her disappointment about the location of her composition course more than anything she learned about writing: "Wow, I'm sorry. I don't really remember a lot about first-year writing. That was my first year at UCI. It was in a trailer [laughter]. I was like, I'm going to university and I'm in a trailer? That's a little disheartening" (pp. 63-64). Knowledge transfer is a complex, multifaceted phenomenon, and here we see how material conditions and associations of feeling inform this student's relation to her writing course and, I would hypothesize, also to the way she relates to and takes up the genres she learned in the course. Agency and genre performance are not only a matter of genre knowledge. Materiality also plays an agentive role, as does emotion, institutional status, cultural capital, and so on. To understand genre uptake, we need to take these factors into consideration.

A recent study by Artemeva and Fox (2010) also reveals the power of uptake memory. They studied the relationship between genre awareness and performance in a first year engineering communications course. At the beginning of the course, they asked students to identify five different texts representing five different genres, one of which was a technical report. 77% correctly identified the technical report and were able to explain why they identified it as such (so they demonstrated genre awareness). However, when asked shortly afterwards as part of a diagnostic exercise to write a technical report, only 11% of the same students were able to do so in ways the instructor and expert deemed a successful demonstration of the genre. It is not surprising that genre awareness alone does not predict genre performance. More interesting, however, is that the majority of students in the study, despite apparently knowing the difference between technical report and English essay (as indicated in their identification of the five genres), nonetheless defaulted to producing traditional high school English essays when asked to write a technical report. Here, we notice how uptake memory can trump awareness when it comes to genre performance. What I find especially interesting, though, is that we learn later in the study that the technical reports written for the diagnostic were graded. This raises a question about the role that grades, and the stakes associated with those, played in leading students to default to producing English essays rather than risk taking up their still tentative knowledge of technical reports. This again points to how uptake is more complex a site of agency than our theories of genre have generally acknowledged. In her call for more research on transfer of prior genre knowledge, Devitt (2004) acknowledges that:

> the mechanism for writers selecting antecedent genres is not...straightforward. Writers may choose their antecedents for many reasons not necessarily related to the similarity of situation, including such reasons as their comfort level with a particular genre or their resistance to a teacher or the genre the teacher promoted. (p. 206)

Artemeva's (2005) research on engineering students' transitions from academic to workplace genres sheds light on the complex agency at work in genre uptake. For one case study student, Sami, his ability to challenge workplace genres early in his professional career is tied, Artemeva explains, to his sense of cultural capital, which allows him to redefine and shape a kairotic moment at work. Sami's cultural capital is an inheritance of sorts, willed to him by his father and grandfather, also engineers, and by this sense of belonging: "My dad passes that information to me, so in a sense I get to carry around years of experience before I even have a career...I have the feeling I've been there before" (pp. 401-402). Here, again, we are reminded of Freadman's (2002) point about the long, ramified, intertextual memory of uptake and how that comes to bear on the performance of genre, in ways that exceed genre knowledge alone.

Not only is uptake a complex site of agency; it is also a site of power. Borrowing from Nowacek's (2011) work on genre and knowledge transfer, we can see how uptakes are brokered: they need to be seen and sold. Certain routinized uptakes follow well-worn, expected lines of motion and are thus habitually received. But other uptakes need to be explicitly "sold" and validated, and here power comes into play in terms of which uptakes are sanctioned, who is granted authority to sell and see uptakes, and so on. Freadman's (2012) case study of a political interview provides insight into this process, in which interviewer and interviewee vie for control over the genre and its desired uptakes, with serious consequences for the interviewee.

Take for instance the following example, in which a student came to me, as writing program director, to complain about her course grade, on the grounds that her instructor's written feedback on her papers throughout the course was consistently too brief and unhelpful. When I followed up with the instructor, the instructor earnestly explained that he was experimenting with providing fewer comments in order to encourage students to develop stronger self-assessment and meta-cognition skills. The problem, I came to learn, is that the instructor did not explain his pedagogical strategy to students enough, so that an important genre in the system of expected uptakes (teacher's end comment on students' papers) was minimized, and nothing else was put in its place. As a result, the student was denied an opportunity to co-participate in an exchange of uptakes between herself and her instructor, as mediated by the teacher comments. In place of the more detailed teacher comment, the instructor needed to create space for the kind of meta-reflection he wanted students to do, perhaps a student memo in which students assess their performance. By not replacing the teacher feedback genre with another genre that would reorient student energy in ways he intended, the instructor underestimated the power of students' uptake memory and the extent to which it informs their genre performances.

This example highlights the extent to which uptake memory informs our genre encounters and performances. In particular, the above example suggests that a change in one genre within the system of genres cannot occur in isolation. If an instructor wishes to reorient the work of assessment from the genre of teacher feedback to, say, the genre of student reflective memo, he or she must also be prepared to redistribute the power dynamics that are maintained in the genre of teacher feedback. This includes making more visible usually occluded meta-genres such as the instructor's grading rubric, so that students can have more access to the meta-generic expectations and values that they will need to guide their self-reflection and assessment. At the same time, and just as importantly, this process requires a co-participant in the discursive exchange who is willing to accept the assessment role offered by the teacher, something that the students' history of participation in school may not prepare them to do. Uptake is at once the result of and the hidden dimension of genre knowledge. While genres condition and secure uptakes, uptakes can also pre-condition or over-determine our encounters with genres, leading us in rhizomatic directions.

As one final example, in a cross-institutional study of how students use prior genre knowledge in first-year composition (FYC) courses, a team of researchers and I found that when students encounter new, less familiar genre tasks, some inaccurately recognized similarities (this is a five-paragraph essay, this is a literary analysis) that allowed them to persist in using prior genres, while others reported instances of "not genres" (this is not like a literary analysis). Our analysis suggests that the recognition of "not" genres allows students to abstract and re-purpose strategies from prior genres. The "not" genre recognition provides insight into why and how some students extract and repurpose strategies from prior genre knowledge earlier than others while some hold on to prior genres to such an extent that they reformulate their perception of the assignment in ways that make it possible for them to draw, even if inaccurately, on prior genres rather than acknowledge "not" genres. Here, we see students' uptake memories at work, as they habitually select from a set of possibilities and, in the process, exclude a range of others which might serve them just as well, if not better. These selections, as we observed, are informed by factors such as confidence, attachments to prior successes and failures, and material conditions (Reiff & Bawarshi, 2011). As these examples suggest, genre uptakes are both ways of knowing and ways of no-ing (see Freadman, 1994; Devitt, 2004).

We need to make uptake more an object of our attention in genre research and teaching (cf. Devitt, this volume; Freadman, this volume). By doing so, we can get at some of the learned, embodied inclinations as well as the material conditions that guide our and our students' encounters with and performances of genre. We need space and time within our genre pedagogies to delay these learned inclinations and default uptakes in order to historicize them and make them a site of critical examination and intervention in our classrooms.

The key is to delay the uptakes long enough for students to critically examine their sources and motivations, as well as for students to consider what is permitted and what is excluded by these uptakes. For example, when we assign a writing task, we might ask students to reflect on their sense of stakes, their investment in it as well as what they think the task is asking them to do, what it is reminding them of, and what prior resources they feel inclined to draw on in completing the task. Because uptake represents its object, how students recognize the task at hand and what they feel is at stake for them is shaped by and shapes how they take it up. In turn, it is valuable to ask students to consider how they come to recognize a task and its timing (see Freadman, 2012, for more on the relevance of timing on uptake), as well as the sense of ambivalence, frustration, and exclusion they might feel in taking it up (Dryer 2008; Kurtyka 2015; Randazzo 2015). Such a metacognitive reflection, itself an important component of uptake, serves to help students interrogate their default inclinations to act in certain ways and not others. This becomes an important first step in encouraging students to examine and make strategic uses of their genre knowledge—as well as to consider how they can broker their uptakes in relation to others. At the same time, we also need to design assignments that invite students to use a wider range of their discursive resources, to mix genres and modalities from different domains, and then to reflect afterwards on the experience of taking up genres across domains (see Gonzales 2015). Such opportunities invite students to experience and confront the affordances (e.g., what uptakes allow to be said and not said) and consequences of particular uptakes. Likewise, they invite students to take up alternative uptakes, both in terms of having students analyze what alternative uptakes offer to the making of meaning and in terms of having students strategically deploy alternative uptakes in order to produce new meanings.

In this chapter, I have tried to describe uptake as a site of agency that invites us to recognize the interlocking systems and forces at play in performances of genre, in ways that exceed genre knowledge alone and get us closer to what Bhatia (2010; this volume) has termed "interdiscursive" performances. As sites of agency, uptakes involve both the instantiation and regulation of power as well as the potential for intervention. A rhizomatic view of uptakes accounts for and allows us to identify not only the relations and meanings that are secured by dominant uptakes, but also to pay attention to the uptakes that are "dismissed or trivialized" (Lu, 2006, p. 613) within and between networks of activity. This approach makes visible the unpredictable uptakes, the sweeps, transversals, the uptakes motivated by emotions, shaped by historical and material conditions as well as long and short term memories. That said, such a "thick" attention to and critical engagement with our uptakes is particularly difficult, because uptakes, as habits of remembering as well as "habits of forgetting" (Trimbur, 2006, 579) that mediate our encounters, are less textually "visible" and predictable and more subject to material and political forces, tied to dispositions, and informed by emotions. We need more robust ethnographic approaches to study uptake. Pedagogically, we need to go beyond the explicit teaching of genre conventions (textual and ideological) and focus also on genre uptakes: why students are inclined to take up certain genres in certain ways, what factors, relations, motivations, and affordances inform these inclinations, etc., so students can examine and negotiate the multiple agencies at work in their genre performances.

References

Applegarth, R. (2012). Rhetorical scarcity: Spatial and economic inflections on genre change. *College Composition and Communication, 63*(2), 453-483.

Artemeva, N. (2005). A time to speak, a time to act: A rhetorical genre analysis of novice Engineer's calculated risk taking. *Journal of Business and Technical Communication, 19*, 389-421.

Artemeva, N., & Fox, J. (2010). Awareness versus production: Probing students' antecedent genre knowledge. *Journal of Business and Technical Communication, 24*, 476-515.

Bastian, H. (2015). Capturing individual uptake. *Composition Forum* 31. Retrieved from http://compositionforum.com/issue/31/individual-uptake.php

Bawarshi, A. (2008). Genres as forms of in[ter]vention. In C. Eisner & M. Vicinus (Eds.), *Originality, imitation, plagiarism: Teaching writing in the digital age* (pp. 79-89). Ann Arbor, MI: University of Michigan Press.

Bazerman, C. (1994). Systems of genres and the enactment of social intentions. In A. Freedman & P. Medway (Eds.), *Genre and the new rhetoric* (pp. 79-101). Bristol: Taylor and Francis.

Bazerman, C. (1997). The life of genre, the life in the classroom. In W. Bishop & H. Ostrom (Eds.), *Genre and writing: Issues, arguments, alternatives* (pp. 19-26). Portsmouth, NH: Boynton/Cook.

Bazerman, C. (2004). Speech acts, genres, and activity systems: How texts organize activity and people. In C. Bazerman & P. Prior (Eds.), *What writing does and how it does it* (pp. 309-339). Mahwah, NJ: Lawrence Erlbaum Associates.

Beebee, T. O. (2010). *The ideology of genre.* University Park, PA: Pennsylvania State University Press.

Bennet, J. (2010). *Vibrant matter: The political ecology of things.* Durham, NC: Duke University Press.

Bhatia, V.K. (2002). Applied genre analysis: Analytical advances and pedagogical procedures. In A. Johns (Ed.), *Genre in the Classroom: Multiple Perspectives* (pp. 279-284). Mahwah, NJ: Lawrence Erlbaum Associates.

Bhatia, V. K. (2010). Interdiscursivity in professional communication. *Discourse and Communication, 4*(1), 32-50.

Bleich, D. (2001). The materiality of language and the pedagogy of exchange. *Pedagogy: Critical approaches to teaching literature, language, composition, and culture, 1*(1), 117-41.

Coole, D., & Frost, S. (2010). *New materialisms: Ontology, agency, and politics.* Durham, NC: Duke University Press.

Deleuze, G., & Guattari, F. (1987). *A thousand plateaus: Capitalism and schizophrenia* (Brian Massumi, Trans.). Minneapolis, MN: University of Minnesota Press.

Devitt, A. J. (1991). Intertextuality in tax accounting: Generic, referential, and functional. In C. Bazerman & J. Paradis (Eds.), *Textual dynamics of the professions: Historical and contemporary studies of writing in professional communities* (pp. 335-357). Madison, WI: University of Wisconsin Press.

Devitt, A. J. (2004). *Writing genres.* Carbondale, IL: Southern Illinois University Press.

Dryer, D. (2008). Taking up space: Genre systems as geographies of the possible. *JAC: Rhetoric, Writing, Culture, Politics, 28*(3/4), 503-534.

Emmons, K. K. (2009). Uptake and the biomedical subject. In C. Bazerman, A. Bonini, & D. Figueiredo (Eds.), *Genre in a changing world* (pp. 134-157). Fort Collins, CO: The WAC Clearinghouse and Parlor Press.

Engeström, Y., Engeström, R., & Kärkkäinen, M. (1995). Polycontextuality and boundary crossing in expert cognition: Learning and problem solving in complex work activities. *Learning and instruction, 5*(4), 319-336.

Freadman, A. (1994). Anyone for tennis? In A. Freedman & P. Medway (Eds.), *Genre and the new rhetoric* (pp. 43-66). Bristol: Taylor and Francis.

Freadman, A. (2002). Uptake. In R. Coe, L. Lingard, & T. Teslenko (Eds.), *The rhetoric and ideology of genre: Strategies for stability and change* (pp. 39-53). Cresskill, NJ: Hampton University Press.

Freadman, A. (2012). The traps and trappings of genre theory. *Applied Linguistics, 33*(5), 544-563.

Gonzales, L. (2015). Multimodality, translingualism, and rhetorical genre studies. *Composition Forum* 31. Retrieved from http://compositionforum.com/issue/31/multimodality.php

Jarratt, S. C., Mack, K., Sartor, A., & Watson, S. E. (2007). Pedagogical memory: Writing, mapping, translating. *WPA: Writing Program Administration 33*(1/2), 46-73.

Kill, M. (2006). Acknowledging the rough edges of resistance: Negotiation of identities in first-year composition. *College Composition and Communication, 58*(2), 213-235.

Kurtyka, F. (2015). Settling into genre: The social action of emotion in shaping genres. *Composition Forum* 31. Retrieved from http://compositionforum.com/issue/31/settling-in.php

Lu, M. (2006). Living-English work. *College English, 68*(6), 605-618.

Massumi, B. (1987). Translator's forward: Pleasures of philosophy. *A thousand plateaus: Capitalism and schizophrenia* (Brian Massumi, Trans.) (pp. ix-xv). Minneapolis: University of Minnesota Press.

Nowacek, R. (2011). *Agents of integration: Understanding transfer as a rhetorical act.* Carbondale, IL: Southern Illinois University Press.

Orlikowski, W. J., & Yates, J. (1994). Genre repertoire: The structuring of communicative practices in organizations. *Administrative Science Quarterly, 39,* 541-574.

Paré, A. (2000). Writing as a way into social work: Genre sets, genre systems, and distributed cognition. In P. Dias & A. Paré (Eds.), *Transitions: Writing in academic and workplace settings* (pp. 145-166). Creskill, NJ: Hampton.

Prior, P. (2009). From speech genres to mediate multimodal genre systems: Bakhtin, Voloshinov, and the question of writing. In C. Bazerman, A. Bonini, & D. Figueiredo (Eds.), *Genre in a changing world* (pp. 17-34). Fort Collins, CO: The WAC Clearinghouse and Parlor Press.

Randazzo, C. (2015). Hearing silence: Toward a mixed-method approach for studying genres' exclusionary potential. *Composition Forum* 31. Retrieved from http://compositionforum.com/issue/31/hearing-silence.php

Reiff, M.J. (2011). The spatial turn in rhetorical genre studies: Intersections of metaphor and materiality. *JAC: Rhetoric, Writing, Culture, Politics, 31*(1/2), 207-224.

Reiff, M. J., & Bawarshi, A. (2011). Tracing discursive resources: How students use prior genre knowledge to negotiate new writing contexts in first-year composition. *Written Communication, 28*(3), 312-337.

"Rhizome." (2010). *Oxford English Dictionary* (3rd ed.). Retrieved from http://www.oed.com.offcampus.lib.washington.edu/view/Entry/ 165259?redirectedFrom=rhizome&

Rounsaville, A. (Fall 2012). Selecting genres for transfer: The role of uptake in students' antecedent genre knowledge. *Composition Forum, 26.* Retrieved from http://compositionforum.com/issue/26/ selecting-genres-uptake.php

Russell, D. (1997). Rethinking genre in school and society: An activity theory analysis. *Written Communication, 14*(4), 504-554.

Russell, D. (2010). Writing in multiple contexts: Vygotskian CHAT meets the phenomenology of genre. In C. Bazerman (Ed.), *Traditions of writing research* (pp. 353-364). New York: Routledge.

Schryer, C. (1994). The lab vs. the clinic: Sites of competing genres. In A. Freedman & P. Medway (Eds.), *Genre and the new rhetoric* (pp. 105-124). London: Taylor and Francis.

Schryer, C. (2011). Investigating texts in their social contexts: The promise and peril of rhetorical genre studies. In D. Starke-Meyerring, A. Paré, N. Artemeva, M. Horne, & L. Yousoubova (Eds.), *Writing in knowledge societies* (pp. 31-52). Fort Collins, CO: The WAC Clearinghouse and Parlor Press.

Seidel, C. K. (2007). Professionalizing the student body: Uptake in a nineteenth century journalism textbook. *Linguistics and the Human Sciences, 3*(1), 67-85.

Spinuzzi, C. (2003). *Tracing genres through organizations: A sociocultural approach to information design* (Vol. 1). Cambridge, MA: Massachusetts Institute of Technology Press.

Spinuzzi, C. (2004). *Describing assemblages: Genre sets, systems, repertoires, and ecologies.* (White Paper Series: #040505-2). Austin, TX: Digital Writing and Research Lab.

Spinuzzi, C. (2008). *Network: Theorizing knowledge work in telecommunications.* Cambridge: Cambridge University Press.

Spinuzzi, C., & Zachry, M. M. (2000). Genre ecologies: An open-system approach to understanding and constructing documentation. *Journal of Computer Documentation, 24*(3), 169-181.

Swales, J. M. (1996). Occluded genres in the academy: The case of the submission letter. In E. Ventola & A. Mauranen (Eds.), *Academic writing: Intercultural and textual issues* (pp. 45-58). Amsterdam: John Benjamins.

Swales, J. M. (2004). *Research Genres: Explorations and Applications.* Cambridge: Cambridge University Press.

Trimbur, J. (2006). Linguistic memory and the politics of U.S. English. *College English 68*(6), 575-588.

Chapter 9

Form Alone: The Supreme Court of Canada Reading Historical Treaties

Janet Giltrow

University of British Columbia (Canada)

In now abundant demonstrations of genres' embedding in social contexts, and in opposition to traditional views, rhetorical genre theory insists that genre is not form alone. Another area of language study, pragmatics, also says *not form alone*:

> The central problem for pragmatics is that the linguistic meaning recovered by decoding vastly underdetermines the speaker's meaning. (Sperber & Wilson, 2002, p. 3)

The sentence is silent on much. While many theorists in pragmatics could be cited along the same lines, Sperber and Wilson's statement in 2002 is telling insofar as their own *Relevance: Communication and Cognition* (1986/1995 2nd ed) had 15 years earlier set out an attention-getting program for understanding the inferential dynamics of meaning. The measure of the problem extends through not only those years but into the present with 3559 entries in an on-line relevance-theory bibliography[1] still battling the issue on many fronts, only a handful of these resorting to genre. It also reaches back to the antecedents of *Relevance*: from at least Wittgenstein (1958) and Austin (1975) at mid-century through Grice (1975), from whose Conversational Maxims the term "relevance" is carried over, and Goffman (1981), and others. The problem is a theoretical orientation, and also a problem in the ordinary sense: a stubborn condition still calling for a solution.

In the broadest terms, the problem is about meaning being inferred not from the utterance alone but from the utterance in context. A particular sentence is unlimited in its potential meanings, depending on context. ("It is 8 o'clock" is a sentence that can be uttered; the meanings to be inferred are potentially unlimited.) Many areas of language study point to something called "context." In pragmatic studies of inference, context means, first, what is unspoken in relation to the utterance; second, what, in the arena of the utterance, can combine with it to produce a functional inference—that is, one which enables addressees to feel they have understood the utterance (what A means by saying "It is 8 o/clock"— in Sperber and Wilson's (1995) term, the relevance of that saying). Third, context is composed of mutual knowledge. The pragmatic view observes the speaker estimating whether the consciousness of the addressee has access to the assumptions that will effectively combine with the utterance for plausible inference (what does the addressee know? what's on his mind?) and, in turn, the addressee estimating not only the speaker's consciousness (what does she know?) but also the speaker's estimate of the addressee's consciousness (what does she know that I know?). Anne says to Bob, "It's 8 o'clock," in a context where they are waiting for a performance to begin. They mutually know that the performance was scheduled to begin at 7.45. The utterance can combine with this assumption to produce the inference *the performance is significantly late getting started.* At home, another time, Anne says to Bob, "It's 8 o'clock," Anne and Bob mutually knowing that they usually have dinner at 7. The utterance can combine with this assumption to produce the inference *let's eat.*

Every utterance is an experiment in estimating the consciousness of another. The uncertainties of these estimates are a far cry from the notion that language works most efficiently when it is identically understood by all. The pragmatics of inference asks, how can the addressee select from the potentially unlimited number of assumptions in a context—in other words, narrow down *to* a context? And, worse, how can interlocutors possibly estimate one another's consciousness swiftly and accurately enough for efficient communication?

Genre theorists have also concerned themselves with context. For genre theory, context is, roughly, a culturally typifiable situation attended by motives and intentions. In pragmatic terms, the motive and intentions would be mutually known, but in all the vicissitudes with which pragmatics concerns itself: how do language users conduct the rapid-fire searches of mutual consciousness? Genre theory has been relatively untroubled by this cognitive puzzle. Unlike pragmatic theorists, genre theorists have not marvelled at the mysterious efficiency of language users' searching and activating areas of consciousness for productive inference, nor have they been troubled by the hazards of mis-fires. Such concerns about mutual consciousness have been covered by Miller's (1984) early proposal for "intersubjectivity," or by loose notions of tacitness—"genre knowledge" is only in small measure explicit—or, in a pinch, by "convention": people are in quiet agreement that this is the thing to say at this time.

The different focus of inquiry in the two fields may account for different levels of concern. Classically, pragmatics has focused on conversational snippets: Anne saying to Bob, "It's 8 o'clock." Genre theory, meanwhile, concentrates on what Bakhtin (1986) called the "secondary," non-conversational genres: those involved in recognizable "spheres of activity"[2] (p. 60). The sphere of activity will in itself narrow the range of assumptions contributing to relevant inference, and begin to answer the pragmatic problem of search and selection. Genre theory may thereby contribute to pragmatics means of understanding how language-users construct mutual consciousness. At the same time, pragmatics may in turn contribute to genre theory an appreciation of the vulnerability of meaning, and its multiplicity and unevenness even in situations of evident communicativeness.

We could say that form is the tip of the iceberg, the visible part, while the mass is underwater, in the unspoken silence of mutual consciousness. But this image only begins to capture the connection between form and consciousness, for, while form is stable and unchanging—literal and exposed for all to see—the submerged silence is not only unfathomable but also unstable: composed of multiple consciousnesses able only to estimate rather than to ascertain one another, and also liable themselves to change—liable to drift, shift, re-focus in the current of experience. Moreover, while it might be tempting to seek stability by bringing more of the unspoken to light, the distribution of speech and silence is itself an efficiency: not simply a concession to the impossibility of saying everything, but an expression of common ground—as Sperber and Wilson (1995, pp. 217-218) say, "the relationship"—such expression and relationship being disrupted by explicitness, and the path of inference derailed.[3] The speech/silence ratio is itself meaningful.

This chapter re-introduces the problem of inference first to a scene where genre conditions are more evident than in pragmatics' typical conversational examples. It then takes the problem to legal genres, where it continues to be perceived as an obstacle to efficiency. The chapter then focuses on a Supreme Court of Canada reading of an historical treaty with First Nations, for implications to be derived for genre study. Amongst these implications is a view of genre change beyond genres' emergence and disappearance and beyond their formal adaptation and innovation. Pragmatics also offers an approach to understanding language-users meaning-seeking behavior when a genre's form survives its original context, for the problem is not only the inscrutability and impermanence of consciousness but the exposure and permanence of form.

The Problem of Inference

In this demonstration of the problem of inference—the silence/speech ratio—the interlocutors, unlike Anne and Bob, are strangers to one another. Unlike Anne and Bob in the "8 o'clock" example, they do not construct a context of mutual assumptions from personal familiarity. Here is a sentence in fact uttered:

A: I have a bag of garbage.

Is the speaker a hoarder on a reality-TV show? Does her utterance combine with assumptions in context about her suffering from hoarding syndrome for the inference that she has taken a courageous step towards mental health? For us overhearers, knowing the actual uptake can begin to contextualise:

B: $5

Inference? A is selling her garbage? A will pay $5? What are A and B doing? A is me, in May 2012. B is a clerk in the lobby of the hotel in a village on the British Columbia coast. A gives B $5, B gives A a strip of yellow tape. A leaves the lobby, ties the tape on a bag, takes the bag to a bin behind the hotel. A's motives? Get rid of garbage— maybe that is inferable from the word-form *garbage*. But why is she carrying garbage around? Why does a hotel take garbage? (The Château Laurier hotel in Ottawa doesn't take garbage.) For the $5? Probably not, maybe to avoid careless dumping ... but why would there be dumping?[4] Without having to ask about intentions or motives, A and B mutually recognise one another's intentions in speaking, and enough of one another's motives to go on. Pragmatics can't say how this happens, but genre theory can. Although strangers to one another, A and B mutually know intentions and motives from their experience in spheres of activity, composing roles and relationships, interests and attitudes. That experience produces the consciousness which makes these few words efficiently silent on what is mutually understood even while A's and B's motives are different. From a pragmatic perspective, spheres of activity afford common ground: mutual recognition of assumptions, histories, and prospects (this has been done before; it will be done again). These horizons of familiarity extend beyond personal acquaintance even to strangers. At the same time, the pragmatic perspective tells us that mutual consciousness is not a perfect match of minds, not a unanimity. Even indemnified by genre, the assumptions populating the silence are not ascertainable. And, while genre study has long observed the trouble outsiders have when all they know are the words, not the content of the silence, pragmatics might be the first to notice the disturbance which can be caused by actually saying *what* goes without saying. For example, B says "$5. This is a hotel." A thinks, *why is he telling me what he knows I already know? Does he mean I should be grateful it's only $5?* The speaking of the silence makes the exchange less rather than more efficient. Pragmatics might also be first to notice the perishability of the phase of consciousness which hosts the silent assumptions. The assumptions live only as long as their host in its current phase: genre stability is a phenomenon of consciousness, not form. And pragmatics might be more likely to anticipate the unevenness of the perishability: A may say *I have a bag of garbage* in 2013, when the social experience of B's counterpart (or even B himself) has changed his material and intentional orientation to the world. *I have a bag of garbage* won't work the same way. Or B may, for his own interests, decide to be literal or awkward and hear form alone: "Oh"/"Lucky you!" (Underdetermination leaves the door open to a range of behaviours.) Pragmatics and genre theory both tell us *not form alone*. Identical form—*I have a bag of garbage*—would mean something different in a different context, engage different intentions, different motives.

The Problem of Inference in Legal Genres

Underdetermination is a theoretical problem—and a practical problem in some spheres of activity. In law, principles of legal drafting seek to reduce the level of underdetermination, guiding the writing of genres where context-dependency is a liability rather than an efficiency, and producing, in their context-wary stance, the sound of legalese as what goes without saying is actually said.[5] Legal reading, as well as legal writing, is also guided by rules to deal with underdetermination. There are guides for judges reading contractual and statutory genres, and, in their opinions, judges often recite the rules—"canons of interpretation." Both the guides and analyses of them tell us that judicial interpretation can favour one of three principles. (1) Textualism—or literalism—reads the sentence (*I have a bag of garbage*) until it coughs up its meaning: form alone, or "plain meaning," which is sometimes but not always distinguished from "ordinary meaning." (2) Intentionalism reads the sentence and finds what the speaker intended—what legislators had in mind— by consulting, for example, hansard. (3) Contextualism extends the search, beyond only legislators' recorded or inferable intention at the time to something like *what would they say now if they knew what we know today?* Opponents of contextualism argue that it is an ungoverned search for desirable outcomes, a scene for judicial activism. Each principle attempts to deal with the perishability of assumptions, in change of scene: as if *I have a bag of garbage* were recorded, then replayed elsewhere, at another time.

In Canada, a principal authority on statutory interpretation is Ruth Sullivan (2008). Heroically and not uncontroversially, Sullivan

(1999) has taken linguistic-pragmatic principles to statutory interpretation. She finds that (1) even literal reading is never context-free—you can't attend to *I have a bag of garbage* without attempting a context; form is never alone, for assumptions will rush or creep in to enable inference; (2) judges should make their assumptions explicit, so their judgements will be more persuasive; (3) "plain meaning" rules in literal textualism are not only confused but also persistent because they are in keeping with common-sense notions of what language is even while they defy people's common experience of language (the efficiency exemplified in the *I have a bag of garbage* exchange is the common experience—so common that we sleep through it). While our usual experience of language is of its silent efficiencies and the inferential character of meaning, we cling to a notion of language being at its best when it is explicit and identically understood by all.

Other scholars have also taken linguistic-pragmatic principles to legal genres. They have, for example, examined judges' uses of dictionaries. Finding a particular word or phrase to be the sticking point, a judge will look it up in the dictionary, for its real meaning—that is, *form alone*. So, Hobbs (2011), observing that the US Supreme Court "has increasingly relied on dictionary definitions" (p. 327), describes *Smith v. United States* where "the defendant was arrested after offering to trade an ... automatic weapon for two ounces of cocaine" (p. 332). The criminal code provides that persons convicted of a drug-trafficking crime are liable to greater penalty if they "[use]... a firearm" in the activity. The judge looked up *use* and found that its meanings include "to convert to one's service" and "to employ," and asserted that the facts "fall squarely within those definitions." Could genre theory have helped? It might have identified spheres of activity: drug-dealing and law enforcement. In their intentional, material orientation to the world, the motives of drug-traffickers can typically be advanced by the use of firearms for intimidation or injury—not barter. Legislators and framers of criminal law, in their sphere of activity protecting people from violent harm, intend *uses a firearm* to mean use for intimidation and injury—not barter. *It goes without saying* that they do not mean barter; had they said so, the law would have been a caricature of legalese, such as "uses ... a firearm, not including for purposes of barter, or decoration, or ambulatory support" (excluding a limping drug dealer who uses a firearm as a crutch). The contemporary scene is thick with contextual assumptions accessible even to readers involved only as mass-media spectators to drug trafficking. The silence of the statute on "uses a firearm *for what*" is a measure of the accessibility of the assumptions. But the state asked for a literal reading of *form alone*, and the judge went along. On pragmatic rather than genre principles, Sullivan might regard the judge as making an inference from an unspoken assumption—for example, that drug dealers are bad and should be punished more harshly—and then masking his inference with a literal reading. That others may silently share this assumption secures the mask. The literal reading is a mask—and also a kind of loophole reading: a reader cannot help but entertain the assumptions circulating in the spheres of activity, but pretends ignorance, as if a Martian with a dictionary.

The drug-deal case is contemporary, affording access to the assumptions on which the utterance itself is silent. Even then, it is stripped to form alone. When time passes, and contemporary motives perish, when there are no original witnesses left to the mutual consciousness by which meaning was inferred—yet the utterance is retrieved—how does form fare?

Courts Reading an Historical Instance of the Treaty Genre

The 1760 Treaty of Peace and Friendship between the Mi'kmaq and the British Crown was re-introduced to readers in the 1990s by (1) the strategic harvesting and sale of eels by Donald Marshall, a Nova Scotia Mi'kmaq, Marshall intending that his action be tried; (2) his being charged with "the selling of eels without a licence and fishing during the close season with illegal nets" (*R. v. Marshall No. 1*, 1999) and (3) his being tried in Nova Scotia Provincial Court, and his appealing to Nova Scotia Court of Appeal, and failing in that appeal, appealing to the Supreme Court of Canada. I noticed the case for its successive and different readings of one statement of the treaty. Speaker intention was obviously "vastly underdetermined" by sentence meaning ("I" is the Mi'kmaq signatory):

> And I do further engage that we will not traffick, barter or Exchange any Commodities in any manner but with such persons or the managers of such Truck houses as shall be

appointed or Established by His Majesty's Governor at Lunenbourg or Elsewhere in Nova Scotia or Accadia. (AANDC, 2010)

I also noticed the case for its revival of what I recognised as an historical genre: the agreement on trade and alliance. From study of the 18th and early 19th century writings of fur traders, I knew that such agreements were commonly reported to London and Paris as arrangements for trade and geo-political alliance:[6] the Cree, for example, would trade with the British through the Hudson's Bay Company (chartered by the Crown), and not trade with the French, when perhaps adversaries of theirs *would* trade with the French. The Company would promise to offer high-quality trade goods. I agree with Supreme Court of Canada Chief Justice McLachlin, in her dissenting opinion, that the Mi'kmaq knew what treaties were ("the Mi'kmaq understood the treaty process as well as the particular terms of the treaties they were signing" [*R. v. Marshall No. 1*, 1999]), that is, knew the genre. In this phase, treaties were not a colonial genre imposed unilaterally by European interests. As a trade genre, they were motivated by well-established spheres of activity, their express terms enabled the goals of those spheres, and their silence on other terms indicated mutual consciousness. And as political alignments and trade agreements, they involved parties with distinct interests (just as the garbage bagger and hotel clerk have distinct interests). Further, just as interests were distinct, perspectives on the genre would have been distinct rather than identical. Moreover, even as the genre *treaty* persisted across epochs, its instantiations could scarcely have been identical in meaning as historical conditions changed. Like the isolated sentence, the genre—even with replications of wording—could not have been unchanged.

250 years later, the utterance presents itself for re-reading, over and over. Because no "ordinary meaning" for *Truck house* survived to the late 20th century, the term had to be defined by specialists as a kind of trading post, and all readers inferred from the definition a benefit for the Mi'kmaq. Involving a fixed schedule of exchange values attractive to indigenous traders, the truckhouse scheme, was short-lived, being disallowed by London authorities for its monopolistic character and being a money-loser in any case (see Gwyn, 2003, pp. 79-80, for discussion of the truckhouse scheme). But

the assumptions of continuing and expanding trade on which the scheme was based would not have expired with its collapse.

Even located in a genre recognisable to 20th century readers, and deemed recognisable to 18th century participants, the sentence got three different readings.

(1) The trial judge found right to trade, and assumed in it, right to harvest, but now there are no truckhouses so right to trade is gone, and with it, right to harvest; he read the treaty's silence on harvest as "goes without saying," given the spheres of activity. The silence is a problem for treaty interpretation, however, in that it left no positive declaration of right to harvest.

(2) The Court of Appeal read the silence literally: no right to harvest, because of difference with a 1752 treaty which did say harvest. Here was a series of instances of a genre (this local series going back 45 years to 1726), with one instance missing some regularities of expression. Was the missing statement so well understood that it fell silent? Or was it deliberately omitted?

Both readings turn to contextualist and intentionalist aids (for example, minutes of the treaty meetings, correspondence with London, historians' testimony as to the military situation), but favour literal textualist readings. The appellant also took a literal, form-alone reading: the truckhouse was a condition for agreeing to restriction on trade; if there were no truckhouses, as agreed, there were no restrictions on trade, or harvest. Literal, form-alone readings may be associated with privileged interests or law-and-order, as in the drug-trafficking case, but they need not be.

(3) The dissenting Supreme Court of Canada opinion found no error in the trial judge's reading. The majority opinion, however, found the right to harvest assumed in the right to trade, and the right to trade assumed in, not contingent on, the agreement to the restriction in view of the truckhouse benefit. (That is, the Mi'kmaq agreed to restriction because *of course* they had the right to trade:

it goes without saying. They didn't get the right from the restriction: the truckhouse was a compensation for the restriction.) The court finds a continuing right to harvest, and trade. The appeal is allowed and acquittals entered on all charges.

But how does the unrestricted right to harvest and trade survive the passage of time? How do Marshall and other Mi'kmaq have this right when I don't? Specialist, contextualist discourse processes come into play to help with *what would they say if they knew what* **we** *know* **now**? Seeking access to the silence, the court turns to two other genres which strategically, deliberately introduce assumptions into the context of interpretation: (a) Section 35 of the Canadian Charter of Rights and Freedoms (1982) distinguishes aboriginal rights from mine, and protects them; (b) the Court reads its own earlier decisions to find a rule for reading. Readings of historical agreements between the Crown and First Nations must, where there is uncertainty (called "ambiguity"), choose amongst plausible inferences the one which entertains First Nations interests and recognises power imbalances and inequities. That is, such readings must execute the Honour of the Crown, a principle from British jurisprudence. This rule for reading prohibits "sharp dealing" (the term originating in the R. v. Badger 1996 SCC decision, and repeated in subsequent judgements): prohibits, that is, textualist readings of form alone which pretend ignorance of the spheres of activity which motivated the original utterance. The Crown cannot seek loopholes by means of literalist readings, as the state did in the American prosecution of the drug trafficker. These reading rules methodically specify two sets of assumptions for reading form alone.

So complex was this reading, and so ripe with inferences which sectors of the public, in *their* spheres of activity, drew from it that non-aboriginal lobster fishers protested violently and vandalised Mi'kmaq property, drawing a lobster inference from an eel decision. Two months after the first decision, the court itself issued "Marshall 2," a controversial and nearly unprecedented clarification. The clarification, however, stirred further controversy and disturbance.

Even with specialist, contextualizing aids to reading, some of them genres themselves—the Charter, the rules for reading treaties—reading *form alone* is a high-risk venture, hazarding the silence, first the silence of the treaty itself and producing an array of different readings, then the silence of judicial assumptions. Sullivan advises Supreme Court Justices to declare their assumptions, in order to improve the persuasiveness of the genre. But when the majority opinion did so, in this case, many people were antagonised rather than persuaded. Possibly the opinion genre depends on silence on some categories of assumptions, and this is what makes literal readings of form alone useful and attractive: their stubbornly pointing to form alone to effectively mask assumptions. Silence may serve differently in different genres.

Silence is dynamic and volatile, especially so because, more than "purpose" or "function", motive is more deeply embedded in the unsaid. It may be easy enough to state the purpose or function of the genre "treaty"—to reconcile the interests of sovereign parties, for example—yet without knowing the motives, the spheres of activity (this is the purpose of a treaty, but why do you want to accomplish that purpose?), one cannot know the meaning. With motive in mind, we can turn again to the case and see that political/trade treaties, while engaging different interests and, in addition, cross-cultural disparities, also engaged mutually recognised motives embedded in spheres of activity. Signatories' experience of the spheres of activity made those motives mutually knowable.

In their history, treaties engaged different spheres of activity. While Chief Justice McLachlin (1999) rejects categories in treaty interpretation—"[slotting] treaties into different categories [peace vs. land cession], each with its own rules of interpretation" paragraph 80 – recent scholarship, both traditional-mainstream and indigenous, shows us three phases of the treaty genre: treaties motivated by (1) geo-political/trade activities; by (2) European settlement; by (3) resource extraction. After Phase 1, the mutuality of consciousness diminishes into increasing disparity—disparity that led Makmillen (2010) to call cross-cultural treaties a limiting case for genre. So in Phase 2 settlement was on the minds of Crown signatories, and First Nations parties to agreement may have had a sense of what settlement meant, for they had experience of entertaining European presence, but they could not know what wide resettlement of their territories would mean, including the racialist assumptions which both accelerated and were accelerated by resettlement. And in Phase 3 they could not know what timber harvest, mining, transportation routes, and today pipelines would mean, and were not told (but who could be said to have known, exactly? who could have known what to say?). So reading protocols are different for treaties from Phases (2)—(3), and delve into cultural disparity—including evidence of Crown negotiators' knowing exploitation of cultural disparity, revealed by recent scholarship.

In the meantime, another aid to reading comes to light, one with robust genre credentials: genre as a phenomenon of mutual consciousness, and consciousness as experience of spheres of activity. Indigenous and indigenous-influenced scholarship has presented, for example, massive documentation of *Treaty No. 7*, 1877 (Hildebrandt et al., 1996)—a settlement treaty—and *Treaty No. 9*, 1905 (Long, 2010), a resource extraction treaty. This documentation attests to the continuity of assumptions in the consciousness of First Nations signatories from the time of the treaties to the present day, a continuity of engagement in spheres of activity which motivated treaty agreements, that is, harvest and trade and the territorial expression of these activities. Similar but so far less organised evidence attests that the 18th century assumptions entertained by Mi'kmaq signatories remain active in community consciousness, experienced in the spheres of activity in which the signatories' descendants engaged: harvest and trade. Expressing this continuity is, for example, Chief Donald Marshall Sr.'s inauguration of "Treaty Day" in 1986, following the Supreme Court of Canada decision recognising the validity of the 1752 Treaty between the Crown and the Mi'kmaq. Treaty Day not only expresses continuity of Mi'kmaq consciousness from the 18th century to the present day but also attempts to revive the historical consciousness of non-aboriginal Canadians: "Throughout the festivities, the Nova Scotia population must become more aware of the Mi'kmaq Nation and our history, which will not only enrich their own cultural and historical knowledge of the Mi'kmaq, but will also enable the Mi'kmaq Nation to be recognized in a manner of which they are deserving" (UNSI, n.d.)—a renewed context, that is, for reading historical treaties. In addition, the Mi'kmaq's uninterrupted reading or hearing of the treaty is attested in a record of petitions to the legislature, to the Crown, to the Colonial office, to government officials, on the terms of the treaty, throughout the 19th and 20th centuries (Coates, 2000, pp. 45-46). For non-aboriginal readers, the Treaty is form alone, even as genre rather than isolated snippet of conversation; for aboriginal readers it is not. It is as if A returns to the hotel in 2013, with garbage, and B's consciousness has in the meantime changed. B takes her literally, or regards her as an anachronism: a disappointment for A, now faced with the unevenness in the perishability of assumptions, and her rights to trade not being protected by the Charter.

Genre and Inference

Genre is not form alone, but at the same time it *is* form. And form is what survives the perishable consciousness. What do people, in their spheres of activity, do to resuscitate these survivals? Are resuscitation efforts peculiar to legal genres, or do we find them elsewhere, as in, for example, literary studies, but with different reading protocols, different "canons of interpretation"? Underdetermination of meaning by form is an efficiency, sometimes a liability, sometimes a resource – and sometimes an excitement, as it is in reading of historical genres by courts, and as it can be in the successive interpretations of literary survivors.

More broadly, genre theory can make a contribution to the work on the pragmatic puzzle of underdetermination: spheres of activity compose common ground, narrowing context to a common ground of accessible assumptions from which to draw inferences. But the donation comes at a cost for genre theory, for now to be reckoned as a main term in genre is mutual consciousness, in all the silent trepidations detected by pragmatics: assumptions unascertainable, uneven, unstable and changeable even when form remains unchanged.

The late 20th century reading of the 1760 Treaty of Peace and Friendship—an instance of a genre formally recognisable to all who come upon it—dramatises both the unevenness and the changeability of the contents of the silence enclosing the form. The interests of the Mi'kmaq and the Crown were different in 1760, but still within the scope of common ground. In the centuries following, these interests diverged more widely, the Mi'kmaq continuing to entertain assumptions attending the signing, the Crown forgetting them and entertaining others when the Treaty presented itself for re-reading. Are the perishability and unevenness peculiar to legal genres—contracts, statutes, treaties—intended both to survive the originating context of the utterance and to reconcile interests? Possibly, the sound of "legalese" signals the peculiar unevenness and volatility in mutual consciousness attending legal genres. But the unevenness and volatility may also be features of all genres, just as the vast underdetermination of meaning is a problem for all utterance (Sperber & Wilson, 2002, p. 3). The problem comes with some benefits, as well as cost, for to observe genre as a phenomenon of mutual consciousness is to open fresh prospects, ones which draw our attention even further away from the traditional view of genre as what is formal, stable, unchanging.

Acknowledgements

Along with all genre theorists, I am grateful to Genre 2012 and its organisers: a compelling event, now unfolding in this volume. For the preparation of this contribution, I owe thanks to fellow researchers and genre theorists Dan Adleman, Dustin Grue, and Donato Mancini, and particular thanks to Futoshi Tachino, for his extraordinarily insightful reading of a draft.

References

Aboriginal Affairs and Northern Development Canada (AANDC). (2010). Treaty of peace and friendship 1760. Retrieved from https://www.aadnc-aandc.gc.ca/eng/1100100028596/1100100028597

Austin, J. L. (1975). *How to do things with words*. Oxford: Oxford University Press. (Original work published in 1955).

Bakhtin, M. M. (1986). The Problem of Speech Genres. In C. Emerson & M. Holquist (Eds.), V. W. McGee (Trans.), *Speech genres and other late essays* (pp. 60-102). Austin, TX: University of Texas Press.

Buchan, B. (2007). Traffick of empire: Trade, treaty and *terra nullius* in Australia and North America, 1750–1800. *History Compass* 5(2), 386-405.

Coates, K. (2000). *The Marshall Decision and Native Rights*. Montreal: McGill-Queen's University Press.

Giltrow, J. (2011). "Curious gentlemen": The Hudson's Bay Company and the Royal Society, business and science in the eighteenth century. In D. Starke-Meyerring, A. Paré, N. Artemeva, M. Horne, & L. Yousoubova (Eds.), *Writing in knowledge societies* (pp. 53-74). Perspectives on Writing. Fort Collins, Colorado: The WAC Clearinghouse and Parlor Press.

Goffman, E. (1981). *Forms of Talk*. Philadelphia, PA: University of Pennsylvania Press.

Grice, H. P. (1975). Logic and conversation. In P. Cole & J. Morgan (Eds.), *Speech acts* (pp. 41-58). New York: Academic Press.

Gwyn, J. (2003). The Miĩkmaq, Poor Settlers, and the Nova Scotia Fur Trade, 1783-1853. *Journal of the Canadian Historical Association, 14*(1), pp. 65-91.

Hildebrandt, W., First Rider, D., & Carter, S. (1996). *The true spirit and original intent of Treaty 7*. Montreal: McGill-Queen's University Press.

Hobbs, P. (2011). Defining the law: (Mis)using the dictionary to decide cases. *Discourse Studies, 13*(3), 327-347.

Long, J. (2010). Treaty No. 9: Making the agreement to share the land in far northern Ontario in 1905. Montreal: McGill-Queen's University Press.

Makmillen, S. (2010). Land, law and language: Rhetorics of indigenous rights and title (Unpublished doctoral dissertation). University of British Columbia.

Miller, C. (1984). Genre as social action. *Quarterly Journal of Speech, 70,* 151-167.

Solan, L. (2010). *The language of statutes: Laws and their interpretation.* Chicago, IL: University of Chicago Press.

Sperber, D., & Wilson, D. (1995). *Relevance: Communication and cognition.* Oxford: Blackwell. Original work published in 1986.

Sperber, D., & Wilson, D. (2002). Pragmatics, modularity and mind-reading. *Mind & Language, 17*(1), 3-23.

R. v. Badger, 1 Canada Supreme Court Reports 771 (1996).

R. v. Marshall #1, 3 Canada Supreme Court Reports 456 (1999).

R. v. Marshall #2, 3 Canada Supreme Court Reports 533 (1999).

Sullivan, R. (2008). *Sullivan on the construction of statutes* (5th ed.). LexisNexis Canada.

Sullivan, R. (1999). Statutory interpretation in the Supreme Court of Canada. *Ottawa Law Review, 30*(2), 175-227.

Union of Nova Scotia Indians [UNSI]. (n.d.). *Treaty day.* Retrieved September 26, 2013, from http://www.unsi.ns.ca/treaty-day/

Wittgenstein, L. (1958). *Philosophical investigations* (3rd ed.). Trans. G. E. M. Anscombe. Englewood Cliffs, NJ: Prentice Hall, 1953. (Original published in 1953)

EndNotes

[1] This figure is derived from Relevance Theory On-Line Bibliographic Service http://www.ua.es/personal/francisco.yus/rt.html by Dustin Grue, personal communication, September 16, 2013.

[2] Bakhtin often pointed to "the professions," and law particularly, in proposing the provenance of secondary genres. Schooling and the marketplace would be other arenas hosting spheres of activity, as would be sports and celebrity entertainment, for other examples.

[3] If Anne were to add to "It's 8 o'clock" the unspoken assumption "the performance was supposed to begin at 7.45," knowing that Bob knew this (Bob has not asked, "when does the performance begin?"), she opens the way to other inferences beyond significant lateness: that waiting is tedious; that she is a stickler for punctuality, for example. If, at home, Anne were to add, "We usually eat at 7," an assumption readily accessible to Bob, he could infer as her meaning that this departure from what is usual is unacceptable. In each case, uttering the unspoken changes the track of inference.

[4] Focus the context to a scene typical on the south British Columbia coast, and engaging several intersecting spheres of activity: cruising boaters tie up to a government wharf adjacent to the hotel; so do cottagers living off the grid and crossing from nearby islands.

[5] Solan (2010) points out the limits of actually saying when he observes how statutory language written "broadly" to include many instances can confuse rather than enlighten juries (p. 214).

[6] As Buchan (2007) writes, "Colonial trade in North America developed throughout the seventeenth and eighteenth centuries as a means both of profit and of diplomacy along sparsely populated and often far distant frontiers" (p. 22). During this period, the Hudson's Bay Company urged on their managers the importance of treating their trade partners with "leniency and mildness," and the managers, in turn, in report of trade talks and alliance, demonstrated their rhetorical command of delicate situations amongst sovereign parties (Giltrow, 2012, p. 59).

Chapter 10

Challenges in the New Multimodal Environment of Research Genres: What Future do Articles of the Future Promise Us?

Jan Engberg and Daniela Maier

Aarhus University (Denmark)

Academic knowledge communication, that is, the communication of domain-specific knowledge generated by researchers for other researchers in order for them to understand and use this knowledge, has been increasingly marked by a shift towards multimodality. Jakubowicz and Van Leeuwen (2010) state that "for at least 90 years there have been attempts to produce intellectual work using media other than the traditional academic paper" (p. 361)[1]. During the last decade, the nature and number of these attempts have significantly increased. The development of easily accessible technologies and the competencies of new generations of multiliterate users who can create and retrieve knowledge across several semiotic modes (i.e., written text, speech, still and/or moving images, sound, music, etc.) and media (i.e., print, video, internet, etc.) serve as the impetus for the increase in and diversification of such attempts. We are witnessing a "fast increase of interest in multimodal communication" (Norris & Maier, 2014b, p. 1).

"Multimodality is gaining momentum" (Norris & Maier, 2014a, p. 382) in academic research across various domains. As a consequence, a growing number of the forms of representation, including semiotic modes other than writing (i.e., academic visual essays, academic video essays), compete today with the traditional research articles (RAs). Additionally, we see the appearance of the first video peer-reviewed academic journals such as the international peer-reviewed journal, *Audiovisual Thinking* (http://www.audiovisualthinking.org/), and the *Journal of Visual Experiments* (JoVE), a peer-reviewed, PubMed-indexed video journal (http://www.jove.com/).

The dissemination phase of the research process is also undergoing rapid changes. In particular, the electronic publication format makes it possible to develop new forms of dissemination (e.g., through the addition of a highly complex interactive layout or the inclusion of moving images and online tools such as *Youtube*). Among others, big publishing houses such as Elsevier (see 2015a)[2] work strategically towards the development of online tools and interactive applications. In the near future, publishing research findings will involve more and more activities that require not only domain-specific knowledge, but also knowledge about various semiotic modes and media.

Given these changes in knowledge making and mobilization, we have conceived a project which systematically explores and maps the multimodal creation, representation, and dissemination of academic knowledge through new generic configurations and across several media. Like Kress (2005), we combine the "notions of convention, of competence, of knowledge, and of authority" (p. 19) in order to investigate the consequences of the new multimodal phenomena. The present chapter reports on parts of this project. In this chapter, we refer to the researcher who attempts to access some of the new generic configurations of research articles as *the user*.

Objective

The prototypical and traditional way of disseminating research results has been through the written research article published in a printed journal, which is designed to be read, that is, perceived mainly through the decoding of a written document (Berkenkotter & Huckin, 1995, p. 27). The goal of the project that we report on is to establish a set of descriptive dimensions and categories for the assessment of the multimodal development of the RA. Below, we present the theoretical background for the development of a set of descriptors, report on the present stage of the development, and discuss central results of two of our previously reported analyses that used the developed set of descriptors (Maier & Engberg, 2013, 2014). The analytical section of the chapter focuses on the shift from the dissemination of research results by way of printed documents to a screen-based way of dissemination while highlighting subsequent interactional opportunities.

The analytical section of the chapter predominantly concentrates on the user's interaction with the document (in a broad sense) and the contribution of this interaction to the rendering of (new) knowledge. Because we are especially interested in the shift from one set of (multi)modal possibilities to another, we focus on the effects of the new possibilities. Specifically, we investigate the relations between the rendering of knowledge in the traditionally dominating written mode and the new multimodal possibilities provided by the shift of medium in the publishing house Elsevier's (2015a) *Article of the Future* project.

The *Article of the Future* project is an ongoing initiative aiming to revolutionize the traditional format of the research article. Over 150 researchers, publishers, and editors have participated in the project. Our present data were collected from among the RAs published through the *Article of the Future* project and include 13 prototype research articles from seven disciplines: business management, materials science, mathematics and computer science, paleontology, parasitology and tropical diseases, psychology, and cognitive science. In the chapter, we focus on those aspects of representation and dissemination of academic knowledge that characterize all the prototype articles.

As mentioned above, the first goal of our study is to develop a set of descriptors for the possible relations between modes that develop through the user's interaction with the multimodal document. Through the developed set of descriptors, we intend to gain access to the process of rendering knowledge in the multimodal document by its creator. We ask, how do possibilities of user interaction contribute to the rendering of knowledge? What types of knowledge are rendered through the interaction? The second goal of the study-based on our qualitative analyses – is to interpret and evaluate the degree of the contribution of the intended interaction to the achievement of the RAs' central goals. The research questions we ask are, do the possibilities of the interaction contribute to a more efficient process of rendering scientific knowledge? Or, are they (also) used for other purposes, for example, in order to reach out to other audiences and to make the RA usable in other settings? Finally, in the concluding section, we discuss some of the consequences of the observed changes in the generic form of the traditional research article.

Theories and Methods

In this section, we present the theoretical and methodological approaches central to our investigation of academic knowledge communication from the perspective of multimodality. Our study has drawn on the theoretical constructs from multimodality, genre, film studies, and knowledge communication theories.

Multimodality

Due to the combination of several semiotic modes (language, images, and sound) in the structure of the observed new generic configurations, we find the multimodality approach relevant in our exploration. Jewitt (2014) explains that multimodality "attends to the full repertoire of resources that people use to communicate and represent phenomena and experiences including speech, sound, gesture, gaze, body posture and movement, writing, image and so on" (p. 127). The shift of the RA publication medium from print to screen representation at least potentially allows the presenter to apply the full repertoire of communicative modes. We investigate the degree to which the repertoire has been appropriately used in the documents under study. Moreover, the multimodality approach allows us to address the interaction and combination of semiotic modes in knowledge construction and meaning creation as well as the manipulation at various levels of the generic structure. According to Kress (2010)

> knowledge is made and given shape in representation, according to the potentials of modal affordances; the process of representation is identical to the shaping of knowledge. Makers of representations are shapers of knowledge. (p.27)

In our context, this approach may help us to describe the multimodal interaction used in the dissemination and development of knowledge. We adopt Kress's (2005) understanding of mode and medium when exploring their roles in academic knowledge communication:

> I use the term "mode" for the culturally and socially produced resources for representation and "medium" as the term for the culturally produced means for distribution of these representations-as-meanings, that is, as messages. These technologies—those of representation, the modes, and those of dissemination, the media—are always both independent of and interdependent with each other. (p. 7)

The notions of modes and media facilitate the exploration of the "resemiotisation" (Iedema, 2003) and "remediation" (Bolter & Grusin, 2002) phenomena that characterize academic knowledge communication in new genre configurations. To sum up, from the perspective of the multimodal approach to communication, it is our aim to investigate what consequences the shift from one medium (aka vehicle of dissemination) to another has for the representation and, thus, for the shaping of scientific knowledge. We focus on the role of the user's interaction with the document and the knowledge it disseminates.

Knowledge Communication

In this chapter, we are especially interested in the communication of academic knowledge among peers. In this context, we base our work on Kastberg's (2007) definition:

> Knowledge communication is strategic communication. As 'strategic' it is deliberately goal-oriented, the goal being the mediation of understanding across knowledge asymmetries. As 'communication' it is participative (interactive) and the communicative 'positions' converge on the (co-)construction of (specialized) knowledge. (p. 8)

In other words, the study of the communication of academic knowledge is the study of how academic knowledge generated by researchers is communicated to other researchers in a participative process leading to (co-)construction of knowledge among producers and users of documents. Kastberg's understanding that the goal of knowledge communication is to mediate understanding *across knowledge asymmetries* is central in our work. Jacobsen (2012) observed:

> More often than not, knowledge asymmetries appear as granitic bastions of permanent difference. However, I argue that they exist, and become real, the moment we recognize them. We recognize them partly because our history compels us to. We recognize them partly as a matter of habit. We recognize them as a matter of convenience. And we recognize them because there are obviously differences in what you and I know. ... I conclude my argument by describing knowledge asymmetries as the differences in knowledges that are *recognized* to exist by participants, including the researcher, in situated interactions. (p. 169, emphasis in original)

Knowledge asymmetry, understood as differences in structure, depth, and breadth of knowledge among participants in the process of knowledge communication, is important for producing a document and for shaping/changing traits of a genre like that of the RA. RAs are typically read when users of the document recognize a (possible) asymmetry between their own knowledge and that of the producer of the research article. For communicative purposes, this asymmetry must be created through the instantiations of relevant modes in the document: the document must show the relevant differences in knowledge and, thus, communicatively create a relevant asymmetry to be recognized by the document user. This is done by using many different modes and following many different (argumentative) strategies, which we will not discuss in this chapter.[3] In our case, we are interested in investigating how the possibilities of making the user interact with the document on the screen are used to make the knowledge asymmetry recognizable to the user. In turn, Scardamalia and Bereiter's (2006) assertion that knowledge is a social fact emerging from discursive interaction informs our understanding of *knowledge building*. For Scardamalia and Bereiter, it means that in education we need to create environments in which the learners understand their task as achieving insights that may (potentially) help the discipline to improve the collective knowledge. According to the authors, this goal may be achieved through using the ways of speaking and communicating that are more *knowledge transforming* (revealing the actual insights and ideas achieved) than merely *knowledge telling* (Scardamalia & Bereiter, 1987). Mutual knowledge building aims at transforming existing knowledge in order to further it rather than merely restating it.

We use the concept of knowledge building to explore concrete ways of creating knowledge asymmetries. Confronted with dynamic multimodal data, we employ a conceptual framework that accounts for the nuances of the knowledge building processes, which occur when the user is accessing the complex generic structures. We have a special interest in assessing if the knowledge that is supposed to be built through a user's navigation options in the prototype articles can be classified as contributing to the *expansion* or to *enhancement* of knowledge, wherein the attempts to show expansion or enhancement are instances of knowledge transforming. However, if we do not find that the interaction offered to the user demonstrates the expansion or enhancement of knowledge, we characterize the interaction as an instance of mere knowledge telling.

The strategy of *knowledge expansion* refers, so to speak, to the breadth of the knowledge to be built. It is important to determine if the knowledge expansion considers the *core knowledge* and, thus, may contribute to the central knowledge transformation process, or if the expanding knowledge is *peripheral*. We view knowledge as belonging to the core knowledge communicated through a document if it directly contributes to the topics seen as central according to the article's title and abstract. Other knowledge intended to be built by the user is defined as peripheral. It may be further characterized as either *necessary and presupposed knowledge* or *supplementary knowledge*. The *necessary and presupposed knowledge* covers the domain-specific knowledge that the users are supposed to possess as part of their background expertise, while the *supplementary knowledge* refers to the information that is not central but may be relevant for further research work and readings.

The notion of *knowledge enhancement* refers to the depth of the knowledge to be built. In order to qualitatively assess the phenomenon of knowledge enhancement, it is necessary to investigate different interlinked ways of presenting knowledge in order to understand if they convey *new* knowledge elements, or if these simply convey *repeated* knowledge in different multimodal ways. Apart from this distinction, our study of the RA prototypes reported in this chapter has shown that it is also important to distinguish between knowledge traditionally belonging to the discipline (new domain-specific knowledge) and knowledge that would not be seen as part of the domain-specific knowledge (*other types of new knowledge*), but which usually appears in other genres. For example, some of the RA prototypes investigated in this study contain "talking heads"—videos in which researchers, either alone or in groups, present their work while maintaining eye contact with their viewers. This representation may cause the building of knowledge about the author's looks, dress, and speech mannerisms as well as about the intent of the author to address the user directly. Neither of these knowledge types are domain-specific, but they may be supporting the overall process of making the user build domain-specific knowledge.

Multimodal Documents and Genre

Having presented the theoretical positions concerning multimodality and knowledge communication, we conclude the theoretical part of the chapter by combining these positions, and presenting the theoretical basis for the analysis of multimodal documents and genres. In accordance with Bateman (2008, 2009), we refer to genres as *multimodal multi-stratal configurations* and subscribe to Hiipalla's (2014) claim that "if multimodal genre is viewed as a stratified phenomenon, then we need analytical tools that could allow us to identify the semiotic choices that contribute to genre structures on multiple strata" (p. 114).

As a part of our study, we adopt Bateman's (2008, 2009) conceptual framework as it allows us to discuss genre in terms of meaning-making 'flows' which organize the generic configurations: the *text-flow*, the *page-flow* and the *image-flow*.

Text-flow refers to when "the visual line of the developing text provides a basic one-dimensional organizational scheme [*sic*]", and when "the spatial nature of the page is not made to carry significant meanings in its own right" (Bateman, 2009, p. 61).

Page-flow is characterized by "the use of the layout space to communicate additional meanings" (Hiippala, 2014, p. 116). For Kress (2005), "in spatially organized representation, the elements that are chosen for representation are simultaneously present, and it is their spatial arrangement that is used to make (one kind of) meaning" (p. 13).

Image-flow is "used to organize sequences of graphical elements rather than the text organized by text-flow" (Bateman, 2009, p. 61); apart from that, it also facilitates the appearance of new meanings that go beyond the meanings that can be found at the level of individual images. In our work, we adopt this concept to explain the sequencing of moving images as well because "it makes a difference for the interpretation of visuals whether an image appears alone or as a part of a series of images" (Holsanova, 2014, p. 349). Kress (2005) also highlights that "time and sequence in time provide the organizing principle for making meaning. Sequence is used to make meaning" (p. 12).

Our understanding of genres as multimodal multi-stratal configurations that can be characterized by the above-mentioned series of flows has to be accompanied by the characterizations of visual essays and video essays stemming from the fields of education and film studies. For example, for Hughes and Tolley (2010), a visual essay is "a text that relies more heavily on images with minimal print text" and that "entails new forms of semiotic processing of the combinations" of various semiotic documents (p. 6). Meanwhile, a video essay has been characterized as a film genre, which "enables the filmmaker to make the 'invisible' world of thoughts and ideas visible on the screen" (Alter, 2003, p. 13). In order to do that, "the traditional coherence strategies like the voice-over commentaries and the succession of images are undermined by the complex mix of various kinds of both still and moving images belonging to various media and other film genres that are edited in loosely constrained ways" (Maier & Engberg, 2014, p. 135).

So far, in this subsection we have looked at how the textual constituents of multimodal genres like the ones investigated here may be relevantly described. Concerning the mechanisms underlying the emergence and development of a genre, on the other hand, we follow Miller's (1984) idea of genre as typified social action. Miller sees genre as a recurrent situated construal of a rhetorical type and a classification that is open rather than closed (pp. 155; 157). Both aspects mentioned here (the rooting of genres in recurrent situational conditions and the open texture of the genres) are relevant in the context of our project. We investigate classes of documents (emerging genres) that fulfill the same purposes as traditional research articles by including elements from other modes than the ones traditionally used in academic knowledge communication between peers. This means that we investigate attempts at realizing the traditional purposes, but under the changed situational conditions of accessibility of more modes, which is, of course, due to the changes in technologically-based affordances of the present media. Our interest lies in investigating the influences of these changed affordances and the ways in which authors recurrently put them to serve academic knowledge communication. And we do this under the assumption that individual instantiations of genres (that is, the individual documents investigated) are not copies of a generic structure, but independent attempts to comply with concrete situations on the basis of conventionalized prototypes (Paltridge 1997) or Generic Structure Potentials (Hasan 1977).

This open approach is especially apt for the investigation of our object of study, because it gives central importance to possibilities of gradual generic transformations through the change in how senders choose from the elements offered by the prototype. The choice of elements is, however, not always free. For the concept of genre as such, the distinction between choice being possible and choice being free may not be relevant. Rather, what is important for the concept of genre as such is that features of the genre respond to and reflect features of the situation that have been sufficiently important for the sender to govern her choice. For our project, however, the distinction is relevant. In the case of academic knowledge communication in the form of traditional RAs and in less traditional forms, we find situations in which the researchers themselves or the research community (e.g., the journal *Audiovisual Thinking*) become the agents of change as well as situations in which the publisher (e.g., *Article of the Future* project) is the agent of change. This influences the freedom of choice of the researcher producing the article. Below, in the section presenting analytical results, we present an in-depth discussion of the repercussions of these different situations.

Analytical Findings

The theoretical approaches described in the previous section form the basis of our qualitative analyses of the academic knowledge communication. In this section, we report some of the project findings. We will first present the data transcription table used as a basis for our analyses of the different (sub-)genres we have looked at. After that, we report results of our analyses. This section focuses on the article prototypes from the *Article of the Future* project, but we also refer to our previously published analyses (Maier & Engberg, 2013, 2014) focused on academic visual essays appearing in the *Visual Communication* journal and academic video essays appearing in the *Audiovisual Thinking* journal. This discussion allows us to touch on not only publisher-induced, but also author-induced challenges in the contemporary context of academic knowledge communication.

Data Transcription Table

Adopting a multimodal approach, we have established a data transcription table, which serves as a guide for our investigation of academic multimodal knowledge communication. The distinctions and categories have been elaborated on the basis of the theoretical ideas we have presented in the previous section and on the basis of our gradually developing insights into the types of situations we are investigating. The categories are, thus, the result of both an interactive process of immersion into theory, and the performance of the preliminary analysis (Table 1).

Table 1

Data transcription table

Change agent / Change types				Author (in *Visual Communication and Audiovisual Thinking*)	Publisher (in *Articles of the Future*)
The multi-flow layout	Text flow (text sequentiality)				
	Page flow (spatial contiguity)				
	Image flow (temporal sequentiality)				
Knowledge processes	Multimodal interaction (knowledge building inside the document)	Concurrence			
		Complementarity			
		Connection			
	Interactivity (knowledge building through reader's navigation options)	Knowledge expansion	Core knowledge		
			Peripheral knowledge		
		Knowledge enhancement	New domain-specific knowledge		
			Repeated knowledge		
			Other types of new knowledge		

The basic distinction in the table is between the change agents, on the one side, and change types, on the other. The change types are based on different theoretical approaches to the study of multimodal communication and the communication of knowledge. The distinction between changes induced by authors and by publishers, respectively, goes back to a difference that we have observed in the drivers behind the change in the different investigated situations. In the case of the visual and video essays, the research communities drove the change. Both times, the research communities, acting as the agents of change, provided thorough descriptions of why they wanted to innovate publishing formats (conglomerates of forms used for presenting textual content) in a particular way (Maier & Engberg, 2014, p. 115). In contrast, in the *Article of the Future* project, the change agent who provided the arguments for the change was the publishing house (cf. section below). It is important to investigate if the difference in the agents of change influences the choice of possibilities offered by the new technological situation. We are especially interested in studying if the shift to multimodal communication has a similar impact upon the target audience in the situations wherein two different types of the change agents act.

Earlier in the chapter, we have presented the basis for drawing a distinction between different flow types and the basis for the development of the system of descriptors that allow us to assess knowledge communication types triggered by the interaction of the user with the multimodal document. The basis for drawing and describing the distinctions concerning multimodal interaction inside the document is presented below. It is our claim that the descriptors may contribute to an explanation of the central features that characterize the developing multimodal RA genre.

Analysing Situational Impact on Genres

In what follows, we present selected issues of both the author-induced challenges in visual and video academic essays and the publisher-induced challenges in the online prototype articles.

Author-Induced Challenges: Academic Visual Essays and Academic Video Essays

We have analyzed the ways in which researchers present their work by exploiting multimodal generic structures that do not yet belong to the traditional academic communication framework and the consequences of these endeavors.

First of all, according to our preliminary findings (Maier & Engberg, 2014, p. 141), based on the range of multimodal documents chosen from the two international peer-reviewed journals, *Visual Communication* (academic visual essays in printed journal) and *Audiovisual Thinking* (academic video essays in an inherently online journal), it is evident that the dynamic network formed by these multimodal documents is characterized by the existence of overlapping transitional and intermediate generic forms that are constantly evolving. We have labelled as "transitional" those forms that do *not* have a relevant number of traits, which the established genre does not possess either. Other forms were labelled as "intermediate" because, although retaining some of the characteristics of the established genre, they *do* have a significant number of unique traits not connected to that genre. This situation is very likely to emerge, due to the influence created by the different flows (Bateman, 2008, 2009), and can be well described by conceptualizing genres as open prototypes to be chosen from in individual situations (Miller, 1984). We found that traditional research articles were organizationally dominated by the text-flow; visual essays by the page-flow; and video essays by the image-flow.

The multimodal analysis of documents has traditionally focused on the interaction among different modes involved in meaning creation. In our data description (Table 1) we call such an interaction *multimodal interaction*, distinguishing between *concurrence*, *complementarity* and *connection*. Our understanding that meaning emerges from multimodal interaction is based on the basic tenet that "each mode is *partial* in relation to the whole of meaning" (Kress & Jewitt, 2000, p. 3). Therefore, meanings develop as the result of a combination of the semiotic contributions from elements in different modes. Our analyses of the interactions are mainly based on Martinec and Salway (2005), Van Leeuwen (2005), and Unsworth (2006). We have described the proposed categories as follows:

The main types of relations employed in this multimodal analysis are concurrence, complementarity and connection. As for *concurrence*, two main subtypes have been identified: elaboration through specification, explanation and similarity, and elaboration through overview and detail. *Complementarity* is realized through extension that can take two forms: augmentation and contrast. Finally, the ideational *connection* is established through circumstantial enhancement: temporal, spatial and causal. (Maier & Engberg, 2014, p. 126; emphasis added)

We have used the descriptors to investigate differences between traditional (printed) research articles, visual essays, and video essays. We have found examples of all types of interaction in the investigated texts. The main overall results of the analyses are (cf. Maier & Engberg, 2014, p. 140):

- While we find that in traditional RAs, multimodal interaction between text and other modes is present mainly in the communication of methods, in the other two genres, the interaction is mainly present in the dissemination of research results.
- In video essays, predominantly, relations of complementarity are intensified in the form of multiple layers of relations between the same verbal and visual elements, creating the possibility of multiple interpretations, which may be detrimental to the communication of specific knowledge. However, such relations also create the possibility of communicating other meanings alongside the central academic knowledge to be disseminated through the document.
- Similarly, visual essays and video essays include additional textual explanations in order to achieve precision and communicative clarity that may be lost through the more intense complementary interaction between modes.

In the academic video essays:

> it is not only the culmination of choices made across semiotic resources in their interaction with other resources that makes meaning, but also the temporal and spatial unfolding of those choices. (O'Halloran, 2004, p. 109)

Therefore, the inclusion of documents dominated by the image flow (e.g., video essays) opens up further possibilities for the interaction of modes that are oriented towards making supplementary meanings. Temporal order and spatial positioning of the presentation of the elements emerge as a supplementary source of meaning.

Publisher-Induced Challenges: *Article of the Future* Project

As already mentioned, publishing houses such as, for example, Elsevier, are also in the process of renewal, proposing new online article formats "to allow for an optimal exchange of formal scientific research between scientists" and "for excellent on-line readability and seamless navigation" (Elsevier, 2015a, para. 1). The prototypes have several display modes: article only, article and outline, article and side view, and full view (both navigation outline and interactive sidebar). They have been designed in order to make it "easier for the users to focus on the article and spend more time reading it on-screen" (Elsevier, 2015b, para. 4).

Each prototype has been designed with a three pane layout:

- A navigation pane in which a table of contents is provided with clickable section headers and thumbnails of images and tables
- A middle pane with the original article which includes hyperlinked access to information about authors, interactive graphs, tables, plates and Google maps
- A right pane where the user can acquire additional information (e.g., the photo, e-mail address and mailing address of the author(s)) and view other features (e.g., figures, references, flowcharts, etc.) that can also be accessed from the other two panes.

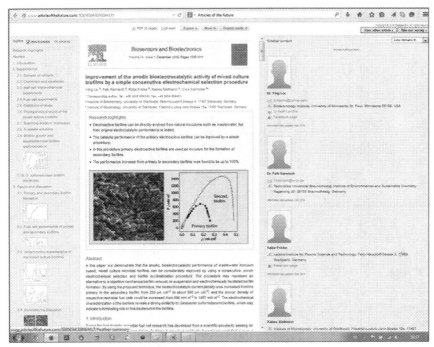

Figure 1. Screen shot of the three pane layout.

The dynamic design allows the users of the prototypes to interact with the content of an article with the assistance of the complex network of hyperlinking and action opportunities. As mentioned above, a user of an article can choose between several display types that resemiotize knowledge to a higher or lesser degree: automatic, article only (with embedded hyperlinks), article and outline, article and sidebar. Even the .pdf version of the article has navigation elements because the left side of the screen displays the hyperlinked bookmarks through which the user can access specific parts of the file. In this context, the reading mode[4] is combined with the navigation mode[5] in all three panes and display modes of the prototypes through hyperlinks.

The prototypes incorporate, apart from the text of the article, interactive tables, plates, and (experimental flow) charts that support the acquisition of *new knowledge.* For example, the interactive affordances existing in interactive and experimental flow charts allow for the access of *new supplementary knowledge* by:

- clicking on hyperlinks, which results in new, complementary information being displayed, so that *new supplementary knowledge* is built in simple interactive charts
- actively modifying the already given information by manipulating elements of the experimental flow charts

Each interactive figure changes color when the viewing mode is changed. The content of the chart can be enriched by the user according to various coordinates. For example, in the article presented in Figure 1, the user can change the dimensions of various axes by clicking a button in Figure 2 of the article, and the curves will then change as well. Consequently, new supplementary knowledge is made available.

Furthermore, the access to *new supplementary knowledge* is facilitated in the reference list through hyperlinking the prototype article to the full texts of the cited articles. As a consequence, users may access the articles cited in the prototype article, which makes the research process that informs the prototype article more transparent, or, as Goldberg (2010) indicates, "the complexities of multi-mediating production encourage the revelation of distributed expertise in interaction, of co-making and interdependence" (p. 381).

As already stated, apart from offering *new supplementary* or *presupposed knowledge*, hyperlinking allows the users to access the same information in different formats (e.g., full document, .pdf, PowerPoint, other windows). The varying formats repeat the same information without enhancing it. Repetition is also manifested in some of the hyperlinking strategies because the same information can be accessed by hyperlinking from various places of the three panes. Several of the possible back and forth reading paths accessible through scrolling and hyperlinking both in the vertical and horizontal planes have the same repetitive function. Still images hyperlinked to accompanying texts that are repeated below the images are also an example of building *repeated knowledge*. Videos in which the authors ("talking heads") orally present their research illustrate a similar resemiotisation process through which more or less the same knowledge is communicated. However, the videos also include *types of new knowledge*, not connected to the *core knowledge* communicated in the article, such as what the researchers look like, what the sound of their voices is, and what their facial expressions are. Having eye contact with the researchers while they explain how they obtained their research results might have a persuasive effect, but according to our interpretation, it does not contribute to enhancing the amount of *core knowledge* communicated through the other modes.

In addition, if "visual and multimodal messages are created according to how an imaginary or hypothetical recipient would perceive the material" (Holsanova, 2014, p. 333), then the identity of the users of these videos appears rather problematic. Because of this *other type of new knowledge* communicated in the "talking heads" videos, the videos might not address any particular audience because according to our impression and to our students' reactions, neither researchers nor teachers or students appear to be interested in looking at close-ups or medium shots of researchers talking about their research presented in the articles already displayed in various formats. The visual and aural information seems to have no interest either for researchers, teachers or students on the same homepage.

It should be noted here that, although we have tried to categorize certain types of knowledge that are made available due to the interactive means, the boundaries of these types of knowledge are not clear-cut because they may partially overlap. For example, the "talking heads" videos communicate multimodally both *repeated knowledge* (as they repeat what is already mentioned in the text of the article) and a new type of knowledge, the *counterproductive knowledge* (related to the researchers' physical appearance). We consider this knowledge to be counterproductive because it might hinder the user to concentrate on the core knowledge that is communicated by the researchers.

Conclusions

In this chapter, we have focused on some aspects of academic knowledge communication related to new generic configurations that are intended to challenge the predominance of the written text in the creation, representation, and dissemination of academic knowledge. We have attempted to map some gains and losses in the increasingly multimodal representations of knowledge and "to provide means of navigating between the Scylla of nostalgia and pessimism and the Charybdis of unwarranted optimism" (Kress, 2005, p. 6).

The asymmetries between several types of knowledge possessed by participants in academic knowledge communications (e.g., authors, professional media experts, users, peer reviewers) have to be reconciled: the researchers' domain-specific knowledge and their knowledge of media usage on one side, and the professional media experts' knowledge of media usage and their knowledge of the researchers' domain-specific knowledge on the other side. Furthermore, in the case of academic visual essays and academic video essays, the asymmetries that have to be reconciled are those between the researchers' domain-specific knowledge and their knowledge of media usage necessary for communicating their domain-specific knowledge. The problems that might appear in these reconciliation processes are bound to have a series of repercussions. Some of them became visible in our analytical work.

In his explorations of the passage from page to screen in communication, Kress (2005) found that because of the multiple reading paths offered by the screen, the reader may become an author too and then, "when everyone can be an author authority is severely challenged" (p. 19). In the case of the academic visual essays and the academic video essays, the authority is challenged by the author's level of expertise necessary to design the new generic configurations, and by the user's and reviewer's levels of expertise necessary to decipher them properly in order to gain the anticipated core knowledge. Taking into consideration the prototype articles, we argue authority is also challenged by the professional media experts who are in the position to influence the representation of the domain-specific knowledge created by researchers.

In the case of the prototype research articles, the intensified use of various processes of resemiotisation (e.g., from written text to speech and gesture) made possible by the usage of several (embedded) media, fosters the appearance of *redundant knowledge*. The result of our analysis is that, due to repeated instances of *redundant knowledge* communication, the primary purpose of the prototype articles, that is, to build and present new domain-specific knowledge, is accompanied by a secondary purpose, namely, an instructive one. In teaching and learning contexts, redundancy may have the purpose of instilling the information in the minds of the multiliterate users. Otherwise, we may claim that this redundancy has a rather limited value in research contexts. So, the usage of the prototype articles for other purposes than disseminating research work is made possible as the prototype article design facilitates teaching activities. This diversification of purposes contributes to the appearance of two other phenomena. First, it provokes a blurring of boundaries in the author's voice from researcher to teacher. Second, it raises the question of the intended target group as it becomes rather uncertain which elements are meant to address the research community and which ones are to be used by students.

The access to several layout displays and media influences the peer-reviewing process. Although definitely enriching in those cases wherein the usage of several media succeeds in facilitating *new core knowledge*—as it has been shown in our analytical findings—this access can undermine an objective peer-review process. First of all, the reviewers' competence in understanding and evaluating multimodal documents is supposed to match the researchers' competence in communicating academic knowledge across modes and media. If this is not the case, the objectivity of the reviewing process might be jeopardized not necessarily or not only because of the reviewers' domain-specific knowledge (as it might happen in traditional academic genre contexts), but also because of the reviewers' expertise in the using media. This also implies the need for a common framework of evaluation. As Jakubowicz and Van Leeuwen (2010) have stressed, because of the appearance of multimedia production, the academic publishing world is confronted with a series of issues, including "the development of an agreed, shared, comprehensible and applicable set of criteria" for the peer review of digital academic publication (p. 362). As far as knowledge communication through moving images is concerned, Pasquali (2007) makes it clear that "the general acceptability of video methods in scientific journals will depend on the quality of the peer-review process for video submissions" (p. 715). Recently, Goldberg (2010), Jakubowicz and Van Leeuwen (2010) have succeeded in developing "a framework for assessing the scholarly quality of multi-media digital production" (p. 380) for two versions of an academic publication. However, there still is a need for more work to be done in the assessment field in order to cover the wide range of such scholarly production. Jakubowicz (2009) also notes that "older mentors have no experience in innovatory multimedia research and publishing and are unable to provide role models" (p. 362) to younger researchers who might try to communicate academic knowledge across semiotic modes and media. Further, the peer-review process might also be influenced by the reluctance to change the constellation of academic genres and dissemination possibilities, namely by a "'shark-net' of resistance to innovation" (Jakubowicz, 2009, p. 362).

The relevance of the analytical work presented in this chapter lies in the fact that a growing range of new communicative competencies is already expected from researchers both as authors and peer reviewers. In the course of their academic careers all researchers will be (and already are) expected to become multiliterate when it comes to developing, presenting, and evaluating academic knowledge communicated in new generic configurations across different modes and media. All modern researchers need to be aware of and prepared for the challenges and the possibilities of the different modes and media in order to improve their communicative efficiency and enhance professional visibility.

References

Alter, N. M. (2003). Memory essays. In U. Biemann (Ed.), *Stuff it: The video essay in the digital age* (pp. 12-13). Zurich: Edition Voldemeer.

Askehave, I., & Nielsen, A. E. (2005). Digital genres: A challenge to traditional genre theory. *Information Technology & People, 18*(2), 120-141.

Bateman, J. A. (2008). *Multimodality and genre: A foundation for the systematic analysis of multimodal documents.* London: Palgrave Macmillan.

Bateman, J. A. (2009). Discourse across semiotic modes. In J. Renkema (Ed.), *Discourse, of course: An overview of research in discourse studies* (pp. 55–66). Amsterdam: John Benjamins.

Berkenkotter, C., & Huckin, T. N. (1995). *Genre knowledge in disciplinary communication: Cognition, culture, power.* Hillsdale, NJ: Lawrence Erlbaum.

Bolter, D. & Grusin, R. (2002). *Remediation: Understanding new media.* Cambridge: The MIT Press.

Elsevier. (2015a). *Article of the Future.* Retrieved from http://www.articleofthefuture.com/

Elsevier. (2015b). *Guiding Principles of Design.* Retrieved from http://www.articleofthefuture.com/

Goldberg, D. T. (2010). Variations on 'The Goldberg Variations': Comments on Jakubowicz and Van Leeuwen. *Discourse & Communication, 4*(4), 379-381.

Hiipalla, T. (2014). Multimodal genre analysis. In S. Norris & C. D. Maier (Eds.), *Interactions, images and texts: A reader in multimodality* (pp. 111-123). Boston, MA: Mouton de Gruyter.

Hasan, R. (1977). Text in the Systemic Functional Model. In W. Dressler (Ed.), *Current Trends in Text Linguistics* (pp. 228-246). Berlin: Walter de Gruyter.

Holsanova, J. (2014). In the eye of the beholder: Visual communication from a recipient perspective. In D. Machin (Ed.), *Visual Communication* (pp. 331-356). Berlin: Mouton de Gruyter.

Hughes, J., & Tolley, S. (2010). Engaging students through new literacies: The good, bad and curriculum of visual essays. *English in Education, 44*, 5–26.

Iedema, R. (2003). Multimodality, resemiotization: Extending the analysis of discourse as multi-semiotic practice. *Visual Communication*, 2(1), 29-57.

Jacobsen, U. C. (2012). Knowledge asymmetries. A situated inquiry in three sites of professional communication. Unpublished PhD thesis. Aarhus University, Aarhus, Denmark.

Jakubowicz, A. (2009). Beyond the static text: Multimedia interactivity in academic journal publishing in the humanities and social sciences (not). In B. Cope & A. Phillips (Eds.), *The future of the academic journal* (pp. 361–376). Oxford: Chandos Publishing.

Jakubowicz, A., & Van Leeuwen, T. (2010). The Goldberg variations I: Assessing the academic quality of multidimensional linear texts and their re-emergence in multimedia publications. *Discourse & Communication*, 4(4), 361-378.

Jewitt, C. (2014). Multimodal approaches. In S. Norris & C. D. Maier (Eds.), *Interactions, images and texts: A reader in multimodality* (pp. 127-136). Boston, MA: Mouton de Gruyter.

Kastberg, P. (2007). Knowledge communication: The emergence of a third order discipline. In C. Villiger & H. Gerzymisch-Arbogast (Eds.), *Kommunikation in Bewegung: Multimedialer und multilingualer Wissenstransfer in der Experten-Laien-Kommunikation. Festschrift für Annely Rothkegel* [Communication in motion: Multimedial and multilingual knowledge transfer in expert-lay communication. Festschrift for Annely Rothkegel]. (pp. 7-24). Berlin: Lang.

Kress, G. (2005). Gains and losses: New forms of texts, knowledge, and learning. *Computers and Composition*, 22, 5–22.

Kress, G. (2010): *Multimodality: A Social Semiotic Approach to Contemporary Communication*. London: Routledge

Kress, G., & Jewitt, C. (2000). *Multimodal literacy*. New York: Peter Lang.

Liu, Y., Harnisch, F., Fricke, K., Sietmann, R. & Schröder U. (2008) Improvement of the anodic bioelectrocatalytic activity of mixed culture biofilms by a simple consecutive electrochemical selection procedure. *Biosensors and Bioelectronics, 24* (1), 1006-1011.

Maier, C. D., & Engberg, J. (2013). Tendencies in the multimodal evolution of narrator's types and roles in research genres. In M. Gotti & C. Sancho Guinda (Eds.), *Narratives in academic and professional genres* (pp. 149-175). Bern: Peter Lang.

Maier, C. D., & Engberg, J. (2014). Tendencies of multimodal gradations in academic genres network. In J. Engberg, C. D. Maier & O. Togeby

(Eds.), *Genre: Encounters between literature, knowledge and developing communicative conventions.* Tübingen: Narr Francke Attempto Verlag.

Martinec, R., & Salway, A. (2005). A system of text-image relations in new (and old) media. *Visual Communication, 4* (3), 337n.

Miller, C. (1984). Genre as social action. *Quarterly Journal of Speech, 70,* 151-167.

Norris, S., & Maier, C. D. (2014a). Conclusions. In S. Norris & C. D. Maier (Eds.), *Interactions, images and texts: A reader in multimodality* (pp. 381-382). Boston, MA: Mouton de Gruyter.

Norris, S., & Maier, C. D. (2014b). Introduction. In S. Norris & C. D. Maier (Eds.), *Interactions, images and texts: A reader in multimodality* (pp. 1-3). Boston, MA: Mouton de Gruyter.

O'Halloran, K. L. (2004). Visual semiosis in film. In K. L. O'Halloran (Ed.), *Multimodal discourse analysis: Systemic functional perspectives* (pp. 109-130). London, UK: Continuum.

Paltridge, B. (1997). *Genre, Frames and Writing in Research Settings.* Amsterdam and Philadelphia: John Benjamins.

Pasquali, M. (2007). Video in science—Protocol videos: The implications for research and society. *EMBO reports, 8*(8), 712-716.

Scardamalia, M., & Bereiter, C. (1987). Knowledge telling and knowledge transforming in written composition. In S. Rosenberg (Ed.), *Advances in applied psycholinguistics* (pp. 142-175). Cambridge: Cambridge University Press.

Scardamalia, M., & Bereiter, C. (2006). Knowledge building: Theory, pedagogy, and technology. In R. K. Sawyer (Ed.), *Cambridge handbook of the learning sciences* (pp. 97-118). New York: Cambridge University Press.

Unsworth, L. (2006). Towards a metalanguage for multiliteracies education: Describing the meaning making resources of language-image interaction. *English Teaching: Language and Critique, 5*(1), 55–76.

Van Leeuwen, T. (2005). *Introducing social semiotics.* London: Routledge.

EndNotes

[1] Pasquali (2007) asserts that "during the early twentieth century, the technological development of 'moving images' was driven more by scientific interests than commercial or artistic ones" (p. 712).

[2] See the next section of the chapter for more details on the project.

[3] See Jacobsen (2012) for an in-depth analysis of the creation of knowledge asymmetries in three concrete sites.

[4] "The 'reading mode' leaves the user in a traditional reader position with sequential reading as the guiding principle (similar to traditional reading, no matter whether the actual reading is strictly linear or not)" (Askehave & Nielsen, 2005, p. 127).

[5] "The 'navigating mode' allows the reader to navigate the site and actively construct his/her own reading path" (Askehave & Nielsen, 2005, p. 127).

Chapter 11

Genre Profiles as Intermediate Analytical Level for Cultural Genre Analysis

Martin Luginbühl

University of Neuchâtel (Switzerland)

Most genre scholars assume that there is an interrelationship between cultural change and genre change. However, in many diachronic or comparative studies this relationship is presented in a very simplistic way: changes or, in the case of comparative studies, differences in the micro level of genres (genre features) are related directly to the macro level of the national, and sometimes even global, culture. Such linking of genre and culture occurs, on the one hand, due to a problematic conceptualization of culture (cf. Humboldt, 1836/1963 and Herder, 1772/1985), and, on the other hand, due to the lack of an intermediate analytical level between the micro level of genre features and macro level of culture. In the first section of this chapter, I briefly discuss how more recent trends in genre studies and the corresponding field of German studies, *Textlinguistik*[1], conceptualize culture. In the following sections, I introduce the concept of *genre profiles*, an intermediate analytical level for genre analysis consisting of genre repertoires, genre frequency, and genre clusters. Further, I illustrate my theoretical considerations by presenting a comparative analysis of the American "CBS Evening News" and the Swiss "Tagesschau" (cf. Luginbühl, 2014). My analysis demonstrates how genre profiles help to understand (journalistic) culture and genre history.

Genre and Culture

Genre change became the focus of genre studies in 1990s (e.g., Bazerman, 1994; Bendel, 1998; Berkenkotter & Huckin, 1995; Fleskes, 1996; Nickl, 2000; Warnke, 1996). These studies often illustrate how genre change is related to many different contextual factors such as community goals or membership, communicative purposes or general discursive practices. More recent studies (e.g., Devitt, 2004, Bawarshi & Reiff, 2010, Gansel, 2011) demonstrate how genre change reflects changes in cultural, situational, and generic contexts. For example, comparative studies of TV news shows (Bourdon, 2008; Hallin & Mancini, 2004) point at various factors related to genre change, such as the differences in media systems and technology, media markets, target audiences, political systems, and so on. In the field of contrastive textology (e.g., Hartmann, 1980; Spillner, 1981), however, it is still quite common to focus on the textual features of genres alone, which then—sometimes rather recklessly—are related to the cultural change or cultural differences at a macro level (e.g., national differences). The approach to genre studies, which still remains widespread, involves comparing textual features of texts belonging to a genre (e.g., obituaries) and relating the differences in these features to the differences in either national or linguistic cultures (see Hauser & Luginbühl, 2012).

The problem with this approach is that the scholars who rely on it often overgeneralize findings of their studies, wherein they often analyze one genre used in two national/linguistic/geographical contexts and attribute differences in the genre and its use to the different mentalities of the inhabitants of these two contexts/ countries (e.g. de Zarobe 2008; Landbeck, 1991; Sandahl, 2008; Schmitt, 2008). These scholars also tend to neglect broader generic contexts by only looking at single genres. But above all, researchers who rely on this approach tend to consider genres as characterized solely by textual features without looking at the situational context. According to Devitt (2009), this approach results in "formalism" (p. 28), which leads to the view of genres as categories of texts characterized by common textual features. If researchers relate these textual features to national cultures, then cultures become conceptualized in a homogeneous and rather static way, similarly to how they are conceived by Herder (1772/1985) or Humboldt

(1836/1963) (cf. Luginbühl, 2014). But of course genre is social action (Miller, 1984) constituted by social practices within a certain culture. Genres rely on social and communicative needs, which are changing and which differ between different communities of practice (Wenger, 1998). As such, they facilitate communication by providing reliable, yet flexible patterns that respond to a communicative need (cf. Devitt, 2004, p. 116; Swales, 1990). Genres also construct recurring situations (Bawarshi, 2000) by structuring verbal interaction and, thus, structuring social reality.

If we understand culture as a set of norms and values of a community (be it a small community like the editorial staff of a TV news show, or a large community like an entire nation), genres with their form, content, and pragmatic function have an important cultural function. In order to negotiate and balance common norms and values, these norms and values must be expressed in a recognizable way (Linke, 2011). In other words, genres are materialized through textual patterns and become recognizable as both cultural artifacts and a symbolic dimension of human action (Barth, 1989; Geertz, 1973; Goodenough, 1964). Culture viewed from this perspective is dynamic (the process of balancing never comes to an end), heterogeneous (the norms and values can be conflicting within and between communities), and semiotically based (the norms and values have to be semiotically materialized). Genre as social and symbolic action thus always serves the process of communitarization.[2] Therefore, culture can be understood as established, stabilized, and yet changing through communicative exchanges, with genres, as habitualized forms of communication, playing an important role. To analyze genres culturally means to look at the overall genre form—not just lexis, grammar, and rhetorical patterns—but everything that can be shaped and has a potential to carry meanings beyond the text, that is, narratives, functions, and situations created by a genre, its material and multimodal aspects (images, colors, sounds), and so on. All these forms can be understood as stylistic forms in a broad way (cf. Sandig, 2006); all of them are able to realize meanings beyond textual propositions as "an aspect of substance on a higher level" (Miller, 1984, p. 160) or a form of "secondary significance" (Linke, 2011, p. 30).[3] As these stylistic choices are not mandatory, they can be understood as cultural "positionings," or as "meaning made visible" (Fix, 2011, p.

72). As a reflection of the actions of a community, stylistic patterns of genre can, thus, be interpreted from the perspective of culture (cf. Devitt, 2009). In the case of TV news genres, similar content is often presented with the intention to inform (and to entertain), however, the forms of presentation may significantly differ between different shows, nations, languages, and the time of production (cf. Luginbühl, 2014). The differences in form, thus, can be related to different (journalistic) cultures, but only when interpreted in their context.

Genre Profiles

Genre Profiles as Intermediate Analytical Level

The relation between genre and cultural change can be understood by developing an analytic meso level between the micro level of a single genre style and the macro level of cultural change. The concept of *genre profiles* serves as an intermediate level, allowing one to both describe the contouring of an entire genre network while also focusing on the genre style, and taking into account a broader empirical basis than just a single genre. Notably, this intermediate level allows one to contextualize changes in specific genres and draw conclusions about the significance of these genres within the analyzed network, which is essential for understanding their cultural value.

Genres can be viewed at different levels of generalization, from an entire TV news show to more specific genres and, further, genres on a very specific individual level. For the analysis presented in this chapter, I will not talk of entire TV news shows as one genre, but rather as a "macro genre" (Bhatia, 2004, p. 57) that entails different more specific genres (like lead-ins, packages, interviews etc.). These genres form different ethno-categories for the journalists producing them (cf. Luginbühl & Perrin, 2011) and these genres have quite distinguishable, different forms and often comprise different rhetorical actions and recontexualize different communicative situations.

The view that genres are in a systematic relationship with each other and do not exist individually or independently is not new and has been acknowledged by other genre studies scholars, who have proposed their own concepts of "inter-genre-ality" (Devitt, 2009, p.

44). Each of these concepts focuses on a different aspect of genre relations: "genre sets" (Devitt, 1991, p. 339) are used to describe sets of genres produced by a particular professional group; "genre systems" (Bazerman, 1994, p. 97) refer to genres interacting in specific settings (like the genre sets of people working together); "genre colonies" (Bhatia, 2004, p. 29) are group genres with similar functions, and "disciplinary genres" (p. 54-55) are genres of a particular discipline or professional domain. Similar concepts have been developed in the German Textlinguistik to describe functional, situational, formal, and topical relations between genres: "genre intertextuality" (Klein, 2000, p. 34) or "genre networks" (Adamzik, 2001, 2004, p. 94-106). Recently, Adamzik (2011) introduced the term "genre field" to refer to a set of topically or functionally interchangeable genres and "genre chains" (Swales, 2004, p. 18). In this view, genre fields and chains form "genre networks" (Adamzik, 2001, p. 27) within genre systems and within interaction systems. Genres are linked to other genres, including genres that precede or follow them in a production process (cf. Bakhtin, 1986), that co-occur within "super- or macro genres" (Bhatia, 2004, p. 57), share similar functions, address similar topics, and are used in similar situations. The significance and value of genres depend on the relations among them and, thus, on the *genre profile* of a community. As these profiles are collectively established, passed on or changed, they become cultural artifacts like the genres themselves. To understand the cultural status of genres, it is not sufficient to analyze single (specific) genres. We need to take into account more complex genres, keeping in mind their sub genres, and complex genre profiles. In other words, we first have to analyze single genres and then groups of genres. A genre profile analysis provides an empirical and comprehensible way to understand genres within a "macro genre" and to analyze the contours of macro genres from different angles.

Analysis of TV News Genre Profiles

This section uses the concept of genre profiles to analyze the macro genre of TV news shows. The analysis (cf. Luginbühl, 2014) is comparative in two ways. First, it compares two different shows, the American "CBS Evening News" and the Swiss "Tagesschau." Second, it compares different stages of these shows from their beginning until

2013. Conducting a synchronic analysis from both comparative and diachronic perspectives helps to understand genres and, especially, observe changes in genres, if any. While genre change has been investigated in many studies (e.g., Bazerman, 1994; Bendel, 1998; Berkenkotter & Huckin, 1995; Berkenkotter & Luginbühl, in press; Campbell & Jamieson, 1990; Fleskes, 1996; Warnke, 1996; Yates, 1989), the intermediate analytical level of genre change has been underexplored (see Adamzik, 2010, p. 31).

The following results are based on the analysis of 17 weeks of TV news; including, one week per decade analyzed for every show, starting with the first archived weeks in the 1950s for "Tagesschau" and in the 1960s for the "CBS Evening News." In decades that included important show format changes (1980s, 1990s), two weeks were analyzed (see Luginbühl, 2014).

Genre Repertoires

The term "repertoire" was originally introduced by Bakhtin (1986, p. 60) and subsequently used by Orlikowski and Yates (1994). Devitt (2004) defines repertoire as a "set of genres that a group owns, acting through which a group achieves all of its purposes, not just those connected to a particular activity" (p. 57). We can analyze the repertoires within single macro genres. This will show what stylistic (not mandatory) choices a community (in our case, the editorial staff of a TV news show) makes at a certain point of time. Comparing the genre repertoires also allows one to trace genre genesis and genre death (cf. Miller, 1984).

In order to analyze genre repertoires, genres must be defined as accurately as possible, which is often difficult given their dynamic character and their ability to bend and mix. In the case of TV news, most genres report on varied content and serve similar functions. I classified the genres first by looking at the modes used and the communicative situation established. For example, I examined whether there was a combination of the anchors voice with news footage and whether the narrator was the animator (Goffman 1981, p. 226) or author. In doing so, I considered the journalist's ethnocategories (cf. Luginbühl & Perrin, 2011). Analyzing the aforementioned corpus, I identified two genre repertoires (see Table 1 for a slightly simplified overview).

Table 1

News repertoires of the "CBS Evening News" and the "Tagesschau"

Genre	CBS Evening News	Tagesschau
Headlines	*realized*	*realized*
Greeting / Goodbye	*realized*	*realized*
Lead-In and Lead-Out	*realized*	*realized*
Anchor Item *Story read by anchor on camera*	*realized*	*realized*
Anchor Voice Over *Anchor item fading to news footage with anchor speaking off camera*	*realized*	*realized*
"Sprechermeldung" [newsreader item] *Story read by a newsreader*	NOT REALIZED	*realized*
Film Item *news footage with voice over by anchor or newsreader*	*realized*	*realized*
Package *story produced and told by a correspondent, who is often visible on scene; usually includes sound bites*	*realized*	*realized*
Statement	*realized*	*realized*
Interview	*realized*	*realized*
Commentary	*realized*	*realized*
Stand Up *story told by a correspondent on camera*	*realized*	NOT REALIZED

Both shows utilize a small genre repertoire. Given that TV news shows have to be produced on a daily basis, the fact that journalists rely on a small repertoire of genres is not surprising. That said, each show has a genre that is not realized in the other: the "Stand Up" in the CBS Evening News and the "Sprechermeldung" (newsreader item) in the Swiss "Tagesschau." The "Stand Up" is a story with a correspondent on screen telling a story (usually at the scene of the event). This genre sees the person telling you the story at the scene of the event, demonstrating her/his closeness to the event. It is a typical way of representing events in the "CBS Evening News."

The "Sprechermeldung" is a news story read by a newsreader in an extremely reserved and distanced way. This detached "proclaiming" of a seemingly objective truth out there was typical of realized genres in the Swiss "Tagesschau" until the early 1980s. These two genres, the "Stand Up" and the "Sprechermeldung," although not realized very often, point at two very different ways of telling news stories: trustworthiness through closeness versus trustworthiness through distance. Examining the (changing) frequencies of genre occurrence (genre frequencies) in the next section allows me to put these initial findings into perspective. Further, I explore crucial differences in the journalistic cultures of the two shows.

Genre Frequencies

While a (synchronic) view of genre repertoires reflects differences and parallels that can be interpreted culturally, it is important to examine the genre frequencies diachronically to better understand the way genres change through time. To accomplish this, I calculated genre frequencies, measured not in absolute numbers but in percentages of the entire show's duration. Of course, a low frequency is not in all cases a sign of irrelevance: greetings and goodbyes are mostly short and thus have in my counting a low frequency, but are nevertheless important when it comes to the journalist's relationship to the audience. That said, a high frequency indicates an important genre, while growing or shrinking frequencies are a sign of changing genre significances. As genres are related to a certain way of reporting an event and, thus, of depicting the world, changes in genre frequencies can be related to changes in journalistic cultures. The genre frequencies characteristic of the Swiss "Tagesschau" can be seen in Figure 1. In this figure, headlines, greetings, goodbyes as well as lead-in and lead-outs are summarized as "news presentations."

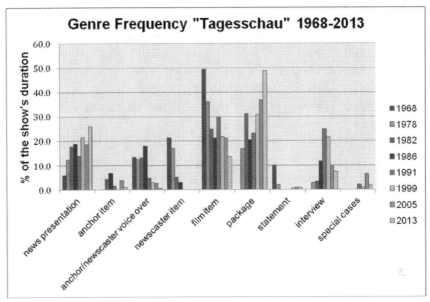

Figure 1. Genre frequency in "Tagesschau," 1968-2013 (genre names presented in Table 1).

Not only can we see that genre frequencies changed significantly during the last six decades in the Swiss "Tagesschau," we can also observe trends in the frequency changes of most genres. It appears that expanding or emerging genres do so at the cost of certain, but not all, other genres, which then become peripheral (as in the case of newsreader items or the anchor voice overs). The package is not realized at all in the 1960s, but becomes pivotal over time (as evidenced by the frequency of nearly 50% in 2013). Similarly, news presentations, which did not exist in 1958, shift from peripheral to pivotal. The trends suggest a changing audience orientation.

As we can see from Figure 1, the growing frequencies of packages and news presentations coincide with a decrease in film items, newscaster items (which disappeared entirely), statements (which re-appear as sound bites in the packages), and anchor/newscaster voice-overs. Further, film items and anchor voice overs have been replaced by packages in the Swiss "Tagesschau," which is worth noting given that the package is a reporting genre and not a presenting one like the lead-in. This change in the form of reporting may be related to different world representations.

In the film items, similarly to the newsreader items mentioned above, facts are declared in a distanced way, mostly following the inverted pyramid style; the newsreader typically remains invisible and anonymous (appearing as a "voice out of nowhere"); the camera work is unremarkable, and there is no obvious perspective of the reporting individual. Film items and newsreader items made up more than 50% of the show's content until the late 1970s. This is noteworthy as film items and newsreader items are typically realizing what could be called, following Hanitzsch (2007), totalitarian objectivism (p. 376), which is a form of reporting known for suggesting that a static and absolute truth is "out there," "independent of the existence of any perceiver" (p. 376). In the totalitarian objectivism reporting, the story itself gives the impression of depicting an unmediated replication of reality. The package, on the other hand, is known for offering a very different representation of the reported events. While film items and newsreader items realize totalitarian objectivism, packages favour what could be called a subjectivist objectivity (Hanitzsch, 2007, p. 376). A package is (at least seemingly) produced by a correspondent, who typically appears at the scene of the reported event. While film items hide their status as crafted products, the packages tend to mark it. Packages are known for having a named and mostly visible correspondent, and for offering a representation of the world that is selectively influenced by the professional interpretation of the journalist. Packages also emphasize the impermanence of the information, acknowledge that it can change with further investigation into the event. Most packages take the form of "donuts" featuring the correspondent live at the scene at the beginning and the end and they also tend to serve as a more dramatic and emotional way of telling stories. In the package, truth appears to be something dynamic and fluid.

Analyzing the genre frequency of the Swiss "Tagesschau" we can observe an important change in the late 1970s and early 1980s. This change is linked to the changes in the show's vision that were publicly acknowledged in 1980 when an entirely new format with an anchor (instead of a newsreader) was introduced. This approach aimed at a more self-reflexive reporting and a closer relation to the audience.

Figure 2 presents the genre frequencies for the "CBS Evening News." As can be observed from the figure, not only are the genre frequencies different, there are also considerably fewer changes over time compared to the Swiss "Tagesschau."

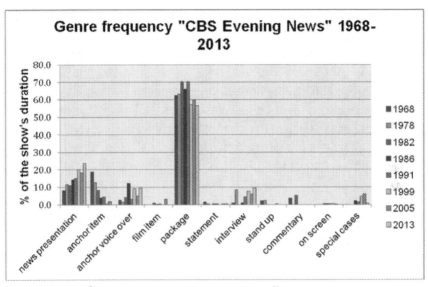

Figure 2. Genre frequency in "CBS Evening News," 1968-2013.

In the "CBS Evening News," the package, with its aforementioned subjectivist objectivity, was the dominant genre since at least the 1960s.[4] Similarly to the Swiss "Tagesschau," changes in news presentations and anchor items can also be found in the "CBS Evening News:" news presentations became more important over time, while the significance of anchor items declined. Compared to the Swiss "Tagesschau," the "CBS Evening News" has a very different genre profile (see Figures 1 and 2). The paradigm change that occurred in the Swiss "Tagesschau" has obviously never occurred in the "CBS Evening News."

A lack of comparative data quite often leads to overgeneralizations in TV news studies as observations of one show are generalized for all shows in a country, a linguistic region or even all TV news shows worldwide (e.g. Landbeck, 1991; Montgomery, 2007; Thussu, 2007). However, my findings presented above demonstrate that genre profiles may evolve very differently in different contexts.

These findings indicate how changes of single genres are interrelated to one another, and can be related to the meaning of the genre form.

Genre Linkings

As mentioned above, genres are structured in genre networks. There are genres with similar functions (like different reporting genres) or genres that tend to build expectable chains (like lead-ins and packages). Intertextual relations between genres can be based on the level of form, function or content. Further, intertextual relations appear in diachronic relations as well as in synchronic and typological ones (Luginbühl et al, 2002, p. 19-25). These intertextual relations characterize genre profiles in addition to repertoires and frequencies. I will illustrate this by analyzing conventionalized genre chains, which I call *genre linkings*. In the analyzed corpus two different kinds of linkings can be found: sequences with a fixed order and sequences with a half-fixed order. An example of a sequence with a fixed order, or a *sequential cluster*, is the sequence of [lead-in – package – interview with correspondent]. An example of a sequence with a half-fixed order, or *serial cluster*, which has more flexibility in the order of sequence, is the sequence of [lead-in – package – anchor item – anchor voice over – anchor item – lead-out]. Examining these clusters allows one to characterize different genre profiles and understand the cultural norms and values they rely upon (Püschel, 1992).

Sequential clusters start to occur more often as an intermediate level of genre organization within the macro genre of TV news shows, leading to a sequentialization of news coverage. In the "CBS Evening News" in 1949 (which did not feature any packages at that time), the film items were broadcast without lead-ins. In 1968, the cluster [lead-in – package] was already sequentialized; no package was broadcast without a lead-in, which made the anchor (introduced in 1962) a seemingly all-knowing presenter of news. In the Swiss "Tagesschau," however, the film items, the crucial genre for the first three decades of the show, were not sequentialized until the 1980s. In the first format of the show in the 1950s, there was not a news presenter at all. Instead, the show featured film items, which were broadcast one after another, without lead-ins, and without newsreader items on different topics between them. The film items included voice-overs, which were read by an invisible, anonymous newsreader. The fact that film items did not have lead-ins enhanced the impression of an unmediated "showing" of "the truth" out there. The cluster [lead-in – film item] was only sequentialized in the late 1970s.

The aforementioned sequential cluster [lead-in – package – interview with correspondent] appeared in both shows in the 1990s, which suggests not only a change in the correspondent's role from reporter to expert, but also a move toward the "conversationalization" (Fairclough, 1995, p. 9) of news coverage. Further, it also suggests a changing orientation to the audience, as it offers viewers a more explicit structure of the coverage by replacing all-encompassing genres like the film item or the package with a stand-up at the end with several genres covering the same event, thus offering the audience different perspectives on an event.

Serial clusters with a half-fixed order only occur when an extended coverage is realized. Such serial clusters typically expand sequential clusters, reduplicating some elements or entire sequential clusters. For example, if a sequential cluster with a fixed order has the structure [lead-in – package – interview – lead-out], then an expanded sequential cluster may have the following structure [lead-in – package – package – interview – lead-out]. In both shows, serial clusters used to be organized following the inverted pyramid style, which meant introducing the most important information and answering the wh-questions in a newsreader or anchor item then elaborating them in more detail in film items or packages, and then offering a commentary. Both shows moved to replacing the inverted pyramid with a cluster of texts reporting an event from different perspectives and thus realizing a multi-perspective coverage. The "CBS Evening News" switched to this structure in the mid-1980s, and "Tagesschau" started to use this structure in the early 1990s.

Discussion

Journalistic Culture

In analyzing the genre profiles of the "CBS Evening News" and the Swiss "Tagesschau," this study sheds light on the semiotic meaning of the genres used in the two news shows and the significance of single genres within these profiles. I argue the genre forms of news coverage are meaningful for a community and important for establishing, passing on and changing norms and values. In turn, I argue that examining the genre profiles of news coverage can provide important information on norms and values of a culture. The main argument of this chapter is that the concept of genre profiles offers an intermediate level of analyzing the relationship between the level of the norms and values of a community and the level of the features of single genres. In turn, this analytical approach allows us to better understand the relationship between genre change and cultural change.

The analysis of genre profiles relies on the analysis of genre style. It is an empirical way to understand the *generic character*, or *contouring* of genres, within a macro genre like TV news shows. Looking at genre profiles allows us to empirically investigate the significance of a genre within a macro genre, which again can be a basis for cultural interpretation. For example, the development of a new genre within a macro genre (similar to the development of the package in the Swiss "Tagesschau" starting in the late 1970s), a long-term frequency change (similar to the decline of the frequency of occurrence of film items in the "Tagesschau" or the development of the genre of the interview in the "CBS Evening News") and changes in genre linkings are suggestive of cultural change. In other words, genre profile changes are indicative of cultural change. Similarly, genre profile stability also suggests cultural stability. As a part of my research, I related interpretations of the data and interpretations of crucial norms and values to the editorial staff, who were responsible for the genre choice and design thus establishing a journalistic culture.

Hanitzsch (2007) mentions different aspects of journalistic culture, including the market orientation, that is, constructing the public as consumers rather than as citizens (see p. 374), and the institutional role of journalists and objectivism. In my analysis, the genre profiles realized in "Tagesschau" (Figure 1) indicate a growing market orientation of the show. For example, the percentage of news-presenting genres (the headline, greeting and goodbye, lead-in and lead-out) starts at 0% in the 1950s and grows to 26% in 2013. At the same time, the packages with their "more intimate" way of telling stories (e.g., correspondents on scene, more dramatic news narratives) replace the film items with their distanced way of proclaiming a truth as the most important genre. This change around 1980 coincides with a public controversy about the form of the Swiss "Tagesschau" and several format changes between 1980 and 1985.

With the change in the percentage of film items and packages, there was also a change in the institutional role of journalists, who started as reserved, partly anonymous proclaimers of a seemingly absolute truth and then changed to active reporters in the news field and experts in various interviews. In analyzing objectivism, I noted a shift from totalitarian objectivity to subjectivist objectivity. That said, the change has been observed only partially as film items are still apparent in the Swiss "Tagesschau." Within the last decade, these trends have been somewhat thwarted as interviews have become less important, and correspondents are no longer seen on the scene of the event in most packages. It is also worth noting that in some cases the packages (e.g., the ones produced by male correspondents) are read by an anonymous female newsreader, which is a return to traditional totalitarian objectivity.

The genre profiles of the "CBS Evening News" (Figure 2) point to a different journalistic culture. In the "CBS Evening News," the market orientation was already high in the 1960s yet continued to intensify over time (with the package serving as a dominant genre, an anchor introducing every package, and an increasing occurrences of news presentations). Anchor items without news footage disappear entirely in the second decade of the 21st century. The role of correspondents as reporters becomes complemented by their role as experts, as they are now more often interviewed by the anchor as experts instead of reporting on the events as observers. The changing share of interviews reflects this new trend. In the "CBS Evening News," the reporter's objectivity was subjectivist from the very beginning.

While these changes and continuities in journalistic cultures are reflected in the genre forms, they can also be observed more clearly in the changes of genre profiles. For example, if we look at genre form and genre form alone, there are some genres, similar to the film item in the Swiss "Tagesschau," that did not undergo fundamental changes since the 1960s. Nevertheless, their significance has changed dramatically.

Genre profiles are influenced by the cultural norms and values of the editorial staff (norms and values regarding market orientation, the role of the journalists and objectivism). These norms and values depend, once again, on the interpretation of a very complex set of influencing factors (cf. Luginbühl, 2010). At the same time, as Devitt (2004) points out, these genre profiles themselves are connected to other factors. Journalistic culture not only influences and shapes genre profiles, the profiles themselves shape the culture (cf. Bawarshi, 2000).

Genre History

Journalistic culture, including the norms and values of an editorial staff, influence TV news genres. As I have demonstrated, journalistic culture can impact the form of single genres and entire genre profiles, including the choice of genres and the frequency of their realization and their alignment. If we agree that culture influences genre forms and profiles, the genres and genre profiles can be seen as materialized expressions of this culture. Both culture and cultural change are influenced by their context, and the existing genres and genre profiles are part of this context. But genres also affect culture, and cultural norms and values emerge (or are stabilized or changed) through the practices of genre and genre profile design.

Analyzing genre profiles allows us to examine the connection between news culture and new situations. We could say that the change in a news culture can be induced by a new situation (cf. Devitt, 2004). New situations arise when contextual factors (e.g., media markets, media systems, media technology, target audiences, political systems) change or are interpreted in new ways. A new situation can lead, for example, to the need to realize a new relationship with the audience, which will lead to new activities such as staging proximity to the audience or showing journalists as active/critical investigators. In order to fulfill these new functions, new or existing genres can be realized at a higher/lower frequency or aligned in new clusters. This can also lead to changes in macro genres, which, in turn, can lead to new situations in which, for example, some genres become interpreted as antiquated or modern.

The analysis of genre profiles allows us to relate, in a methodologically controlled way, the micro level of genre form to the macro level of cultural norms and values of a community. Genre profiles build an analytical meso level, allowing the researchers to describe and understand the value of a single genre within a bigger, complex and culturally situated network of genre relations. Analyzing genre profiles also allows us to determine the significance of single genres within macro genres. Genre forms and profiles are thus part of the aforementioned contextual factors, and part of a community's culture. As such, it is important to take into account an independent potency of culture in the dynamics of genre change: not only the factors of news production, market orientation, technical innovations or journalistic role models and so on are relevant to genre change, but also the existing genre profiles and, thus, cultural artefacts as well.

References

Adamzik, K. (2001). Die zukunft der text(sorten)linguistik. Textsortennetze, textsortenfelder, textsorten im verbund [The future of text(type)linguistics. Text type networks, text type fields, text types in conjunction]. In U. Fix, S. Habscheid & J. Klein (Eds.), *Zur kulturspezifik von textsorten* [*About Cultural Characteristics of Text Types*] (Vol. 3, pp. 15-30). Tübingen: Stauffenburg.

Adamzik, K. (2004). *Textlinguistik. Eine einführende darstellung* [*Text linguistics. An introduction*] (Vol. 40). Tübingen: Niemeyer.

Adamzik, K. (2010). Texte im kulturvergleich. Überlegungen zum problemfeld in zeiten von globalisierung und gesellschaftlicher parzellierung [Texts in cultural comparison. Reflections on the topic in times of globalization and social fragmentation]. In M. Luginbühl & S. Hauser (Eds.), *MedienTextKultur. Linguistische beiträge zur kontrastiven medienanalyse* [*MediaTextCulture. Linguistic contributions to contrastive media analysis*] (pp. 17-41). Landau: Verlag Empirische Pädagogik.

Adamzik, K. (2011). Textsortennetze [Text type networks]. In S. Habscheid (Ed.), *Textsorten, handlungsmuster, oberflächen. Linguistische typologien der kommunikation* [*Text types, action patterns, surfaces. Linguistic typologies of communication*] (pp. 367-386). Berlin, New York: de Gruyter.

Bakhtin, M. M. (1986). The problem of speech genres. In C. Emerson & M. Holquist (Eds.), *Speech genres and other late essays. Trans. Vern W. McGee* (pp. 60-102). Austin: University of Texas Press.

Barth, F. (1989). Analysis of culture in complex societies. *Ethnos, 54(3-4)*, 120-142.

Bawarshi, A. S., & Reiff, M. J. (2010). *Genre: An introduction to history, theory, research, and pedagogy*. West Lafayette, Ind.: Parlor Press.

Bazerman, C. (1994). Systems of genres and the enhancement of social intentions. In A. Freedman & P. Medway (Eds.), *Genre and new rhetoric* (pp. 79-101). London: Tayler & Francis.

Bendel, S. (1998). *Werbeanzeigen von 1622-1798. Entstehung und entwicklung einer textsorte* [*Advertisments from 1622-1798. Emergence and development of a text type*] (Vol. 193). Tübingen: Niemeyer.

Berkenkotter, C., & Huckin, T. N. (1995). *Genre knowledge in disciplinary communication - cognition/culture/power.* Hillsdale, NJ: Lawrence Erlbaum Ass.

Berkenkotter, C., & Luginbühl, M. (2014). Producing genres: Pattern variation and genre development. In E.-M. Jakobs & D. Perrin (Eds.), *Handbook of writing and text production* (Vol. 10) (pp. 285-304). Berlin, New York: Mouton de Gruyter.

Bhatia, V. K. (2004). *Worlds of written discourse. A genre-based view.* London, New York: continuum.

Bourdon, J. (2008). Imperialism, self-inflicted? On the Americanization of television in Europe. In W. Uricchio (Ed.), *We Europeans? Media, representation, identities* (pp. 93-108). London: Intellect.

Campbell, K. K., & Jamieson, K. H. (1990). *Deeds done in words. Presidential rhetoric and the genres of governance.* Chicago: University of Chicago Press.

Devitt, A. J. (1991). Intertextuality in tax accounting: Generic, referential, and functional. In C. Bazerman & J. G. Paradis (Eds.), *Textual dynamics of the professions: Historical and contemporary studies of writing in professional communities* (pp. 336-357). Madison WI: University of Wisconsin Press.

Devitt, A. J. (2004). *Writing genres.* Carbondale: Southern Illinois University Press.

Devitt, A. J. (2009). Re-fusing form in genre study. In J. Giltrow & D. Stein (Eds.), *Genres in the internet* (Vol. 188, pp. 27-47). Amsterdam: Benjamins.

Fairclough, N. (1995). *Media discourse.* London etc.: Arnold.

Fix, U. (2011). Fraktale narration. Eine semiotisch-textstilistische analyse [Fractal narration. A semiotic-text stylistic analysis]. In J. G. Schneider & H. Stöckl (Eds.), *Medientheorien und multimodalität. Ein TV-werbespot - Sieben methodische beschreibungsansätze [Media theories and multimodality. One TV commercial - Seven methodological approaches]* (pp. 70-87). Köln: Halem.

Fleskes, G. (1996). *Untersuchungen zur textsortengeschichte im 19. Jahrhundert. Am beispiel der ersten Deutschen eisenbahnen [Investigation on the text type history in the 19th century. The example of the first German railways]* (Vol. 176). Tübingen.

Gansel, C. (2011). *Textsortenlinguistik [Text type linguistics].* Stuttgart: Vandenhoeck & Ruprecht.

Geertz, C. (1973). Thick description: Toward an interpretive theory of culture. In C. Geertz (Ed.), *The interpretation of cultures: Selected essays* (pp. 3-30). New York: Basic Books.

Goffman, E. (1981). *Forms of talk.* Oxford: Blackwell.

Goodenough, W. H. (1957/64). Cultural anthropology and linguistics. In D. H. Hymes (Ed.), *Language in culture and society. A reader in linguistics and anthropology* (pp. 36-40). New York: Harper & Row.

Hallin, D. C., & Mancini, P. (2004). *Comparing media systems. Three models of media and politics.* Cambridge etc.: Cambridge University Press.

Hanitzsch, T. (2007). Deconstructing journalism culture: Towards a universal theory. *Communication Theory, 17:* 4, 367-385.

Hartmann, R. R. K. (1980). *Contrastive textology. Comparative discourse analysis in applied linguistics.* Heidelberg: Groos.

Hauser, S & Luginbühl, M. (Eds.) (2012). *Contrastive media analysis. Approaches to linguistc and cultural aspects of mass media communication.* Amsterdam: Benjamins.

Herder, J. G. (1772/1985). *Ueber die neuere deutsche Literatur. Fragmente.* [*On newer German literature. fragments*], ed. by Regine Otto. Berlin, Weimar: Aufbau-Verlag.

Humboldt, W. v. (1836/1963). *Über die verschiedenheit des menschlichen sprachbaues und ihren einfluss auf die gestige entwicklung des menschengeschelchts* [*On the differences of human language structures and their influence on the intellectuel development of mankind*]. In *werke in fünf bänden* [*Collected works in five volumes*], ed. by A. Filtner & K. Giel. Volume III: Schriften zur Sprachphilosphie. Darmstadt: Wissenschaftliche Buchgesellschaft.

Klein, J. (2000). Intertextualität, geltungsmodus, texthandlungsmuster: Drei vernachlässigte kategorien der textsortenforschung - exemplifiziert an politischen und medialen textsorten [Intertextuality, mode of application, text action patterns: Three neglected categories of text type research – illustrated by text types from politics an mass media. In K. Adamzik (Ed.), *Textsorten, reflexionen und analysen* [*Text types, reflections and analysis*] (Vol. 1, pp. 31-44). Tübingen: Stauffenburg.

Landbeck, H. (1991). *Medienkultur im nationalen vergleich: Inszenierungsstrategien von Fernsehnachrichten am Beispiel der Bundesrepublik Deutschland und Frankreichs* [*Media culture in national* comparison: *Staging strategies of TV news exemplified at the Federal Republic of Germany and France*]. Tübingen: Niemeyer.

Linke, A. (2011). Signifikante Muster – Perspektiven einer kulturanalytischen linguistik [Significant patterns – perspectives of cultural-analytical linguistics]. In E. Wåghäll Nivre, B. Kaute, B. Andersson, B. Landén & D. Stoeva-Holm (Eds.), *Begegnungen. Das VIII. Nordisch-Baltische Germanistentreffen in Sigtuna vom 11. bis zum 13. 6. 2009* [*Encounters. The VII. Nordic-Baltic meeting of Germanists in Sigtuna from 11. to 13. July 2009*] (Vol. 74, pp. 23-44). Stockholm: Acta Universitatis Stockholmiensis.

Luginbühl, M. (2010). Sind textsorten national geprägt? Nachrichtensendungen im vergleich [Are text types nationally charaterized? TV news shows in comparison]. In M. Luginbühl & S. Hauser (Eds.), *MedienTextKultur. Linguistische Beiträge zur kontrastiven Medienanalyse* [*MediaTextCulture. Linguistic Contributions to Contrastive Media Analysis*] (pp. 179-207). Landau: Verlag Empirische Pädagogik.

Luginbühl, M. (2014). Medienkultur und medienlinguistik. Komparative textsortengeschichte(n) der amerikanischen "CBS Evening News" und der schweizer "Tagesschau" [Media culture and media linguistics. Comparative text type history of the American "CBS Evening News" and the Swiss "Tagesschau"] (Vol. 3). Bern: Lang.

Luginbühl, M., Baumberger, T., Schwab, K., & Burger, H. (2002). *Medientexte zwischen autor und publikum. Eine studie zur intertextualität in presse, radio und fernsehen* [*Media texts between author and audience. A study on the intertextuality in press, radio and TV*]. Zürich: Seismo.

Luginbühl, M., & Perrin, D. (2011). "Das, was wir in der Tagesschau den rausschmeißer nennen": Altro- und ethno-kategorisierung von textsorten im handlungsfeld journalistischer fernsehnachrichten ["That what we call a kicker in the Tagesschau": Altro- and ethno-categorizations of text types in the area of journalistic TV news]. In S. Habscheid (Ed.), *Textsorten, handlungsmuster, oberflächen. linguistische typologien der kommunikation* [*Text types, action patterns, surfaces. Linguistic typologies of communication*] (pp. 577-596). Berlin, New York: de Gruyter.

Miller, C. R. (1984). Genre as social action. *Quarterly Journal of Speech, 70*, 151-167.

Montgomery, M. (2007). *The discourse of broadcast news. A linguistic approach.* London: Routledge.

Nickl, M. (2000). *Gebrauchsanleitungen. Ein beitrag zur textsortengeschichte seit 1950* [Instruction manuals. A contribution to the text types history since 1950] (Vol. 52). Tübingen: Narr.

Orlikowski, W. J., & Yates, J. (1994). Genre repertoire: The structuring of communicative practices in organizations. *Administrative Science Quarterly, 39,* 541-574.

Püschel, U. (1992). Von der pyramide zum cluster. Textsorten und textsortenmischung in fernsehnachrichten [From the pyramide to the cluster. Text types and text types blends in TV news]. In E. W. B. Hess-Lüttich (Ed.), *Medienkultur - Kulturkonflikt. Massenmedien in der interkulturellen und internationalen kommunikation [Media culture - Culture conflict. Mass media in intercultural and international communication]* (pp. 233-258). Opladen: Westdeutscher Verlag.

Sandahl, D. (2008). Textmuster als dispositionstypen. Deutsche und Schwedische harte nachrichten und hintergrundberichte im vergleich [Textual patterns as disposition types. German and Swedish hard news and background reports in comparison]. In: H.-H. Lüger & Lenk, H. E. H. (eds): *Kontrastive medienlinguistik [Contrastive media linguistics]* (pp. 211-224). Landau: Empirische Pädagogik.

Sandig, B. (2006). *Textstilistik des Deutschen [Text stylstic of the German language].* Berlin: de Gruyter.

Schmitt, Holger (2008): Illokutionsdichte und illokutionskomposition deutscher und englischer pressetexte. Die FAZ im Vergleich mit der International Herald Tribune [Illocution density and composition of German and English newspaper texts. The FAZ in comparison to the Internation Herald Tribune]. In: H.-H. Lüger & Lenk, H. E. H. (eds): *Kontrastive medienlinguistik [Contrastive media linguistics]* (pp. 305-323). Landau: Empirische Pädagogik.

Spillner, Bernd (1981). Textsorten im sprachvergleich. Ansätze zu einer kontrastiven textologie [Genres in language comparison. Approaches to contrastive textology]. In W. Kühlwein, G. Thome & W. Wilss (eds): *Kontrastive linguistik und Übersetzungswissenschaft [Contrastive linguistics and translation studies]* (pp. 239-250). München: Fink.

Thussu, Daya Kishan (2007): *News as entertainment. The rise of global information.* Los Angeles: Sage.

Warnke, I. (1996). Historische dimensionen pragmatischer textorganisation - Analytische konzeption und empirische untersuchung am beispiel der intertextualität in spätmittelalterlichen reichslandfrieden [Historical dimenstion of pragmatic text organization - Analytical conceptualization and empirical analysis in the caso of late medieval 'Reichslandfrieden']. In S. Michaelis & D. Tophinke (Eds.), *Texte - Konstitution, verarbeitung, typik [Texts - Constitution, processing, typicality]* (Vol. 13, pp. 131-148). München, Newcastle: Lincom Europa.

Yates, J. (1989). *Control through communication. The rise of system in american management.* Baltimore: Johns Hopkins University Press.

de Zarobe, Leire Ruiz (2008): "Le fait divers" in der spanischen und französischen Regionalpresse [The "fait divers" in the Spanish and French regional press]. In: H.-H. Lüger & Lenk, H. E. H. (eds): *Kontrastive medienlinguistik [Contrastive media linguistics]* (pp. 193-210). Landau: Empirische Pädagogik.

EndNotes

[1] Text(ual) Linguistics
[2] Human communities require semiotic signs and mechanisms that allow them to adjust their norms and values in order to communicate successfully with each other and with other groups of humans. Community norms adjusted for successful intra- and inter-group communication become part of the group's "common sense" and, hence, part of the community. I use the term *communitarization* to describe this process.
[3] All translations are the author's.
[4] My corpus includes a show from 1949, but none of the 1950s as there is no archive from that time.

Chapter 12

Genre and Identity in Social Media[1]

Natasha Rulyova

University of Birmingham (UK)

This chapter examines how identities are constructed in social media, particularly, in the blog, and how a variety of genres are used by the blogger to shape a range of identities. The blog helps the blogger to establish a contract between her and her audiences, and, in turn, to reach out to specific communities of followers. The focus of my case study is a blog that has been written in Russian by the Russian opposition leader Alexei Navalny, who has kept his blog on the LiveJournal website at http://navalny-en.livejournal.com/ since 2006. My analysis is informed by the understanding of genre as *social action* (Miller, 1984) and a discursive conception of identity (Butler, 1990; Fairclough, 2003; Hall, 1990, 1992, 1996). To examine the blog as a multimodal text, I apply Kress's (2010) social semiotic approach to communication (p. 26). I also draw on van Leeuwen's (2008) understanding of discourse as the *recontextualization* of social practice, which allows me to examine how identity is constantly recontextualized—or re-shaped through the use of genre—in response to changing contexts.

Currently, most researchers view the blog as a publishing platform (Miller & Shepherd, 2009; van Dijk, 2004), not a genre. However, this was not the case when the blog just emerged. Initially, researchers considered the blog as a genre because most early bloggers used it to write a kind of personal journal/diary. Since then, bloggers have explored and enjoyed a great variety of genres (for more info, see Rulyova, in press). Although the majority of blogs are produced by and represent individual agents, there are also blogs written by groups of people. There are personal, political, institutional, corporate and other types of blogs (see Giltrow & Stein, 2009). The blog examined in this chapter is written in a variety of genres and mainly, though not exclusively, by the owner of the blog, Alexei Navalny. During the time when Navalny was not allowed to have access to his blog due to allegations against him by the authorities the blog was run by his wife and his close allies.

Any analysis of social media websites including the blog presents a number of methodological challenges. First, the content of such websites is complex: still and moving images, multi-lingual content, and intertextuality (e.g., links to other texts/websites and un/ acknowledged quotations). Second, this multi-faceted content is produced by users who act as producers, consumers, writers, readers, listeners, viewers, and reviewers. Third, the analysis of the content of social media websites needs to be done in relation to social organization.

In his approach to social communication, Kress (2010) acknowledges both the complexity of online communication and its relation to the social sphere. Further, he focuses on three main notions: discourse, genre and mode, which are defined in the following way:

> *discourse* offers meanings to be realized; it shapes the world of knowledge as ideational 'content'; and provides a social-conceptual location. *Genre* offers the means for contextualizing /locating/situating that meaning in social spaces and at the same time provides an account of the social characteristics of those spaces. *Mode* offers meaning-laden means for making the meanings that we wish or need to make material and tangible—'realizing,' 'materializing' meanings. (Kress, 2010, p. 114, emphasis in original)

In other words, Kress explains that the "two terms, discourse and genre, make it possible to refer to 'the what' and 'the how' of meaning-making and of meanings in the world" (p. 114). The distinctions between the functions of discourse, genre and mode are helpful not only to see how communication is conducted but also to identify the role of agency in the process of communication:

Discourse answers the questions: 'What is the world about?' and 'How is it organised as knowledge?' Genre answers the question: 'Who is involved as a [sic] participants in this world; in what ways; what are the relations between participants in this world?' Mode answers the question: 'How is the world best represented and how do I aptly represent the things I want to represent in this environment?' (Kress 2010, p. 116)

Kress's approach further positions genre not only in relation to agency but also in relation to social organization (1985; also see Bazerman, 1988; Swales, 1990). In genre studies, this view of genre has been developing since the 1980s. Genre can be viewed as social action (Miller, 1984) and can also be described as "forms of life," as "ways of being," as "frames for social action," and as "the familiar places we go to create intelligible communicative action with each other and [as] the guideposts we use to explore the familiar" (Bazerman, 1997, p. 19). Given that genres reflect and are reflected in patterns in the social sphere, genre analysis has become a helpful methodology to examine the content of social media, a space where social practices take place recurrently, and in great numbers. The forthcoming volume *Emerging Genres in New Media Environments* edited by Carolyn Miller and Ashley Kelly provides further evidence of how genre approaches are productively applied to the analysis of new media texts. The popularity and extensive use of social media websites makes it possible to observe how social practices and rhetorical actions occur across the world and in different languages, as users access the same global social media websites (e.g., LiveJournal, Facebook, Twitter).

It is useful to distinguish between these social media websites/platforms, and genres, in which users communicate. Social media platforms provide users with a fairly homogeneous space and rules for communication. Facebook, LiveJournal and Twitter provide similar affordances to users in different national languages. Genres, on the other hand, are influenced by cultural and linguistic specificity, as demonstrated below.

The concept of *recontextualization*, which was developed in the sociology of education (Bernstein, 1990), allows us to shed light on the differing ways genres are used in linguistic, cultural and semiotic discourses. This concept has been employed in Bernstein's discussion of "curriculum" and "school science" as the recontextualization of the practices that took place in the laboratory. Fairclough (2003) has also employed the concept in his discussion of textual transformation from one discourse (e.g., academic) to another (e.g., managerial. Further, van Leeuwen (2008) explored how recontextualisation could help to theorize the effects that discourse has on social practice. van Leeuwen views all texts as the presentations of social practices, demonstrates how social practice is (re)shaped through texts.

In this chapter, I use the concept of recontextualization to examine how the genre utilized by the social media user/agent depends on the communicative purpose. Bloggers choose a genre of communication and self-representation depending on who they wish to reach out to and what they wish to achieve through this act of mass (self)communication, to use Castells's (2011) term. Recontextualizing oneself and one's writing is a necessary part of the blogger's activity, as the blog is an ever-changing entity. The blog has a beginning but no definitive end. It is non-finite, and, therefore, it has a capacity for endless recontextualization. The blog is in constant motion and change; it consists of texts and is an arena for discourses to interact. In a true Bakhtinian (1986) sense, the blog represents a variety of discourses which co-exist in their multiplicity and complexity, and are often in dialogue with each other. This representation of a variety of discourses in a blog is more spontaneous and varied than, say, in a novel, which Bakhtin (1981) used as his object of examination, because blogs are more open to external forces. They can be edited in an on-going fashion; they are inherently intertextual and have looser boundaries than other texts, such as novels. What the blog is to the novel could be compared to Bakhtin's description of how the novel relates to the epic. (Bakhtin, 1981). The novel for Bakhtin engages with contemporary reality in the ways in which no other genre could previously do. The novel is adaptable to changing conditions; it is open-ended; it allows for different discourses to coexist in one piece of writing; it is dialogic and polyphonic. The blog provides affordances for all these qualities to be taken to a new level: the blog allows for any contemporary discourses to be included; the blog is unfinalised in that as long as it is online it can be accessed by online users who can add comments and create references to the blog. The blog provides affordances to adapt to fast-changing social reality and makes it possible for the blogger to reshape online identity. The blog's capacity to provide intertextual references including to visual and other types of texts is limitless.

It is also productive to briefly compare the role of the blogger/the agent with that of the novelist. The blog has the affordances to create the plurality of voices and consciousnesses that Bakhtin admired in the work of Dostoevsky (1984). However, unlike the author of the novel, the blogger is under constant pressure to review and reshape her texts and entries in reponse to online users. In other words, on the one hand, the social practice of blogging "articulates" discourses (Fairclough, 2003, p. 25); on the other hand, texts in the blog shape blogging as a social practice and create the blogger's online identity. As such, blogging encourages the blogger's or the agent's regular self-recontextualization.

The blog, a site where discursive practices take place over time, provides an opportunity for continuous identity formation. With the blog's archiving functions, which allow for the storing of all entries, blogging identities have a past and a future. The blogging identity fits the definition of identity provided by Hall (1990): a "'production,' which is never complete, always in process, and always constituted within, not outside representation" (p. 222). Hall argues that there is no such thing as one unified identity because identity can only be perceived as such through a coherent narrative of the self about oneself (1990). In social media, we face exactly what Hall described as "a bewildering, fleeting multiplicity of possible identities" (1992) with which the user can identify for a certain period of time. This discursive concept of identity echoes the understanding of identity developed in both social sciences and the humanities in recent years (Butler, 1990; Fairclough, 2003; Hall, 1990, 1992, 1996).

Butler's concept of performativity is also instrumental in understanding the role of genre in identity formation. According to Butler (1990), identities are shaped by performative actions and behaviours. Performativity is an act through which speech and gestures are internalized. Identity is constructed through the process of repetition of speech acts and reiteration of social actions. Butler's focus is on gender construction. She argues that gender is no more than a "stylish repetition of actions" (1990). Butler's understanding of identity construction through performance and repetition is reminiscent of the way, in which identity is linked to genre in genre studies (in Education and Linguistics, in particular).

Like Butler, who says that identity is caused by the repetition of speech acts and gestures, Schryer (2002), a genre studies scholar, insists that identity is shaped through the use of genre where genre is a response to a recurrent rhetorical situation (Miller, 1984). Schryer's conclusions about the role of genre in identity construction are similar to Butler's definition of performativity. Schryer writes:

> we genre our way through social interactions, choosing the correct form in response to each communicative situation we encounter—and we are doing it with varying degrees of mastery. At the same time 'we are genred'. (p. 95)

In other words, identity, including gender identity, is constructed through the use of existing genres by the agent in response to recurrent rhetorical situations.

The production of identity can also be understood in the context of broader contemporary debates about subjectivity, self, and self-realisation. Friedman (1999) argues that in contemporary society individuals appear to have an increasing choice of horizontal options for identity construction which are replacing vertical relationships inherited through family and genetics (though with genetic modification and other gene manipulation it is possible to widen horizontal options on the level of genetics too). Vertical identities are those which children inherit or learn from their parents, such as the colour of the skin, language, religion, tastes, etc. Horizontal identities refer to differences between children and their parents; it is possible to acquire a horizontal identity. For example, being transsexual, deaf or multilingual could be examples of horizontal identities (for further information, see Solomon 2012). In the globalized world of increasing horizontal options for identity construction, education (in a wider sense) plays an increasingly important role. Instead of "inheriting" or accepting features of our identities as given, individuals can choose and "perform" (within limits) not only social class but also race, gender and sexuality. By broadening their range of available genres, individuals increase their chances for successful communication.

Educationalists and English for Specific Purposes (ESP) genre studies scholars emphasise an increasingly important role of genre and learning in the process of self-identification. Kress (1999) makes this point very succinctly: "After all, it is impossible to be authentically 'me' in my writing if I do not have anything resembling real command of the resources of writing (in this language)" (p. 463). Kress makes explicit the connection between using semiotic resources and expressing the self, which is especially pertinent in the context of social media. Kress also underscores that literacy is multimodal. To successfully communicate their identities, individuals not only need to learn how to write, but also to learn how to utilize sounds, images and moving images.

Some educationalists are sceptical about the role of genre in identity construction. Kress (1999) recognises some potential problems with the increasing power of generic interactions:

> The impulse for writing has shifted: from desire to power, from the individual to the social, from expression to communication, from creativity to conventionality, from authenticity (a question of fit with personal truth) to appropriateness. (pp. 463-464)[2]

In the world of globalised media, when conventions and patterns of communication are constrained by dominating social media formats, such as Facebook and Twitter, it seems difficult to see much space for individual creativity. While some suggest that technology forces users to shape their identities in particular ways, I argue that there is space for creative interpretation of genres (see Tardy, this volume) as long as the authorities, with the help of technology, do not start punishing those who avoid prescribed ways of behaving online.

In my analysis of Navalny's blog below, I explore the potential for creativity when pre-existing genres are localised, updated, and adapted to local contexts. I argue that the potential for creativity is located in the individual's capacity for interpretation within the laws of the genre. While Bakhtin (1981) posits "each word tastes" (p. 293) of previous users, this does not prevent new users from using the word anew (with different levels of creativity). In the same way, pre-established genres carry meanings that can be re-interpreted by new users when the genre is pushed into a new linguistic and cultural environment. Bawashi and Reiff (2010) describe genre as an "actualizer" of discourse; however, genre can become an actualizer only through its unique and individual performance by the subject who inevitably brings spontaneity to the genre performance (p. 27).

When users start their blogs or social media accounts, they seemingly have the possibility of creating their identities from scratch. They can write under different names. They can pick their gender, age, social group, make up their biography and background, and create a number of believable identities online. The physical body of the user and her virtual identity do not have to correspond to each other. That said, the user is restricted by her semiotic resources and ability to use technology. By choosing a language to write in the blogger finds herself in a particular cultural and linguistic environment, restricted by its boundaries and conventions. The choice of language and discourse predetermines the audience and, therefore, identity is constructed in response to the particular social milieu, a particular segment of internet users.

Bakhtin's (1981) notion of dialogism is crucial to understanding this process of identity construction. The blogger's identity emerges within a particular discourse (which is informed by local practices), in certain rhetorical situations, and always in response to the potential audience. The online identity is located at a certain website or a platform and, therefore, is also, to some extent, shaped by the global platform. So, the identity, say, of a Russian-language blogger informed by local discourses is channelled through global online formats. By employing a genre, an individual user establishes a contract with a particular social group or a segment of social media users. By writing in an existing genre, the blogger responds to the expectations of her potential readers/viewers. Sometimes new media users create new genres in response to a need or a gap created in social reality. For example, the emergence of a new technology, such as dashboard cameras (dashcams) has led to the advent of a new media subgenre, which can be described as contribution to the "fail genre". Before the appearance of dashcams, Russian drivers were not represented as a group on the internet (Rulyova, in press). Now Youtube is full of the videos of car crashes that take place on Russian roads[3]. Dangerous driving in Russia has become a globally known phenomenon due to its representation in online space. Now individual Russian drivers with dashcams in their cars have a choice of constructing their own identities vis-à-vis this new subgenre referred to as the "fail" genre.

Coming into being in dialogue with the prospective audience, the social media user's identity is performed through genre. Bazerman (2002) argues that genres shape "intentions, motives, expectations, attention, perception, affect, and interpretive frame" (p. 14). He explains:

> when you start writing in those genres you begin thinking in actively productive ways that result in the utterances that belong in that form of life and you take on all those feelings, hopes, uncertainties, and anxieties about becoming a visible presence in that world. (p. 14)

The success of the blog (if we assess it by the number of followers) depends on how well bloggers negotiate appropriate genres to reach out to audiences and to shape their own identities. As these identities are in the process of constant re-production, they need to be recontextualised and re-shaped amid changing circumstances.

There are two sides to bloggers' identities: bloggers as they appear to other internet users in their blogging entries, that is, as products of their own blogs, and bloggers as agents. The latter can be subdivided into *the rhetor* and *the designer*, according to Kress (2010). The rhetor's task is political—he assesses:

> the social environment for communication as a whole. . . . to shape [the] message such that the audience will engage with it . . . [t]he designer assesses what semiotic—representational— resources are available, with a full understanding of the rhetor's needs and aims . . .. Th[at] is a semiotic task. (pp. 49-50)

The agent as rhetor chooses the discourses and genres of representation, the agent as designer is in charge of choosing the material resources (e.g., what platforms to use, what visual or written texts to produce). Acting as a rhetor and a designer, the agent produces a discursive/textual identity or multiple identities, depending on their communication aims. These identities are in constant process of re-production; are communicated with the help of available semiotic resources, and are re-shaped in response to the audience and to changes in the social context.

To summarize my conceptual framework, the social media/ blogging identity comes into being in a particular discourse (which has particular social, cultural and linguistic characteristics), and *in response* to existing discourses and potential audiences. The blogger's identity is inherently dialogic: predetermined by the potential audience and *performed* through genres. The genres, of course, provide a potential contract between the blogger and other users while also acting as a link between local discourses and global online formats. The blogger's identity is continually re-contextualised in response to the changing aims and purposes of mass (self) communication.

Case Study: Alexei Navalny's Blog

The emergence of Alexei Navalny's public persona is strongly associated with his active presence on social media. He has been blogging in Russian since 2006, according to the archive of his blogging website (Navalny, n.d.f). Since 2011, Navalny's blog has also been available in English (Navalny, n.d.g). In addition, Navalny has a Facebook account (Navalny, n.d.e). He has a Twitter account (Navalny, n.d.h) with over 1.03 million followers as of 12 April 2015. In addition, in 2013 when he was running for the Mayor of Moscow he acquired a website (Navalny, n.d.a).

Navalny is a prominent critic of President Putin and a renowned critic of corruption among Russian politicians. He emerged as a leader of the opposition during the presidential elections in 2012 at a time when anti-Putin protests were organized primarily through social media websites, and when the opposition protested against the allegedly unfair election. In his blog, Navalny published documents disclosing corruption of State Duma (the Russian Parliament-like body) deputies and other Russian politicians. Following this, Navalny was accused of money-laundering by the authorities and tried in court more than once. In July 2013, he was sentenced to five years in prison before the sentence was suspended. In October of the 2013, he was again convicted to a five-year term for embezzlement, and, again, this sentence was suspended. Shortly after, new money-laundering charges were brought against Navalny and his brother. In February of 2014, Navalny and his brother were prosecuted on embezzlement charges and Navalny was placed under house arrest and restricted from communicating with anyone but his family. In December of 2014, he was sentenced with another suspended prison term of three and a half years while his brother received an actual three and a half-year prison sentence.

As mentioned above, Nalvany's participation as a candidate in the Mayoral election in Moscow, the capital of Russia, marked his emergence as a politician. He started his campaign the day after his five-year jail sentence was suspended when he was able to run for the Mayor's office. At the beginning of his campaign, he was supported by 2% of the vote. As a result of a very well organized campaign, he took 27% of the vote against 51% taken by the Kremlin-supported Sobianin in September of 2013. During his campaign, Navalny received very little coverage in the national government-controlled media (including main TV channels), where the majority of publications about him were negative. Alternative media, such as *Dozhd.ru* (*Rain.ru*, an independent TV channel and website), and *Ekho Moskvy* (*The Echo of Moscow*, an independent radio station), supported Navalny's campaign. In the Western media, Navalny is often portrayed in a positive light as the strongest opposition figure to Putin.

It has long been acknowledged that Navalny's political and public persona was formed through his well-coordinated and persuasive online and off-line activities. In turn, my research asks: How does the rhetor and designer, Navalny, shape his identity in a blog? What discourses, genres, and modes has he used since 2006? Have they changed depending on the social and political context? What are the genres wherein he performs his identity?

Discourse of Navalny's Blog

Since starting his blog in 2006, Navalny positioned himself within alternative and informal discourses. His early blogging contains some informal expressions from the Russian internet slang known as *Olbansky language* or the *language of padonki* (scumbags' slang). This slang is characterised by the phonetic spelling of Russian words and by ignoring conventional spelling and grammar rules. The very appearance of this slang in the Russian-language internet is associated with alternative discourses, youth sub-cultures opposing the official and "grown-up" discourse (see Böökli, 2009; Zvereva, 2012).

With time, Navalny's discourse has remained alternative but less marked by *Olbansky*. Instead, Navalny turns to the use of metaphorical language, poetic references, and the use of some derogatory language for satirical effect. For example, during his Mayoral campaign, Navalny attacked his main competitor, the incumbent candidate to the mayor of Moscow from the government-supported United Russia party by making references to the poems by Vladimir Mayakovsky (1893-1930), a Russian writer known as the poet of the Bolshevik revolution. Navalny writes, "To take the chord that would 'send rumblings' and be heard in each Moscow flat, especially in the 308 square meters apartment at 13 Rochdel'skaya st." (Navalny, n.d.f). This alludes to Mayakovsky's lines: "Frightened, a Neva aristocrat is wincing / And Narva and Vyborg and Okhta areas / will hear the bursts of provocative laughter"[4] (1917/1939).[5] Navalny critiques Sobyanin, who used his position to acquire a very large apartment on Rochdelskaya street, by comparing him to the frightened aristocrats forced out of their properties by the Bolsheviks.

In the tradition of late Soviet *steb*, a peculiar type of late-socialist discourse of humour based on the aesthetics of the absurd (Yurchak, 2005, pp. 249-50) and post-Soviet irony, Navalny plays with Soviet and post-Soviet jargon. For example, the following sentences use the Soviet discourse of five-year economic plans and achievements to speak with light humour about the success of his Mayoral campaign: "Strengthen our activities in cubes. Earlier we organised 30-50 cubes per day. From Thursday onwards we will deliver 146 cubes." "Cubes" here refer to his mobile mayoral campaign stalls manned by his supporters with the purpose of distributing published materials in support of Navalny.

Navalny ironically applies other well-known Soviet clichés and phrases, such as the often quoted hyperbole, ascribed to Vladimir I. Lenin, the leader of the 1917 Bolshevik revolution, by Maksim Gorky, a well-known Soviet author, according to whom Lenin describes Leo Tolstoy as *chelovechishe* (a giant of a man) (Gorky, 1924/2002). Navalny uses the term satirically to describe Vladimir Yakunin, the president of the Russian Railways company and a high profile government official (Yakunin is also physically a rather large person), whom Navalny accused of being involved in corrupt activities.

Navalny often writes his blog with strong ironic and even satirical undertones to expose many corrupt officials, such as the controversial leader of the Liberal Democratic Party, Vladimir Zhirinovsky. For example, the title of one of Navalny's blog posts was "Zhirinovsky's little son and his Dubai apartment with seven bathrooms." Navalny uses the diminutive form "a little son," which has a strong negative connotation when used to denote a grown-up person, especially a politician. Navalny often uses metaphors (e.g., similes: "thief-emperor" / "vor-amperator" [sic] to express his attitude toward the Russian government's position on Ukraine [posted on 12 March 2014[6]]), metonymies, and other figures of speech).

At times, his satire borders on being ethically questionable, especially when—in order to provide evidence of officials' corrupt and illegal activities—Navalny publishes photographs of their relatives and children, and includes copies of documents, passports, and other identity documents that became available to him without the owners' permission. As another example, in a blog post styled in a folk fairytale genre and titled "A Christmas Fairy-Tale 'A Fox's Vine for a male Cinderella'" (n.d.f), Navalny leaks copies of documents showing that a member of the State Duma[7] owns a €2 million property in France. Navalny attaches pictures of the property, maps, quotations from the Facebook correspondence of the Duma member's son, the son's picture with the Eiffel Tower in the background, copies of the Property Purchase Contract and other supporting materials.

Overall, there are some recurrent features in the way Navalny employs discourse. His language is subversive, highly critical of the government, oppositional, and satirical. So, his blogging identity is informed by alternative oppositional discourses, and it is shaped within those discourses both in response to and for the users of these discourses. As his campaign has shown, young educated professionals are his main audience and supporters.

Genre and Identity in Navalny's Blog

The most noticeable change that Navalny's blog has undergone is a massive proliferation of genres through which Navalny chooses to communicate in his blog since 2006 (Navalny, n.d.f). At the beginning, he started, as many other bloggers, using the blog as a *personal journal* by entering relatively short postings, some of which were of a personal nature and some, political. However, step by step, Navalny the rhetor begins to employ other genres, for example, that of investigative journalism. In the Russian context, this genre can be traced back to the late Soviet period and, in particular, *perestroika*. For Russian people, this genre is associated with television programmes, such as *Vzglyad* [*Glance/Point of View*], and with magazines and newspaper articles, such as the *Ogonyok* [*Little Light*], the *Argumenty i fakty* [*Arguments and Facts*]. In his blog, Navalny uses techniques characteristic of this style of writing, including direct speech, quotations from official documents and from others' speeches, and personal commentary. For example, on 6th November, 2013, Navalny added a posting, "Watch it once again" (Navalny, n.d.f), which was a re-posting from a year before featuring a video about the liberal Russian journalist Oleg Kashin, who reported on controversial social and political issues, being beaten up. The blog features the violent scene as recorded on a security camera. Republishing the materials, Navalny comments on the lack of progress with the investigation into this case, and calls for police accountability to people instead of to the leading authorities. The genre of this blog post is similar to the write-ups of investigations, which emerged as a genre during *perestroika*. These genres have the same social motive (to reveal problems with police corruption), and employ similar rhetorical and linguistic strategies (e.g., persuasion, ellipsis, quotation, repetition). While writing in this style, Navalny acts as a *journalist-investigator*.

Along with acting as a journalist-investigator, Navalny also acts in accordance with his professional training as a *lawyer*. In his blog, he conducts a *legal investigation* by publishing legal papers and procedures. He also performs as a lawyer when he engages with the genre of drafting laws. One of the recent laws that he proposed stated that the State Duma members (deputies) should not buy cars worth more than 1.5 million Russian rubles (at the time, 1 ruble was roughly equal to $0.33 US). In addition, in his legal work published on the website, he comments on existing laws and legal documents, translating them into the vernacular. Writing in this genre, he acts as a *legal consultant* or *adviser*. Navalny also continues to use his blog as a *personal journal* to some extent. In it, he shares his impressions from his travel abroad (Italy, for example), and reflects on daily occurrences. So, Navalny acts both as a *legal consultant/adviser*, translating legal documents, and a *personal journal writer,* narrating about himself, his life, and his family.

Of all the genres that Navalny has used, he is most successful at attracting attention to the blogs about his campaigns against Putin and against "crooks and thieves," as he calls members of the United Russia, a leading pro-government party associated with President Putin and his supporters. While writing in this genre he acts as a *campaign organizer.* For example, he has been running a few campaigns on his websites: (1) the "Rospil" Project, a non-commercial project to control state purchases (Navalny, n.d.a); (2) RosYama, an internet project aimed at improving the quality of Russian roads (Navalny, n.d.b); and (3) RosZH K Kh, an internet project aimed at improving the quality of housing services (Navalny, n.d.c). Each project has its own individual goals and strategies. One common feature shared by all three projects is their participatory structure. Each project's website invites users to submit their complaints (whether they are about bad roads or about the lack of water pressure), to distribute the project's leaflets, and so on. These projects are not confined to the internet and their strategies rely on both online and off-line resources and activities. The projects are also used as political resources. For example, on 30th May 2013, a banner reading, *Putin is a thief,* appeared in the main square of a Russian city. This led to the city authorities calling on the police and issuing to the citizens an administrative protocol for defacing municipal property. Responding to this, Navalny used his campaign website to urge city volunteers to respond to the actions of the authorities by measuring and listing all of the multiple potholes on the roads in the centre of the city.

During the Mayoral campaign in Moscow, the range of genres which Navalny used to engage with his electorate further increased. As a *Mayoral candidate,* he was giving public speeches, which were consequently posted online and distributed through his blog, Facebook, Vkontakte (a Russian counterpart of Facebook, https://vk.com/) and Twitter. As a *Mayoral campaign organizer,* in his blog he published questionnaires, polls, graphs, posters and videos. Off-line he also introduced a few new genres of political agitation, some of which were interpretations of Western election genres adapted to the post-Soviet context or variations of early Soviet propaganda techniques, such as agit-trains (agit[ation]-trains, or trains covered in political slogans) (see Taylor, 1979). Navalny admits that he borrowed some ideas for his campaign from President Barack Obama's election campaign and from the US television series *The Wire* (2002-2008).

In February of 2014, Navalny was put under house arrest, and banned from using any media including the internet. Shortly after that, his blog posts were resumed by the so-called "collective Navalny." Navalny instructed his wife to run his Twitter account and members of his Foundation for Fighting against Corruption to run his Facebook and Vkontakte accounts.

Adjusting Genres to Local Needs

As mentioned above, there are two sources of genres from which Navalny has been borrowing in his online and offline political campaigns. The first source is the early Soviet (Bolshevik) propaganda and the second one is contemporary Western political campaigns.

The Bolshevik political propaganda (preceding and immediately following the 1917 Bolshevik revolution in Russia) was varied and creative. It was inspired by artistic Russian avant-garde movements (e.g., Cubo-Futurists, Constructivists) and conducted in a great variety of genres, including posters, political agitation trains, political agitation boats, traveling theatrical performances, documentary and feature films (Golomstock, 1990). Mayakovsky was one of the founders of *the Okna ROSTA* (*Windows of the Russian Telegraph Agency [ROST]*) project (1919-1921), which was known for inventing a new genre of the political poster to promote the Bolshevik revolution and its values (see ROSTA windows, n.d.). Russian avant-garde artists and constructivists, in particular, worked in a number of modes: photography, poster, photomontage, and some others.

Early Soviet genres and constructivists' stylistics are now used by both anti-government protesters (such as Navalny) and pro-government supporters (for example, in videos promoting the pro-government youth movement, *Nashi [Our]*). Navalny re-interpreted some of these political agitation genres during his election campaign by employing new ways of fostering collective social action; including, the "cubes" (mobile campaign stalls), campaign posters in the subway, and campaign slogans on private cars. As mentioned above, the mobile campaign stalls were used to distribute campaign newsletters and leaflets, and to recruit new volunteers. Offline activities involving volunteers and Navalny himself were digitally recorded and posted on his blog with comments and calls for support. These comments were complemented with visual maps showing support for Navalny in Moscow by district as well as with sociological data about the campaign, reports on Navalny's meetings with supporters, photo evidence, information about financial support received for the campaign, and appeals to voters to support him.

In addition to written texts, pictures, and videos posted by Navalny himself, his blog also includes materials posted on behalf of his supporters (e.g., a cartoon). During his mayoral campaign, Navalny's blog included texts in a variety of genres, such as Facebook reports on volunteers' work, LiveJournal and Twitter updates on the campaign, photo evidence of Navalny's meetings with voters, copies of the relevant articles in the mass media (both positive and negative) with commentary, and television appearances in shows about election debates on both pro-government and alternative channels. His blog also included appeals to voters, reminders to vote, updates on polls in the media, information about online polls, complaints from supporters about the current Mayor, and so on.

The genres used in contemporary Western political campaigns have been familiar to Russian politicians since the 1990s when, among other organizations, the National Democratic Institute for International Affairs and the International Republican Institute both arrived in Moscow to promote democracy and disseminate knowledge about the ways in which political campaigns are organised in the West. It has long been acknowledged that the former Russian President Boris Yeltsin's victory in 1996 was to some extent attributed to the help provided by Western political consultants as well as the support of the Russian media oligarchs (for more information on the role of the media in politics under Boris Yeltsin, see [Zassoursky, 2004]). Throughout the 1990s, Western genres unknown to Soviet audiences also appeared in popular culture, including, television and film. One such example is the adaptation and subversion of the Western genre of the television quiz show which saw the *The Wheel of Fortune* being transformed into the Russian *Pol'e Chudes* (*Field of Miracles*), which then led to the form and content of the show being changed beyond recognition (Rulyova, 2007).

In analysing Nalvany's blog, we also observe a hybridization of genres, or genre mixing (Fairclough, 2003, p. 35), that is, the phenomemnon of several genres being mixed and used in one text, in addition to the proliferation of genres. Instead of using the genres discussed above in their original form (if there is such a form, as genres constantly transform and adapt to new social conditions and new technologies), Navalny's blog uses hybridized and mixed genres. The genres are also adapted to the more vernacular or colloquial speech, which is characteristic of blogging and writing for other social media.[8]

In the course of his blog, Navalny, the rhetor and the designer, has chosen a variety of genres to shape his identities. Each genre, such as the genre of investigative journalism or a legal genre, has been used by the rhetor, Navalny, to communicate with the audience with a particular purpose in mind. The choice of the genre in each case has allowed Navalny to perform in a particular social role: as a citizen journalist, as a public lawyer, as a citizen of Russia, as a Mayoral candidate, and as an opposition leader. All of these roles are constructed through informal vernacular discourses which permeate all Navalny's texts. Hybridized (or mixed) genres, such as a vernacular form of a public lawyer speech (which is afforded by the platform of the blog), allows Navalny to shape himself as a new type of a public lawyer who is enagaged with social media and is comfortable to bring visual means to support his arguments.

Navalny the rhetor uses various genres to recontextualize his identity while, in turn, enhancing his social presence. Depending on the changing context and his communicative goal, Nalvany recontextualizes his identity and communicates his selfhood by employing a variety of genres. Put another way, his discursive identity is constantly being recontextualized and reshaped in genres that are relevant and available to him. The choice of genre determines his audience (and vice versa) while creating links between Navalny the agent and Navalny the product of discursive practices. By performing a range of available identities, which Navalny uses to deliver messages to certain online communities, he achieves greater authority and emerges as a leader of the Russian opposition.

Conclusion

Focusing on the blog of the Russian opposition leader, Aleksei Navalny, this chapter has examined how bloggers use genres to shape their online identities in social media. This chapter has demonstrated how Navalny, the rhetor and designer, used an increasing number of genres to construct corresponding identities, depending on his communicative purpose. While he started as a private blogger, writing about his personal life, in and through his blog, he developed and performed a range of identities, including that of public figure, journalist, lawyer, politician, and organizer of civic campaigns. All these identities are performed through genres, which are hybrid in that they combine features of other genres. When Navalny the rhetor chooses campaigning genres and techniques borrowed from the US context, he adapts and mixes them with early Soviet political genres. In the process of adapting to contemporary online discourses, these genres become hybridized and often localised. The Navalny case study demonstrates that social media platforms provide affordances for agents, or new media users, to creatively shape new horizontal identities. Internet users have access to limitess linguistic, cultural, rhetorical, historical, literary and other resources which they can pick and choose from in order to create messages and identities. Genres play a crucial role in the construction of horizontal identities by offering some channels through which new identities could be performed.

Social media identities are shaped by local discourses and performed through genres. First, these genres act as contracts between bloggers and their audiences. Second, these genres act as links between global online platforms and local discourses. For example, Navalny, as we explored, uses global online platforms to channel his messages and his identity with the help of the genres that are familiar to his audiences; the genres are transformed by his creative use of local discourses.

References

Bakhtin, M. (1981). *The dialogic imagination: Four essays* (M. Holquist, Trans.). Austin, TX: University of Texas Press.

Bakhtin, M. (1984). *Problems of Dostoevsky's poetics.* Minneapolis, MN: University of Minnesota Press.

Bawarshi, A. S., & Reiff, M. J. (2010). *Genre: An introduction to history, theory, research, and pedagogy.* West Lafayette, IN: Parlor Press.

Bazerman, C. (1988). *Shaping written knowledge: The genre and activity of the experimental article in science.* Madison, WI: University of Wisconsin Press.

Bazerman, C. (1997). The life of genre, the life in the classroom. In W Bishop & H. Ostrom (Eds.), *Genres and writing: Issues, arguments, alternatives* (pp. 19-26). Portsmouth, NH: Heinemann.

Bazerman, C. (2002). Genre and identitiy: Citizenship in the age of the internet and the age of global capitalism. In R. Coe, L. Lingard & T. Teslenko (Eds.), *The rhetoric and ideology of genre: Strategies for stability and change* (pp. 13-37). Creskill, NJ: Hampton.

Bazerman, C., Bonini, A., & Figueiredo, D. (Eds.). (2009). *Genre in a changing world.* West Lafayette, IN: Parlor Press.

Bernstein, B. (1990). *Class, codes and control Vol. 4: the structuring of pedagogic discourse.* London, Routledge.

Böökli, J. (2009, May). Russian internet slang: "Олбанский язык" or "Язык падонков." [The "Olbansky language" or the "Language of scumbags"]. Retrieved from http://blogs.transparent.com/russian/russian-internet-slang-олбанский-язык-or-жаргон-падонк/

Butler, J. (1990). *Gender trouble: Feminism and the subversion of identity.* New York /London: Routledge.

Castells, M. (2011). *Communication power.* Oxford: Oxford University Press.

Fairclough, N. (2003). *Analysing discourse: Textual analysis for social research.* London: Routledge.

Friedman, L. (1999) *The horizontal society.* London: Yale University Press.

Frow, J. (2006). *Genre.* London: Routledge.

Gillmor, D. (2004). *We the media: Grassroots journalism by the people, for the people.* Sebastopol, Canada: O'Reilly Media.

Giltrow, J., & Stein, D. (Eds). (2009). *Genres in the internet: Issues in the theory of genre.* Amsterdam/Netherlands/Philadelphia: John Benjamins.

Golomstock, I. (1990) *Totalitarian art in the Soviet Union, the Third Reich, Fascist Italy and the People's Republic of China.* (R. Chandler, Trans.) New York: Haper Collins.

Gorky, M. (2002). *V. I. Lenin.* (Transcribed by D. Walters). Lenin Museum and Maxim Gorky Internet Archive. Original work published in 1924. Retrieved 29 June 2015 from https://www.marxist.org/archive/gorky-maxim/1924/01/x01/htm

Hall, S. (1990). Cultural identity and diaspora. In J. Rutherford (Ed.), *Identity: Community, culture, difference* (pp. 222-237). London. Lawrence Wishart.

Hall, S. (1992). The question of cultural identity. In S. Hall, D. Held & A. McGrew (Eds.), *Modernity and its futures* (pp. 273-326). Cambridge: Polity Press.

Halls, S. (1996) Introduction:Who needs identity? In S. Hall, P.du Gay (Eds.), *Questions of cultural identity* (pp. 1-17). London: SAGE.

Kress, G. (1985). *Linguistic processes in sociocultural practice.* Geelong, Victoria: Deakin University Press.

Kress, G. (1999). Genre and the changing contexts for English language arts. *Language Arts, 76*(6), 461-469.

Kress, G. (2010). *Multimodality: A social semiotic approach to communication.* London: Routledge.

Mayakovsky, V. V. (1939). Netrudno landyshami dysha [It's not difficult, while breathing in the scent of lilies of the valley]. In N. N. Aseev, L. V. Mayakovsky, V. O. Pertsova, & M. I. Serebryansky (Eds.), *Mayakovsky, V.V. Polnoe sobranie sochinenii: Stikhotvoreniia, poemy, stat'i, 1912-1917* [Mayakovsky, V. V. Complete works: Poems and essays, 1912-1917], vol 1. Moskva [Moscow]: Khudozhestvennaia literatura. Original work published in 1917.

Miller, C. (1984). Genre as social action. *Quarterly Journal of Speech, 70,* 151-167.

Miller, C., & Shepherd, D. (2009). Questions for genre theory from the blogosphere. In J. Giltrow & D. Stein (Eds.), *Genres in the internet: Issues in the theory of genre* (pp. 263-290). Amsterdam: John Benjamins.

Miller, C. (2014, February). The Round Table: Genres from Multiple Perspectives. Presented at the international conference *Writing Across Borders*, Paris, Université Nanterre-Defence.

Miller, C. & Kelly, A. R. (Eds.). (forthcoming) *Emerging Genres in New Media Environments*.

Navalny, A. (n.d.a). Alexei Navalny [Mayoral page]. Retrieved April 1, 2015 from: http://navalny.ru

Navalny, A. (n.d.b). The Rospil Project. Retrieved April 1, 2015 from http://rospil.info/

Navalny, A. (n.d.c). The RosYama Project. Retrieved April 1, 2015 from http://rosyama.ru/

Navalny, A. (n.d.d). The RosZH K Kh Project. Retrieved April 1, 2015 http://roszkh.ru

Navalny, A. (n.d.e). Timeline [Facebook page]. Retrieved April 1, 2015 from https://www.facebook.com/navalny.

Navalny, A. (n.d.f). The Blog of Navalny [LiveJournal page]. Retrieved April 1, 2015 from http://navalny.livejournal.com/

Navalny, A. (n.d.g). The Blog of Navalny in English. [LiveJournal page]. Retrieved April 1, 2015 from http://navalny-en.livejournal.com/

Navalny, A. (n.d.h). Tweets. [Twitter page]. Retrieved April 1, 2015 from https://twitter.com/navalny and has over 1.03

ROSTa windows: The art of satirical poster. (n.d.). Retreived April 1, 2015 from http://tass.ru/en/russia/747405

Rulyova, N. (2007). Subversive glocalisation in the game show Pole chudes (The Field of Miracles). *Europe-Asia Studies, 59*(8), pp 1367-1386.

Rulyova, N. (forthcoming). Genre and identity in Russian New Media users' response to a meteor shower in Chelyabinsk in 2013. In C. Miller & A. R. Kelly (Eds.), *Emerging Genres in New Media Environments*.

Schryer, C. F. (2002). Genre and power: A chronotopic analysis. In R. Coe, L. Lingard, & T. Teslenko (Eds.), *The rhetoric and ideology of genre* (pp. 73-102). Cresskill, NJ: Hampton.

Solomon, A. (2012) *Far from the tree: Parents, children and the search for identity.* New York, London: Chatto & Windus.

Swales, J. (1990). *Genre analysis.* Cambridge: Cambridge University Press.

Taylor, R. (1979) *The politics of the Soviet cinema: 1917-1929.* Cambridge: Cambridge University Press.

van Dijk, J. (2004). Composing the self: Of diaries and lifelogs. *The Fibreculture Journal.* Retrieved from http://journal.fibreculture. org/issue3/issue3_vandijck.html

van Leeuwen, T. (2008). *Discourse and practice: New tools for critical discourse analysis.* New York, NY: Oxford University Press.

Yurchak, A. (2005). *Everything was forever, until it was no more: The last Soviet generation.* Princeton: Princeton University Press.

Zassoursky, I. (2004). *Media and Power in Post-Soviet Russia.* New York: M. E. Sharpe.

Zvereva, V. (2012). *Setevye razgovory: Kul'turnye kommunikatsii v internete* [*Network conversations: Cultural communication on the Internet*]. Bergen: Department of Modern Languages, University of Bergen.

EndNotes

[1]   I would like to express gratitude to Professor Gunther Kress for reading a draft of this chapter and providing me with very helpful and insightful feedback.

[2]   From personal communication with Gunther Kress (email dated 23 March 2014), I understand that his view has since changed. He is now thinking of writing in multimodal environments in terms of *design,* and, therefore, the concept of creativity needs to be reviewed.

[3]   See http://www.youtube.com/watch?v=itMdLTd1l4E; http://www.youtube.com/watch?v=taqHJ9U-Vts .

[4]   Editors' note: "Neva aristocrat" alludes to Russian aristocrats who, prior to the 1917 Bolshevik revolution, used to live in spacious apartment buildings on Neva Drive, one of the most prestigious areas in the imperial St. Petesrburg. "Narva, Vyborg, and Okhta areas" refer to poor parts of St. Petersburg where the working class used to live. With the advent of the Bolshevik revolution, the majority of aristocrats were expelled from their large apartments, and murdered or sent to GULAG, while the Communist Party leaders moved to their apartments; some working class families were allowed to live in these apartments, one family per room, at times allowing the original owner to retain one room.

[5]   This and other translations from Russian are the author's.

[6]   Editor's note: the post is no longer available on-line.

[7]   Editor's note: The lower house of the Federal Assembly of Russian legislature.

[8]   For further discussion of increasing conversational discourses in public sphere, see (Gillmor, 2004).

Chapter 13

Genre, Knowledge and Pedagogy in the Sydney School

David Rose

University of Sydney (Australia)

Generations of Genre

The idea of language as meaning in social context has been explored for over six decades in the systemic functional tradition. The roots of this project can be traced to Halliday's teacher, Firth, who foresaw its key directions with remarkable prescience. Firth's particular field was phonology, but by the 1930s he had already developed a model of how meaning could be described in strata, from the sounds of words all the way up to social contexts:

> I propose to split up meaning or function into a series of component functions. Each function will be defined as the use of some language form or element in relation to some context. Meaning, that is to say, is to be regarded as a complex of contextual relations, and phonetics, grammar, lexicography, and semantics each handles its own components of the complex in its appropriate context. (1935, p. 45)

Meaning for Firth was function in context; the context of phonology was grammar and lexis; the context of grammar was semantics.

As a grammarian, Halliday set out to describe the semantic functions of grammatical patterns, by examining their functions in discourse, in the texts that people actually speak and write with each other. Perhaps his greatest contribution is the description of three layers of grammatical patterning, simultaneously serving *interpersonal*, *ideational* and *textual* functions in each clause of a text. The description he has given us of these grammatical "metafunctions" in Halliday and Matthiessen (2004), is thorough, elaborate and immensely useful, but the idea of meaning as function in context started with Firth. The same may also be said for the idea of language as systems of functions, which Firth (1935) elaborates for phonological systems:

> The phonetic function of a form, of a sound, sound-attribute, or sound-group is then its use in contradistinction from other 'sounds'; the phonetic value or use of any sound is determined by its place in the whole system. (p. 55)

This is the genealogy of the term "systemic functional linguistics" or SFL; language is organised as systems of contrasting options for making meaning (Saussure's [1966] *valeur*), at the levels of phonology, lexico-grammar and discourse semantics; elements at each stratum serve functions in the context of higher strata with the social contexts of language modelled as a further stratum of meaning.

Halliday proposed intrinsic relations between the three metafunctions of language and three dimensions of social contexts, modelled as types of realisation: interpersonal functions enact patterns of social relations, or *tenor*; ideational functions construe patterns of social activity, or *field*; textual functions present interpersonal and ideational functions as relevance in context, or *mode*. But Firth (1935) had also foreshadowed such a tripartite contextual model: "The central concept of the whole of Semantics considered in this way is the context of situation. In that context are the human participant or participants, what they say, and what is going on" (p. 64). Critically, Firth interposed a semantic stratum between grammar and context:

> ...if you want to bring in general cultural background, you have the contexts of experience of the participants... when phonetician, grammarian, and lexicographer have finished, there remains the bigger integration, making use of all their

work, in semantic study. And it is for this situational and experiential study that I would reserve the term "semantics." (p. 65)

For this stage of the research, Halliday's grammatics provided the foundations for his student, Martin, to describe interpersonal, ideational and textual systems of discourse semantics that realise variations in tenor, field and mode (Martin, 1992; Martin & Rose, 2003). Martin used the term *register* to denote this contextual stratum, and proposed general options for its systems of meanings that are observable in discourse. With respect to tenor, relations between interactants are most generally either equal or unequal, and close or distant. Fields are focused on activities and/or entities that are specific or generalised. With respect to mode, discourse is either dialogic or monologic, and either accompanies what is going on or constitutes its own field. As each of these parameters may vary independently, Martin referred to tenor, field and mode as *register variables*. The advantages these explicitly articulated parameters have provided for research cannot be overstated.

As outlined in his chapter for this volume, Martin also built on work by Gregory (1967), Hasan (1984), Plum (1998), Rothery (1994, 1996) and others to propose *genre* as a more abstract stratum of social context, phasing together unfolding patterns of tenor, field and mode. In the terms of SFL, genre is defined as recurrent configurations of meanings, and a culture can be described as an evolving system of genres. As they are recurrent configurations, each genre is recognisable to members of a culture by way of repeated experience, and empirically describable to the analyst. Again this approach to genre is presaged by Firth (1935) as:

> an empirical rather than a theoretical analysis of meaning. It can be described as a serial contextualization of our [linguistic] facts... all contexts finding a place in what may be called the context of culture. It avoids many of the difficulties which arise if meaning is regarded chiefly as a mental relation. (p. 72)

Firth's "contexts of experience of the participants" above is also crucial here as experience varies between members of a culture.

Following Bernstein (2000), we can view culture as a reservoir of semiotic resources, at the levels of genre, register and language, and the set of resources that each member variously acquires and deploys as our repertoire (p. 158).

This model of genre has been prodigiously fruitful for empirical research, using Halliday's grammatics and Martin's discourse semantics to analyse text after text in multiple social institutions, building descriptions of the genres in which participants enact their social relations and construe their experience. The best known of these institutions, that is most often associated with the so-called "Sydney School" research, is education. But as it reaches beyond language into institutional contexts, this research has not relied simply on linguistic analysis, but on sociology of education. Firth also foresaw this: "Sociological linguistics is the great field for future research," which must address "the very difficult problem of describing and classifying typical contexts of situation within the context of culture, and secondly of describing and classifying types of linguistic function in such contexts of situation" (p. 65). What Firth called "typical contexts of situation" include not only the genres of classroom discourse in school, but also the genres in which knowledge is written and read in school. At this point, his "context of situation," derived from Malinowski's anthropology (1935), must be left behind as written genres constitute their own fields, and the situations in which they are learnt are another set of genres, discussed below. There are no ethnographic contexts beyond genre, only other genres.

A major goal of the project has been to describe "types of linguistic function" in pedagogic genres, so they can be made explicit for teachers and learners. Bernstein's (1990, 2000) sociological theory of "pedagogic discourse" has been essential for this project. His sociological use of the term "discourse" is broadly parallel with SFL's fields of social practice, but includes social relations. He also uses "practice" interchangeably, so we will substitute "practice" for his "discourse" when possible, to avoid confusion with discourse as a stratum of language. Bernstein has given us the structuring of pedagogic practice, in terms of social relations between teachers and learners, and types of knowledge they exchange. The task of educational linguists has been, firstly, to describe how these social relations and types of knowledge are realised as texts and hence elaborate Bernstein's model; and, secondly, to recontextualise what has been found in a form that is directly useful for teachers and their students.

Describing Knowledge Genres

The first stage of the education project described the genres typically written by primary school students through large scale textual analyses in collaboration between educators and linguists (see Rose, 2008). These descriptions were recontextualised for teachers with names for the genres and their stages along with synopses of their primary social functions (as in Table 1). Naturally, any text has multiple social functions, but its primary goal expects the stages through which the goal is achieved.

Table 1

Genres described in the first phase of research

	genre	function	stages
Stories	**recount**	*recounting events*	Orientation Record of events
	narrative	*resolving a complication*	Orientation Complication Resolution
Factual texts	**description**	*describing specific things*	Orientation Description
	report	*classifying & describing general things*	Classification Description
	explanation	*explaining sequences of events*	Phenomenon Explanation
	procedure	*how to do an activity*	Purpose Equipment Steps
Arguments	**exposition**	*arguing for a point of view*	Thesis Arguments Reiteration
	discussion	*discussing two or more points of view*	Issue Sides Resolution

As these are genres in which school knowledge is typically written and read, I will refer to them as *knowledge genres*. Their fields vary from specific (recounts, narratives, descriptions) to generalised (report, explanation, procedure), and their tenor may be more distant than the discourse that children are familiar with. These types of registers lie outside the experience of most primary school children, who require careful scaffolding to master the language resources that realise them. They must learn how to engage readers through literary devices in stories, to generalise experience as technical fields in factual texts, and to negotiate evaluations of issues and positions in arguments. In terms of Bernstein's (2000) knowledge types, their repertoire must expand from "horizontal discourses" that are "local, segmentally organised, context specific and dependent" to "vertical discourses" that "take the form of a coherent, explicit, and systematically principled structure" (p. 157).

Alongside the description of knowledge genres, a classroom genre was designed, principally by Rothery (1994, 1996), for guiding students to write these genres successfully. Dubbed a teaching/ learning cycle or TLC, it included three stages. The first was termed *Deconstruction*, in which a teacher guides students to identify and name the stages of a model text in the genre under focus, along with some pertinent language features. The second is *Joint Construction*, in which the teacher guides students to construct a new text with the same stages, but about a field that the class has been studying. The third is *Independent Construction*, in which each student writes their own text following the model they have practised together. I will use the term *curriculum genres* for genres of classroom practice, following Christie (2002).

The designed TLC curriculum genre represented a significant departure in teaching practice as it explicitly guides students to do a writing task through joint practice before they are expected to do individual writing tasks. A more typical pattern in schools and further education is for teachers to set writing tasks, with more or less explicit instructions, and then evaluate each student's attempts, perhaps with feedback. The genre writing TLC reversed the pedagogic focus, to first prepare all students to do the task successfully rather than repairing less successful attempts afterwards. In terms of tenor, the teacher's authority is essential to guide students, but their outcomes are less unequal than in other pedagogies. These include both traditional pedagogies in which teachers' authority and students' rankings are explicit, and progressive/constructivist pedagogies that proscribe teachers' authority and prescribe each student to progress at their own unequal levels.

With respect to knowledge, an explicitly labelled description of the knowledge genres under focus was an essential component of this pedagogy. Teaching this knowledge about language was embedded in the practice of writing about the curriculum topics under focus in contrast to more traditional practices of teaching language systems in isolation. In genre pedagogy, students acquire two fields simultaneously: knowledge about the curriculum topic and knowledge about the language that realises it as written texts. In terms of mode, this was accomplished by dialoguing about written texts that could be seen and shared by all, pointing out features of the model, and constructing the joint text on the board.

The project's second phase extended the description of knowledge genres across the secondary school curriculum and beyond to further education and associated workplaces. For example, research on science and related school curricula was reported in Martin and Veel (1998) while Rose, McInnes and Korner (1992) tracked written genres in science based industries from procedures for manual tasks through technical notes written by technicians to research articles written by industrial scientists. Relations between genres and the fields in which they are acquired and deployed were thus thoroughly explored together with the social hierarchies of knowledge and power they enact (Rose, 1998). Genres described for school curricula are listed in Table 2. These and other knowledge genres described in the research are discussed in detail in Martin and Rose (2008).

Table 2

Genres described in the second phase

	genre	purpose	stages
Stories	recount	recounting events	Orientation Record of events
	narrative	resolving a complication	Orientation Complication Resolution
	exemplum	judging character or behaviour	Orientation Incident Interpretation
	anecdote	sharing an emotional reaction	Orientation Remarkable event Reaction
	observation	commenting on an event	Orientation Event description Comment
	news story	reporting current events	Lead Angles
Chronicles	autobiographical recount	recounting significant life events	Orientation Record of stages
	biographical recount	recounting stages of a life	Orientation Record of stages
	historical recount	recounting historical stages	Background Record of stages
	historical account	explaining historical stages	Background Account of stages

Explanations	sequential explanation	explaining a sequence	Phenomenon Explanation
	conditional explanation	alternative causes & effects	Phenomenon Explanation
	factorial explanation	multiple causes for one effect	Phenomenon:outcome Explanation:factors
	consequential explanation	multiple effects from one cause	Phenomenon:cause Explanation:consequs.
Procedures	procedure	directing activities	Purpose Equipment Steps
	protocol	prescribing and proscribing actions	Purpose Rules
	procedural recount	recounting procedures	Purpose Method Results
Reports	descriptive report	classifying & describing an entity	Classification Description
	classifying report	describing types of entities	Classification Description:types
	compositional report	describing parts of wholes	Classification Description:parts
Arguments	exposition	arguing for a position	Thesis Arguments Reiteration
	discussion	discussing two or more positions	Issue Sides Resolution
Text Responses	review	evaluating a literary, visual or musical text	Context Description of text Judgement
	interpretation	interpreting the themes of a text	Evaluation Synopsis of text Reaffirmation
	critical response	challenging the message of a text	Evaluation Deconstruction Challenge

Table 2 expands the genre options outlined in Table 1 in three dimensions. More specific types of explanations and reports were identified, story and procedural families were extended with contrasting options, and chronicle and text response families were added, netting in curricula in Science, Geography, History, Technology and Literature Studies. Ongoing research continues to expand these options. For example, Figure 1 elaborates the procedural family systemically as a network of contrasting choices beginning with a prospective option for directing activities vs a retrospective option for recounting activities. Procedures direct sequences of activities with sub-types common in industrial workplaces and protocols that prescribe and proscribe activities common in institutions as various as homes, schools, bureaucracies and corporations. Recounted procedures range from school science reports to technical notes in industry, to research articles recounting academic activities and case studies recounting various types of institutional activities. Descriptions of these procedural genres have fed into language teaching in fields such as School Science, Technical Training, Engineering, Law, Business and Medicine while a major focus of genre research in other traditions has been on just one of the options in Figure 1, the academic research article.

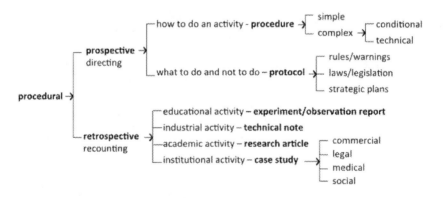

Figure 1. Expanded procedural family.

Alongside these typological perspectives on knowledge genres, Figure 2 presents a topological perspective, in which genres are clustered along two axes: the extent to which their primary purpose is to provide information or to engage readers' feelings and judgements; and the extent to which they present things and events as natural or to contest viewpoints about them. Genres in the top left tend to present scientific or technological information as fact—more natural than contestable—so that contested science stands out as newsworthy. In contrast, we expect the chronicles in the top right to take a position in relation to other views, more or less explicitly. For example, if history is presented merely as fact it may be regarded as either dull or one-sided. Arguments and text critiques by definition contest other voices, but in deft hands their conclusions can flow so naturally that they appear uncontestable. And stories can weave their writers' judgements into the events so seamlessly that the reader scarcely realises they are moralising. Any particular text may be positioned along axes like these, depending on its settings in field, mode and tenor.

Figure 2. Topological perspective on genre families and functions.

This perspective also brings out genre preferences of contrasting pedagogic theories and practices. As informing genres are deployed in fields of economic production and social management, they are a particular focus of traditional pedagogies. For example, in sciences and social science, progressive/constructivist theories often privilege story genres as they are vehicles for personal expression and growth; critical theories privilege the persuasive functions of arguments and critiquing functions of text responses, reflecting these theories' roots in literary criticism. Genre pedagogy, on the other hand, merely equips teachers to scaffold any genre expected of their curricula and students' needs, furnishing descriptions to do so.

Analysing Curriculum Genres

The third phase of the project extended the design of the pedagogy from the tasks of writing to reading. Central to this development was the recognition that reading is a fundamental mode of learning in the school, that many if not most school students are unable to read at the levels they need for academic success, and that teachers are inadequately trained to teach reading effectively to meet these needs. Moreover, the primary function of writing tasks in school and university is to demonstrate what students have learnt from reading for the purpose of evaluation.

These institutional criteria suggested a sequence of designed curriculum genres that commence with reading to learn and culminate with learning to write. The series of curriculum genres would need to address each stratum of the language task (e.g., genre, register, discourse, grammar, graphology), and to integrate teaching these skills with teaching the curriculum. They would need to be applicable to all stages of schooling across curriculum fields, and they should meet the needs of all students to achieve success.

With respect to this last goal, Bernstein's (2000) analysis of "pedagogic discourse" makes plain that inequalities in education outcomes are consequences of "social biases in education. These biases lie deep within the very structure of the educational system's processes of transmission and acquisition and their social assumptions" (p. xix). The school's exchange of knowledge is embedded in the social order it serves:

> Pedagogic discourse embeds rules which create skills of one kind or another and their relationship to each other, and rules which create social order. We shall call the discourse which creates specialised skills and their relationship to each other instructional discourse, and the moral discourse which creates order, relations and identity regulative discourse... Fundamental to my argument is that the regulative discourse is the dominant discourse. In one sense this is obvious... it tells the children what to do, where they can go, and so on. It is quite clear that regulative discourse creates the rules of social order. However, I also want to argue that regulative discourse produces *the order in the instructional discourse.*

There is no instructional discourse which is not regulated by the regulative discourse. If this is so, the whole order within pedagogic discourse is constituted by the regulative discourse... Therefore I argue that the regulative discourse provides the rules of the internal order of instructional discourse itself. If this argument holds, much can be derived from the notion that we have *one discourse* and *the regulative discourse is dominant* [emphasis in original]. (pp. 33-35)

Bernstein's instructional discourse (practice) covers both pedagogic activities and relations, and the knowledge that is exchanged by teachers and learners. His regulative discourse (practice) is clearly far broader, and oriented more to social relations, including social hierarchies in society and the school, relations between participants, and their social identities. Genre and register theory is powerful enough to describe Bernstein's order in instructional practice empirically, to reveal the rules of social order in the regulative practice that constitutes it, and to subvert dominant rules by re-designing instructional practice.

Instructional practice can be described in terms of register variables, including pedagogic activities (field), pedagogic relations (tenor) and pedagogic modalities (mode) together with the fields of knowledge that are exchanged through these activities, relations and modalities. Pedagogic activities are structured as sequences of lessons composed of lesson activities that are composed of learning cycles. Pedagogic relations between teachers and learners, and between learners, are more or less hierarchical and more or less inclusive. The teacher/learner pedagogic relation may be explicit, as in traditional ('didactic') modes, or implicit, as in progressive ('socratic') modes. Pedagogic modalities include spoken, written, visual and manual modes of meaning, and relations between modalities as learning activities unfold. Knowledge exchanged includes both the fields of the curriculum, and knowledge about the language in which these fields are written and spoken. However, this knowledge is not equally acquired by all students as Bernstein (2000) points out:

The school necessarily produces a hierarchy based on success and failure of students... failure is attributed to inborn facilities (cognitive, affective) or to the cultural deficits relayed by the family which come to have the force of inborn facilities. (p. xxi)

What students acquire from school is not just unequal shares of knowledge, but unequal identities as more or less successful or failing learners. This configuration of pedagogic activities, relations, modalities, knowledge and identities constitute a curriculum genre, modelled in Figure 3.

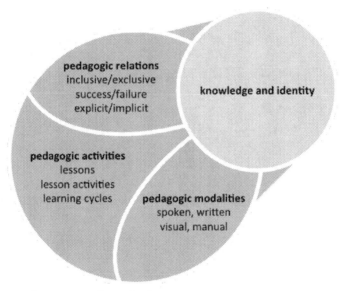

Figure 3. Configuration of curriculum genres.

One further model is required to design the sequence of curriculum genres outlined above, that is, the structure of pedagogic activities. The core phase of any pedagogic activity I will call the learning task. Only the learner can do this task, but in education institutions each task is typically initiated and evaluated by a teacher, either directly or through a written medium. The initiating phase can be called the Focus. The nucleus of a pedagogic activity thus includes Focus, Task and Evaluate phases, as in Figure 4.

Figure 4. Nucleus of pedagogic activities.

This nucleus can be expanded with two optional phases. The learner may first be prepared to do the task successfully by some form of demonstration, synopsis or explanation. Once the task is successfully completed, it may be elaborated with a further step, such as a definition, explanation, or discussion of its significance. Prepare and Elaborate phases are thus more marginal elements of a pedagogic activity (as in Figure 5).

Figure 5. Expanded potential of pedagogic activities.

We can refer to these as *phases* of a pedagogic activity. To prepare all learners to succeed with each learning task, it is essential for teachers to understand the nature of the task. This is obvious with manual activities, in which an expert physically demonstrates each step in the task and hands control to the novice to practice the step with guidance before moving on to the next step. Indeed this "apprenticeship" mode of demonstration and guided practice appears to be a fundamental mode of learning in human cultures, and may be a defining feature of our species (Rose, 2006). It is less obvious with semiotic activities, which require close analysis using a social semiotic model to reveal the structuring of pedagogic activities.

This structuring is evident in studies of children learning their mother tongues by Halliday (1975) and Painter (1986, 1991, 1999). Language actually begins with the sets of sounds and gestures that infants start using from around nine months, known as protolanguage, before the mother tongue takes over. Language teaching may involve drawing the child's attention to phenomena, or following the child's attention, as in the following example at 14 months old, from Painter (1986, pp. 81-82).

Table 3

Learning the mother tongue

Child	*dae* [pointing at a bird in the garden]	Identify
Mother	*Yes*	Affirm
	Bird	Elaborate
Child	*da* [pointing]	Identify
Mother	*Bird*	Elaborate
Child	*da* [pointing]	Identify
Mother	*That's a bird.*	Elaborate
Child	*ba; ba* [pointing]	Identify

As the child initiates the exchange here, there is no Focus phase, but the pointing and naming activity is prepared by thousands of instances of caregivers pointing and naming the world long before infants start to do so themselves. The task is to identify elements in the context, and eventually to articulate their mother tongue names, a universal pattern of human language learning. The mother capitalises on the child's attention by first affirming and then elaborating with the mother tongue word.

It is this evaluation and elaboration that marks this as a pedagogic exchange, in which the mother is the teacher and the child the learner. The affirmation evaluates the child's utterance as success with a learning task, rewarding the child with positive emotion. Expectation of this reward is the child's motivation for pointing and naming, and for engaging in pedagogic exchanges in general. In this instance, the reward encourages the child to repeat the identifying act again and again. On the mother's side, she knows intuitively that success and affirmation enhance the child's capacity for learning, which she capitalises on by repeating her elaboration, initially just with the word, but then with a whole clause. Elaborations such as these provide models of mother tongue language features such as lexical items ('bird') and grammatical structures ('that's a bird'), at the precise moment when the child is most ready to recognise and remember them. These links between cognition and emotion are explained neurologically by Edelman's (1992) Theory of Neuronal Group Selection, but understood intuitively by all teachers from parents to peers to professional educators. In this example, the outcome of repeated success and elaboration is that the child begins to replicate the mother tongue word. Painter comments that "[a] few days later 'ba' became the regular form for bird" (Painter, 1986, pp. 81-82).

In terms of pedagogic activities, each of these repetitions of Identify, (Affirm) and Elaborate phases is a learning cycle. The sequence as a whole is an informal lesson activity, which is made explicit by the mother's repeated elaborations, and culminates with the child's acquisition and production of a new item of knowledge. At the level of lesson activity, this culminating utterance is the Task, for which the preceding learning cycles Prepare. This utterance would undoubtedly have been affirmed by the mother, but was not recorded in Painter (1986). That is, the structure of pedagogic activities applies at each level of learning cycle: lesson activity, and lesson. We can refer to these as *ranks* of pedagogic activity, with a fractally repeated structure of phases (Prepare) (Focus) Task (Evaluate) (Elaborate).

The pedagogic relation in this instance is one-on-one, so maximally inclusive; it is explicit, and consistently evaluated affirmatively. The pedagogic modalities are spoken and gestural. The initial source of meaning is in the world, which the child brings into the exchange by pointing and vocalising, the mother assigns it a name, and then refers to it exophorically as "that," reconstruing the acts of pointing and vocalising as mother tongue words. We will use the term *source* for the origins of meanings in pedagogic modalities, and the term *vector* for the ways in which meanings are brought into the discourse such as by pointing, naming and referring. The knowledge exchanged is the word "bird" for the entity the child identifies, which is repeated and approximated with "ba."

At this point, we can make the discursive realisations of pedagogic register variables explicit. Pedagogic activity is realised as lesson activities, each phase of which is composed of one or more learning cycles, that are also composed of phases. Pedagogic relations are realised as teacher/learner exchanges, in which one or more learners participate. Pedagogic modalities are realised as sources and vectors of meanings. Knowledge exchanged is realised as lexical items, and relations between items as an activity unfolds. Relations between these pedagogic register variables and discourse semantic systems are schematised as follows (Table 4).

Table 4

Relations between pedagogic register variables and discourse semantic systems

register	pedagogic activities	pedagogic relations	pedagogic modalities	knowledge
discourse	phases in learning cycles & lesson activities	participation in classroom exchanges	sources & vectors of meanings	items & their relations as activity unfolds

The model can now be applied to expand the analysis of pedagogic exchanges, illustrated in Table 5.

Table 5

Expanded analysis

exchange		cycle phases	sources & vectors	items & relations	activity phases
Child	*dae* [pointing at bird]	Identify	point at entity		
Mother	*yes*	Affirm			Prepare
	bird	Elaborate	name entity	*bird*	word
Child	*da* [pointing]	Identify	point at entity		
Mother	*bird*	Elaborate	name entity	repeat *bird*	
Child	*da* [pointing]	Identify	point at entity		
Mother	*that's a bird.*	Elaborate	refer & name entity	refer & repeat *bird*	
Child	*ba; ba* [pointing]	Identify	point & name entity	repeat *bird (ba)*	Propose
Mother	...	(Affirm)			word

The analysis helps us to see precisely how knowledge is negotiated, presented and construed in a curriculum genre. Cycle phases specify learning tasks (e.g., identifying phenomena or proposing wordings), evaluations (affirming or rejecting), and elaborations of knowledge. Sources and vectors specify where meanings originate and how they are imported into the discourse. Items and relations specify the meanings exchanged, and how they are accumulated as activities unfold. Activity phases specify the pedagogic functions of learning cycles. In this instance, the pedagogic functions of repeatedly pointing, referring and naming an entity, coalesce as preparations for the child's final task of proposing the name himself, "ba; ba."

This close analysis of the "order in instructional practice" can then be applied to interpret the regulative practice that produces it. This is an instance of a curriculum genre that is probably shared across human cultures. For example, I have frequently observed similar exchanges in the Indigenous culture of Australia's Western Desert (Rose, 2001, 2010). Its broad social function is intergenerational reproduction of mother tongue language. In this instance, the mode is dialogic and ancillary as it refers to an entity outside the discourse (the bird) using gesture, gaze and a pronoun "that." Although the field is initially a specific entity (the bird), the pedagogic goal is to generalise a class of similar entities. With the noun "bird;" the mother is giving the child a resource to classify his experience. The pedagogic activity is clearly built on oft repeated experience, as the child expects affirmation for identifying the entity, recognises the pedagogic function of elaborations, and eventually repeats the class term himself as he points at the bird. As the pedagogic relation is inclusive, affirming and explicit, it is maximally effective at achieving the goal of the genre, i.e., acquisition of language knowledge. In Bernstein's terms the familial "rules of social order" are visible and explicit in that the child recognises the mother's authority to evaluate him, and to provide knowledge for him to acquire. The "social relation" is hierarchical but nurturing; the "social identity" it produces is a successful learner who is confident and motivated to display what he has learnt.

Now let's apply the analysis to a curriculum genre in the school, which is intended to help prepare children for the task of reading. Shared Book Reading involves teachers reading picture books to young children, and discussing meanings in the text and images. The exchange in Table 6 is a snippet of shared book reading of *Jack and the Beanstalk* (from Williams, 1995, p. 501). As participation in classroom exchanges is unequally distributed, a column is added specifying which students are addressed by the teacher, and which students respond.

Table 6

Shared book reading

	exchange	participation	cycles	sources	knowledge	activity phase
T	*Long ago in a far away land lived a widow and her son Jack.*	class		read text	*widow, her son Jack*	Task listening
T	*What's a widow?*	class	Focus	student knowledge	*widow* repeat	Evaluate knowledge
	It looks like a lady to me. [pointing to picture]	class	Prepare	refer & point image	*lady* class	
	What's a widow?	class	Focus	student	*widow*	
	Rhianna?	Rhianna		knowledge	repeat	
S	*An old woman.*	Rhianna	Propose	student knowledge	*old woman* member, synonym	
T	*Well she doesn't look too old.*	Rhianna	Reject	refer image	*not old* negate class	

The lesson activity begins with the teacher reading the first sentence of the book to the class, whose task is to sit and listen. She then directs a Focus question at the class, asking for a definition of "widow," the source for which must be the children's own knowledge. As there is no immediate response, the teacher prepares by giving the class the entity she wants, "lady," and points to the image in the book. Students now have their hands up and she selects Rhianna, who proposes "an old woman." This is consistent with the preparation, as *woman* is synonymous with *lady*, and *an old woman* is a member of that class. But this is not what the teacher wants and she rejects it by referring to the image (*doesn't look*) and negating the classifier *old*. This is a qualifying type of rejection that does not explicitly negate the entire response but is clearly not affirming. It may be argued these are not rejections, but students always know when a response is rejected.

Following Rhianna's failed response, the teacher provides a further clue (in the next extract), with a Focus question that all students can answer successfully, "Is there a daddy there?—No." On the basis of this successful response, she then asks them to guess what has happened to the daddy. Unfortunately, as she is giving this clue, one child is still trying to identify the answer in the picture. Each cycle is separated by a horizontal line, as follows.

Table 7

Shared book reading continued

	exchange	participation	cycles	sources	knowledge	activity phase
T	*Is there a daddy there?* [pointing to picture]	class	Focus	point image	*daddy there* co-class	Evaluate knowledge
Ss	*No.*	class	Identify			
T	*What do you think has happened to the daddy?*	class	Focus	student knowledge	*happened* class *to daddy* repeat	
S	*Looks like... a cow.*	David	Identify	refer image	*cow*	
T	*David?*	David	Focus			
S	*It's it's it's a little cow.*	David	Identify	refer image	*little cow*	
T	*No no.*	David	Reject		*not cow*	
T	*When there's a widow, something's happened to daddy.*	class	Focus	teacher knowledge	*widow,* repeat *happened to daddy* repeat	
S	*He died? Miss, he died?*	Student3	Propose	student knowledge	*died* member	
T	*Yes that's right.*	Student3	Affirm			
	A widow means that her husband has died.	class	Elaborate	teacher knowledge	*define widow = husband died*	Elaborate knowledge

David appears to be focused on the teacher's continual pointing at the image for criteria. As Rhianna's "woman" has been rejected, and there is no "daddy," the only other option in the image, aside from Jack, is the cow. He even repeats "looks like" which seems to be the teacher's criterion for interpreting images. Despite this achievement in reasoning and following the teacher's cues, the teacher explicitly negates David's proposal. She then repeats her Focus, but this time as a statement, giving rather than demanding information. This provides sufficient criteria for one student to recognise that the required answer is a member of the class of activities "happened to daddy," i.e., "he died." At last the teacher has a response she can affirm, and elaborate with an explicit definition from her own knowledge instead of the students'.

This rigmarole of asking the class to "guess-what's-in-the-teacher's-head" derives from the teacher's progressive/constructivist training not to tell students, but to encourage them to make inferences for themselves as inferencing is purported to be a cognitive skill in reading that children must acquire. The guessing game is part of a collection of activities sometimes called 'discovery learning' that is held to be learner-centred in contrast to teacher-centred traditional practices. The teacher has also been trained to encourage students to try and infer the meaning of words by looking at the accompanying pictures. Again this is widely touted as an early reading strategy, but is highly misleading as David's struggle illustrates. These practices are associated with representational and cognitivist theories of meaning that Firth was warning against 80 years ago, where "meaning is regarded chiefly as a mental relation" (1935 p.72), but remain pervasive in reading and learning theories.

What is the social order, relations and identities behind this instructional practice? The shared book reading genre is closely related to the parent-child reading genre with which it has co-evolved in middle class culture along with early childhood schooling (Bernstein, 1975). Their similarities are described by Williams (1995, 1999), and contrasted with parent-child reading practices in non-middle class families. Their continuities and disjunctions with mother tongue language learning are also discussed in Rose (2010), and Rose and Martin (2012). Their primary social function is to engage children in the pleasure of reading picture books, but other functions are shaped by the theories and practices of the school, such as encouraging inferencing above. Shared book reading is also used to train infants in behaviours such as sitting still and quietly, attending, responding to teacher questions, raising hands to speak, and giving relevant answers. The mode is dialogic; it is ancillary to the field of the story being read, but uses spoken, visual and manual modalities to engage children in written stories' monologic mode (detailed in Rose, 2010).

In this instance, the field of knowledge is initially the setting and characters of the story in its first sentence, but the teacher abruptly shifts this to knowledge of word definitions. The connection is the teacher's word level theory of meaning, in which she has been trained to teach vocabulary. At the rank of learning cycle, the task is to propose a definition, which David mis-reads as identifying an image. Two responses are rejected before one can be affirmed and finally elaborated. At the rank of lesson activity, the children's task is to comprehend the story as it is read aloud. The teacher may consider the function of the following cycles is to expand their comprehension by encouraging them to infer the meaning of "widow," but the regulative function is also to evaluate their knowledge. The elaboration of knowledge only becomes explicit when the teacher finally provides the definition. Such confusion of evaluation and learning activities is endemic in schools. In progressive/ constructivist theory, it is legitimated as learners constructing their own meanings, but the texts they produce are always still subject to evaluation. Pedagogic relations in this case are not inclusive as only a few children respond, two responses fail and only one is successful. So relations between students are hierarchical, as is the teacher/ student relation. Despite the theory of learner-centred practice, in which children are encouraged to guess for themselves, the teacher's institutional authority to evaluate and elaborate is always final.

Bernstein refers to this practice as "invisible pedagogy," in which criteria are known only to the teacher, and hierarchies are masked. In contrast to the exchange in Table 5, the social order in this practice (Table 6 & 7) is implicit and invisible, as it must be to mask its regulative function, which is to continually and relentlessly evaluate children on the ladder of success and failure, creating differentiated identities as successful or failing learners. This regulative practice appears to have evolved along with early years schooling, and the rise of the new middle class in the late twentieth century (Bernstein,

1975). It depends on universal features of children's primary socialisation in mother tongue language learning to engage and respond to the adult. Yet unlike mother tongue language learning, it functions to legitimate the inequality of participation and outcomes between children from middle class and other families in the school years that follow. It does so by socialising children into internalising their positions on the ladder as part of their personal identities. As Bernstein (2000) makes plain, "these biases can reach down to drain the very springs of affirmation, motivation and imagination" (p. xix).

Designing Curriculum Genres

Now let's turn to alternatives—to a sequence of curriculum genres informed by genre and register theory that are explicitly designed to enable all students to continually succeed at learning tasks no matter what their class, language or cultural backgrounds, and our analysis of pedagogic activities. This is the sequence of curriculum genres in the program known as *Reading to Learn* (Rose, 2014; Rose & Martin, 2012).

The first genre in the sequence is known as Preparing for Reading, the function of which is to enable all students to follow a text with general understanding as it is read, and to participate successfully in elaborating activities during and after reading. The preparation stage includes two elements: a synopsis of the field of the text to be read, and a step-by-step summary of how the field unfolds through the genre. This can be done at any stage of school or university with any text in any field. Its effect is that no student need struggle to follow the text as it is read. Telling learners what to expect as the text unfolds reduces their semiotic load, allowing them to attend to the field without overload. The text may then be read aloud, which further reduces the semiotic load as they need not struggle to decode unfamiliar words. Some longer texts such as novel chapters or short stories may be read all at once, but denser texts may be read paragraph-by-paragraph, in which case each paragraph may be briefly prepared, read and elaborated. Preparing for reading *Jack and the Beanstalk* could begin as follows.

This is a story from a long time ago. It's about a young boy named Jack who lived with his mother. His mother was a widow. That means her husband, Jack's father had died. They were very poor. The only money they got was by selling the milk from their cow. But the cow stopped making milk, so Jack's mother told him to take the cow to the market and sell it for money. On the way, he met an old man who had some magic beans, and he persuaded Jack to swap the cow for the beans. When Jack got home without any money, his mother was very angry. She threw the beans on the ground outside, and sent Jack to bed. The next morning, when Jack woke up, the beans had grown into an enormous beanstalk that stretched right up into the sky...

Whereas academic texts may require prior introduction to the field, stories generally require no synopsis other than a summary of the field (i.e., plot) unfolding through each phase of the story genre. In addition, key lexical items are included in the preparation, such as the definition of widow. The preparation is analogous with a roadmap for following the text with certain lexical elements as sign-posts that students recognise. Planning requires teachers to analyse a text's structure phase-by-phase, and note essential items to include in the preparation. Such analyses are facilitated by knowledge about genres and their structures. *Jack and the Beanstalk,* for example, is a recount, consisting of a series of episodes, and many episodes include a setting, problem and solution phase. Recognising such patterns is invaluable for teachers to plan Preparing for Reading. With multimodal texts such as children's picture books, the illustrations are also used to support the preparation. This may be done for the whole text before reading or one page at a time. After reading, key elements of a text may be discussed to reinforce and extend students' understanding of the field. Again these elaborations may follow reading the whole text or after reading each paragraph.

The second curriculum genre in the sequence is Detailed Reading, in which the teacher guides students to read an extract from the reading text sentence-by-sentence, identifying and discussing each element of meaning as they go. Detailed Reading functions to enable all students to read the passage with complete comprehension and fluency, and to recognise the language choices the author has made, so they can recognise such choices in other texts and deploy them in their own writing. Detailed Reading uses carefully designed learning cycles that enable the teacher to engage every student in a class in recognising the meanings under focus, and to benefit equally from elaborations. This type of design can be illustrated with the opening sentence from *Jack and the Beanstalk*. The exchange begins with the teacher preparing the sentence with its function and a simple synopsis before reading it, and then preparing each element of meaning before asking students to identify them.

Table 8

Detailed Reading

		participat.	cycles	sources	knowledge
T	*This is the setting of the story. The first sentence says that Jack lived with his mother. Look at the words and I'll read it.*	class	Prepare sentence	refer text	*setting, first sentence, jack, his mother*
	'Long ago in a far away land lived a widow and her son Jack.'	class		read text	repeat
T	*Now, right at the beginning of that sentence it tells us when the story happened.*	class	Prepare	refer text	*that sentence when happened*
	S1, can you see the words that say when it happened?	student 1	Focus	"	class
S	*Long ago*	student 1	Identify	read text	instance
T	*That's exactly right*	student 1	Affirm		
	Let's all highlight the words "long ago."	class	Direct	refer text	repeat
	Long ago means many years ago, before you or your parents or even your grandparents were born. Fairy stories often start like this.	class	Elaborate	teacher knowledge	define function in genre
T	*Who can tell me another way fairy stories start by saying when it happened?*	class	Focus	student knowledge	*when happened* class
S	*Once upon a time*	student 2	Propose	"	instance
T	*Exactly*	student 2	Affirm		
	Once upon a time also means long ago.	class	Elaborate	teacher knowledge	repeat

T	Then it tells us where the story happened.	class	Prepare	refer text	*where happened*
	S3, can you see where it happened?	student 3	Focus	"	*class*
S	*In a faraway land*	student 3	Identify	read text	instance
T	*Excellent*	student 3	Affirm		
	Everyone highlight the two words faraway land.	class	Direct	refer text	repeat
	That's another way fairy stories often start. It's long ago and far away because it's very different from how we live now.	class	Elaborate	teacher knowledge	explain functions in genre
T	*Next it tells us the two main characters in the story.*	class	Prepare	refer text	*characters class*
	S4, who is the first one?	student 4	Focus	"	*who class*
S	*A widow*	student 4	Identify	read text	instance
T	*Right*	student 4	Affirm		
	Let's highlight the word widow.	class	Direct	refer text	repeat
T	*Who remembers what widow means? S5?*	class	Focus	remind prior lesson	repeat
S	*Jack's daddy died*	student 5	Propose	recall prior lesson	define *widow*
T	*Exactly right*	student 5	Affirm		
	A widow is a woman whose husband has died.	class	Elaborate	adjust	re-define *widow*
T	*Who's the next character, S6?*	student 6	Focus	refer text	*character class*
S	*Her son Jack*	student 6	Identify	read text	instance
T	*Yep*	student 6	Affirm		
	Highlight son Jack.	class	Direct	refer text	repeat
	So there's just the two of them. So that's the setting of the story, it tells who it's about and where and when it happened.	class	Elaborate	"	enhance field define story phase

Detailed Reading in Table 8 unfolds in highly predictable cycles of Prepare, Focus, Identify, Affirm, Direct and Elaborate. The predictability of the pedagogic activity enables all students to engage in a complex discussion of the text's register and language patterns.

With regard to participation, preparations and elaborations involve the whole class, but focus questions and affirmations are directed at individuals by name, to ensure that every student is actively and successfully engaged. In this instance, six students are affirmed in the space of just one sentence, but the whole class successfully performs the identifying and highlighting tasks, so all are prepared for the elaborations. What prepares them for elaborations is their semiotic work in identifying the wordings from the teacher's meaning cues, and this learning activity rapidly orients students to recognising related patterns in other texts. Note also that student responses need not be entirely accurate to be affirmed, as the teacher then directs the class precisely what to highlight.

Sources of meanings are generally the text itself, and teacher knowledge in elaborations. Student knowledge is elicited when the teacher is confident that students can respond successfully, such as recalling prior lessons. There is an elaborate interplay of modalities here from the spoken preparation to focusing visual attention (*Can you see the words?*), to the written wording that students identify, to the manual practice of highlighting, and back to the spoken mode in elaborations. Each cycle is a wave of information with peaks in the preparation and elaboration when attention is focused on what the teacher and students are saying, and a trough in the identifying phase, allowing students to focus their attention on the written text. Martin (2006) describes the textual and interpersonal patterns of Detailed Reading cycles as follows.

> ...we can recognise a wave of information structure with lots of information at the beginning and end of the complex and a much narrower band of relatively redundant information at its centre—a pulse of preparation content which wanes from an initial peak towards a central trough and then waxes again in the culminative extension. And beyond this it is important to recognise a prosody of positive affect radiating through the exchange complex... and amplified in the [affirmations of] successful identifications by the class. (p.215)

These tiers of ideational, textual and interpersonal structure are outlined in Figure 6.

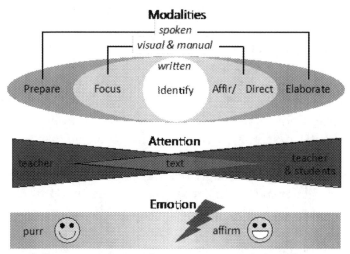

Figure 6. Modalities, attention and emotion in Detailed Reading.

Knowledge exchanged includes both the field of the text and knowledge about language at the levels of genre, register and discourse (*fairy story, setting, characters, often start this way, first sentence*). Preparation cues often give a general class of meaning (*main characters, who, when it happened, where*), and Focus questions repeat these cues. The students' task is then to identify instances of these semantic categories in the sentence. They are supported to do so by position cues (*right at the beginning of that sentence, then, next*) as they highlight each element in turn. Elaborations capitalise on their success to discuss meanings at the more abstract levels of genre, register and discourse. The teacher may give the elaboration or ask students to propose one from their knowledge (*Who can tell me another way fairy stories start? Who remembers what widow means?*). The final elaboration reinforces and extends explicit knowledge about the genre (*setting of the story*). Such abstract elaborations are given after students have control of the text's field, embedding knowledge about language within knowledge about the field of study. While the field in this instance is a children's fairy story, the same practice can be applied to any text at any level of education.

These designed learning cycles are related to the standard classroom practice of asking questions to engage students in the construction of knowledge. But this is an evolved, universal, intuitive practice that teachers acquire and deploy tacitly. Although it is a fundamental mode of classroom teaching, involving a complex set of skills, teachers are rarely trained to do it, beyond general protocols for "questioning techniques." Typically only a handful of students consistently respond (Nuthall, 2005; Rose & Martin, 2012), and teachers use their responses to elaborate with items of knowledge they want the whole class to acquire. The broad pedagogic function of this practice is to reduce students' semiotic load by breaking up the acquisition of knowledge into manageable segments, guiding students to apply their own knowledge to the field. The practice is a feature of most curriculum genres to a greater or lesser extent (see, for example, Alexander, 2000, who describes international practices). At one extreme is the academic lecture, where knowledge is transmitted in a continuous stream and the learning task is to listen and interpret independently; next are tutorials or secondary school lessons, in which the transmission of knowledge is interspersed with questions to the class; more interactive are primary school classes, in which knowledge is continuously negotiated with questions and responses. The shared book reading (Table 6 & 7) illustrates a maximally interactive variant of the practice in the early school years.

One reason that so few students consistently respond in any class is that questions typically demand interpretations of the field from students' own knowledge. Inevitably only a few students can provide appropriate responses successfully, while other students learn to avoid rejection by remaining silent. As the shared book reading (Table 6 & 7) illustrates, this socialisation starts at the beginning of school and continues relentlessly over the years that follow. Detailed Reading resolves this problem in three ways: firstly, the initial source of responses is the text that is available to all rather than a few students' exclusive knowledge; second, the task is prepared with meaning and position cues that all can understand and apply; third, the task of articulating the identified wording is directed at individual students by name, so that all get an equal opportunity to respond. This practice has the added advantage of managing students' attention and behaviour through success and affirmation, rather than control and admonishment. No one knows who will be asked next, so all are continually ready, and the expectation of success and public affirmation is a powerful motivator for every student.

This regulative practice is closer to that of the exchange in Table 5 than the shared book reading in Table 6 and 7. Pedagogic relations are deliberately inclusive and equal between students, guided by the teacher's explicit authority. The knowledge exchanged is explicitly beyond that of any student, but is made equally accessible to all by the teacher's interactive guidance. This is accomplished by a carefully designed traversal of pedagogic modalities, managing students' attention and emotion through the phases of each learning cycle and culminating in elaborations of knowledge that all students are prepared to acquire.

Practice with planning and managing the complexities of the Detailed Reading genre gradually gives teachers the skills to confidently deploy its design of pedagogic activities, relations and modalities in other curriculum genres in the *Reading to Learn* sequence. It can be used in paragraph-by-paragraph reading, to guide students to identify key information in each paragraph, and in the elaborating discussion that follows reading. It can also be used to guide writing. Following Detailed Reading, the sequence can proceed down the language strata to focus on grammar and graphology or it can go straight to writing new texts.

The writing genre that follows Detailed Reading is known as Joint Rewriting, in which the teacher guides students to appropriate the language resources from the Detailed Reading passage to write a new text. For stories, these resources are the literary language devices in each sentence. For arguments and text responses, they are the patterns of appraisal that evaluate an issue, position or text. For factual texts, they are the ideational elements in each sentence. For stories, the preparation stage involves generating a new field for the text. The teacher guides students to propose options by pointing to the original passage, and asking students to consider what innovations in plot, setting and characters would fit its patterns. Students then take turns to scribe the new text, as the teacher guides the class to propose new elements for each sentence. For example, as *Jack and the Beanstalk* is a fairy tale, its discursive patterns could be appropriated to write a different story in the same register as follows.

> Long ago in a far away land lived a widow and her son Jack. All they owned was a cow. Every day they sold some of the cow's milk. Then one day the cow stopped giving milk. Jack's

mother said to him, "Take the cow to the market. Sell her and bring me the money."

Rewrite:

> Once upon a time, in a village near a wood, lived a woman and her daughter Red Riding Hood. In the wood in a little cottage lived her grandmother. Every week Red Riding Hood took some food to her grandmother. One day they packed a basket of food. Red Riding Hood's mother said to her, "Take the basket to Grandma. Give the food to her, but don't talk to any strangers on the way."

And so on. Learning cycles in Joint Rewriting are prepared by pointing to each sentence element in turn, and considering alternatives that would fit the overall discourse and grammar patterns of the sentence and passage. The students' tasks are to propose options, and take turns scribing. Elaborations include rephrasing students' proposals, and discussing language features at the levels of genre, register, discourse, grammar, and graphology as students scribe the chosen elements on the board.

Following Joint Rewriting, students attempt their own versions, in the activity known as Individual Rewriting. For stories, they choose their own plot, setting and characters, and follow the same literary patterns as the original and joint rewrite. This is a powerful technique for learners to appropriate the culture's reservoir of literary language devices into their own repertoire. This is, of course, what experienced readers and accomplished writers do more or less intuitively. Explicit guidance in these curriculum genres brings this practice to consciousness, so that both the stronger and weaker writers in a class acquire the literary resources of accomplished authors. Rewriting may be compared to the *imitatio* tradition of classical rhetoric except that the guidance provided in Detailed Reading and Joint Rewriting ensures that every student succeeds in the tasks. The effect extends well beyond the particular patterns in any one passage as repeated guided practice gives all students a conscious orientation to recognising and appropriating language resources as they read.

The language focus of Detailed Reading and Rewriting is on the discourse and grammar patterns that instantiate the register of particular texts. In the next curriculum genre in the sequence, Joint Construction, the focus is on patterns of genre and register. In the original genre writing TLC outlined earlier, model texts were deconstructed as far as their generic stages, and characteristic language features. In the *Reading to Learn* sequence, deconstruction goes further to appropriate the structures of phases within each generic stage of a model. Martin in this volume presents an example which used an extract of Mandela's *Long Walk to Freedom* as a model. The Joint Construction by a class of Indigenous university students followed the phasal structure of Mandela's autobiographical recount precisely, as follows (Table 9).

Table 9

Joint construction of class

phases	Mandela's model	Joint Construction
setting	*born free*	*adventures of life*
comment	*obeyed my father*	*listened to my elders*
episode1	*as a young man*	*started school*
episode2	*as a student*	*from my first day at school*
episode3	*as a young man in Johannesburg*	*as a teenager in high school*
episode4	*my brothers and sisters were not free*	*my family also needed a role model*
episode5	*joined the African National Congress*	*decided to go to university*
comment	*Freedom is indivisible*	*Education is indispensable*

The obligatory staging of a recount is simply Orientation and Record, as set out in Tables 1 and 2. But phases within stages are more variable, depending on the genre and register. In this instance the Orientation includes a setting and comment phase while the Record includes a series of episodes that are stages in the author's life, concluding with a comment (see Rose, 2006; Martin & Rose, 2008, for more detail on types of phases). Joint Construction in *Reading to Learn* follows the phasal patterns of model texts for the same reason that Joint Rewriting follows the sentence patterns of

Detailed Reading passages; it is a powerful technique for guiding students to appropriate the repertoires of accomplished authors into their own at the levels of register unfolding through genre. In this particular lesson, Rewriting was combined with Joint Construction, but typically Rewriting is done with short passages, and Joint Construction with whole texts.

Martin also presents the sequences of curriculum genres in the *Reading to Learn* program diagrammatically, as a series of nested cycles. The sequence is re-presented below with glosses for the functions of each genre, their language focus and scale of text.

curriculum genres	functions	language focus
Preparing for Reading	Understanding texts as they are read	Patterns of field unfolding through genre
Detailed Reading	Reading literary, abstract and technical language in depth	Patterns of meaning within and between sentences
SentenceMaking Spelling SentenceWriting	Embedding foundation literacy skills in reading and writing curriculum texts	Functions of word groups in sentences, words in groups, letter patterns in words
Joint Rewriting	Appropriating literary, abstract and technical language from reading	Grammatical structures as sentences are rewritten
Joint Construction	Constructing successful texts for assessment	Stages and phases of genres explicitly labelled

(Left-hand vertical labels: whole text; passage; sentence)

Figure 7. Genre functions and language focus.

Knowledge

I have outlined one trajectory of research in the work of the "Sydney School" from the description of a handful of knowledge genres in the primary school, and design of a curriculum genre for teaching students to write them, to far more elaborate descriptions of knowledge genres across education institutions, and more detailed descriptions and designs of curriculum genres for reading and writing.

I have also shown how genre and register analysis can be applied to any curriculum genre to display its configurations of pedagogic activities, pedagogic relations and pedagogic modalities, and their roles in the exchange of knowledge and creation of identities. I have illustrated how genres of mother tongue language learning have evolved to be maximally effective by means of continual affirmation and elaboration of a child's communicative acts. We have also seen how the curriculum genres of the school have evolved to be instructionally effective for some students more than others by means of continually unequal distributions of affirmation and unequal preparedness for elaborations of knowledge. In terms of regulative practice, these genres are effective for the reproduction of social hierarchies through unequal acquisition of knowledge in school, and internalisation of learner identities along the ladder of success and failure. This is the regulative practice of the school, no matter what the ostensible instructional theory, traditional, behaviourist, progressive, constructivist, critical. Finally I have shown how this regulative practice can be subverted by deliberate redesign of pedagogic activities, relations and modalities, informed by genre and register theory. But this is no mere theoretical exercise; these redesigned curriculum genres have been achieving results for over fifteen years across education sectors, and are on average four times more effective than standard practices for the least successful students and one and a half times more effective for the most successful (Culican, 2006; Rose et al., 2008; Rose & Martin, 2013). In currently fashionable parlance, they are phenomenally effective at closing the gap in education outcomes.

One strand of "Sydney School" research that I have only touched on is the knowledge exchanged through the school's curriculum genres. We have seen that this knowledge is of two orders: knowledge of curriculum fields, and knowledge about the language that realises them. The school has evolved to provide at least one group of students with types of knowledge that are remote from the everyday experience of most children, and that have and are evolving in institutions that control the social and natural worlds. The language that has evolved to realise these fields, primarily in written modes, is abstract, technical and condensed. To participate in the controlling institutions of modernism through professional education, students must learn to control these patterns of meaning.

If we wish to provide all students with access to these resources, and hence to the knowledge structures of these institutions, then teachers require two orders of explicit knowledge: knowledge about the semiotic structures of their curriculum fields and the language that realises them; and knowledge about the semiotic structures of their own instructional practice. Research in the "Sydney School" has gone a long way to describing the first (Halliday & Martin, 1993; Christie 1999; Christie & Martin 1997, 2007; Martin & Veel, 1998; Martin & Rose, 2003/2007, 2008; Christie & Maton, 2011); the latest generation of research is focusing on the second (Christie, 2002; Rose, 2004; Martin, 2006, 2012; Rose & Martin, 2012; Martin & Maton, 2013).

Genre pedagogy is designed to integrate each of these domains of knowledge in pedagogic practice. In popular terms, language and literacy learning is embedded in learning curriculum content, and both are embedded in a designed pedagogic practice. The school's dis-integration of these dimensions of learning serves its stratifying regulative functions. Independent reading and writing skills are supposed to be acquired at the start of school, making way for the learning of curriculum content, construed as systems of concepts. While learning is construed as a generic cognitive activity; both content and learning are imagined apart from their actual contexts in knowledge and curriculum genres. If students do not acquire the requisite literacy skills early, they may be assessed as lacking cognitive abilities to acquire curriculum concepts, and may be prescribed generic literacy or numeracy remediation. Similarly, if they arrive at school with a different mother tongue, they may be prescribed generic language remediation separate from the curriculum content their peers are studying. These institutional practices may be traced to the divorce of language and subject knowledge in the trivium and quadrivium of the classical and medieval academies; they distort the integral relations between knowledge, language and learning. Sydney School research has aimed to describe the complexes of knowledge genres and semiotic modes that constitute curriculum fields, and the curriculum genres through which they are acquired. The outcome is a pedagogy that enables teachers to guide successful acquisition of knowledge through reading the curriculum, and displays of knowledge in writing, not just for the elite but for every student in the school.

References

Alexander, R. (2000). *Culture & pedagogy: International comparisons in primary education.* Oxford: Blackwell.

Bernstein, B. (1975). Class and pedagogies: Visible and invisible. *Educational Studies, 1*(1), 23-41.

Bernstein, B. (1990). *Class, codes and control 4: The structuring of pedagogic discourse.* London: Routledge.

Bernstein, B. (2000). *Pedagogy, symbolic control and identity: Theory, research, critique.* London: Taylor & Francis.

Christie, F. (Ed.). (1999). *Pedagogy and the shaping of consciousness: Linguistic and social processes.* London: Cassell.

Christie, F. (2002). *Classroom discourse analysis.* London: Continuum.

Christie, F., & Martin, J. R. (Eds.). (1997). *Genre and institutions: Social processes in the workplace and school.* London: Cassell.

Christie, F., & Martin, J. R. (Eds.). (2007). *Language, knowledge and pedagogy: Functional linguistic and sociological perspectives.* London: Cassell.

Christie, F., & Maton, K. (Eds.). (2011). *Disciplinarity: Functional linguistic and sociological perspectives.* London: Continuum.

Culican, S. (2006). *Learning to read: Reading to learn, A middle years literacy intervention research project.* Catholic Education Office: Melbourne. Retrieved from http://www.readingto learn.com.au

Edelman, G. (1992). *Bright air, brilliant fire: On the matter of the mind.* New York: Basic Books.

Firth, J. R. (1935). The technique of semantics. *Transactions of the Philological Society, 34*(1), 36-73.

Gregory, M. 1967 Aspects of varieties differentiation. *Journal of Linguistics* 3. 177-198.

Halliday, M. A. K. (1975). *Learning how to mean: Explorations in the development of language.* London: Edward Arnold.

Halliday, M. A. K .& Matthiessen, C. M. I. M. (2004). *An introduction to functional grammar.* London: Arnold. Originally published in 1985.

Halliday, M. A. K., & Martin, J. R. (993). *Writing science: Literacy and discursive power.* London: Falmer.

Hasan, R. (1984). The nursery tale as a genre. *Nottingham Linguistic Circular* 13 (Special Issue on Systemic Linguistics). 71-102.

Malinowski, B. 1935 *Coral Gardens and their Magic.* London: Allen & Unwin.

Martin, J. R. (1992). *English text: System and structure.* Amsterdam: John Benjamins.

Martin, J. R. (2006). Metadiscourse: Designing interaction in genre-based literacy programs. In R. Whittaker, M. O'Donnell & A. McCabe (Eds.), *Language and literacy: Functional approaches* (pp. 95-122). London: Continuum.

Martin, J. R. (2012). *Forensic linguistics.* In W. Zhenhua's (Ed.), *Vol. 8: Collected Works of J. R. Martin.* Shanghai: Shanghai Jiao Tong University Press

Martin, J. R., & Maton, K. (Eds.). (2013). Cumulative Knowledge-building in Secondary Schooling. *Linguistics and Education* (Special issue), *24*(1), 38-49.

Martin, J. R., & Rose, D. (2003). *Working with discourse: Meaning beyond the clause.* London: Continuum.

Martin, J. R., & Rose, D. (2008). *Genre relations: Mapping culture.* London: Equinox.

Martin, J. R., & Veel, R. (Eds.). (1998). *Reading science: Critical and functional perspectives on discourses of science.* London: Routledge.

Nuthall, G. A. (2005). The cultural myths and realities of classroom teaching and learning: A personal journey. *Teachers College Record*, *107*(5), 895-934.

Painter, C. (1986). The role of interaction in learning to speak and learning to write. In C. Painter & J.R. Martin (Eds.), *Writing to mean: Teaching genres across the curriculum* (pp. 62-97). Applied Linguistics Association of Australia (Occassional Papers 9).

Painter, C. (1991). *Learning the mother tongue* (2nd ed.). Geelong, Vic.: Deakin University Press.

Painter, C. (1999). *Learning through language in early childhood.* London: Cassell.

Plum, G. 1998 *Text and Contextual Conditioning in Spoken English: a genre-based approach.* Nottingham: University of Nottingham (Monographs in Systemic Linguistics 10). *minerva.ling.mq.edu.au/ network/SysWorld/sflist/gplum_v1.pdf*

Rose, D. (1998). Science discourse & industrial hierarchy. In J.R. Martin & R. Veel (Eds.), *Reading science: Critical and functional perspectives on discourses of science* (pp. 236-265). London: Routledge.

Rose, D. (2001). *The western desert code: An Australian cryptogrammar.* Canberra: Pacific Linguistics.

Rose, D. (2004). Sequencing and pacing of the hidden curriculum: How indigenous children are left out of the chain. In J. Muller, A. Morais & B. Davies (Eds.), *Reading Bernstein, researching Bernstein* (pp. 91-107). London: Routledge Falmer.

Rose, D. (2006). Reading genre: A new wave of analysis. *Linguistics and the Human Sciences, 2*(2), 185–204.

Rose, D. (2008). Writing as linguistic mastery: The development of genre-based literacy pedagogy. In R. Beard, D. Myhill, J. Riley & M. Nystrand (Eds.), *Handbook of writing development* (pp. 151-166). London: Sage.

Rose, D. (2010). Meaning beyond the margins: Learning to interact with books. In J. Martin, S. Hood & S. Dreyfus (Eds.), *Semiotic margins: Reclaiming meaning* (pp. 177-208). London: Continuum.

Rose, D. (2014). *Reading to learn: Accelerating learning and closing the gap.* Sydney: Reading to Learn. Retrieved from http://www.readingtolearn.com.au

Rose, D., & Martin, J. R. (2012). *Learning to write, reading to learn: Genre, knowledge and pedagogy in the Sydney School.* London: Equinox.

Rose, D., & Martin, J. R. (2013). Intervening in contexts of schooling. In J. Flowerdew (Ed.), *Discourse in context: Contemporary applied linguistics (Volume 3)* (pp. 447-475). London: Continuum.

Rose, D., McInnes, D., & Korner, H. (1992). *Scientific literacy (Write it right literacy in industry research project - stage 1).* Sydney: Metropolitan East Disadvantaged Schools Program. 308 pp. [reprinted Sydney: NSW AMES 2007]

Rose, D., Rose, M., Farrington, S., & Page, S. (2008). Scaffolding literacy for indigenous health sciences students. *Journal of English for Academic Purposes, 7*(3), 166-180.

Rothery, J. (1994). *Exploring literacy in school English (Write it Right Resources for Literacy and Learning).* Sydney: Metropolitan East Disadvantaged Schools Program [republished 2007 by Adult Migrant Education Service NSW]

Rothery, J 1996 Making changes: developing an educational linguistics. R Hasan & G Williams [Eds.] 1996 *Literacy in Society.* London: Longman. 86-123.

Saussure, F. (1966). *Course in general linguistics.* New York: McGraw-Hill. (Original work published 1916)

Williams, G. (1995). *Joint book-reading and literacy pedagogy: A socio-semantic examination.* Unpublished doctoral dissertation. MacQuairie University: Department of Linguistics.

Williams, G. (1999). The pedagogic device and the production of discourse: A case example in early literacy education. In F. Christie's (Ed.), *Pedagogy and the shaping of consciousness* (pp. 88-122). London: Continuum.

Chapter 14

Bending Genres, or When is a Deviation an Innovation?

Christine M. Tardy

University of Arizona (USA)

I'd like to begin by sharing an excerpt of a text. As you read it, consider what genre you feel the text belongs to and what aspects of the text give you that impression.

A Brief Introduction to the Artist and His Education

As the records show, Juan Tauber was born in 1978 in a small city named Rio Cuarto in the province of Cordoba, Argentina. The artist completed his elementary and secondary education in that town. At the age of 19, presumably fleeing from the law with a much older lover, he moved to the capital of that country, Buenos Aires. There, Tauber enrolled in the UBA (University of Buenos Aires) pursuing a degree in textile design. Three years later, in 1999, Tauber found his passion in the fine arts and began painting.

In December of the year 2000, for reasons still unknown, the artists relocated to the United States of America. Soon after he's arrival to the city of Chicago, we found records of the artist's efforts to become acquainted with the English language. During January 2001 documents show his enrollment to the Lakeview Learning Center, ESL program, where he was placed at a 102 level.[1] Tauber finished these language lessons relatively quick graduating from this institution in December of the same year. Five years later, the artist joined the {Midwest University} community. In January 2007, he enrolled in this institution pursuing a degree in fine arts.

[1]This shows that Tauber's first efforts to communicate in English happened relatively late in life and explain some of the major flaws on his writing techniques. It is common, and valued, in Spanish writing to create very long sentences where an arrangement of multiple ideas are linked by commas. This is a mistake that we not only see in the amount of run on sentences present in every draft, but also in the awkward transitions of ideas separated by periods in certain paragraphs.

While reading, you may have found yourself trying to identify its purpose, exigence, and audience; indeed, you may have found the text to be a bit perplexing in terms of genre. It seems to have elements of a biography or historical narrative, but also includes features that seem bound to a school context. What is the text responding to? This excerpt was taken from a reflective cover letter submitted in a writing portfolio by a student named Juan Tauber in my first-year composition course a few years ago. Juan was an art student from Argentina, and he was not one to write within the box. For each course assignment, he took an unconventional approach, but when assembling his portfolio at the end of the term, he decided to bend pretty much all the rules. His portfolio was presented as a collection of archival documents written by a famous, now deceased, artist (Juan Tauber) but assembled by an art historian or biographer. The cover letter is re-purposed into a prologue describing the newly discovered writings of the artist. Juan even re-designed his papers for the portfolio so that they resembled crumpled artifacts rather than freshly submitted student papers (Figure 1). What is particularly inventive about Juan's portfolio is its ability to resist the traditional generic norms and expectations while still addressing the reflective and educational goals of the assignment.

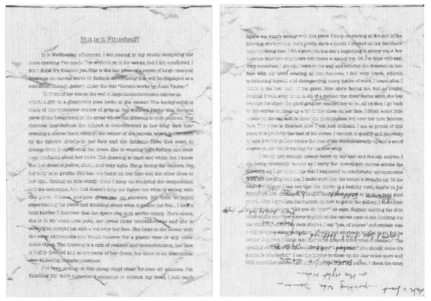

Figure 1. Pages from Juan's writing course portfolio.

Juan chose to respond to this classroom assignment in a unique and somewhat risky way. In this case, his text was lauded as innovative and successful, later winning a university-wide writing award, but in other circumstances it might have been considered an inappropriate response to the assignment. It is this question—when and why an unconventional text might be perceived as innovative versus deviant—that I take up in this chapter.

Genre Innovation

Contemporary genre theory has led to greater understandings of many aspects of texts and writing. We know a fairly good deal about the conventions that characterize certain genres and discourse communities (Halliday & Martin, 1993; Hyland, 2000; Swales, 1990, 2004), as well as how conventions come into being and how they, in turn, shape the values and practices of communities (Bazerman, 1988; Berkenkotter & Huckin, 1995). We now have excellent studies of genre change over time (Yates & Orlikowski, 1992) and, more recently, of emerging genres (Giltrow & Stein, 2009). We also know a fair bit about how genre systems and activity systems coordinate and carry out the work of social groups (Berkenkotter, 2001; Russell, 1997), and how genres travel through communities and organizations (Spinuzzi, 2003). We are also learning more about how writers of different language backgrounds and literacy contexts develop knowledge of genres and an ability to use them in rhetorically effective ways (Artemeva, 2008; Gentil, 2011; Tardy, 2009). Since at least the 1990s, genre theory has cautioned us to view genres as dynamic and fluctuating, referring to them through metaphors such as *life forms, agents,* or *actants* (Devitt, 2011). But despite this acknowledgement—or perhaps insistence—that genres are not constraining templates, very little scholarship has directly explored how writers effectively *flout* or *bend* generic conventions. Schryer (2011) and Devitt (2011) have both suggested viewing genres metaphorically as *improvisation* or *play,* yet we know less about how far these metaphors can stretch in various literacy contexts—particularly in the stereotypically stodgy sites of academic writing.

Taking on this issue in its entirety is obviously well beyond the scope of a single paper, so I'd like to focus in on a more modest set of questions: To what extent can and do student academic writers play, improvise, or innovate with genres? What kinds of innovations are valued by teachers, if any? To answer these questions, in my mind, we need a set of theoretical constructs to help understand what is going on when genres are bent, and we then need to look, systematically, at actual writing contexts.

Before diving into the theoretical waters, I first need to address the definitional issue of *genre innovation,* a term which I'll use throughout this chapter. For the purposes of my discussion here, I use this phrase to refer to departures from genre convention that are perceived as effective and successful by the text's intended audience or community of practice. There may be some argument for understanding innovation even more broadly, encompassing both successful and unsuccessful norm-departures, but because of the typically positive connotation of the term innovation and because of my interest in understanding *perceptions* that a norm-departure is "innovative" (as opposed to deviant), I have opted for a somewhat more contained use of the term.

Many theoretical constructs are relevant to understanding genre innovation, but in an attempt to create a fairly straightforward framework, I focus on just three here, drawing on creativity theory, systems theory, and Bourdieu's (1991) social theory of symbolic capital.

Creativity studies is a field of inquiry largely situated within psychology but also interdisciplinary in scope and encompassing several different orientations. This diversity of thought notwithstanding, one very common view of creativity characterizes it by *originality or novelty* and *usefulness, appropriateness, or value* (Kozbelt, Beghetto, & Runco, 2010; Pope 2005; Sawyer 2012). Scholars generally agree that creativity tends to be the result of formal training, conscious thought, hard work, and high productivity. Whether it be a poem, a sonata, or a scientific study, creative products work *within the boundaries of genre,* bending certain conventions but by no means all. As psychologist Sawyer (2012) notes, "We don't expect every aspect of a creative work to be novel. All creative works liberally draw on shared conventions, and that fact alone doesn't make us question the creativity of the work" (p. 237). When applying this concept to genre theory, then, we might expect that creative or innovative uses of genre are novel in some ways but still conventional in many ways. Experience with genres may, then, be an important aid in genre innovation.

Within the broader field of creativity studies, sociocultural approaches align best with genre theory. These approaches emphasize the social nature of creativity and the extent to which a product or idea is not inherently creative but, rather, is *judged* as creative (i.e., novel and appropriate) by specific people in specific spaces and historical moments. As Amabile (1982) stated, "...a product is creative when experts in the domain agree it is creative" (p. 1001).

Psychologist Csikszentmihalyi (1999) has proposed the use of systems theory to understand the interacting levels that influence the sociocultural process and evaluation of creativity: the *individual* who serves as the source of the innovation; the *field*, defined specifically as the social networks or gatekeepers who initially evaluate the product's novelty and appropriateness; and the *domain*, made up of the larger system for conventions and common practices from which individuals draw. This system serves as a useful heuristic for analyzing specific literacy contexts and judgments of genres as innovative or deviant—though there is a case for adding one more component to the system for our purposes, and this is *genre* (see Figure 2). While some genres may be relatively open to innovation, others seem more resistant to norm-departing. Bhatia (2006) refers to these as liberal and conservative genres, respectively. Taking the nature of the genre into account—within the context of a larger social system—can help explain why the same writer within, say, a writing classroom, can "get away with" flouting conventions in a memoir assignment but not in a research paper.

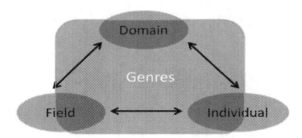

Figure 2. Adaptation of Csikszentmihalyi's (1999) system theory of creativity.

One criticism of this systems-based approach is that it does not foreground how power operates within the system and, therefore, judgments of creativity. For this, we may usefully turn to Bourdieu's (1991) economic metaphor of the linguistic market. For Bourdieu, an utterance must satisfy three "ritual conditions" (p. 113) in order to be granted social power: It must be produced *by* a legitimate authority, *within* a legitimate situation, and *in* legitimate forms. So, who can be considered a "legitimate authority"? According to Bourdieu, legitimacy is granted through the accumulation of linguistic, symbolic, or cultural capital. It is not surprising that many examples of innovation in academic writing come from authors who have already established their linguistic and disciplinary competence and who hold relatively high status within their field. These writers can exchange their accumulated capital for the right to depart from dominant norms because they already have what Bourdieu calls a *profit of distinction*—that is, they have access to scarce linguistic competences (language varieties, genres, discourses) that hold social power. The relative scarcity of these competencies makes them more valuable or profitable. But "legitimate" writers likely also bring with them other forms of accumulated capital, such as professional and/or cultural capital.

So far, I've offered three theoretical concepts that could be useful in understanding what I'm calling genre innovation, or in helping us consider the question of *when is a deviation an innovation?* I turn now to an academic literacy context to explore the extent to which these concepts can be productively employed to help us understand genre innovation.

Classroom Example: *Research Methods* in Environmental Science

I wanted to examine this issue within a context in which particular disciplinary conventions are explicitly taught and usually expected, at least to some degree, and one in which writers often face challenges in terms of being perceived as legitimate. While there certainly are school settings that encourage experimentation with traditional genres, it is likely more common for students to find themselves in classrooms in which they are expected to emulate— rather than innovate—privileged genres. My choice of context for this research, then, was a setting that I believe is fairly typical in undergraduate education in many countries: a discipline-specific research course.

The course I observed was an upper-level environmental science class, titled *Research Methods*. As stated in the syllabus and by the instructor, the course was intended to prepare students to complete their required senior research projects within about one year after the *Research Methods* course. The major course assignment consisted of a proposal for this research project. The course, however, was not focused solely—or even primarily—on proposal writing. From my perspective as an observer, it might best be characterized as a course on "how to think like a scientist." Students read articles on the nature of science, research design, and ethics; they discussed scientific practices like publication and collaboration; they heard various environmental science faculty members describe their research; and they shared articles related to their own proposed projects while the instructor modeled analysis of these articles.

The class met twice per week for a 10-week term as was required for all environmental science majors. Most of the 13 students in the class were nearing the end of their third year, just preparing to start their final-year research project. The course was taught by a senior faculty member, whom I will refer to here as Professor Hanson (a pseudonym). Reflecting the more general demographics of students in the program, all class members were English-dominant users, and 10 of the 13 were women.

Again, the primary aim of my research was to learn more about how genre innovation or creativity is described, carried out, and perceived within the context of a university course that aims to teach, primarily, convention. I will focus here on three of the questions that I explored:

1. What kinds of generic norms are taught in the course?
2. To what extent (and why) do students aim to meet or flout the norms that they learn?
3. When are norm-departures judged as innovative?

Adopting an ethnographic approach, I observed and recorded each class session, taking field notes throughout and transcribing portions of the class that later became relevant to my analysis; I collected and analyzed all course documents, including the syllabus, assignment guidelines and other handouts, and all readings; I interviewed Prof. Hanson near the beginning of the term and again after the final proposals had been graded; collected 11 student proposals; and I interviewed five of the 13 students at the end of the course. All seven interviews (two with the instructor and five with the students) were transcribed and then analyzed using Atlas.ti, a qualitative coding software program, along with the other data.

What Kinds of Generic Norms are Taught?

Given the primary aim of *Research Methods* to prepare students to undertake their senior research project, it is not surprising that the norms and conventions taught in class went far beyond text formats. While genre forms were addressed, more time was devoted to teaching other aspects of research genres, such as disciplinary values, research practices, and writing practices.

Class readings selected by Professor Hanson addressed issues such as research ethics, research design, and data analysis. Through class discussions of these texts, students were taught to view science as a neutral and objective evidence-based exploration of how the world works. In addition, each student presented one research article related to their own area of research, and these reading presentations were followed by discussion of the study, during which Prof. Hanson encouraged students to consider the study's design and findings as well as alternative approaches or follow-up studies. As students offered ideas in these discussions, the professor often rewarded their comments with statements like "You sound like a scientist!"

Through these reading discussions and also more general and informal discussions that took place in class, students were also taught how these disciplinary values of objectivity and neutrality are carried out through *research practices*. They learned, for instance, about the importance of developing field-specific knowledge and creating research designs that would be considered rigorous and sound. Early in the class, Prof. Hanson said, "I'm going to ask you to develop a research project in which any outcome is intriguing," emphasizing the value of not being wed to a hypothesis and searching for truth through evidence. Discussions like this helped to familiarize students with dominant practices for research in their field early on, so that as they began their first independent research they were already mindful of the expectations and norms.

To a lesser extent, the issue of *writing practices* came up in the course as well. Through several class discussions, Prof. Hanson shared with students the typical processes for publishing research articles, including the notion of blind peer review and issues of fraud in the publication of data. Students learned the importance of locating appropriate sources and using those sources to identify a research story in their paper. Only one student in class had been involved in the practice of "writing up" research (as a research assistant with another faculty member in the department), but many class members asked questions about the process, which was largely unfamiliar to them.

Although this was not a writing class per se, there were some discussions of the actual *written form* of research genres in science, particularly research articles and proposals. The guidelines for the students' research proposals stated that they should include an introduction section (which would be the bulk of the paper) followed by a short proposed methods section and a timeline. While formal conventions for the methods and timeline sections were not discussed in class, Prof. Hanson did spend some time talking with students about the conventional structure of an introduction section. One particular discussion was very explicit, with Prof. Hanson drawing an upside-down triangle on the whiteboard to represent a conventional introduction. She explained to students that "all introductions work the same way, like an inverted triangle," (field notes, 28 April 2011), and she described the typical stages of an introduction (see Figure 3). Another class discussion focused on the use of passive voice, with Prof. Hanson explaining that active voice is increasingly common and that students could use it in their own writing. Occasionally, Prof. Hanson used the readings to discuss generic form, drawing students' attention to the structure of the research articles from class and particularly noting introduction sections that did *not* conform to a traditional format. For example, she drew attention to papers that did not include a hypothesis at the end of the introduction, a convention that Prof. Hanson encouraged students to adopt. In addition to these in-class discussions on form, Prof. Hanson provided individual feedback on students' proposal drafts. In an interview, she shared that her feedback emphasized the importance of telling a story about the research and at times also referred to conventions for citing sources.

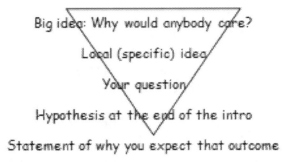

Figure 3. Prof. Hanson's recommended structure for introductions.

While Prof. Hanson presented some norms as fairly rigid and inflexible (such as the rhetorical structure of introductions or the values that guide scientific research), she also told students that there was room for stylistic variation. She told them she preferred to use passive voice and third person, but "gave them permission" to use active voice and first person. In an interview, she described how one student's early draft of the proposal was written "very conversationally." Prof. Hanson explained:

> I struggled a little bit with whether to ask her to, to change the style. And, I finally told her that it's not the, the standard style, but that that it was fine, as long as she understood that. And she ended up changing it. I didn't want to force her to write in a style that was different, especially when we had read some of the papers that talked about, you know, having more personality in a paper, I thought, I shouldn't try to strip her of her personality. But she ended up stripping herself of her personality. [laughs] Yeah, she ended up changing the, the tone of the paper to be more conventional. (Interview #2)

In sum, the norms of research genres that were taught and expected by the instructor tended to be related to disciplinary thought and practices rather than to form. This example can perhaps serve as an important reminder that genres are best understood as social practices or actions rather than as forms. For Prof. Hanson, the written proposal, and the conventions associated with it, were more of an afterthought or at least just a trace of the research practices. Educating undergraduate students to "do science" then was more about learning the norms of epistemology and practice than it was learning to adhere to a particular textual structure.

To What Extent (and Why) Do Students Meet or Flout Norms That They Learned?

Overall, the students' approaches to generic research practices—including their written texts—might be best characterized by conformity, or at least they were guided by the *aim* of conforming. When discussing their written proposals at the end of the term, four of the five students I interviewed explicitly stated that they tried to design their research projects and written proposal within the boundaries of what they perceived to be the expected conventions:

> ...there's probably places where I broke unintentionally. But like I was saying, like I really like this like style of scientific writing. So I would—I tried to, umm, make it sound very like professional and like what I read (Ingrid)

> I never really thought outside the box when I was writing . . . for me—it's—I basically just kind of stuck with—Yeah. I didn't want to be too risky. (Hannah)

> when I was writing, it seemed easiest to me if I just stuck with kind of the formatting that I thought that Dr. Hanson was looking for. Yeah, and also, I, I think in science I don't really know how I would deviate from like what I'm supposed to be talking about or, I guess conventional writing methods, or, whatever. Because I've never really seen any scientific writing that's not really structured all the same way. So, I don't really think I deviated too much from anything. (Cathy)

Represented by the above comments, the most common reasons for adhering to written norms were a desire to align with the teacher's expectations, a perception that science writing does not allow for many norm-departures, and a lack of understanding of how one might effectively bend the genre.

One student, however, did break from formal convention, and his work offers some interesting insight into genre innovation. The student, Frank, worked within the proposal genre but also took ownership over it and bent it in both subtle and sometimes more jarring ways, particularly in his introduction. As described earlier (and shown in Figure 3), Prof. Hanson had encouraged students to adopt a particular structure for their introduction sections, one that was fairly similar to the typical Create a Research Space (CARS) model (Swales, 1990), though Prof. Hanson used slightly different language to describe it. This model did characterize many of the articles read in class (and Samraj, 2002, also found it to be generally adopted in environmental science research articles), so students were exposed to it repeatedly throughout the term. For the most part, Frank's proposal followed this structure, yet he incorporated non-traditional moves as well, emphasizing his personal investment in the issue.

Rather than beginning the proposal with Prof. Hanson's suggested "big idea" or by "establishing a territory" (Swales, 1990), Frank began with a paragraph that essentially plopped the reader down into the south side of Chicago and the community controversies regarding urban agriculture. Similarly, he ended his introduction not with the suggested statement of why he expected the outcome that he had hypothesized but instead by demonstrating his personal investment in the project. Table 1 displays much of Frank's introduction with the rhetorical moves labeled. Moves that were not taught in class or demonstrated through class readings (i.e., Frank's innovative moves) appear in italics and include "depicting the local context," "personalizing the problem," and "demonstrating personal investment in the problem."

Table 1

Move analysis of Frank's proposal

On the south side of Chicago, unused plots of land are being transformed into small-scale urban farms. These urban farms are designed to supply community members with healthy, locally grown, organic produce. In some cases, urban farms are developed on land that was abandoned for environmental health-related reasons. It has been observed that communities do not always respond to the availability of fresh produce the way one would expect. Despite the transformation of these urban sites into land suitable for growing food, some residents are hesitant to purchase this food because they fear it is unsafe due to the previous contamination of the land on which food is grown. . . .	*Depicting the local context*
The contamination of soil due to heavy metals is usually prevalent anywhere time-honored industry is found. Alas, it would be very likely to find high concentrations of lead, copper, and iron in the soil surrounding a train yard or a foundry (Nabulo, et. al. 2010). Lead was also a component of gasoline, paint, and other widely consumed products before its dangers were fully understood. . . . Despite the known hazards of lead, many children grow up playing soccer and digging up worms in the contaminated soil of their back yard and the empty lot down the street. It is crucial these children are not exposed to any more invisible lead in the food they eat. When planting a garden, it is very possible that a fruit or vegetable could absorb unhealthy amounts of any toxic substance. In a 2003 study, scientists from Northwestern University analyzed the lead concentrations of soils and subsequent edible plants grown in a Chicago neighborhood (Finster, et. al. 2003). They found varying amounts of lead in every species. The findings showed the highest concentration of lead in edible shoots (mint, coriander, cilantro, etc.) and root vegetables (carrot, onion, radish, etc.). . . .	Big idea/ Establishing the territory

Over the past 30 years or so, a number of studies have been done that analyze the effects of local, organic agriculture. These studies include ideas of improved nutritional value and sustainability. A 2004 Iowa study found that the average distance conventional produce traveled to reach Des Moines was 1,494 miles (Pirog, 2004). The same study found that the average distance for (the same species/type of) locally grown produce to reach Des Moines was only 56 miles. . . . The nutritional benefit of eating organic in contrast to conventional produce is debatable. A 2001 study compared and analyzed 41 different published experiments that have tried to answer this question (Worthington, 2001). The conclusion was that . . .	
On the South side of Chicago there lies a three-acre environmental oasis within the Fuller Park community. Eden Place Nature Center is bordered by a train yard to the west and the Dan Ryan expressway to the East. The local soil has one of the highest lead concentrations in the city (edenplacenaturecenter.com). At one point the grounds were used as a local dumping site of construction materials, burnt-out cars, and sometimes, dead bodies (Smith G., 2011). When Eden Place founder Michael Howard's nine-year-old son tested positive for lead poisoning, Howard suspected a link between the abandoned lots his son and friends thought of as playgrounds. A 2002 Children's Memorial Hospital study in Chicago found that 46 percent of Fuller Park community's young children tested for high lead levels. Howard dedicated his life to educating his community about environmental problems by creating Eden Place and 'greening' one of the most unlikely places in the city. In the last 10 years Eden place has flourished, educating thousands of students, parents, and family's about the importance of urban ecology.	*Personalizing the problem*

Last year Eden Place decided to incorporate a small raised bed garden and a single hoop house. The goal being to make healthy, organic, and competitively priced fruits and vegetables available to the community members. The farmer's market held at Eden Place was not a success. Organizer's suggested that community members are fearful of eating the produce because of the local history of contamination, even though the garden beds are completely separated from the ground and filled with healthy soil. Perhaps scientific evidence can support that the produce grown at Eden place is very safe to eat and that it is in fact a healthier and tastier alternative to the conventional produce sold in the local supermarket. This information coupled with creative marketing has the potential to educate more community members about urban agriculture and potentially lead to a demand for more abandoned lots to be used beneficially. Vegetables with edible leaves appear to be susceptible to lead contamination (Finster et. al. 2003).	Local question/ Establishing a niche
I have chosen to study leafy greens specifically.	Your question/ Occupying the niche
I hypothesize that the leafy greens grown at Eden Place have safe lead concentrations as well as better taste and nutritional value than the conventionally grown leafy greens that are available.	Hypothesis
If I find my results do not support this hypothesis I am determined to understand why, and propose solutions to the problem.	*Demonstrating personal investment in the problem*

Together these unconventional moves give Frank's research an exigence that is personal and in which he is invested as a human being. By weaving together traditional and innovative moves, Frank works largely within a conventional paradigm of thought while incorporating less traditional content. In doing so, he establishes a research problem in both objective (scientific) and personal (human) terms. And his use of unconventional rhetorical moves is augmented by numerous linguistic features that Hyland (2008) has identified as expressions of stance and engagement. Frank's proposal, for example, includes first person, attitude markers, hedges and boosters, and vivid and personalized description in unique ways (found most commonly within his non-traditional moves).

Despite these interesting—and, arguably, creative—approaches to the genre's form, it was not Frank's move structure or use of language that caught the eye of Prof. Hanson. In fact, she never mentioned these features when discussing the proposal with me. Instead, what made the proposal stand out to Prof. Hanson was what she described as the creative scientific thinking. She was particularly impressed with Frank's inclusion of a logic tree, a heuristic used to follow the possible outcomes of one's findings. Students had read about logic trees in class, and the professor suggested during one class session early in the term that they apply these to their own research; Frank was the only student who did so, including a figure of a logic tree at the very end of his introduction. To Prof. Hanson, Frank's use of the logic tree demonstrated how his research would be "interesting no matter what the outcome was" (Interview #2).

In contrast to Frank's proposal, Prof. Hanson identified two other proposals in the class as relatively weak, and these cases give some further insight into the issue of genre bending. Unfortunately, neither of these student-authors volunteered to be interviewed for my research, but they did share their proposals with me. The professor seemed particularly surprised by the weaknesses of one of the proposals; the author, Kurt, stood out in class discussions as bright, active, and very invested in scientific research, but Prof. Hanson described his proposal in this way:

> Kurt's [proposal] was weak. He had a hard time wrapping his mind around the project. [...] He knew he wanted to work with fossils, but he had no idea what he wanted to do and he couldn't tell a story [in the introduction]. And even at the end he had a hard time telling the story. I think he finally was able to get it, he just ... he ... I think a lot of it is that telling the story. [...] I mean the first three or four pages of his five or six page proposal were, were references from—were information from one citation. And it's just—it's hard to imagine how you can build a story that way. It just—it doesn't seem like it

should work that way. The final draft wasn't that way, but for a long time it was. (Interview #2)

Given her characterization of the proposal as having difficulty "telling a story," I looked again at the rhetorical moves of Kurt's introduction section. Surprisingly, this proposal actually adhered much more closely to Prof. Hanson's proposed structure than Frank's proposal, and it incorporated many phrases that are fairly conventional for signaling rhetorical moves. Prof. Hanson's original concern that Kurt had cited only one reference in the introduction had been eliminated by the final draft (Kurt draws on five references here—not much different from Frank's seven references), and the introduction clearly identifies a problem, though certainly not in language as colorful and engaging as Frank's.

When Are Norm-Departures Judged as "Innovative"?

This comparison of Frank's and Kurt's texts and Prof. Hanson's comments on those texts piqued my interest. Why was Frank's proposal, with its minor norm-departures, judged to be innovative rather than deviant or unsuccessful? In contrast, why was Kurt's work not considered successful despite seeming to adhere to generic expectations, at least on the surface? The common definition of creativity shared earlier offers a useful starting point for answering this question: a product is creative when it is both *novel* and *appropriate*. In other words, the object is recognizable as belonging to the appropriate genre, and the author shows knowledge of that genre but does not follow the conventions too rigidly. A creative text offers something new, something that allows it to stand out, to surprise the reader but in a way that the reader values. Kurt's proposal follows structural conventions fairly closely, generally adhering to a typical move structure. The norm-departures in Kurt's work discussed by Prof. Hanson included limited references and the lack of a persuasive research narrative; these features seemed to suggest to her gaps in Kurt's content knowledge and were, therefore, judged as deviations rather than innovations. Frank's proposal incorporates more non-traditional elements: he plays with formal conventions by including non-traditional moves and atypical linguistic features such as vivid, emotive, and personal language; he demonstrates his own personal investment in and attitudes toward the research, including an advocacy-like rhetorical stance; and, most importantly to Prof. Hanson, Frank's work demonstrated sophisticated and creative thinking by laying out several possible outcomes to his research. To Prof. Hanson, Frank's proposal (and research project) was smart and creative, while Kurt appeared to lack a strong grasp of his research.

A systems-based perspective on creativity (see Figure 2) allows us to also see how the process of perceiving creativity or innovation in this case is not simply a response to textual features but occurs instead through a complex sociocultural system. In the background lie the *genres* of research articles and proposals. Through class discussions, text models, readings, and assignment guidelines, students were given the message (intentionally or not) that the genres of scientific research, in their written instantiations, are generally not forms they could play with. Students were encouraged to understand the research article or proposal form itself to be mostly conventional. Yet, at the same time, they were encouraged to consider the thinking and planning that *leads to* the proposal (also, of course, part of the genre) as an opportunity for creativity and innovation.

To apply the system-based model further, we can see that the *domain*—in this case, scientific research and the culture of the environmental science department—values an investment in and passion for research. In the *Research Methods* class, this value was demonstrated to students through guest speakers' presentations, Prof. Hanson's comments in class, and many of the readings. Students were repeatedly told that scientific creativity came out in the *thinking about* and the *design* of research; creativity in written form was not discussed nor were examples provided. The *field*—the immediate context of the *Research Methods* class, with Prof. Hanson in the role of gatekeeper—influenced students' work by making clear the expected conventions of research and research writing. Although students may have felt that the professor gave them freedom, they also felt constraints: as in any university course, they were expected to demonstrate knowledge of conventions and, in the end, they would receive a grade based at least partially on how well they demonstrated this. Finally, the *individual* plays an important role in the system. In this case, the proposal writers were novices who had limited or no previous experience in reading research articles, conducting independent research, and writing about their own research. This background often served as a constraint to creativity, as few students felt as though they had the confidence or desire to take ownership over their work and find ways to innovate in field-appropriate ways. In general, they wanted to play it safe. Frank's sense of personal investment in the work may have encouraged him to be more innovative; in contrast, Kurt's apparent struggles to make sense of his new research area may have steered him toward a more conservative approach to the proposal genre. Perhaps more importantly, Prof. Hanson perceived Frank as knowledgeable in his research but saw Kurt as not quite grasping the questions or story of his research.

It is possible that Prof. Hanson's *perceptions* of each writer's content knowledge—and, thus, his legitimacy—influenced her judgments of the proposals. Put another way, her perceptions of the proposals could be attributed in part to differences in accumulated capital. As Prof. Hanson explained, Frank "had no experience with the system, [but] he just could think it out." On the other hand, she felt that Kurt had "a hard time wrapping his mind around the project." Even though she admitted that Kurt's proposal became stronger with revision, her perception that he did not quite grasp the story behind the research seemed to continue to influence her judgment of the proposal, even after revisions. It is also possible that Frank's more sophisticated use of language granted him more authority, or more right to innovate. Or that his use of the logic tree—a heuristic taught in class—persuaded Prof. Hanson of his investment and scientific knowledge, building his symbolic capital. In other words, in various ways, Frank seemed to accumulate the capital that could lend legitimacy to his research and written text, bolstering the perception that his norm-departures were innovative.

Implications for Genre Theory and Pedagogy

It may be impossible to understand definitively why people judge certain genre departures as innovative and others as deviant—certainly, a wide range of factors influence any given context or "system"—but the concepts explored here highlight some of the complexities that go into such judgments and the ways in which they function as part of a larger sociocultural system. Understanding more about innovation, importantly, offers several insights into genre and genre theory.

First, as genre scholarship has repeatedly emphasized, genres are themselves not equivalent to text form but are, rather, constellations of practices, values, epistemologies, and beliefs that are instantiated through repeated, "typified" forms. The example from the environmental science *Research Methods* course demonstrates that genre innovation, too, is not limited to generic form. Departures to formal conventions certainly offer one possibility for innovation, but they are not the only route. Instead, innovation is likely to begin much before the text itself is produced, through the thinking, acting, and interacting of writers and readers within a social setting. To understand genre innovation, then, we need to look at, but also beyond, texts.

Taking a sociocultural and systems-based orientation to innovation or creativity also re-frames the notion of genre innovation as not simply something that a writer or text *does* but as something that a reader or other gatekeeper *judges*. And such perceptions—of a genre as innovative or deviant—are likely to be linked to perceptions of genre knowledge. If a writer, like Frank, is perceived as knowledgeable in disciplinary content, research practices, or even writing practices, a reader (teacher, advisor, editor) may be more likely to view norm-departures positively, as intentional and skilled innovations. Atypical genre instantiations may be perceived more negatively, as unintentional errors, when readers feel that the writer lacks the sophisticated genre knowledge that informs (successful) innovation. The proverbial cry for "more research" applies here: though anecdotal evidence abounds, we need to know more about how genre expertise relates to authors' perceived rights to depart from dominant norms, whether those be norms of content, procedures, rhetoric, or form.

The example explored here also suggests that not all genres, writers, and contexts are equal in terms of innovation potential, thus potentially tempering the playful, creative, and improvisational aspects of genre. Developing a more robust framework for understanding *which* genres can be improvised, *in which* contexts, *by* whom, and *for* whom can inform notions of genre-as-play. As a second language writing scholar, I am particularly interested in the potential for innovation within multilingual and transnational literacy contexts—and I think much work needs to be done here, particularly as these contexts become the norm in many domains. As texts traverse geographic, social, political, and linguistic spaces, judgments and perceptions of convention, innovation, and error become unstable and fluid, a point nicely elucidated by Blommaert (2010). Understanding the centrifugal forces (Bakhtin, 1981, p. 272) that act on genres in such contexts will require research that takes into account texts, communities, language, and power—and their interactions.

The complexities of genre innovation, of course, also raise questions for teaching and learning genres in classroom environments. Genre-based pedagogy, at least in some forms, has been critiqued for teaching conventions at the cost of perpetuating dominant norms that marginalize some writers (e.g., Freedman, 1993; Luke, 1996). In some contexts, it is fair to say that convention has been given a rather poor reputation, aligned with rigidity and stability. One pedagogical response in US-based composition studies has been to turn students' attention directly to the normalizing properties of academic language and encourage students to challenge conventions by meshing languages and discourses within academic genres (Canagarajah, 2006; Horner, Lu, Royster, & Trimbur, 2011). While I support the principles and aims behind these initiatives— particularly the call to recognize and draw on the plurilingual reality of students' lives—I also worry that they may not take into full account the kinds of social and generic complexities involved in such innovations. For example, it is not clear that student writers are *allowed* to bend genres in the same ways that "expert" writers are. Teachers often look for signs that a student *knows* a genre before accepting their attempts to modify or play with it (to be recognized as legitimate, to return to Bourdieu's terms). Furthermore, some research suggests that instructors often value innovations to content over innovations to generic form (Allison, 2004; Thaiss & Zawacki, 2006), again reinforcing the importance of considering innovation beyond textual form. And then there is the issue of *which* genres can be manipulated and *how*. Many arguments for encouraging innovation in writing, for example, draw on examples from composition classrooms in which students are composing essays rather than research-based writing in disciplines that tend to value textual convention. In classrooms like *Research Methods*, for example, textual or rhetorical innovation is unlikely to be rewarded but research innovation may well be.

What I hope to have offered here, then, is not necessarily a call for teaching genre innovation (while I believe there are appropriate contexts for that goal, it is unlikely to always be the most valuable or suitable approach) but rather a call for more in-depth study of genre innovation, particularly as it influences student writing and genre learning. If teachers want to help students eventually take ownership over genres that matter in their lives, perhaps even to appropriate them in new ways, they need to explore with students what is allowable and rewarded in different disciplines and different genres. In turn, teachers and students alike may benefit from explorations of when adhering to convention is a wiser option than breaking from it. With the increasing mobility of genres and their users across geographical, political, cultural, and linguistic spaces, understanding the possibilities and cautions of genre innovation is a timely and worthwhile endeavor.

References

Allison, D. (2004). Creativity, students' academic writing, and EAP: Exploring comments on writing in an English language degree program. *Journal of English for Academic Purposes, 3*(1), 191-209.

Amabile, T. M. (1982). Social psychology of creativity: A consensual assessment technique. *Journal of Personality and Social Psychology, 43*, 997-1013.

Artemeva, N. (2008). Toward a unified theory of genre learning. *Journal of Business and Technical Communication, 22*, 160-185.

Bakhtin, M. M. (1981). *The dialogic imagination: Four essays* (M. Holquist, Ed., C. Emerson & M. Holquist, Trans.). Austin, TX: University of Texas Press.

Bakhtin, M. M. (1986). *Speech genres and other late essays* (C. Emerson & M. Holquist, Eds. & Trans.). Austin, TX: University of Texas Press.

Bhatia, V. K. (2006). Genres and styles in world Englishes. In B. B. Kachru, Y. Kachru, & C. Nelson (Eds.), *The handbook of world Englishes* (pp. 386-399). Oxford: Blackwell Publishing.

Bazerman, C. (1988). *Shaping written knowledge: The genre and activity of the experimental article in science.* Madison, WI: University of Wisconsin Press.

Berkenkotter, C. (2001). Genre systems at work: DSM-IV and rhetorical recontextualization in psychotherapy paperwork. *Written Communication, 18*, 326-349.

Berkenkotter, C., & Huckin, T. (1995). *Genre knowledge in disciplinary communication.* Hillsdale, NJ: Lawrence Erlbaum Associates.

Blommaert, J. (2010). *The sociolinguistics of globalization.* Cambridge: Cambridge University Press.

Bourdieu, P. (1991). *Language and symbolic power* (G. Raymond & M. Adamson, Trans.). Cambridge, MA: Harvard University Press.

Canagarajah, A. S. (2006). The place of world Englishes in composition: Pluralization continued. *College Composition and Communication, 57*(4), 586-619.

Cheng, A. (2007). Transferring generic features and recontextualizing genre awareness: Understanding writing performance in the ESP genre-based literacy framework. *English for Specific Purposes, 26*, 287-307.

Csikszentmihalyi, M. (1999). Implications of a systems perspective for the study of creativity. In R. J. Sternberg (Ed.), *Handbook of creativity* (pp. 313-335). Cambridge, UK: Cambridge University Press.

Devitt, A. (2011). *Creating within genres: How genre metaphors shape student innovation.* Paper presented at the Conference on College Composition and Communication, Atlanta, GA.

Freedman, A. (1993). Show and tell? The role of explicit teaching in the learning of new genres. *Research in the Teaching of English, 27,* 222-251.

Gentil, G. (2011). A biliteracy agenda for genre research. *Journal of Second Language Writing, 20,* 6-23.

Giltrow, J., & Stein, D. (Eds.). (2009). *Genres in the internet: Issues in the theory of genre.* Philadelphia, PA: John Benjamins.

Halliday, M. A. K., & Martin, J. R. (1993). *Writing science: Literacy and discursive power.* Bristol, PA: Taylor & Francis.

Horner, B., Lu, M. Z., Royster, J. J., & Trimbur, J. (2011). Language difference in writing: Toward a translingual approach. *College English, 73*(3), 303-321.

Hyland, K. (2000). *Disciplinary discourses: Social interactions in academic writing.* London: Longman.

Hyland, K. (2008). Disciplinary voices: Interactions in research writing. *English Text Construction, 1*(1), 5-22.

Kozbelt, A., Beghetto, R. A., & Runco, M. A. (2010). Theories of creativity. In J. C. Kaufman & R. J. Sternberg (Eds.), *The Cambridge handbook of creativity* (pp. 20-47). Cambridge, UK: Cambridge University Press.

Luke, A. (1996). Genres of power? Literacy education and the production of capital. In R. Hasan & G. Williams (Eds.), *Literacy in society* (pp. 308-338). New York, NY: Longman.

Pope, R. (2005). *Creativity: Theory, history, practice.* New York, NY: Routledge.

Russell, D. (1997). Rethinking genre in school and society: An activity theory analysis. *Written Communication, 14,* 504-554.

Sawyer, K. (2012). *Explaining creativity: The science of human innovation* (2nd ed). Oxford: Oxford University Press.

Samraj, B. (2002). Introductions in research articles: Variations across disciplines. *English for Specific Purposes, 21,* 1-17.

Schryer, C. F. (2011). *Genre as generative.* Paper presented at Writing and Rhetoric Across Borders Conference, Fairfax, Virginia.

Spinuzzi, C. (2003). *Tracing genres through organizations: A sociocultural approach to information design.* Cambridge, MA: MIT Press.

Swales, J. M. (1990). *Genre analysis: English in academic and research settings.* Cambridge, UK: Cambridge University Press.

Swales, J. M. (2004). *Research genres: Explorations and applications.* Cambridge, UK: Cambridge University Press.

Tardy, C. M. (2009). *Building genre knowledge.* West Lafayette, IN: Parlor Press.

Thaiss, C., & Zawacki, T. M. (2006). *Engaged writers and dynamic disciplines: Research on the academic writing life.* Portsmouth, NH: Boynton/Cook-Heinemann.

Yates, J., & Orlikowski, W. J. (1992). Genres of organizational communication: A structurational approach to studying communication and media. *The Academy of Management Review, 17,* 299-326.

Chapter 15

Students as Genre Scholars: ESL/ EFL Classroom Approaches

Ann Johns

San Diego State University (USA)

In his well-researched 2012 volume, *What the best college students do,* Bain points out that successful university students who become creative and contributing adults draw from their past and current experiences, their "models of situations"(p. 56); but they tend to go way beyond these, finding new or different insights in what they read, write, or encounter. As they develop these insights, often consulting a variety of sources, they remain invested in their work (see Norton, 2011) and motivated to move towards a specific goal. Keeping this goal in mind, they remain focused as they attempt to achieve it. Much of this should be of no surprise to genre theorists or teachers, who know that figuring out what a text is and does is enabled by efforts to come to terms with past experiences with the genre and its conventions, combined with goal direction and an openness to the situated nature of a specific text (Prior, 1998, p. xi). This endeavor requires flexible thinking;, for student analysts need to consider the various centripetal forces that contribute to text prototypicality and, conversely, the centrifugal forces (Bakhtin, 1981) buffeting the specific situation in which a text from a genre is processed and produced (Berkenkotter & Huckin, 1995). Thus, as Prior (1998) has noted, writing a text should be viewed as:

> [happening] in moments that are richly equipped with tools (material and semiotic) and populated with others (past,

present, and future). When seen as a situated activity, writing does not stand alone as the discrete act of a writer, but emerges as a confluence of many streams of activity: reading, talking, observing, acting, making, thinking and feeling as well as transcribing words on paper. (p. xi)

All too often though, even in what are identified as genre-based classes, texts are taught as sterile and rigidly formatted, removed from the often messy, complex situations in which they are produced. And this, as Freedman (1994) famously pointed out, is a major problem facing teachers and curriculum designers. There are a number of reasons for this problem, two of which are teacher misunderstandings about the nature of genres, thinking of them principally as texts with immutable moves or structures; as well as imposed curricula or assessments that promote "context-free," often template-driven writing.

However, it does not need to be this way, particularly if we consult the work of the modern genre theorists who suggest involving the students in active problem-solving as they attempt to unravel the mysteries of a genre (see Bazerman, 2009, p. 295). Here, I will argue that this can be done through drawing from students' prior knowledge of the many forces that may influence a text, by enhancing students' confidence in their abilities to read or write familiar and then challenging pieces in a genre, and by providing group-based activities that encourage exploration and experimentation. Among many, particularly novice, English as a second language (ESL) or English as a foreign language (EFL) students, it may be only under these circumstances that they are sufficiently invested and focused to devote the time necessary to purposefully read and analyze a text and its context or carry on with the sometimes lengthy and frustrating writing process of producing a product in a genre deemed satisfactory for the audience(s) addressed.

How can we entice students to become genre scholars, to be curious about and invested in texts and their contexts of all kinds (print, visual), and to become sufficiently focused and "noticing" to complete deep readings or draft and revise challenging written pieces? After discussing the contributions of the two genre "schools" with which I am most familiar[1], I will suggest some approaches to encouraging novice or ESL/EFL students to become deeply invested in genre studies—perhaps for the rest of their lives.

Contributions of Two Genre "Schools"

I'll begin here with the genre "school" (see Hyon, 1996; Swales, this volume) into which I have been thoroughly initiated, English for Specific Purposes (ESP). In their introduction to an ESP handbook, Paltridge and Starfield (2013) identify the principal pedagogical goal of this "school":

> A key feature of an ESP course is that the content and aims of the course are oriented to the specific needs of the learners. ESP courses, then, focus on the language, skills and genres appropriate to the specific activities the learners need to carry out in English. (p. 2)

The needs analyses to which these writers refer should be both pre-course and on-going, and if seriously pursued, broad in scope, as Hyland (2006) has noted:

> "Needs" is actually an umbrella term that embraces many aspects, incorporating learners' goals and backgrounds, their language proficiencies, their reasons for taking a course, their teaching and learning preferences, and the situations they will need to communicate in. Needs can involve what learners know, don't know or want to know and can be collected and analyzed in a variety of ways. (p. 73)

When conducting a needs analysis, what might curriculum designers do to identify genres (and appropriate texts from the genres) for teaching? As Price and I point out in our ESP overview (2014), the most effective methods require working with those in the target situation in which students need to use the language. This might include job-shadowing, interviews, or collecting texts and exploring the contexts for writing from people already initiated into a target discourse community. The next steps are to analyze and classify the findings. Bhatia, a major contributor to the ESP literature, suggested three levels at which genres could be explained and grouped in a needs analysis for curriculum design: by *rhetorical/*

generic values[2] (e.g., evaluation, narration, description), by a *genre colony* (e.g., "promotional"), of which specific named genres are a part, and finally by the *individually identifiable generic constructs*, that is, *the names* used by community members for their genres (e.g., book blurbs, sales letters, job advertisements) (2002, p. 281). Once this research has been initiated, ESP curriculum designers turn to the selected texts, linking their lexical, grammatical and discourse features to the goals of the discourse communities in which students will be using the language. It is the reliance upon specific, situated, named genres (and features of texts within them), combined with an analysis of students' needs, that makes the development of ESP curricula challenging and on-going and which, in the ideal, empowers the students themselves to conduct some of the research, especially now that corpus linguistics is available to all (see Reppen, 2010).

Not surprisingly, the curricula developed from needs analyses vary considerably among locales. Thus, for example, our curriculum project for a private university in Lebanon (Eid & Johns, 2011) was, by necessity, considerably different, in terms of needs analyses conducted, as well as focus, activities, content, and genre exemplars, from the academic curricula I developed for courses in South Africa (Johns & Makalela, 2011) and in California (Johns, 2009).

But whatever its efforts to bring in context (e.g., Swales, 1998) and to view genres not solely as texts but as metaphors (Swales, 2009), much of ESP pedagogy and research remains text internal, as students and their teachers analyze written pieces from a target situation for their moves and other linguistic and structural features, aided, in many cases, by corpus studies (see Johns, 2013). Although this text-based work is very useful, some students, especially those for whom academic reading and writing in English are particularly difficult, enjoy and benefit from beginning their analysis with the context in which a text is written, particularly if this context is familiar. So I now turn for insights to the second "school" discussed here, Rhetorical Genre Studies (RGS) (see Barawarshi & Reiff, 2011), which, rather than being a "linguistic," text-focused approach like ESP (Flowerdew, 2010) focuses first on the social nature of text, its situatedness. Bawarshi and Reiff (2010) make the following comment about the importance of recognizing writing contexts and their complexities as we study genres, [texts] exist in a dynamic, inter-dependent, mutually-constructing relationship with the genre systems they situate so that through the use of genres and other mediational means, we enact context as we function within it. (p. 95)

Because the pedagogical focus in this paper is on novice ESL/EFL university students, who tend to be challenged by the culture and assignments in their English-dominant academic classrooms (e.g., MacBeth, 2006), it draws especially from the insights of Devitt, Bawarshi, and Reiff (e.g., 2004), whose RGS textbook asks students to focus first on the "scenes" in which texts from genres are embedded. With a revised, pedagogical focus, Prior's work (2004) is also applied to the discussion that follows. .

Pedagogical Possibilities

Who are the students for whom this type of pedagogy is designed? For many years, I have been teaching first year academic reading and writing classes for bilingual and ESL college students in California, most of whom have been classified as "remedial" by their educational institutions. These students are similar to many others I have met around the world. Most are the first in their families to be enrolled in college. Not surprisingly, they are taking academic classes to progress, to graduate, and, they hope, to earn a decent living. In most cases, they are not happy about being in my "remedial" class for which they will not be given credit towards graduation. Thus, it is important for them to recognize the benefits of their "remedial" instruction to their futures and to view what they already know about texts as important. Two of my first responsibilities, then, are to demonstrate respect for their ideas, cultures, language and texts, and to promote active learning. Lecturing is definitely not the route to take! Though the approach suggested here, when modified, has benefited students in other classroom contexts, the texts and activities presented have been selected after extensive needs assessments for this first year, "remedial" population, which, in the United States, comprises more than 60% of the entering university students (Higher Education Policy Institute [HEPI], 2010). All of the students involved in this discussion have signed a "human subjects" consent form, approved by the San Diego State University Institutional Review Board.

What, then, can be done to assist these students to come to terms with genre complexity, motivate them to read and write difficult texts, and perhaps enhance their investment in a life-long interest in genre and its place in their academic and professional lives ? The discussion that follows presents a teaching process that draws from the works of ESP and RGS experts as well as upon my own extensive classroom and curriculum design experiences.

Initially, elicit a known genre and activate student schemata. There seems to be considerable agreement in educational circles that eliciting background knowledge is essential to effective reading and writing (Donovan, Bransford & Pellegrino, 1999; Fisher & Frey, 2009). In many cases, advice to teachers centers on the two traditional, and apparently separate, types of schema that represent this knowledge in the literature: content and formal (structural) features of text. As we know from genre studies and activity theory (Russell, 1995), there is much more to a person's prior knowledge of a text and text production than these two apparently dichotomous schemas represent; and as academic writers, researchers, and future genre scholars, our students need to dig into the complexities, in a way that supports their own understandings of texts and text production.

Begin with texts from familiar genres. In her ground-breaking article, "Genre as social action," Miller (1984) spoke of the importance of "homely" genres, the texts we live by every day. Following Miller's lead, I have long been asking students to include in their literacy portfolios a homely genre in their first or second (or third) language (Johns, 1997). Some of their favorites are newspaper obituaries and wedding invitations from their home cultures (pp. 39-45), but a number of others have appeared as portfolio entries as well: sermon outlines, event announcements, ads (often posted on bulletin boards), blogs, feature articles in women's magazines, and notes for talks that they have presented. One student brought in a paper she had written for a previous class, upset because it was jam-packed with the instructor's red marks. She viewed these marks as an intrusion into her creative writing rather than an essential part of the student-teacher "conversation" in the writing process.

Provide students with opportunities to reflect as much as possible on the ecology of the situation (see Prior, 2004) in

which the text selected was produced. Once students have chosen a text from a homely genre for their portfolio entry, I ask them to discover everything possible about the situation in which their text was processed and produced. Those students who wrote the texts themselves come up with some creative and interesting observations and remembrances: about their personal motivations or the power structure within the text-writing situation, about genre choice, about events or people that influenced the writing, and about their readings of their cultures and languages as realized in the text. If the text is not their own, they are encouraged, if possible, to interview the person(s) who wrote it. After this research and remembrance activity, which is followed by a written reflection for the portfolios, students work in groups to analyze what they discovered and then develop questions that we can ask of their selected texts, particularly those that focus on the writing situation. Here are some of the "situatedness" questions developed, several of which are similar to the more formal, academic text production categories provided by Prior (2004):[3]

- Why was the text written? Was it assigned by someone? Thought up by the author? Or what?
- What did the writer want to achieve by writing this text? What were his/her purposes?
- How much "say" did the writer of this text have? What kinds of choices did the writer get to make about the genre, text structure, the content, the stance,[4] and the argument? Or were some of the elements of the text fairly well set and couldn't be changed?
- What events were going on when this text was written that influenced the writing of the text? In what ways was the writing influenced? For example, did the situation tell the writer what the language should be?
- Who were the audiences for this text? How do we know? Does the author "speak" to the audience in some way? How?
- What questions does the text address? Why does the author and his/her audience/community address them? (See also Bean, 2004)
- What do we know about the writer's process? For example, how long did it take to write the text? Who did the writer talk

to about the text? Did these persons influence it? How? What got in the way of finishing the text, if anything? What did the writer read, see, or experience that can be found in the text? How many drafts did the writer produce? Who read it before it was "published"? Did the author correct the text as s/he went along, or correct the errors at the end of the process? Did someone else edit the text before it was "published" or presented? (see Johns, 2002)

- What happened to this text? Was it successful in achieving what the writer wanted to get done? Did people use it in some way—or forget it? Did people misunderstand what the writer was trying to achieve?

The students then ask these questions of their chosen texts from "homely" genres, and we discuss their answers. Only after these questions have been addressed do we turn to the features of the texts themselves. The students' internal analyses of their texts are based on the principle of "noticing," which has long been an important contribution to language acquisition (Schmidt & Frota, 1986). Organized in groups, students exchange their selected homely texts and "notice" and classify what is there. They often come up with observations about use of visuals, font type, text structure, thesis/claim, support/evidence, author credibility/ethos (as evidenced in text), lexicon (especially repeated nouns and adjectives), grammar (verb tense), syntax, metadiscourse, quality of paper, and corrections or comments found on the texts. The groups contribute to a class list of possible categories of features to notice in their own selected texts—and in other texts as well.[5]

After considering both context questions and text features, students prepare individual posters, including both a visual representation of the activity surrounding the text production and features noticed within their chosen texts. Students from other classes, as well as teachers and administrators, are invited to a poster display and discussion with the students about what they noticed in their "homely" genres and, of course, about the situations in which the texts they selected were produced.

Move into texts from genres prominent in the target situation. Students now have a sense of the messiness and depth of the context in which a text is created, and some ways to examine text features and the processes of the writer. At this point, they have the opportunity to apply their knowledge to a genre that is directly relevant to their academic work: common in history, composition, and social science courses, according to our needs analysis, the *opinion editorial* (OE). When introducing the OE, I begin with a text in the genre that I wrote, one that critiques the goals of our local university (Johns, 2004), a topic that has proven to be of considerable interest to these students since it involves "remedial" instruction in which they are enrolled (see Appendix A). I pass out the text and students read it silently without marking it. Then, using the "situatedness" questions that they have developed for their own "homely" texts, listed above, they interview me about both the situation for my OE and my writing process. The students take notes on the interview; and as an assignment, they google "talking points," a useful genre for organizing the information in their notes. Fortunately, there are a variety of instructions for writing talking points (not always in agreement, not surprisingly) and a number of exemplars that they can download. After bringing their "research" on talking points to class, they meet in groups and prepare five to eight points that include what they view as the most important ideas from the interview about both the context for the OE and my quite long writing process. This is followed by a short group oral report or collaborative paper (1-2 pages) indicating their results.

Study a second text in the same genre. By this time, the students have begun to feel quite comfortable with the sometimes jumbled, interactive nature of the situation in which a text may be processed or produced. Most no longer believe in the rigid, non-recursive writing process taught in many of their previous classes (see Appendix B). With a second OE text, we turn to the issue of prototypicality, the shared features of both OE texts and contexts that instantiate our schemas, assisting us to relegate both texts to the same genre category. It is important to note that one of the central purposes for studying conventions of a genre, what is prototypical, is to help students to read. If they recognize that they have read a text from the genre before, they are more able to see how its prototypical features assist them to comprehend: that is, they are better able to predict the context and some of the text features. .

But here's the rub, an important point that appears to have been lost in a number of genre curricula: what is typical or conventional in a genre is not merely found in the text itself. Prototypicality appears in elements of the situation (e.g., type of publication, writer's status, the type of audience, the physical context), as well as in the text's more common purposes, its structure, its visual appearance, its content, its language, or its tone. These various possibilities, among others, should be clear to the students, who will again participate in an exploration of text.

But first, students need to become comfortable with a second OE. For this discussion, I have selected an OE text on a topic that is of considerable interest to secondary school students these days, bullying (Boyd & Marwick, 2011). The students read the text silently. Then, they place my OE piece next to the OE text on cyberbullying as I pose some open-ended questions for their group work:

- What can you hypothesize about similarities between the contexts in which these texts were written? For example, where were they published? In what part of the publication do they appear? Why were they written? What other similarities might there be? What other questions did you pose earlier about the texts you studied that can be posed, and answered, for these texts?
- Look at the texts themselves. In what ways are they similar? Consider all possibilities: use of visuals, fonts, paragraphing, language, placement of the claim, types of evidence, tone, author ethos....

Some of the students are then assigned to try to contact the authors of the bullying text in order to answer some of the questions, e.g., about their processes and the situations in which the text was written.

Before the students go on, the class is divided into two groups, one of which is to "chart" my OE, and the second is assigned to "chart" the cyberbullying piece. What is charting? It is an approach to close reading of the text in which students work together to discover how a text is organized functionally (by "moves," [Swales, 1990]), the language indicating that organization, and finally, what the text says.[6] Students are given blank "charting" grids, pre-"chunked" by me into functional categories; and, if it is their first experience with this activity, I model how it is done by completing a few of the sections (see Appendix C). Students are given a list of possible "doing/function" words,[7] though they are encouraged to go beyond these for other possibilities. The two groups of students then work with pre-chunked grids and an assigned OE text (either mine or the bullying one) first deciding what the author is doing in the text (functional sections) then how they know (the language indicated) and finally summarizing the same section in the "saying" column.

Prompt students to write. Much of the classwork described so far involves reading, analyzing and situating texts. Without it, students have difficulty developing academic writing skills. Now, they begin their preparation for writing, that is, organizing their thoughts. For this, the class is divided into two groups: the "Prototypicals" and the "Situateds," with each group completing a chart as seen in Appendix D, depending upon their groups' assignment, that is, to either list similarities between the two OE texts (possible prototypical features) or the differences between them. Once they have completed this work, each group makes a presentation of their findings, while members of the other groups take notes. Then, all the students make two lists: one of what they believe to be the key features of the situation that made one text different from the other and another of what they believe to be conventional or prototypical in an OE text, that is, what makes them similar. Sometimes the class becomes a bit noisy, especially if the students disagree; however, noise indicates investment in their texts, and that is what I am looking for.

Finally, it is time to turn to a prompt addressed to an important audience, in this case, the department chair:

Prompt. Write a memo to the chair of the department in which you explain your experiences with the opinion editorial assignment in the "remedial" classes. To demonstrate what you learned, compare and contrast the two OEs you were assigned. Discuss what, in your view, were the most important elements in the writing situation that caused these two texts to be different and what the major differences are. Then, discuss what the two texts have in common, that is, why both texts can be classified as members of the same genre. Finally, point out what you learned about reading and writing from this assignment that you might be able to apply to other classes.

Conclusion

This particular set of activities was designed for first year college students, novices and/or ESL/EFL students in one of the many "remedial" programs that exist in the United States and elsewhere. However, I have used variations upon this approach for graduate students, teacher trainees and EFL students in other countries, and all seem to appreciate gaining an understanding of the remarkable complexity of a writing situation and its influence upon writers and their texts. As indicated here, students' prior knowledge of genres and their curiosity about them is honored and becomes an integral part of their study and assessment of homely genres for their writing portfolios. After they have developed questions about the writing situation of these homely texts and analyzed them, they are encouraged to present their findings to students, teachers, or administrator audiences. Only then do the students turn to a comparison and contrast of genres that are characteristic of the literacy situations in which they will be working, identified through an on-going needs analysis. Here, the Opinion Editorial (OE), characteristic of several academic classes, was employed to assist the students to consider what is characteristic (or varied) in writing situations and the texts themselves as well as what may be conventional or prototypical in a genre across situations. I find that these kinds of activities motivate students and enhance their learning—leading to very close readings of texts as well as heated discussions in class about contexts for writing

For many years, I have been arguing that one of our principal goals is to destabilize students' theories of genre (Johns, 2002)—to encourage students to become text (and context) researchers as well as more sophisticated readers and writers. Reviews by my students, and their comments years after they have taken my class, indicate that they find this approach useful and motivating. One of the results has been that the more assertive students interview faculty about the texts that they write, using the "situatedness" questions.

In my view, one of our chief responsibilities is to make genre theory accessible. Drawing from the well-respected theorists mentioned in this article, I have devoted my classes to this aim and am pleased by the results.

References

Bain, K. (2012). *What the best college students do.* Cambridge, MA: Harvard University Press.

Bakhtin, M. M. (1981). *The dialogic imagination.* Austin, TX: University of Texas Press.

Bawarshi, A. S., & Reiff, M. J. (2010). *Genre: An introduction to history, theory, research, and pedagogy.* West Lafayette, IN: Parlor Press and WAC Clearinghouse.

Bazerman, C. (2009). Genre and cognitive development: Beyond writing to learn. In C. Bazerman, A. Bonini & D. Figueirredo (Eds.), *Genre in a changing world* (pp. 283-298). Fort Collins, CO: Parlor Press and WAC Clearinghouse.

Bean, J. C., Chapell, V. A., & Gillam, A. M. (2003). *Reading rhetorically: Brief edition.* New York, NY: Longman.

Beers, K., & Probst, R. E. (2012). *Notice and note: Strategies for close reading.* Boston, MA: Heinemann.

Berkenkotter, C., & Huckin, T. N. (1995). *Genre knowledge in disciplinary communication: Cognition/Culture/Power.* Mahwah, NJ: Lawrence Erlbaum.

Higher Education Policy Institute. (2010). *Beyond the rhetoric: Improving college readiness through coherent state policy.* Retrieved January 1, 2014, from http://www.highereducation.org/reports/college_readiness/gap.shtml

Bhatia, V. K. (2002). Applied genre analysis: Analytical advances and pedagogical procedures. In A. M. Johns (Ed.), *Genre in the classroom: Multiple perspectives* (pp. 279-284). Mahwah, NJ: Lawrence Erlbaum.

Boyd, D., & Marwick, A. (2011, September 23). Bullying as true drama. *The New York Times.* Retrieved from http://www.nytimes.com/2011/09/23/opinion/why-cyberbullying-rhetoric-misses-the-mark.html?_r=0

Devitt, A., Reiff, M. J., & Bawarshi, A. (2004). *Scenes of writing: Strategies for composing with genres.* New York, NY: Pearson/Longman.

Donovan, M. S., Bransford, J. D., & Pellegrino, J. W. (Eds.). (1999). *How people learn: Bridging research and practice.* Washington, DC: National Academies Press.

Dudley-Evans, T., & St John, M. J. (1998). *Developments in ESP: A multi-disciplinary approach.* Cambridge, UK: Cambridge University Press.

Eid, C., & Johns, A. M. (2011). *Teachers' guide to English language courses: 2010-2015.* Beirut: Antonine University.

Fisher, D., & Fry, N. (2009). *Background knowledge: The missing piece of the comprehension puzzle.* Portsmouth, NH: Heinemann.

Flowerdew, J. (2011). Reconciling contrasting approaches to genre analysis: The whole can equal more than the sum of the parts. In D. Belcher, A. M. Johns & B. Paltridge (Eds.), *New directions in English for specific purposes research* (pp. 119-145). Ann Arbor, MI: University of Michigan Press.

Freedman, A. (1994). "Do as I say": The relationship between teaching and learning new genres. In A. Freedman & P. Medway (Eds.), *Genre and the new rhetoric* (pp. 191-210). London: Taylor & Francis.

Hyland, K. (2006). *English for academic purposes.* London: Routledge.

Hyon, S. (1996). Genre in three traditions: Implications for ESL. *TESOL Quarterly, 30,* 693-722.

Johns, A. M. (1997). *Text, role, and context: Developing academic literacies.* New York, NY: Cambridge University Press.

Johns, A. M. (2002). Destabilizing and enriching novice students' genre theories. In A. M. Johns (Ed.), *Genre in the classroom: Multiple perspectives* (pp. 237-248). Mahwah, NJ: Lawrence Erlbaum.

Johns, A. M. (2004, March 24). The SDSU of the future. *San Diego Union Tribune,* p. 10.

Johns, A. M. (2009). *AVID college readiness: Working with sources.* San Diego, CA: AVID Center.

Johns, A. M. (2013). The history of English for specific purposes research. In B. Paltridge & S. Starfield (Eds.), *The handbook of English for specific purposes* (pp. 5-30). Oxford, UK: Wiley-Blackwell.

Johns, A. M., & Makalela, L. (2011). Needs analysis, critical ethnography, and context: Perspectives from the client—and the consultant. In D. Belcher, A. M. Johns & B. Paltridge (Eds.), *New directions in English for specific purposes research* (pp. 197-221). Ann Arbor, MI: University of Michigan Press.

Johns, A. M., & Price, D. (2014). English for specific purposes: International in scope, specific in purpose. In M. Celce-Murcia, D. M. Brinton & M. A. Snow (Eds.), *Teaching English as a second or foreign language* (4th ed.) (pp. 471-487). Boston, MA: National Geographic Learning.

LeMaster, J. (2011). Charting a text. *Critical reading.* San Diego: AVID Center.

MacBeth, K. P. (2006). Diverse, unforeseen, and quaint difficulties: The sensible responses of novices to learning to follow directions in academic writing. *Research in the Teaching of English, 41,* 108-207.

Miller, C. (1984). Genre as social action. *Quarterly Journal of Speech, 70,* 151-167.

Norton, B. (2011). The practice of theory in the language classroom. *Issues in Applied Linguistics, 18*(2), 1-10.

Paltridge, B., & Starfield, S. (2013). Introduction. In B. Paltridge & S. Starfield (Eds.), *The handbook of English for specific purposes* (pp. 1-4). Oxford, UK: Wiley-Blackwell.

Prior, P. (1998). *Writing/Disciplinarily: A sociohistoric account of literate activity in the academy.* Mahwah, NJ: Lawrence Erlbaum.

Prior, P. (2004). Tracing process: How texts come into being. In C. Bazerman & P. Prior (Eds.), *What writing does and how it does it* (pp. 167-200). Mahwah, NJ: Lawrence Erlbaum.

Reppen, R. (2010). *Using corpora in the language classroom.* New York: Cambridge University Press.

Russell, D. (1995). Activity theory and its implications for writing instruction. In J. Petraglia (Ed.), *Reconceiving writing, rethinking writing instruction* (pp. 51-78). Mahwah, NJ: Lawrence Erlbaum.

Schmidt, R., & Frota, S. (1986). Developing basic conversational ability in a second language: A case study of an adult learner of Portuguese. In R. R. Day (Ed.), *Talking to learn: Conversation in second language acquisition* (pp. 237-326). Rowley, MA: Newbury House.

Swales, J. M. (2009). Worlds of genre—metaphors of genre. In C. Bazerman, A. Bonini & D. Figueredo (Eds.), *Genre in a changing world* (pp. 1-13). W. Layfayette, IN: Parlor Press.

Swales, J. M. (1998). *Other floors, other voices: A textography of a small university building.* Mahwah, NJ: Lawrence Erlbaum.

"The writing process: The steps to writing success." (n.d.). Retrieved April 15, 2014 from http://www.time4writing.com/writing-resources/writing-process/

Appendix A: The SDSU of the Future

This appeared in the *San Diego Union-Tribune* on March 24, 2004 ©
Ann M. Johns

Ann M. Johns

1) What should the educational and service roles of San Diego
State University be? How should SDSU, the most comprehensive
California State University (CSU) in the region, balance teaching
and research, graduate and undergraduate programs, and its
regional, state, and international interests?

2) The answers to these questions were clear when our family
arrived in San Diego nearly forty years ago: SDSU was a teaching
institution devoted principally to serving local undergraduates.
Students with baccalaureate degrees generally remained in the
region, so our local businesses, educational institutions, and
political offices are now filled with more than 100,000 SDSU
alumni. The campus also offered a few region-appropriate
graduate programs in the 1960s, including those credentialing
public school teachers.

3) In the past twenty years or so—and with accelerating speed in the
last ten—the university has shifted its priorities dramatically. The
campus administration has encouraged departments to propose
doctoral programs, with plans to have more than twenty-five in
place during the coming years. New tenure-track faculty are hired
principally for their research potential; their tenure depends, in
large part, upon their abilities to bring prestige to the campus
through grants, publications, and even private donations. Because
major efforts are underway to enhance graduate education,
undergraduates are finding themselves in much larger classrooms,
with many General Education courses enrolling 100, 200, and even
500 students. In recent years, up to 40% of the General Education
classes have been taught by non-tenured faculty or teaching

assistants, since permanent faculty must devote time to their laboratories, advanced students, or their professional growth.

4) To achieve its goal of "world-class status," the university is determined to shed its regional standing and recruit more students from other parts of the state, the nation, and the world. (University President Stephen Weber uses the term "import" rather than recruit, according to Neil Morgan, *San Diego Union-Tribune,* March 3, 2004.) Since the campus is turning away more than 10,000 applicants each year, local students must be discouraged from attending. So because it is a CSU mandate that qualified local students be given priority, the campus has established a Dual Admissions Program: those who are CSU qualified but do not achieve sufficiently high scores on English or math placement examinations are accepted, but they must attend the already overburdened community colleges until they have met the designated competencies. Of the 860 students who were designated as Dual Admits in fall 2002, 303 attended community college classes, and 180 were fully enrolled on the SDSU campus in fall 2003, a 21% success rate. Though the campus continues to be involved in regional educational efforts such as the City Heights Project and Compact for Success (with the Sweetwater Union High School District), a large number of students applying from high schools in these areas are designated Dual Admits or rejected outright. But it must be more than Dual Admission that is discouraging students in the region from attending. In fall 1999, 43.9% of the freshman class came from San Diego or Imperial Counties; by fall 2002, this percentage had declined to 35.8%.

5) Its other world-class goal, to become a top research institution, will also divert the campus from its original mission; and even if this goal were a worthy one, it is unlikely to be realized. Because the campus is part of the CSU system, SDSU is required to have a higher student-faculty ratio than the University of California (UC) campuses, and its doctoral degrees can only be offered in conjunction with doctoral granting institutions. Particularly in these times of severe budget cuts, many campus departments cannot afford to give faculty the kinds of travel, released time, or grant monies required to pursue extensive research.

6) Are these efforts to import large numbers of students and "increase intellectual capital" in the region appropriate for SDSU? Are the benefits accrued worth a decline in local student enrollment and diversion of funds from undergraduate education? At a time when business leaders in the region are complaining that SDSU graduates have trouble communicating, are larger undergraduate classes that result in fewer writing assignments and speaking opportunities acceptable to the community?

7) In a recent *Academe* article, Philip G. Altbach noted that efforts to achieve world-class status by universities that are not well-endowed or research-designated can "divert energy and resources from more important—and more realistic—goals." Could this diversion of efforts be the reason why SDSU is still found in the fourth tier of the annual *U. S. News and World Report* campus poll, well below a number of its sister CSU campuses?

8) At this point, it would be inappropriate for the campus to return to policies of the 1960s. However, there may be a middle way: rather than attempting to attain UC-like, world-class status, SDSU could refashion itself as an outstanding regional campus. It could be more selective about its doctoral programs, advancing only those that are region-appropriate. At the same time, it could enhance recruitment of CSU-qualified local students, providing additional access and support to young people already in the region, a number of whom, for family or financial reasons, cannot leave to attend another CSU. Those students could bring a richness not measured by test scores to the campus—and to the community after graduation.

Appendix B: (Putative) Steps in the Writing Process.
One of many, almost identical versions online.

(Reproduced from http://www.time4writing.com/writing-resources/writing-process/by permission of www.Time4Writing.com).

Time4Writing.com (n.d.) describes the following steps in the writing process,

1. *Pre-writing:* This is the planning phase of the writing process, when students brainstorm, research, gather and outline ideas, often using diagrams for mapping out their thoughts. Audience and purpose should be considered at this point, and for the older students, a working thesis statement needs to be started.

2. *Drafting:* Students create their initial composition by writing down all their ideas in an organized way to convey a particular idea or present an argument. Audience and purpose need to be finalized.

3. *Revising:* Students review, modify, and reorganize their work by rearranging, adding, or deleting content, and by making the tone, style, and content appropriate for the intended audience. The goal of this phase of the writing process is to improve the draft.

4. *Editing:* At this point in the writing process, writers proofread and correct errors in grammar and mechanics, and edit to improve style and clarity. Having another writer's feedback in this stage is helpful.

5. *Publishing:* In this last step of the writing process, the final writing is shared with the group. Sharing can be accomplished in a variety of ways, and with the help of computers, it can even be printed or published online" (see "The writing process: The steps to writing success," n.d.).

Appendix C: Charting Grid: "The SDSU of the Future"

Para numbers	Doing: What are the functions of sections in which these paragraphs are found?	Language: How do you know that this is what the author is doing?	Saying: Briefly, what does the author say in this section?
1	Raising questions about the role of the university.	Use of question words and question marks.	We need to ask some questions about SDSU's roles.
2.	Giving some history about SDSU's previous roles.	Use of past tense verbs; "forty years ago"	Forty years ago SDSU's role was to train teachers and educate local undergraduates.
3			
4.			
5.			
6.			
7.			
8.			

Appendix D: Similarities (or Differences)
Between the Two Opinion Editorials

Group number: What's your job? _____		
"SDSU of the future"	"Bullying as true drama"	Important?

EndNotes

1   Though I am aware that "The Sydney School," influenced by Systemic Functional Linguistics, has been very active in producing genre-based curricula for a number of school populations and academic levels, I do not feel sufficiently familiar with its work to include it here.

2   Typically referred to as "rhetorical modes" in composition classes.

3   The students' own language is retained.

4   A word I teach students, and teachers—and they like to use it. I try to take "bias" and "opinion" out of the student lexicon.

5   See Beers and Probst (2012) for additional assistance in these activities.

6   An extensive discussion of this approach can be found in LeMaster (2011) and LiteracyTA.com.

7   The list is long. Here are a few examples: *analyzing, arguing, synthesizing, defining, clarifying, interpreting, introducing, suggesting, questioning, justifying, predicting, differentiating between.*

Chapter 16

Translating Practice into Theory in Genre Studies

Amy Devitt

University of Kansas (USA)

Between the idea
And the reality
Between the motion
And the act
Falls the Shadow

—T.S. Eliot, "The Hollow Men"

In a 2002 article, Johns commented on the lack of pedagogical focus in the invited papers at the Second International Genre conference in Vancouver in 1998. She wrote, "some of the essential pedagogical issues were sidestepped or downplayed during most of the conference. Why is this? Why do some of the finest minds in genre theory eschew discussion of the pedagogical implications of their work?" (p. 237). As one of the speakers invited to the Vancouver conference, I disagree that we eschew pedagogical discussions. But I find intriguing her hypothesis about why: "There are direct contradictions between what the theoreticians and researchers continue to discover about the nature of genres and the everyday requirements of the classroom" (p. 237). In this chapter, I wish to explore the extent to which that is so. In what ways have our developing theories about genre contradicted—or at least made more difficult—our developing genre-based pedagogies?

I also wish to explore the reverse: In what ways have our classroom needs contradicted our theoretical understandings? And, if our classroom needs do contradict our theoretical discoveries, how might those classroom discoveries inform our theories? That is, the contradictions between theory and pedagogy make not just pedagogy but also theory more complex. In general, I think scholars of pedagogy have more fully addressed the challenges of theory than scholars of theory have addressed the challenges of pedagogy. Genre theory should work to incorporate the knowledge about genre that we have gained from genre teaching.

Allow a few qualifications first. I do not intend to chastise theoreticians and praise teachers. Rather, I argue for each hearing the results of the other. Martin and Rose (2008) point out the gap between the "abstract academic written discourse" (p. 260) of critical theory and "the language of the disempowered voices it purports to speak for" (p. 259). Our theoretical talk about genre, even about genre learning in the classroom, does not necessarily address the people it might intend to support through that theory, whether disempowered students or practitioners and teachers. Differences in language, however, derive from differences in rhetorical situations. Theory and pedagogy have different purposes, methods, and, too often, audiences. Each also draws from different bodies of scholarship. Most notably, perhaps, genre theory must account not only for classroom genres but also for professional and everyday genres.[1] We have gained a great deal of our theoretical understanding of genres through our study of communicators in workplace settings (see Paré, 2002, for one significant and often cited example), and our knowledge is expanding as we examine digital and multimedia genres as well (see Miller and Shepherd, 2004, for example). We have been more attentive to and more successful at incorporating our knowledge from non-classroom applications into our developing genre theories, with less unexplored shadow in between. When we shift our attention to *teaching* those who write workplace or everyday genres, though, or those who write academic genres, the shadow grows darker[2]. Our study of genre pedagogies, like our study of non-academic genres, can enlighten our genre theory.

My argument here is also about more than just the difficulty or inappropriateness of translating theory into teaching, difficult as that movement might be. With some thirty years of research under our belts, we are surely not "premature," not moving from theory to teaching too soon. A number of sophisticated curricula and pedagogical strategies have developed using genre theories in various classrooms (see, for example, the overviews in Devitt, 2014; Tardy, 2006; Feez, 2002). The notion of translating theory into practice, however, moves one direction only. I am arguing not just for translating theory into practice but also for translating practice into theory.

Finally, my argument is also about more than just the privileging of theory over teaching, or of teaching over theory. We need both, certainly, for they serve different needs. The benefits of bringing the two together and of engaged scholarship in general are becoming apparent in many fields. Barge and Shockley-Zalabak (2008) argue that connecting theory and practice "necessitates bringing members of scholarly and practitioner communities into conversation with one another. Engaged scholarship privileges the diversity of perspectives that theorists and practitioners bring to making sense of a problem and honors their unique knowledge and expertise as valid" (p. 253). The teaching that has developed from listening to genre theory is rich, complex, and substantial. Because genre scholars have developed and enacted such significant genre pedagogies, the discoveries from that teaching can in turn enrich genre theories. It is time to let the knowledge flow both ways, to work not from theory to teaching alone but from teaching back to theory. The space between our theories and our pedagogies raises challenges for both. It is time to work more often between the two.

Elaborating on Johns' hypothesis, then, I would ask two questions: In what ways have our developing theories made genre-based pedagogies more complex? In what ways might our classroom discoveries make genre theory more complex? From there, I'll raise some suggestions of what we might explore if we were to work in the space between.

Because genre has become so much more complex a theoretical concept, the teaching of genre has become comparably more complex. As theory has moved genre from primarily formal patterns of rhetorical and textual features to primarily social actions in cultural contexts, genre has moved from eminently teachable to teachable with great difficulty, if at all. The genre knowledge that students must have now includes not just features of text—whether organizational patterns, rhetorical moves, or stylistic qualities—but also features of context—whether group identities, intertextual genre sets, or institutional settings. The relevant context for any particular genre is highly situated, and no common definition or set of contextual features has emerged to narrow down the possibilities. As an at best loosely defined concept, context includes institutional, material, and cultural settings; roles, identities, and relationships; community functions and individual motives; and anything else that matters for any particular genre in any particular situation. Genre knowledge thus includes knowledge of highly specific and ever-shifting contexts. That fact has created difficulties for all scholars, whether focusing on theory or practice. Context continues to prove elusive for those writing theory. Those studying particular settings, especially professional and workplace settings, have used qualitative methods for investigating the relevant contextual variables. Teachers of writing in classrooms who wish to help students learn more than classroom genres, however, must teach genres divorced from their settings. Our best theories demand that genre be embedded in complex contexts, but our best teaching demands that generic contexts be simplified.

It is not that many teachers haven't tried to teach more complex genre knowledge. The "teaching-learning cycle" from Macken-Horarik, Martin, and the Sydney School has increasingly emphasized students' research into and understanding of context (see Feez, 2002). Teachers of English as a Second Language (ESL) and English for Specific Purposes (ESP) courses emphasize the social functions of the genres they teach, and teachers like Johns send students into the field to do ethnographic research to contextualize their genres (Johns, 1997). In trying to highlight context over textual features, my own textbook, written with Bawarshi and Reiff, *Scenes of Writing* (2004), sends students to do interviews and observations, and itemizes the elements of the "scene" and rhetorical situation for students to analyze and consider when they write. But how fully does any student's inventory of a genre's setting, subject, participants, and purposes capture the rich context that theory tells us created and shaped that genre? We know that what students can gain of an understanding of context is superficial and overly broad, no matter how much research they conduct. Genre-based pedagogies suffer from the weakness of having to teach genres in isolation of their situations, leading scholars like Freedman (1994) to argue for situated learning alone, for learning genres when encountered in their contexts. I have argued for teaching genre awareness rather than particular genres (Devitt, 2004), and I believe that approach benefits from being able to teach students how to identify contextual elements when they encounter a new genre, rather than having to teach the contexts themselves. But genre awareness pedagogies still suffer from the indeterminacy of context, our inability to identify the elements of context that need investigation in every situation or for every genre. Our richer theoretical understanding of genre context has illuminated the poverty of de-contextualized genre teaching.

Another complication our theory brings to our pedagogy involves ideology and critique. Ever since Freedman and Medway reminded us, in their two collections (1994a, b) after the first Ottawa Genre conference in 1992, of the need not just to analyze but also to criticize genre, they have headed us toward a more critical genre studies. Theories of genre now incorporate the understanding that genres not just reflect but shape their rhetorical situations and the social and cultural contexts in which they are situated. As critical discourse has informed genre studies, theories have worked to critique the given and "common sense" nature of existing genres and their established power relationships, identities, and encouragement of conformity. After the 1998 genre conference in Vancouver, the one Johns referred to in her initial complaint about too little attention to pedagogy, Coe, Lingard, and Teslenko (2002) focused genre scholars' attention on *The Rhetoric and Ideology of Genre*. With all these theoretical advances toward a critical genre studies, teachers today are expected to help students not only see how genres shape their perceptions and actions but also change or resist genre's ideological pull. Attempting to incorporate this new theoretical understanding of the ideological nature of genres, in *Scenes of Writing* my co-authors and I tried to take a critical stance toward all the genres we used as examples, and we included a chapter on Critiquing and Changing Genres. The teaching-learning cycle includes "creative exploitation" of genre possibilities as one stage in learning a genre (see Macken-Horarick, 2002). Peters (1997) encourages students to write "antigenres," and Brooks (2002) reports teaching students to "reinvent" a genre rather than placidly accommodate to it.

Yet we add genre critique to our curricula even as our theory tells us that resistance may be futile. How do we get students to resist the ideologies in which they are embroiled? Perhaps we teach them about genres of power. But then Luke (1996) presents such a focused, detailed, and complex article on the multiple meanings of power from multiple philosophers and theorists that I surely despair of ever adequately incorporating notions of power into my courses. Further complicating the ideological mix are all the theoretical advances we've had in agency, identity, consciousness, uptake, and materiality, to name just a few of the theoretical concepts that impact our understanding of genre and, preferably, our teaching of genre. It already takes weeks of dedicated instruction, scaffolded activities, and exploration and reflection in a course design to begin to help students toward an understanding and use of genre as something other than textual formula, much less to help them generate writing within genres that is varied, purposeful, unique, rhetorically aware, deliberate, and critical. Yet genre pedagogies, working to incorporate these current theoretical understandings, develop assignments, activities, and curricula that attempt to address genre's ideological nature and help students develop a critical awareness of the genres they write.

To some extent, I am simply describing the perennial problem of teaching writing—writing of any kind and from any pedagogical approach. Both theory and teaching of writing involve the complex interaction of so many elements that we can't possibly manage/define/design/address them all. We can only get bits and pieces at a time. In spite of some scholars arguing that we should abandon altogether the project of teaching writing in writing classrooms (Crowley, 1998, most directly), many people continue to teach writing and to believe that they can teach writing well. Researchers can, at times, discover ways of teaching writing that are more or less effective for students. And some ways of teaching writing are more theoretically sound than others. Teachers of writing generally acknowledge that they aren't teaching students the full complexity of writing in theory or teaching students all that they need to learn about writing forever. Somehow teachers design curricula to teach writing in different ways in different institutional settings to different student populations, even though there might seem to be direct contradictions between what they are teaching and what theory might have discovered. In teaching writing, perhaps, we may have more helpfully discovered the space in between theory and practice. To incorporate genre into those writing classrooms, genre-based pedagogies also need to work in that space between, to incorporate significant discoveries of genre theory in ways that recognize the needs of learners. Teachers continue to work in their classrooms and pedagogies to help students recognize genre's power for all writers, but they also need to recognize the limitations of what student writers can do with that power. Teachers continue to help students recognize the influence of context and become aware of how local those contexts are in their particular writing situations, but they also need to prepare students to adapt when encountering new genres in their full contextual glory. In spite of the difficulties that genre theory brings to genre pedagogy, then, engaged scholars continue to design curricula that reflect such theoretical complexities and to revise their curricula as new theories emerge, while also staying realistic about how context, ideologies, and, in fact, genres operate differently in the classroom.

While such work recognizes that theory has made teaching more complex, I do not see many scholars adequately recognizing that genre teaching must make our genre theory more complex, that practice can and should be translated into theory. Note Johns' comment again, which speaks to theory that doesn't meet the needs of teaching: "There are direct contradictions between what the theoreticians and researchers continue to discover about the nature of genres and the everyday requirements of the classroom" (Johns, 2002, p.237). There are also direct contradictions between what the teachers continue to discover about the nature of genres and the requirements of theory. Not just the *requirements* of the classroom but also the *discoveries* of the classroom are contradicting theory. As teachers using genre-based pedagogies continue to teach genre and genre-learners, they discover more about how genre works. As I have been describing, teachers using genre-based pedagogies have been complicating their curricula to address ever more complex theories of genre context and ideology. How have theorists been adapting their genre-based theories to incorporate discoveries from teaching?

One significant but perhaps unrecognized example of theory adapting to teaching is Freedman's study of the effectiveness of explicit teaching of genres. Freedman's 1993 critique, which raised such a firestorm of controversy, allowed teaching experience to lead her to a gentler conclusion than theory alone would demonstrate. Theory and research alone, Freedman argued, supported her Strong Hypothesis: "explicit teaching is unnecessary; for the most part, not even possible; and where possible, not useful (except during editing, for a limited number of transparent and highly specific features). Further, whenever explicit teaching does take place, there is risk of overlearning or misapplication" (p. 226). But in the end Freedman moves from her Strong Hypothesis to the Restricted Hypothesis: "It is similar in stating that explicit teaching is neither necessary, nor for the most part possible or useful, and it acknowledges as well the potential for harm in such teaching. However, the Restricted Hypothesis allows that, under certain conditions and for some learners, explicit teaching may enhance learning" (p. 226). She moves to the Restricted Hypothesis in part because, as she writes, "while it is true that the formulation of the Strong Hypothesis is buttressed by theory (based on extensive research) from first and second language acquisition," other research and theory can support a more qualified version that "may provide a better fit with some teachers' personal experience or practical wisdom" (p. 241). She recognizes, in this comment, that our pedagogical experiences do not necessarily support our theoretical claims. In fact, she offers both models "to practicing teachers as hypotheses to be tested in the crucibles of their own experience and classrooms" (p. 226). Here then is a model of a scholar making two significant moves: modifying her conclusions based on an interaction of some theory and research and some pedagogical knowledge; and proposing that teaching experience should test the accuracy of theoretical hypotheses. She finds a space between the two for a more complicated answer to her research question. However controversial her conclusion might be for other reasons, Freedman illustrates how teaching might complicate theory productively—and illustrates what working the space between theory and practice might produce.

One area of genre studies where theory has begun incorporating practice most aggressively is the nature of genre knowledge, drawing especially on discoveries about transfer. The work on transfer emerges in part from teachers' recognition that students cannot routinely or easily draw on knowledge of genres they have studied or used previously. A great deal of research has examined the transferability (or lack thereof) of genre knowledge from school context to outside, or even from one classroom context to another (see, for example, Artemeva & Fox, 2010; Nowacek, 2011; Reiff & Bawarshi, 2011; or Wardle, 2007). This body of scholarship has led teachers and other curricula designers to begin attending to how to help students learn to transfer genre knowledge. It has also led theorists to begin reconsidering the nature and production of genre knowledge. These new discoveries about pedagogical transfer still need to be incorporated more fully into theory. Our theories may need to further distinguish different components of genre, for example, to account for the complexities of what does and does not remain with writers as they move from one context to the next, perhaps discriminating different types of genre knowledge or even different knowledge for different genre types. Different learners transfer genre knowledge differently (see Reiff & Bawarshi, 2011, for example), leading theory back perhaps to the role of genres in inculcating ideology or agency in genres. Some theorists and researchers have recently turned to cognitive knowledge of genres (see Bazerman, 2009, for example), and this cognitive turn benefits from considering what teachers and pedagogies have discovered about genre learning. Cognition would seem a likely topic to approach the space between theory and practice since cognition sits between theory and teaching. It encompasses ideas of the learner interacting with what is learned. It includes perception and knowledge. It looks at how as well as what, not as two separate entities but as interwoven components. Much of our work in transfer edges toward the space between, though it has more often been taken up for its pedagogical implications than its theoretical ones. Building on that research leads to a better understanding of the nature of genre and opens our theorizing of genre as contextualized cognitive as well as social action.

Cognitive genre theory might also address the ways genres encourage or inhibit certain actions, including students' actions. Students' resistance to critique has already been noted, but some students also resist variation from or innovation within genres. In her study of a first-year writing course that attempted to encourage innovation, Heather Bastian (2010a) discovered how reluctant students can be to critique genres or to innovate generically. She analyzed what motivates or inhibits students' willingness to write innovatively within genres, delineating the influence of both external motivators and individual variations. Such classroom-based research and the similar experiences reported by teachers everywhere should combine well with theories of cognition, uptake, and agency. Both theory and practice together can help us understand more fully and work more successfully within generic creativity and constraint.

Classroom-based knowledge also contributes to our understanding of ideology and genre. Our experiences as teachers with our students demonstrate that what students want (models and formulae to follow) conflict with what we try to give them (rhetorical understanding and critique). As Bastian (2010b) argues in another piece, students have a very difficult time critiquing genres foreign to them, much less ones with which they are familiar. Perhaps Johns is correct that, "Critical pedagogues, most of whom are highly educated, encourage critique of the system before the students can understand it and negotiate it" (quoted in Swales, 2004, p. 247). If so, how would that affect our theoretical understanding of the ideologies of genre? The effects of ideology through genres might be more layered and nuanced than current theories describe.

Perhaps the largest elephant in the room between theory and practice is the role of textual form in genre. Teaching students to shift their thinking about genres from formulas and texts to rhetorical situation and actions is difficult. For our students (and colleagues in other disciplines and most of the general populace), genre equates comfortably with textual patterns. For rhetorical genre theory, those textual patterns have been relegated to a supporting role, at best. Of course, what is commonly believed is not necessarily true, nor should it replace scholarly investigation. But our theories should be challenged by how sticky generic form is in the classroom and for most users of genres. If form does not constitute genre, as most genre theory would have it, then what is the relationship between genre and form? What is it about genres that they seem so formal and formulaic to the people who use them? Why do generic formulas have such high visibility? In our move to redefine genre rhetorically and semiotically, our theories have left form perhaps too far behind, refusing to acknowledge substantially what our classroom and everyday experience tells us: that the forms of genres play a significant role in the understanding and use of genre. Since scholars have developed multiple methods of discourse analysis to describe those textual patterns with considerable complexity, form need not be grossly oversimplified. The formal identification of genre in the classroom and everyday use persists, and that persistence, the stickiness of that conception, should lead us to develop a fuller and more well-defined role for textual form in theories of the nature, operation, and significance of genre. Overall, our theories need to find a place for generic form as well as action.

In fact, students and novice writers can live on genre form alone, and that knowledge from practice may be the riskiest elephant in the room to acknowledge. Not only do students and novice writers in general want to follow formulas but also students want and need more straightforward understandings of the genres we ask them to write than our theory posits. In the classroom and classroom research (as well as outside academe), we discover that many writers get along just fine with simplified versions of genres, with the most basic understandings of what a particular genre is; many writers imitate genres and do okay. They fake it till they make it. I may bemoan that fact, but I also think that fact should tell us something about our theories. At some level, in some ways, genre must be simpler than we're making it out to be. A theory that attempted to address that reality might tease out the multiple layers of generic action, including some that do in some contexts operate more formulaically.

Combine multiple discoveries from teaching—that students equate genres with forms, that students crave formulas and models, that formulaic writing works to some degree, that students struggle to innovate or critique genres, that students have difficulty using genre knowledge from one context in another context—and we have practice that deserves to be translated into theory. Those facts must be meaningful. I suspect that the meaning connects back to the ideological nature of genres. To understand how genres act ideologically, we may need to understand how repeated forms trigger ideology—or at least how they connect. What makes the formal nature of genres so sticky with our students may be the stickiness of ideology. But I would not attribute those discoveries from teaching to the ideological nature of genre alone and call it done. The challenges from classroom experience to theory are multiple and should be ongoing. Our pedagogical experience should be complicating our theories, just as our theories complicate our pedagogies. We need to design theories that reflect such quotidian and even undesired realities of writing and teaching as we see in every study of the classroom. Our theory needs to address what we see in teaching.

Please note that I am not arguing that pedagogy should lead us to theorize a much-reduced version of genre. Rather, the theory that incorporated discoveries from teaching and classroom-based research would have to be much more complicated and probably messy to include different levels of understanding and skills, the wide variation of genre use from one population to the next and within populations, and the quotidian meaning of genre to most writers and readers. There are also realms within genre pedagogy that remain heavily under-theorized. Which theories tackle genre-based writing processes, for example? In *Scenes of Writing* (Devitt, Reiff, & Bawarshi, 2004), my co-authors and I wrote a chapter on genre considerations in writing processes, but we found relatively little explicit theory of genre as process to draw from for this chapter (in contrast to the rich theory that influenced our instruction in genre contexts and critique). Examining common pedagogical issues through theory can enrich both.

Note, too, that I do not intend to place the entire burden back in the realm of theory. I don't mean to be chiding theorists, myself among them, but rather pointing out spaces of possibility for us all. I'm seeking the place between theory and practice, the fuller understanding and exploration of genre that can come from the two interacting. How do we, theorists and teachers alike, work between the two, instead of accepting one and rejecting the other or limiting our scholarship to separate realms? The notion of genre that emerges from the space in between would be theoretically rich and pedagogically practical. Perhaps that would lead to immersion programs, as Freedman so long ago advocated, with genre locally situated at every turn. Or perhaps it would lead to a notion of genre as textually grounded social actions with curricula that extend through different levels of cognitive development and across the curriculum. I suspect my imagination here is too limited. Perhaps our theories and curricula are not yet well developed enough to find the spaces between, but I suspect we simply have not been focusing our eyes on the in-between spots.

The next advances in genre studies might come from looking in between. Work in professional genres may indicate some focuses, for that applied work has often led to theoretical discoveries and vice versa. Working on the issue of context between theory and teaching is needed. Although theories of context are now much richer than they once were, context is still undertheorized. Working to make genre context a more teachable subject, one that students could learn to apply in multiple settings, could lead to improvements in both genre theory and teaching. Studies of emerging genres, like those Miller and Shepherd (2004) are pursuing, could work in the space between, helping us to see what happens as people, including students, take up new contexts. The concept of uptake is certainly high theory, and Bawarshi has shown us a great deal about genre through his theoretical work with that concept. But he has also shown us the effects of genre uptake in the world, whether in political disputes or students' taking up of teachers' assignments (Bawarshi, 2003; this volume). He has shown us how materiality sits in between and offers rich new territory to explore.

It is that new territory that I am seeking in the space between. There are hidden motives to our work that we might discover if we work between. There are aspects of genre that we've been overlooking as we look at just theory or teaching. It may take our continuing to develop our theories and our pedagogies until they are each advanced enough for us to move between them. It will certainly take many of us keeping an eye on the in-between-ness to begin developing the rich genre studies I'm envisioning: a genre studies that has not contradictions between its theories and its pedagogies (and its other settings of practice) but rather interplay; a genre studies that translates theory into practice and practice into theory and enjoys the motion. Between the idea and the reality in genre studies lies the shadow, not necessarily a harbinger of death and destruction but an opportunity for discovery and enlightenment.

References

Artemeva, N., & Fox, J. (2010). Awareness versus production: Probing students' antecedent genre knowledge. *Journal of Business and Technical Communication, 24*(4), 476–515.

Barge, J. K., & Shockley-Zalabak, P. (2008). Engaged scholarship and the creation of useful organizational knowledge. *Journal of Applied Communication Research, 36,* 251-265.

Bastian, H. (2010a). *Disrupting conventions: When and why writers take up innovation* (Unpublished doctoral dissertation). University of Kansas.

Bastian, H. (2010b). The genre effect: Exploring the unfamiliar. *Composition Studies, 38*(1), 27-49.

Bawarshi, A. (2003). *Genre and the invention of the writer: Reconsidering the place of invention in composition.* Logan, UT: Utah State University Press.

Bazerman, C. (2009). Genre and cognitive development: Beyond writing to learn. In C. Bazerman, A. Bonini, & D. Figueiredo (Eds.), *Genre in a Changing World* (pp. 283-298). Fort Collins, CO: WAC Clearinghouse and Parlor Press.

Brooks, K. (2002). Reading, writing, and teaching creative hypertext: A genre-based pedagogy. *Pedagogy, 2*(3), 337–356.

Coe, R., Lingard, M. L., & Teslenko, T. (Eds.). (2002). *The rhetoric and ideology of genre: Strategies for stability and change.* Cresskill, NJ: Hampton Press.

Crowley, S. (1998). *Composition in the university: Historical and polemical essays* (1st ed.). Pittsburgh, PA: University of Pittsburgh Press.

Devitt, A. J. (2004). *Writing genres.* Carbondale, IL: Southern Illinois University Press.

Devitt, A. J. (2014). Genre pedagogies. In A. Rupiper-Taggart, K. Schick, & B. Hessler (Eds.), *Guide to composition pedagogies.* (pp. 146-162). Oxford and New York: Oxford University Press.

Devitt, A., Reiff, M. J., & Bawarshi, A. (2004). *Scenes of writing: Strategies for composing with genres.* New York, NY: Longman.

Feez, S. (2002). Heritage and innovation in second language education. In A. M. Johns (Ed.), *Genre in the classroom: Multiple perspectives* (pp. 43-69). Mahwah, N.J: Lawrence Erlbaum.

Freedman, A. (1993). Show and tell? The role of explicit teaching in the learning of new genres. *Research in the Teaching of English, 27*(3), 222-251.

Freedman, A. (1994). 'Do as I say': The relationship between teaching and learning new genres. In A. Freedman & P. Medway (Eds.), *Genre and the new rhetoric* (pp. 191–210). London: Taylor & Francis.

Freedman, A., & Medway, P. (Eds.). (1994a). *Genre and the new rhetoric.* London: Taylor & Francis.

Freedman, A., & Medway, P. (1994b). *Learning and teaching genre.* Portsmouth NH: Boynton/Cook.

Johns, A. M. (2002). Destabilizing and enriching novice students' genre theories. In A. M. Johns (Ed.), *Genre in the classroom: Multiple perspectives* (pp. 237-246). Mahwah, N.J: Lawrence Erlbaum.

Johns, A. M. (1997). *Text, role and context: Developing academic literacies.* New York, NY: Cambridge University Press.

Luke, A. (1996). Genres of power? Literacy education and the production of capital. In R. Hasan & G. Williams (Eds.), *Literacy in society* (pp. 308-338). London: Longman.

Macken-Horarik, M. (2002). "Something to shoot for": A systemic functional approach to teaching genre in secondary school science. In A. Johns (Ed.), *Genre in the classroom. Multiple perspectives* (pp. 17-42). Mahwah, NJ: Lawrence Erlbaum.

Martin, J. R., & Rose, D. (2008). *Genre relations: Mapping culture.* London /Oakville, CT: Equinox.

Miller, C., & Shepherd, D. (2004). Blogging as social action: A genre analysis of the weblog. In L. J. Gurak, Antonijevic, S., Johnson, L., Ratliff, C., & Reyman, J. (Eds.), *Into the blogosphere: Rhetoric, community and culture of weblogs.* Retrieved from http://blog.lib.umn.edu/blogosphere/ blogging_as_social_action_a_genre_analysis_of_the_weblog.html

Nowacek, R. S. (2011). *Agents of integration: Understanding transfer as a rhetorical act.* Carbondale: IL: Southern Illinois University Press.

Paré, A. (2002). Genre and identity: Individuals, institutions, and ideology. In R. Coe, L. Lingard & T. Teslenko (Eds.), *The rhetoric and ideology of genre: Strategies for stability and change* (pp. 57-71). Creskill, NJ: Hampton.

Peters, B. Genre, antigenre, and reinventing the forms of conceptualization. In W. Bishop & H. Ostrom (Eds.), *Genre and writing: Issues, arguments, alternatives* (pp. 199-214). Portsmouth, NH: Boynton/Cook.

Reiff, M. J., & Bawarshi, A. (2011). Tracing discursive resources: How students use prior genre knowledge to negotiate new writing contexts in first-year composition. *Written Communication, 28*(3), 312–337.

Swales, J. M. (2004). *Research genres: Explorations and applications.* New York, NY: Cambridge University Press.

Tardy, C. M. (2006). Researching first and second language genre learning: A comparative review and a look ahead. *Journal of Second Language Writing, 15*(2), 79–101.

Wardle, E. (2007). Understanding 'transfer' from FYC: Preliminary results from a longitudinal Study. *WPA: Writing Program Administration, 31*(1-2), 65–85.

EndNotes

[1]   I am grateful to Anthony Paré for pointing out my neglect of this area of genre studies, which is in many ways already working in between theory and practice.

[2]   I am speaking in this chapter from the perspective of a scholar working in what has been called Rhetorical Genre Studies, or North American genre studies. While I think my argument applies as well to all who teach and study a rhetorical view of genre, I recognize that my bias lies with the aims and theoretical groundings coming from rhetoric and from teaching writing to native speakers.

Chapter 17

A Genre-Based Approach Underlying Didactic Sequences for the Teaching of Languages

Vera Lúcia Lopes Cristovão

State University of Londrina (Brazil)

Researchers in different parts of the world have worked on (re) conceptualizations of the notion of genre for many decades (e.g., Bakhtin, 1986; Miller, 1984). For example, the well-known article by Hyon (1996) (see Swales this volume) describes three genre studies traditions which continue to be viewed as the most recognized in the areas of Linguistics, Applied Linguistics, Language Studies, and Writing Studies. These three traditions include English for Specific Purposes (ESP), Rhetorical Genre Studies (RGS), also known as North American genre theory or New Rhetoric genre theory, and the Sydney School, based on Systemic Functional Linguistics (SFL). More recently, Motta-Roth (2008) noted that in the Brazilian context, in addition to the three traditions in genre studies identified by Hyon (1996) and Bhatia (2004), it is important to consider a fourth tradition, the socio-discursive interactionism (SDI) (see also Araújo, 2010; Bawarshi & Reiff, 2010). To Motta-Roth (2008), genre research "developed in Brazil in the 1990s can be identified with these four genre schools," which inform "pedagogical practices" (p. 345) in language teaching (cf. Motta-Roth & Heberle, 2015; Vian Jr. this volume). Based on Bakhtin's view of genre as the use of language in all areas of human activity, genres are taken as references to our (oral or written) text productions in order to interact, communicate

403

and construct meanings in the world. This assumption is crucial to the SDI perspective and as the core construct to the *National Curriculum Parameters* (*Parâmetros Curriculares Nacionais,* or PCN) and curricular reforms in terms of assuming genres as mediational tools for language teaching in secondary education. In their review of genre studies, Bawarshi and Reiff (2010) recognized the fourth tradition in genre studies as "the Brazilian educational model or *didactic* approach. This pedagogical approach, informed by the Swiss genre tradition and theories of socio-discursive interactionism, has influenced curricular initiatives and genre pedagogy in Brazil" (p. 177). In Bawarshi and Reiff's definition:

> the Brazilian [pedagogical] model begins with early production of the genre based on writers' previous knowledge and experience, then moves to analysis of genre within rhetorical and social contexts, culminating with (re) production of the genre, thus bringing together a focus on genre awareness, analysis of linguistic conventions, and attention to social context. (p. 177)

It is these features of the Brazilian model that allowed Bawarshi and Reiff to characterize it as an example of interactive genre pedagogy which promotes a reciprocal relation between an individual's cognitive abilities and the complexity of the text being produced.

Araújo (2010) grouped research studies of Brazilian genre scholars into four main traditions: social interactionism, social rhetoric, social semiotics, and critical discourse analysis (cf. Vian Jr., this volume). As she has recently observed (2010), SDI is "the most preferred approach to analyze genre" used in Brazilian foreign/additional language education (p. 51). The objectives of this chapter are to: (a) present an overview of Brazilian genre approaches rooted in socio-discursive interactionism (Bronckart, 1999, 2006; Dolz & Schneuwly, 1998); and (b) discuss the principles underlying genre-based pedagogical interventions developed by Brazilian English teachers. These pedagogical interventions, known as *didactic sequences* (DS), are a group of school activities systematically organized in teaching modules within a class project and aimed at developing students' language capacities, viewed as the skills necessary to produce texts appropriate to the context of interaction (Dolz, Pasquier & Bronckart, 1993).

In this chapter, first, I contextualize some of the latest curriculum changes in the Brazilian secondary education system, which have allowed for the introduction of genre-based initiatives. Second, I offer an overview of the main theoretical and methodological concepts used in this chapter, including SDI, language, genre, language capacities and didactic sequences. Third, I discuss some implications of the genre-based approach for language teaching in secondary school.

Historical Contextualization of Genre-based Initiatives in Brazilian Education

Over the last twenty years, the study of genres in Brazil has developed substantially. To contextualize the expansion, this section provides a brief socio-historical background for the development and dissemination of the SDI-based genre approach and its Brazilian versions (cf. Motta-Roth & Heberle, 2015; Vian Jr. this volume).

In the early 1990s, the Catholic University of São Paulo (PUC-SP) in Brazil started a collaboration with the Faculty of Psychology and Education Sciences at the University of Geneva (FAPSE-UNIGE) in Switzerland. As a part of this collaborative venture, researchers conducted SDI studies related to pedagogical interventions in educational contexts. Genres were examined as mega-instruments for teaching, and contributing to pedagogical material development by the Ministry of Education (MEC), a public body of the federal government of Brazil in charge of planning, proposing and executing decisions related to education. One of MEC's responsibilities is to propose and manage educational policies such as the implementation of the Law of Guidelines and Basis for National Education (*Lei de Diretrizes e Bases da Educação Nacional,* or LDB, Brasil Ministério da Educação, 1996). For example, LDB made it compulsory for elementary and secondary schools to offer foreign language training.

In 1997, following the launch of the latest LDB at the end of 1996, MEC implemented National Curriculum Parameters (Brasil Secretaria Da Educação Fundamental, 1997), which aimed at guiding mother tongue (Portuguese) teaching at primary levels. The content for teaching was selected in agreement with the learning objectives established by the PCN (Rojo, 2000). Further, the PCN have fostered the use of genres as teaching tools and content of teaching, or *teaching objects*. In other words, genres have a dual-level function in language pedagogy. On the one hand, they work as teaching tools in the sense that students engage with genres to participate in specific sociocultural worlds. On the other hand, the very features that compose genres, such as rhetorical choices, organization, etc. are topics covered in a course. As a national guide for the teaching of Portuguese, the PCN have led to changes in school curricula and in teachers' pedagogical practices, as well as the development of instructional materials, school projects, and in-service teacher education programs based on the SDI principles (Schneuwly, 1994).

The PCN for foreign language teaching were launched in 1998 (Brasil Secretaria Da Educação Fundamental, 1998). Although the concept of genre was not explicitly mentioned in the document, examples of genres were provided as a possible type of knowledge to be learned by students. As well, in 1998, the Secretariat of Education of the state of Paraná distributed genre-based instructional materials for the teaching of English to and learning of English by students enrolled in the Adequacy Program. The Adequacy Program aimed at reducing student failure rates and raising retention rates, as well as at placing students in the school year most appropriate to their ages. The instructional materials developed for this program were based on the key concepts of SDI, such as language capacities and didactic sequence. Scholars involved in the program found that, in the program's two-year history, fewer students evaded school, failed a school year, or were mistakingly placed in a school year not appropriate to their age.

Another program partially based on the SDI theoretical and methodological notions was "Writing the Future". The program was offered in 2002, 2004, and 2006 before it became affiliated with an official Portuguese writing contest, the Olympiad. This affiliation helped to expand the program, and since 2008, the program has been offered under the auspices of MEC. Tailored to elementary and secondary school students, the program offers materials focusing on the didactic sequences in four different genres: poetry, memoirs, chronicles, and opinion articles. The program includes material on language capacities, didactic sequences, and student self-assessment. Alongside these efforts in the educational sector, genre studies were also used in other spheres, including academic, journalistic, and everyday ones.

In 2003, a SDI-affiliated research group[1], "Language and Education," working at the State University of Londrina (UEL), organized the first Brazilian Conference on Genre Studies, SIGET. After the first three Conferences at three different universities in the south of Brazil, the Conference became bi-annual and attracted well-known international scholars from different theoretical perspectives. The conference has fostered research in several genre traditions, including ESP, RGS, the Sydney School, SDI (the Geneva School and its Brazilian reconfigurations), perspectives on the Bakhtinian approach to genre, and Critical Genre Analysis.

Due to the fruitful use of genres in educational settings, *Revista Nova Escola,* Brazil's second most popular educational journal, also started publishing articles on genres. The magazine introduced a section entitled Didactic Sequence. Although the theoretical basis for the journal's use of this term is not the same as the one proposed by the SDI (see Anjos-Santos, Lanferdini & Cristovão, 2011), the term didactic sequence introduced in the journal has become popular among Brazilian school teachers and has been used in different types of teaching materials. Along with the aforementioned developments, there has been an increasing adoption of genre-based approaches in curricula from primary to higher education as well as in the State Curriculum Guidelines. For example, educational materials from the state of Paraná (2008) integrated the concept of genre, viewing both (multi)literacies and language as social practice.

More recently, two foreign languages were included as disciplines of study in the National Program of Textbooks (PNLD)[2]. The PNLD aims to solicit pedagogical collections from publishers, evaluate and select textbooks (didactic textbooks) for the public school sector in Brazil, and distribute the selected textbooks. In evaluating potential academic resources, the PNLD looks not only at how the texts support written comprehension and oral production, but at whether the texts use a variety of written and spoken genres.

Moving forward, I review some of the main concepts of SDI. I also consider what it means for genres to be central in teaching and learning, and how curriculum guidelines can transform the educational sector through reflection, awareness, autonomy, and empowerment. I consider efforts to improve the quality of textbooks and, in turn, the quality of education.

Socio-Discursive Interactionism (SDI)

SDI, originally developed at the University of Geneva, promptly reached locations beyond Switzerland. When SDI emerged, it was best known for a) having an epistemological basis and b) taking a didactic, or pedagogical, approach based on empirical studies in educational contexts (Bronckart, 1999; 2006; 2008; Dolz & Schneuwly, 1998).

SDI is viewed as a human science comprised of biological, psychological, sociological, and linguistic dimensions that interact and constitute the human being and human capacities (Bronckart, 2011). This approach aims to contribute to the social life of society through education. According to Bronckart (2011), the SDI views language and human social history as determining factors in the constitution and development of both individual psychological capacities and collective culture. Further, Bronckart (2011) observes that SDI is known for its monist philosophical foundation and for its roots in various social sciences and humanities concepts (see Bronckart, Clémence, Schneuwly & Schurmans, 1996 for a detailed historical discussion of the roots that shape and inform SDI philosophical foundations). SDI views genres both as language practices embodied in texts and as part of social practices responsible for an individual's participation in different social activity spheres (Schneuwly & Dolz, 1999). Further, SDI asserts that it is through language practices that people produce, comprehend, and interpret meanings. Along with their socio-cultural, purposeful, and situated features, genres are also recognized as recurrent language forms produced in a communicative context that may be produced, reproduced and consumed by people (Miller, 1984). Yet, genres are not static as they are adapted to socio-communicative situations (Bronckart, 1999). More specifically, they are adapted to the socio-subjective and physical context, which is composed of individuals' objectives and individuals' roles (e.g., reader/listener, writer/speaker), as well as the context, time, and space of interaction and the socio-cultural values underlying the situation. Genres are flexible forms of language functioning in socially situated practices and in particular, concrete communicative situations. They are also forms of social action whose usage is essential to communicative and practical activities (Bronckart, 2006). As Bronckart described in a 2011 video, genres are "the various culturally oriented ways of constructing and organizing significations (or meanings)." In sum, interventions related to language didactics and the didactics of genres are socially and politically useful.

In this sense, the presented above theoretical conceptualization of genres greatly resembles the one put forward by Miller (1984), Bazerman (1994) and other RGS-affiliated authors. Historically, both the SDI and the RGS conceptualizations of genres as important symbolic tools that mediate and afford social action evolved in different geographical locations. The lack of academic conversation between the approaches seems to have been precluded by the fact that SDI authors rarely published their ideas in the English language (a few exceptions are Bronckart [1995, 1996] and Schneuwly [1994]), and by the fact that they were most interested in different sociocultural contexts. For example, while RGS studies focused on writing in the professions and in higher education (cf. Bazerman, 1988; Freedman and Medway, 1994; Miller, 1984), SDI focused on reading and writing in primary and secondary schools.

Language Didactics

As mentioned above, language capacities and didactic sequences are two important concepts in the field of language didactics. To employ a genre-based approach for pedagogical purposes means to use tasks or activities intended to explore the activity sphere(s) in which the target text is produced and circulated. Further, employing this approach means examining the immediate context of text production or, in other words, the text producer, target reader/listener, objective, content, time, and place.

Genres are used as tools for mediation and teaching. As mentioned above, for didactic purposes, the concept of *language capacities*[3] is defined as "required skills for the production of a text in a determined situation of interaction" (Dolz, Pasquier & Bronckart, 1993, p. 30). This definition acknowledges action capacities, discursive capacities, and linguistic-discursive capacities. Action capacities refer to the context of production and are related to situational objectives. They focus on the micro situation (e.g., taking into account the writer/speaker of the text), the target audience, and the objective among other foci. Discursive capacities refer to the text's organization, and are related to discursive objectives. Linguistic-discursive capacities refer to linguistic units, and are related to discursive-linguistic parameters that help construct the text.

Machado and Bronckart (2009) see identifying the context of production (before the textual analysis) as crucial, as it refers to

> the wider *socio-historical context* in which a text is produced, in which it circulates and is used; the *means* in which the text is made available; the *immediate language context*, that is, the text(s) that follow, in the same *means*, the text to be analysed; the *intertext*, that is, the text(s) with which the text has relations easily identifiable even before the analysis; the *situation of production*, that is, the representations of the producer that influence the text form, distributed in eight parameters - emissor, receptor, local, time, social role of the enunciator and receptor, social institution and objective of the production (Bronckart 1997). (p. 46-47, emphasis added)

Here Machado and Bronckart make it explicit that the language action is materialized in a text while also drawing attention to the importance of both the socio-historical context and the immediate context. Due to the crucial importance of exploring the macro context in the construction of meaning, more recently, Cristovão (2013) and Stutz (2011) proposed, for didactic purposes, the concept of *signification capacities*. The signification capacities make it possible for individuals to construct meanings from the representation and/ or knowledge about social practices (e.g., ideological, historical, sociocultural, economic contexts). Their understanding of the signification capacity also calls attention to spheres of human activity, to praxiologic activities interacting with the content in different human experiences, and their relationship with language activities. Such capacities work together in a system.

Applying a genre-based approach in education could support students in performing genre-related language operations. The teacher would facilitate tasks related to action, discursive, linguistic-discursive, and signification capacities. A school syllabus may benefit significantly from a genre-based approach due to the learning situations it may provide. Text production, for example, may be recursively improved. In developing an awareness of one genre, students may be able to re-articulate such knowledge in producing other genres (cf. Millar, 2011).

As for didactics of genres, a type of tool used for didactic transposition may be the pedagogical material in the form of didactic sequences (Dolz & Schneuwly, 1998). DS, which have been defined above as a group of systematically organized pedagogical language activities within a class project, involve: (1) specific communicative situations that the written production is directed to; (2) clear objectives; (3) appropriate content; (4) the use of authentic, socially-circulated texts as sample references for students; (5) effective text organization; and (6) meaningful activities that involve different types of interacting with and understanding language.

The Geneva School of genre studies (e.g., Bronckart, 2006; Schneuwly & Dolz, 1999) posits that the didactic sequence-based curricula (1) allows for adaptation based on the kinds of classes and diverse communicative situations students and teachers encounter collectively; (2) relates to the content and objectives of the educational system (e.g., official Curriculum Guidelines, school policies, and teachers' instructional materials); and (3) integrates activities which may provide curricular progression and skills integration.

Recommendations for an SDI genre-based approach

In terms of the key elements of the SDI genre-based approach, I have five key recommendations. First, the starting point of a didactic intervention should be based on a communicative situation with a clear objective to be achieved and a purposeful prompt for text production. Second, the diagnosis of student strengths should be conducted on the basis of an initial textual production to identify students' difficulties and plan specific activities. For example, conducting an early diagnosis can support students in overcoming issues related to the genre studied, the language capacities needed to be mastered, and students' socio-cultural profiles. Third, I recommend teachers and students use a checklist/control list to evaluate the main characteristics of the kind of text they are to produce and how they can best achieve their purpose and respond to the communicative situation they are involved with. Fourth, I recommend the final version of the text be produced in a way that makes it possible for students to act purposefully in that communicative situation and, ideally, achieve their goals. Last, make the texts available for circulation. Figure 1 represents an example of a didactic sequence and the use of evaluative procedures to assist the rewriting process.

Figure 1. Didactic device.

The theoretical framework underlying the SDI teaching and learning practices focuses on three key concepts, that is, language as a social action composed of different dimensions; language teaching/learning as a social activity mediated by tools (e.g., language, genres, didactic sequences); and language teaching as an interactive process of meaning construction.

Implications for the teaching of languages through didactic sequences

The use of didactic sequences in language teaching has a few key implications. As advocated by SDI language didactic scholars, the teaching of language is informed by the view of language as a social action, language teaching/learning as a social activity, and language teaching as an interactive process. Further, the teaching of language is concerned with providing tools and performance uptake (for a discussion of uptake, see Bawarshi, this volume; Freadman, 1994, 2002, this volume) in social practices to help students act in the world. This approach to teaching writing also involves stages of planning, writing, reviewing, rewriting and producing a final version (Hyland, 2003a, 2003b).[4]

In Brazil, professionals—including material designers, academics, lecturers, researchers and teachers—produce didactic sequences for various school levels, school subjects, and professional areas. To illustrate the ways didactic sequences can be developed and used to teach English as a foreign language in Brazil, I use a Material Design Project. This project involved in-service English teachers from the public sector of Modern Foreign Languages Centre of the State of Paraná (CELEM)[5] working under the guidance of teachers from three universities in Brazil, hired by the Secretariat of Education of Paraná as consultants to the Project.

In 2010, all foreign language (e.g., English, French and Spanish) teachers from the state sector of Paraná were invited to submit a genre-based unit to contribute to the Project of Material Design. The project coordinator analyzed the submitted genre-based units and selected ten English teachers, five French teachers, and eight Spanish teachers as material designers for this CELEM Project. From there, the materials were produced between March of 2010 and July of 2012 through group face-to-face seminars and individual long distance work. The first face-to-face group meeting focused on outlining theoretical assumptions and establishing guidelines for the production of the didactic material.

This project was informed by the understanding that foreign language is a human right, a condition for global citizenship as well as a tool to widen an individual's perception and awareness of linguistic diversity. Further, I view language as a system that constitutes identity construction, relationships and social practices, and as a means for education and critical literacy (Bazerman, 2013). As a part of the project, consultants contributed macro elements (to be covered and explored in the materials) and suggestions for the types of tasks and objectives for the activities. The macro elements underlying the didactic materials produced for CELEM included: (1)

social action and contextual features of a communicative situation; (2) texts/genres; (3) practical activities; (4) critical features of the context and the content; (5) text types; and (6) lexico-grammatical elements constituting the texts belonging to the genre in focus.

One DS that was developed as a result of this project focused on urban legends. *The Encyclopedia of Urban Legends* (Brunvand, 2001) defines urban legends as stories that

> abound in contemporary culture, both in 'folk' (oral-traditional) and in 'popular' (commercial media-disseminated) versions. In fact, the Internet has become a major conduit for the spread of once-strictly-oral urban legends, as well as a useful source of information about them. Urban legends have interested journalists and academic folklorists for decades, and many of these stories eventually found their way into literature, film, television, and even popular music, often with creative artistic variations and sometimes involving gross misunderstanding of their status as 'folklore'. (p. xxi)

Besides these reasons for a growing interest in this genre, one of our objectives to use them as a learning tool was to search for their origins and purposes for their transmission as well as provide grounds for students to produce comments, a survey or even new legends. Contemporary legends provide students with the opportunity to develop their aesthetic and literary capacities not only in relation to the consumption of popular culture but as active producers of such texts in a society that is densely mediated by popular culture and their embedded values. Below I present an example of the development of a DS on contemporary legends available on the Internet (Table 1).

Table 1

Macro elements underlying the didactic material produced for CELEM

	Macro elements
Social and contextual features of a communicative situation	The recognition of the usage of contemporary legends on the Internet and the possible motivations for their creation and circulation.
Genre	Contemporary legends
Practical activity	Production of an oral or written version of a local contemporary legend
Critical aspects of context and content	The relation between fun and fear; consequences and beliefs involving the spreading of contemporary legends
Text types	The typical narrative structure (orientation, complication, resolution, final situation, possible evaluation) (see Bronckart, 1999) and possible variations
Lexico-grammatical features constituting the texts belonging to the genre in focus	Lexical choices to introduce the theme and the characters, to present the plot, time adverbials, past tenses and vocabulary of senses

As we can see from Table 1, the scope of macro elements ranged from socio-cultural aspects to specific language resources and formats of organization. The aforementioned macro elements also correspond to particular types of knowledge intended to be built in order for the development of language capacities. Table 2 presents the main activities proposed for the development of each type of language capacity expected to be developed by the students.

Table 2

Language capacities and the main types of corresponding activities

Language capacities	Main activities
Signification	discussing genre as a cultural, socio-historical artifact; discussing the genre's underlying ideologies; reflecting on the meanings made by the students based on their previous experiences; discussing the macro context; thinking critically
Action	exploring the micro situation of the production of the related texts; focusing on the micro context; thinking critically
Discursive	exploring the content organization; reflecting on multimodality; thinking critically
Linguistic-discursive	exploring language resources; referring to lexico-grammatical features (e.g., cohesion, coherence, verb tenses, vocabulary, pronunciation); thinking critically

Based on Tables 1 and 2, the consultants also produced guidelines, suggesting compulsory content to be explored and objectives to be achieved with the activities proposed. Table 3 presents the guidelines, showing what instruction the in-service-teachers (material designers) received to guide their production.

Table 3

Content and objectives of the activities

Content	Objective(s) of the activities
1. a. Previous knowledge about the situation of the production of the genre as well as the theme	Finding out about communicative situations/ contexts
b. Initial Text Production	Working on text production
2. Initial contact with the genre	Reflecting on the genre
a. Activities aiming at exploring the context of production (who produced the text, for whom, what for, when, etc.)	Reflecting on the context
b. Questions on text comprehension	Reflecting on the content
c. Discussions to anticipate discursive aspects (general text organization etc)	Reflecting on the organization
d. Discussions to anticipate linguistic-discursive features	Reflecting on language
3. Activities to explore discursive features	Working on text organization
4. Activities on linguistic-discursive features	Reflecting on the language
5. Text Production	Working on text production
6. Self-assessment or peer evaluation of oral and written production	Evaluating using the checklist, editing and rewriting
7. Final production - rewriting the text	Producing a final text and making it available for circulation

As can be seen from Table 3, the guidelines cover the types of activities related to the different language capacities. They also promote studying and reflecting on different language dimensions while using an instructional approach based on the concept of language use as social practice. I must also mention that text production is integrated throughout the didactic sequence, including the initial textual production, rewritten drafts, and final versions. As a part of the approach, the process of rewriting can be aided by the use of the checklist, which relates the characteristics being studied (e.g., if the text is organized argumentatively or narratively depending on the genre) to different language capacities. Table 4 illustrates the checklist created for students to use when analyzing their text production in the DS on contemporary legends, in order to be able to produce their last version of the text.

Table 4

Text production checklist for the contemporary legends DS

Prompt	Yes	No	Partially
1. I fulfilled the objective(s) of scaring or entertaining or warning people			
2. I organized the content in a narrative form by setting the scene, introducing the characters, presenting a complication, showing the resolution and concluding with an ending.			
3. I used local references to make my text sound closer to my local reality.			
4. I used vocabulary of senses and adjectives to describe places and people.			
5. I used the past tense and time adverbials.			
6. I managed to make the evaluation/ message clear.			
7. I used other resources like images and/ or sounds.			

Moreover, the collective production of didactic material, as in the Materials Design Project, provides in-service-teachers with an opportunity to construct knowledge in the areas of didactic context, foreign/additional language understanding, language use, evaluation, methodology, research on genres (e.g., language, texts, students skills), theories, practice, literacy, and procedures for teaching. Tomlinson (2003) remarks, "focusing on materials development is the most effective way of . . . helping language education professionals to articulate and develop the skills which they need to apply these theories to practice." (p. 460).

Final Remarks

This chapter has focused on the Brazilian genre-based approach rooted in the theory of socio-discursive interactionism. This chapter has also introduced the framework underlying the didactic sequences for the teaching of languages, including foreign/additional languages. Whenever we use language, we create ways to act in the world through discourse, and, in turn, reproduce and transform it. Primary and secondary school is, of course, the formal locus of intervention providing students with tools to act in the world in a more conscious way. Students do this by developing the necessary language capacities (Cristovão & Nascimento, 2006). This chapter has described Brazilian educational policy guidelines, which position genre as a key teaching concept and SDI as a possible framework for language didactics. To illustrate this, I have described the materials development process used by in-service foreign language teachers in the state of Paraná, Brazil. Much like the experience of Pereira, Aleixo, Cardoso and Graça (2010) in Portugal has demonstrated, the didactic sequence has proved to be a pedagogical approach that contributes both to individual and collective improvement.[6]

References

Anjos-Santos, L.M., Lanferndini, P.A.F., & Cristovão, V.L.L. (2011). Dos saberes para ensinar aos saberes didatizados: uma análise da concepção de sequência didática segundo o ISD e sua reconcepção na Revista Nova Escola. [From knowledge to teach to didactized knowledge: an analysis of the notion of didactic sequence according to the SDI and its reconfiguration by the New School Journal]. *Linguagem em (Dis)curso*, [Language in (Dis)course], *11*(2), 377-400.

Araújo, A. D. (2009). Mapping genre research in Brazil. In C. Bazerman, R. Krut, K. Lunsford, S. McLeod, S. Null, P. Rogers, & A. Stansell (Eds), *Traditions of Writing Research*. London: Routledge.

Bakhtin, M. (1992). Estética da criação verbal. [An aesthetics of verbal creation]. (M. E. G. G. Pereira, Trans.). São Paulo: Martins Fontes.

Bawarshi, A.S., & Reiff, M.J. (2010). *Genre: An introduction to history, theory, research, and pedagogy*. Indiana: Parlor Press.

Bazerman, C. (1988). *Shaping written knowledge: The genre and activity of the experimental article in science* (p. 59). Madison: University of Wisconsin Press.

Bazerman, C. (1994). Systems of genre and the enactment of social intentions. In A. Freedman & P. Medway (Ed.), *Genre and the new rhetoric*. (pp. 79-101). London, Bristol: Talyor & Francis.

Bazerman, C. (2013). *A Rhetoric of Literate Action: Literate Action Volume 1*. Perspectives on Writing. Fort Collins, Colorado: The WAC Clearinghouse and Parlor Press.

Brasil Ministério da Educação. (1996) *Lei de Diretrizes e Bases da Educação Brasileira*. [Law of Guidelines and Basis for National Education]. Brasília: Ministério da Educação.

Brasil Secretaria Da Educação Fundamental. (1997). *Parâmetros Curriculares Nacionais: Introdução aos Parâmetros Curriculares Nacionais* [National Curricular Parameters: Introduction to the National Curricular Parameters]. Brasília: Ministério da Educação.

Brasil Secretaria Da Educação Fundamental. (1998). *Parâmetros curriculares nacionais: Terceiro e quarto ciclos do ensino fundamental: Língua estrangeira*. [National Curricular Parameters: Third and fourth cycles of primary school: Foreign language.] Brasília: Ministério da Educação.

Bronckart, J.-P. (1995). Theories of action, speech, natural language, and discourse. In J.V. Wertsch, P. del Rio, & A. Alvarez (Eds.), *Sociocultural studies of mind*. (pp. 75-91) Cambridge: Cambridge University Press.

Bronckart, J.-P. (1996). Units of analysis in psychology and their interpretation: Social interactionism or logical interactionism? In A. Tryphon & J. Vonèche (Eds.), *Piaget-Vygotsky: The social genesis of thought*. (pp. 85-106) New York:Erlbaum, Taylor & Francis.

Bronckart, J-P. (1999). *Atividade de linguagem, textos e discurso: por um interacionismo sócio-discursivo* [Language activity, texts and discourse: towards socio-discursive interactionism]. São Paulo: EDUC.

Bronckart, J-P. (2006). *Atividade de linguagem, discurso e desenvolvimento humano*. [Language activity, discourse and human development]. Campinas: Mercado de Letras.

Bronckart, J-P. (2011). *The language system at the heart of the systems that make up the human being*. Plenary Session at the International Systemic Functional Congress, Faculty of Letters, University of Lisbon, Portugal. Video.

Bronckart, J-P., Clémence, A., Schneuwly, B., & Schurmans, M-N. (1996). Manifesto: Reshaping humanities and social sciences: A Vygostkian perspective. *Swiss Journal of Psychology, 55* (2/3), 74-83.

Brunvand, J. H. (2001). *Encyclopedia of urban legends*. ABC-CLIO, California.

Cristovão, V.L.L., & Nascimento, E.L. (2006). Gêneros textuais e ensino: contribuições do interacionismo sóciodiscursivo. [Text Genre and teaching: contributions of the socio discursive interactionism] In A.M. Karwoski, B. Gaydeczka, & K.S. Britto (Eds.), *Gêneros textuais: Reflexões e ensino*. [Text Genre: Reflections and teaching]. (pp. 37-59). 2ª ed. Rio de Janeiro: Lucerna.

Cristovão, V.L.L., & Stutz, L. (2011). Sequências didáticas: semelhanças e especificidades no contexto francófono como L1 e no contexto brasileiro como LE. [Didactic Sequences: similarities and specificities in the Francophone context as L1 and in the Brazilian context as FL.] In P.T.C. Szundy, et al. (Eds.), *Linguística Aplicada e sociedade: Ensino e aprendizagem de línguas no contexto brasileiro*. [Applied Linguistics and society: Teaching and learning of languages in Brazilian context]. (pp. 17-40). Campinas, SP: Pontes Editores.

Cristovão, V.L.L. (2013). *Para uma expansão do conceito de capacidade de linguagem.* [For the expansion of the concept of language capacities] In L. Bueno, M. A. P. T. Lopes & V. L. L. Cristovão (Eds.), *Gêneros Textuais e Formação Inicial: uma homenagem à Malu Matencio.* [Text Genres and Pre-Service Education: a Tribute to Malu Matencio]. (pp. 357-383). Campinas, SP: Mercado de Letras

Dolz, J., & Schneuwly, B. (1998). *Pour un enseignement de l'oral. Initiation aux genres formels à l'école.* [Towards the teaching of oral. Introduction to formal genres at school.] Paris: ESF ÉDITEUR.

Dolz, J., Pasquier, A., & Bronckart, J.P. (1993). L'acquisition des discours: émergence d'une compétence ou apprentissage de capacités langagières diverses? [The acquisition of discourse: raising of a competence or learning diverse language capacities?] *Etudes de Linguistique appliquée, 92,* 23-37.

Freedman, A., & Medway, P. (Eds.). (2003). *Genre and the New Rhetoric.* Taylor & Francis.

Hyland, K. (2003a). *Second language writing.* Cambridge, UK, Cambridge University Press.

Hyland, K. (2003b). Genre-based pedagogies: A social response to process. *Journal of Second Language Writing, 12*(1), 17-29.

Hyon, S. (1996). Genre in three traditions: implications for ESL. *TESOL Quarterly, 30*(4), 693-722.

Millar, D. (2011). Promoting genre awareness in the EFL classroom. *English Teaching Forum, 2,* 2-15.

Miller, C. R. (1984). Genre as social action. *Quarterly Journal of Speech, 70*(2), 151-167.

Motta-Roth, D. (2008). Análise crítica de gêneros : contribuições para o ensino e a pesquisa de linguagem. [Critical Genre Analysis: Contributions to language teaching and research.] *D.E.L.T.A., 24*(3), 341-383.

Motta-Roth, D. & Heberle, V. M. (2015). A short cartography of genre studies in Brazil. *Journal of English for Academic Purposes.* doi: 10.1016/j.jeap.2015.05.006

Murray, D. (1972). Teach writing as process not product. *The Leaflet,* 11–14.

Pereira, L.A., Aleixo, C., Cardoso, I., & Graça, L. (2010). The teaching and learning of writing in Portugal: The case of a research group. In C. Bazerman, R. Krut, K. Lunsford, S. Macleod, S. Null, P. Rogers, & A. Stansell (Eds.), *Traditions of writing research.* (Pp. 58-70). New York: Routledge.

Schneuwly, B. (1994). Contradiction and Development: Vygotsky and Paedology. *European Journal of Psychology of Education, 9*(4), 281-291.

Schneuwly, B., & Dolz, J. (1999). Os gêneros escolares: das práticas de linguagem aos objetos de ensino. [The school genres: from language practices to teaching objects.]. *Revista Brasileira de Educação, 11*, 5-16.

Tomlinson, B. (2003). *Developing Materials for language teaching.* London: Continuum.

EndNotes

[1] Founded in 2002, the research group, Language and Education, was coordinated by the author of this article.

[2] In 2011, students from the 6th to 9th grade studying English or Spanish (as a compulsory foreign language taught at school level) received didactic material from MEC to mediate their learning process. In 2012, the same occurred at the high school level.

[3] Despite the usual meaning of the word "capacity," which refers to an innate ability an individual possesses, SDI has used the term "capacity" to denote the skills an individual needs to learn socio-culturally in order to produce and use language.

[4] An editor's note: this approach to teaching writing is known among Anglophone teachers and researchers as the process approach (e.g., Murray, 1972).

[5] The Centro de Línguas Estrangeiras Modernas do Estado do Paraná [Center of Modern Foreign Languages of the state of Paraná] offers free extracurricular foreign language courses to the local community in the public schools of Paraná.

[6] I would like to thank Natasha Artemeva, Janna Klostermann and Lucas Moreira dos Anjos Santos for the critical reading and the corrections suggested. Any misunderstanding, though, is of my entire fault.

Chapter 18

The Traps and Trappings of Genre Theory[1]

Anne Freadman

The University of Melbourne (Australia)

> ...most rules are liable to be altered by the nature of
> the case, circumstances of time and place, and hard
> necessity itself.
>
> – Quintilian (1920/1989, II, xiii, 2)

Since approximately 1990 ...ah! But I'm getting ahead of myself. As Bawarshi opens his book on *Genre and the Invention of the Writer* (2003) with a reflexion on "beginnings," so shall I. This is no mere imitation, but an acknowledgement that we begin by taking our place in a continuing conversation, that beginnings are generic. How one starts indicates not only the topic, but the genre of writing one is undertaking. Since 1990, then, the opening gambit of books and articles on genre has shown a remarkable regularity: they announce a "new conception of genre" (Devitt, 1993, p. 573), "a radical reconception of genre" (Coe, Lingard & Teslenko, 2002; cf. Bawarshi [2000] for whom it is "dramatic" [p. 335]), or a "newly emerging field in genre studies" (Freedman & Medway, 1994, p. 1). The "crux of the new genre theories" (Coe & Freedman, 1998, p. 41) requires explaining, because the development being signaled is variously a decade (Hyland, 2007, p. 148), 15, 20, or 30 years old (Bawarshi & Reiff, 2010, p. 3).

The reference point of these openings—broadly, the 1980s—dates the renewal, or rediscovery of genre to the period which saw, first, the publication in English of two key works by Bakhtin (1981,1986), and the publication of an article by Miller (1994) widely deemed "seminal" or "groundbreaking."[2] Alongside these, a second motivating factor is evident: this is the work of the "Sydney School" in which, through the decade of the 1980s and beyond, Halliday's systemic functionalist model of language and discourse was developed for the purposes of literacy instruction. Kress (1987), writing within this paradigm, considers that genre is "now" firmly established in educational debates:

> Now that genre is firmly on the agenda of educational debate, the focus of theoretical concern has moved to other, further questions. These are predominantly of a political/pedagogical and a linguistic/formal kind. (p. 35)

In stark contrast with the announcements of "radical reconceptualization" of genre, Kress implies in this passage that no further work is required on the theory of genre. The post-1990 proclamation of newness thus refers to a nascent debate concerning theories of genre put forward to contest the systemic functionalist work. Reid (1987) points to this in the introduction to his collection, *The Place of Genre in Learning: Current Debates*, in which the careful dialectical arrangement of chapters is designed to stage a polemical conversation.[3] The Introduction to Freedman and Medway (1994) shows a reorientation of this polemic: where Reid is at pains to discover common ground between the participants in the debate, Freedman and Medway—while acknowledging that there is "considerable overlap"—are concerned to unravel "implicit differences in theorizing" (p. 9) between systemic functional linguistics (SFL) and new rhetorical work, which display, they argue, "fundamentally different conceptions of genre" (p. 10). These two decades of debate culminated in a restatement of Reid's hope: in July 2012, the "Rethinking Genre" conference was held at Carleton University, two of whose objectives were to "create a dialogue" and to "explore possible convergences" among the three major "traditions" of genre studies.[4]

Notwithstanding the assumption that the genre theory that matters is a mere pup, we are told elsewhere that there exists a much older tradition of genre theory, but that its aims and conceptual apparatus, not to mention its assumptions, are radically discontinuous with current work. Thus:

> Our reconception will require releasing old notions of genre as form and text type and embracing new notions of genre as dynamic patterning of human experience ... (Devitt, 1993, p. 573)

> Traditional definitions of genre focused on textual regularities. In traditional literary studies the genres— sonnet, tragedy, ode, etc.— were defined by conventions of form and content. (Freedman & Medway, 1994, p. 1)

> Until the late 1980s . . . [genre] seemed to be an arhetorical prestige term reserved largely for literature. (Coe & Freedman, 1998, p. 41)

I could add Berkenkotter (2009, p. 10) and Giltrow and Stein (2009, p. 8). With the notable exception of Devitt who seeks "integration" (Devitt, 2000), business cannot be done with this older tradition because, by and large, it is identified with literature. The rationale for this is formulated by Swales (1990), who, seeking a definition of genre and relying principally on the concept of social purpose, argues that literature is the exception:

> There remain, of course, some genres for which purpose is unsuited as a primary criterion. Poetic genres are an obvious example . . . Poems, and other genres whose appeal may lie in the verbal pleasure they give, can thus be separately characterized by the fact that they defy ascription of communicative purpose. (p. 47)

This assessment is probably misplaced even for the Western tradition. The trouble arises, I think, from the homogenizing force of the category "literature," but this is a field of genres; purpose is evident once we differentiate genres within it. "Literature" has acquired its unity in the proclamation of futility only since the 19th century. Besides, is pleasure private, a- or anti-social? Surely not. Like epideictic rhetoric in the ancient world, the pleasure afforded by the arts is instrumental in community formation, though the communities effected and affected by it be plural, heterogeneous, and constantly changing.[5]

I have strayed from "beginnings:" let me return to whence I came. The claim to newness—to a "[break] with older, traditional notions of genre" (Devitt, 2004, p. 3) and to a more or less sharp contrast between the traditional and the contemporary—is a modernist gesture. It doubles the equivalent move in literary studies during the 1970s from the aesthetic to the social and from text to context. No longer contemplating forms, we engage with the significance of genre for "people's lives" (p. 1), "highly articulated social systems" (Bazerman, 1994, p. 79), or "communicative social spaces" that constitute who we are on any occasion (Bazerman, 2002, p. 13). As against "romantically individualistic concepts of writing," "the new theories of genre" focus on "writing as social process" (Coe & Freedman, 1998, p. 41). I remark in passing that modernist gestures traditionally attract postmodern challenges. Nevertheless, my challenge is not post-modern, but "post-structural," for reasons that will become clear. More modestly, it is a simple challenge addressed to some of the work on genre with which I am most in sympathy, that is, the new rhetorical account that has burgeoned since the 1990s.

When Reid introduced his collection in 1987, he rather cheekily remarked that the regularities apparent in the published writings of the systemic functionalist school of genre theory indicated that those writings were generic. By pointing out the regularity of the beginnings in writings from the "North American" movement in genre theory, I do likewise. But let me make something quite clear: by pointing out that the openings to research publications from this quarter are generic, I am by no means suggesting that their assertions concerning the history of genre research in writing pedagogy are in any way false. I am drawing attention to the *force* acquired by this assertion in its generic setting. That force goes to an issue in disciplinary politics: this is a discursive act that purports to found a paradigm. And like any foundation narrative, it rests on an overthrow of its enemies and a forgetting of its ancestral roots. In what follows, I shall not be addressing or characterizing theoretical enemies, but I shall be retrieving ancient rhetoric in the figure of

Quintilian the Schoolmaster, who wrote the first—and longest-serving—systematic curriculum for writing for special purposes, for rhetoric and composition all based in the notion of genre.[6] Writing and composition teachers were urged to do just this by Clark, who opens his 1957 book by writing that his book is "about teaching," written for teachers, in the hope that "the modern reader . . . will be enabled better to understand and to evaluate modern discussions of the same problems in the teaching of rhetoric" (p. 4).

In histories, or uptakes, of ancient rhetoric it is often overlooked that "genre" is not merely a topic, as at Quintilian (1920/1989, III, iv); it is the presupposition of all rhetorical treatises. It was simply inconceivable that there might be a generalized rhetoric outside of the settings specified by the kinds.[7] Indeed, until the 20th century, accounts of language did not abstract from its uses.[8] The structuralist revolution introduced this conception in its postulates of a synchronic system. The discipline of linguistics, and with it, applied linguistics, protests that it is no longer structuralist, and in many ways this is true. However, the presupposition of synchrony, and sometimes of system, persists as a silent underpinning of a great deal of its work. This is self-evidently so in systemic functionalist linguistics, but it is also *de facto* true of any theory that thinks of genre as the "shaping" of form to suit a "surrounding" context. Applied linguistics, particularly in second language (L2) settings, is also *de facto* synchronic in its focus on contemporary usage. As against this presupposition of synchrony, genre is always diachronic (see Bazerman's histories of professional genres [e.g., 1988], and Miller and Shepherd's [2004] study of the blog as examples); the pattern was set by Aristotle (2007), whose *Poetics* pays particular attention to the evolution of tragedy to its then present form. Any genre, then, alludes to, or carries, the history of its own practice, and rhetoric is always a study of practice. The pedagogical question of a rhetorical account of genre is how to bring a student to take her or his place in this history—to discover how something has been done before, and how it can be adapted to particular needs as occasions arise. This is quite different from the applied linguistics question: how to teach a language through its uses. For these reasons, I suggest, the recourse to rhetoric is *ipso facto* post-structuralist. My challenge to my colleagues drives this home, insofar as it relies on winkling out structuralist—systemic or synchronic—presuppositions that threaten to undermine the force of their work. This will be so wherever rhetoric is used as an alternative term to "use," "parole," "performance" or "discourse" when these are understood as complementary to "system," "langue," or "competence." It will equally be so where rhetorical accounts of genre rely on an implicitly synchronic sociology. Again, this is self-evidently the case for systemic-functionalist linguistics.

Part of what has been forgotten in "traditional" conceptions of genre is the way rhetoric and poetics did business together in the cultivation of the arts of reading and writing (see Quintilian, 1920/1989, II & X). So—being the literary kind of bird that I am—I shall also pursue my challenge through the deployment of literary analysis with its characteristic ways of going about its work. This means that I will dwell carefully on an individual text—here called a "discursive event"[9]—and ask how its rhetoric works out in the details of its conduct.[10] Together with ancient rhetoric, I use modern literary analysis to raise some questions without in the least supposing that I have generalizable answers for those questions. These questions have to do, first, with the consequences of the assertion that I shall presently attempt to justify that genre theory is a genre; and, secondly, with the consequences for genre theory of the close description of the practice of a single discursive event.

"Genre Theory Is A Genre"

One of the most important books about genre to appear in the past 30 years is Lyotard's *Le Différend* (1983). The book is not exactly "on" genre, but on the ethical and political implications of taking genre seriously. However, Lyotard rejected the possibility of a "general theory" of genre, and he was very forthright in his rejection of structuralism. To grasp the import of this position, we need to understand that he means by "theory" a predictive generalization, and by structuralism, a synchronic system.[11] In the *Differend*, for example, he proclaims polemically that there is no such thing as a language, except as the object of a special theory. His view of genre is similar, but there are generic practices, the pragmatic and political upshot of which can—indeed must imperatively—be described.

Lyotard's rejection of a general theory of genre arises from the aporia he discerns for philosophy. It is subject to "Russell's aporia" (Lyotard, 1983, p. 200). For Lyotard, philosophy is the genre that denies its own status as a genre. In order to write his book—consisting of philosophical reflexions—he has to give up this denial, hence limiting the scope of what he can say, and about what. I discussed the problem this raises in my book on Peirce's semiotics (Freadman, 2004). There, I set Lyotard alongside James:

> Lyotard's point is that conversations . . . take place within genres . . . there is no language in which they could take place, no genre, however abstract, however theoretical, however universal its pretensions, that would do the trick. There is no temple on the hill, to use William James' metaphor for a certain style of philosophy, where we could avoid what Quintilian calls "the heat and dust of the forum". . .

> Whether in the form of a general linguistics, a semiotics, or indeed a rhetoric of genre, the problem remains the same. There can be no theory of the sign outside the local conditions of the genre within which it is posited and whose purposes it serves. Equally, however, there can be no general theory of genre. (p.p. xxx- xxxi)

What follows from this proclamation? My answer regarding sign theory, and now, regarding genre, relies on Lyotard's distinction between "special" and "general" theories: whereas a general theory claims universal applicability, a special theory serves the needs of particular domains. The concept of genre, I argue, is an instrument devised and honed differently to do particular kinds of work.

This point is implicit throughout Hyon's (1996) survey of the "three traditions" she discerns in work on genre "in the past 15 years" (p. 693). The three schools—English for Specific Purposes (ESP), SFL, and the new rhetoric—have "developed genre-based pedagogy in different directions and with different goals and educational sites in mind" (p. 698). Two specific contrasts invite examination. The first bears on the privileged examples of genre submitted to analysis, and the second, on the pedagogy derived from the definitions and their exemplification. With regard to the examples, to what counts as "a" genre, ESP instruction and new rhetorical instruction work with "fairly specialized" genres, whereas SFL work privileges "elemental" genres, that is, "much broader categories such as procedure, report, explanation, discussion, exposition, recount and narrative" (p. 715; also see Martin, this volume). This approach claims to generalize over all genres. However, this level of generality is such as to all but eliminate contextual exigence, and certainly does not lend itself to ethnomethodological or discursive-cultural description or analysis (p. 712). We find a parallel debate between Quintilian and Cicero:

> There is . . . a dispute as to whether there are three kinds or more. But it is quite certain that all the most eminent authorities among ancient writers following Aristotle . . . have been content with the threefold division. Still, a feeble attempt has been made by certain Greeks and by Cicero in his De Oratore, to prove that there are not merely more than three, but that the number of kinds is almost past calculation: and this view has almost been thrust down our throats by the greatest authority of our own times. Indeed, if we place the task of praise and denunciation in the third division, on what kind of oratory are we to consider ourselves to be employed, when we complain, console, pacify, excite, terrify, encourage, instruct, explain obscurities, narrate, plead for mercy, thank, congratulate, reproach, abuse, describe, command, retract, express our desires and opinions, to mention no other of the many possibilities? As an adherent of the older view, I must ask for indulgence and must enquire what was the reason that led earlier writers to restrict a subject of such variety to such narrow bounds. (Quintilian, 1920/1989, III, iv, 1–4)

The answer provided by Quintilian is that "all other species fall under these three genera: you will not find one in which we have not to praise or blame, to advise or dissuade, to drive home or refute a charge, while conciliation, narration, proof, exaggeration, extenuation, and the moulding of the minds of the audience by exciting or allaying their passions are common to all three kinds of oratory" (III, iv, 15–16). I remark that if this is so, then Quintilian's answer must rest on the matter of curricular convenience, as does that, I have no doubt, of the SFL paradigm. The more or less open or closed sets of genres brought into various kinds of classrooms are determined by pragmatic considerations. It is important for us not to confuse a classificatory decision made for pedagogical purposes with a claim as to the ontology of genres.[12]

Notice that Cicero's list as reported by Quintilian cannot bring itself to an end. It is potentially unmanageable. This is in the nature of lists, of course, and Quintilian's art at this point consists in performing this unmanageability in order to demonstrate the neatness of the three-fold division that he prefers. But the "constitutive infinity of lists" (Eco, 2009) makes a significant point in the following two examples:

> Review the multiplicity of language-games in the following examples, and in others:
>
> Giving orders, and obeying them—
>
> Describing the appearance of an object, or its measurements—
>
> Constructing an object from a description (a drawing)—
>
> Reporting an event—
>
> Speculating about an event—
>
> Forming and testing a hypothesis—
>
> Presenting the results of an experiment in tables and diagrams—
>
> Making up a story, and reading it—
>
> Play-acting—
>
> Singing catches—
>
> Guessing riddles—
>
> Making a joke; telling it—

Solving a problem in practical arithmetic—

Translating from one language into another—

Asking, thanking, cursing, greeting, praying.

-It is interesting to compare the multiplicity of the tools in language and of the ways they are used, the multiplicity of word and sentence, with what logicians have said about the structure of language. (Including the author of the *Tractatus Logico-Philosophicus*.) (Wittgenstein, 1967, p. 23)

Bakhtin (1986) agrees, insisting on "the extreme heterogeneity of speech genres:"

The wealth and diversity of speech genres are boundless because the various possibilities of human activity are inexhaustible, and because each sphere of human activity contains an entire repertoire of speech genres that differentiate and grow as the particular sphere develops and becomes more complex. (p. 61)

Neither Bakhtin nor Wittgenstein is theorizing genre for the purposes of a pedagogy; they are intervening into their own disciplines, Bakhtin into literary theory by contesting rigid classifications and by insisting on the imbrication of the literary genres in the broad field of discourse, and Wittgenstein into the philosophy of language, by contesting the homogeneity of its account of semantics. Both, moreover, stress the "forms of life" (Wittgenstein, 1967, p. 226) or the "spheres of activity" (Bakhtin, 1986, p. 62) that correct the decontextualized accounts of language to which they object. The fact that the infinity of their lists cannot be directly translated into a curriculum or a syllabus is of no moment. If we recognize the impossibility of a general taxonomy, then we do not ask if a given piece of writing belongs to the class of report, of recount, or of narrative according to a deductive application of *a priori* criteria; we ask the rhetorician's questions concerning what Lyotard calls the "stakes" of the genre, what the consequences are if it fails to accomplish its task in a specified functional framework.

And then we deal with (collections of) examples, choosing them in function of the precise teaching contexts in which we use them. ESP teaching, primary school literacy teaching, and tertiary level writing instruction are, we might say, the forms of life or spheres of activity that determine the generic status—the function and the uptake—of genre theory.

Let us return to Quintilian's objection to lists such as Cicero's, Bakhtin's and Wittgenstein's: they seem to be random, not based on firm criteria as to what is or is not a "genre," or a "language-game" (Wittgenstein, 1967, p. 23), or a way of "using language" (Bakhtin, 1986, p. 60). Accordingly, Miller (1994) tries to tidy up. Acknowledging that taxonomy is impossible, because "genres change, evolve, and decay" (Miller, 1994, p. 31), and that the number of genres current in any society is "indeterminate," she sets out five criteria on which some groupings count as genres and others do not. Genre is an open set, but criteria for membership can be stated. There are three major ways in which a "genre claim" (p. 37) can fail:

> First, there may fail to be significant substantive or formal similarities . . . Second, there may be inadequate consideration of all the elements in recurrent rhetorical situations ... The third way a genre claim may fail is if there is no pragmatic component, no way to understand the genre as a social action. (p. 37)[13]

I note that Miller's specification, too, has a pragmatic pedagogic rationale. Her discipline is rhetoric, defined by its competence to analyze and to teach the place of the language arts in the conduct of social affairs.

So I reiterate my point, that genre theory is an instrument, honed for particular purposes, where these purposes are a function of the institutional parameters that group together students and define their needs. This may count as a warning that a general theory of genre—this ambition—may well sacrifice its pragmatic purchase on the tasks at hand.

My argument holds not only for the use of genre in recent work in language and writing pedagogies, but also for the ancient tradition. If we distinguish between poetics and rhetoric, it is because a different account of genre is useful for each of the two broad fields of genres, to their place as defined by the way in which culture was represented in the ancient world. The poetic genres were those differentiated by two sets of criteria—their compositional and prosodic forms on the one hand, and their audience on the other (located, in Roman poetics, on the scale of public to personal); the rhetorical genres were differentiated on the basis of the kind of work they accomplished in public affairs: hence a difference between "formal" and "strategic" criteria. Their places in the education system—one in the first stage of training, the second in more advanced work—were complementary (Clark, 1957, p. ix).[14] Within rhetoric, differences of opinion—and hence of curricular focus—between the more philosophical and the more pragmatic of theorists and practitioners bear more than a passing resemblance to the debates between the liberal arts focus of the New Rhetoric and the pragmatic focus of ESP.[15] The debate, here, is between Isocrates and Plato:

> To Plato the sophists were dishonest in their pretensions to wisdom and their claim that they could teach wisdom. Moreover, they were ignoble because they were devoted to the practical arts of getting on in the world instead of to the disinterested search for abstract and theoretical truth. (Clark, 1957, p. 6)

> [For Isocrates] only a few [students] will become champions in the contests of oratory, but all will claim some intellectual training, all will become better educated. (p. 9)

Efforts have been made in the new rhetoric to bring these two objectives together. Devitt (2009) quotes Bazerman to the effect that "rhetorical awareness is . . . critical," leading to "enlightened participation" rather than disengaged distance (pp. 337–338).

Since this is not a treatise in ancient rhetoric, I rest my case: the schools of thought, or paradigms, evident in genre theory since its beginnings are governed by the pragmatics of its uptake, its use, by professionals in specifiable settings. The overarching, "disinterested" theory sought by Plato is subject to this rule within the context of the contest for control of education, whether in ancient Greece, in post-reformation Europe, or between the proponents of liberal education and the proponents of professional skills teaching. Does this mean that genre theory is a single genre evolving over the centuries or that it is a collection of genres, each governed by institutional parameters? The answer does not matter a great deal, but I note a remarkable continuity in the contentious issues across two millennia, wherever "genre" is taken up for discussion: classification and the selection of examples, normativity and the place of imitation, the inclusion or exclusion of literature from the arts of discourse, and the relation between precept and practice. I draw the inference, first, that it is the debates themselves that characterize the genre of genre theory, and, secondly, that the concept of genre lends itself to instrumentalization in a variety of other genres.[16] These are often educational, but include policy-making on issues such as censorship and in the regulation of broad-, tele-, and web-casting.

A further series of contrasts arising from Hyon's survey concerns the pedagogical upshot of the various paradigms of genre theory. Since these are generally explicit in both SFL and ESP, I will not dwell on them, merely remarking that the exemplification and classification issues discussed above correspond to decisions as to the needs of specified student groups. The "elemental" genres of SFL are not recognizable as genres in literary or rhetorical teaching. Hyon (1996) and Johns (2008) among others have rebuked the new rhetoricians for their failure to provide an account of genre directly translatable into the classroom. I suggest that what the rhetoricians bring to the debate is not a set of precepts about teaching so much as a way of thinking about genres, about how they organize our worlds, about how they make objects available for knowledge, and about how they make things happen. How genres work is the major focus of the rhetoric and poetics teachers, how to teach people to work genres is that of the language teachers, and what it is to work a genre is where those concerns meet. I suggest that the pedagogy of genre is an uptake of the analysis of genres whether the focus of that analysis be the networks of relations among them that organize a discourse community (Bazerman, 2004), the emergence of a genre and generalizations over its instances (Miller & Shepherd, 2004), or—being one of those scholars who merely study discourse, the literary sort, moreover—my modest attempts to describe the rhetoric of examples.

A Case Study

...the orator frequently prepares his audience for what is to come, dissembles and sets a trap for them and makes remarks at the opening of his speech which will not have their full force till the conclusion.

- Quintilian (1920/1989, X, I, 21)

My case is a televisual political interview. Like genre theory, the interview is a genre that can lend itself to a variety of purposes according to the institutional and media setting within which it is used. Its stakes vary in function in these settings, or to put it another way, both the uptakes that propel its development as well as the uptake the completed interview secures—in whom, and with what consequences—are sometimes widely different. Police interviews, job interviews, psychiatric interviews, celebrity interviews, ethnographic interviews, and political interviews have in common their participant structure, but differ according to the kind of information elicited and for what use. Most significantly for my purposes, political interviews are a collaborative genre with each participant seeking to pursue some agenda, but they are also for this reason agonistic in that the two agendas compete, and it is likely that one will win while the other will be discredited or disempowered. We will see the conflict of two agendas played out.[17]

Theo Theophanous was a member of the Australian State of Victoria's Legislative Assembly. He presents himself as the incarnation of the "little Aussie battler:" from a modest immigrant background, he had worked his way into the political class, representing a constituency for the left-leaning Labor Party. But he had been charged with committing rape in his Parliamentary office. The interview was conducted immediately following his formal exoneration at a preliminary hearing, which ruled that the plaintiff was unreliable and that he had no case to answer. It went to air on a Friday evening. His agenda was to publicize his innocence as widely as possible. However, the presenter, Heather Ewart, true to her calling, was more concerned with his political future.[18]

At the start, the interviewer goes over the charge and the hearings, as if she too had to test her interviewee's innocence.

Theophanous does not object; he responds as if he is happy to be able to restate his innocence in a more public forum. That is clear in his response:

> EWART: The police felt that it was serious enough to charge you with rape. Has this forever damaged your reputation?
>
> THEOPHANOUS: Look, I think that's a matter for people to consider. Obviously it's had an enormous impact on me. I think that in the scheme of things, people will have to also consider all of the things that I have done and my achievements.

But it is also at this point that he gives Ewart an opening to change the direction of the interview: "people will have to also consider all of the things that I have done and my achievements." Why exactly?

The answer is that a second context has come into play. The political party to which Theophanous belonged had been deliberating on his future: it was time for him to go. Whether or not he was acquitted in the judicial context, he was effectively to be condemned in this political context. The presenter's introductory remarks have alluded to this situation in a sentence ("the political future of former State Cabinet Minister Theo Theophanous hangs in the balance tonight, after a magistrate this afternoon threw out a rape charge against him") whose logical inconsistency is blatant. The presenter leads into this topic quite explicitly: "where does this leave your political career?" and Theophanous allows the question (see Freadman, 2012b for supplementary data online, 10–12). However, he insists that the decision is his own, and that he will not be pushed into making it on television. At this point there ensues a struggle for control over the interview; it is marked by a disagreement over the appropriate class name for the event the two participants are involved in: "Is this a farewell? ...It is an interview."

Note that Ewart's question is motivated by an interpretation of Theophanous' preceding response, and that she justifies her interpretation on the basis of lower-order features: "That sounded like a farewell." It is a crucial point in the work I have been doing recently that "uptake" includes this metadiscursive, or meta-generic, level (Freadman, 2002). When we respond to an utterance or text, we take it as a certain genre. "Is that a threat or a promise?" we might ask, in order to respond "in kind." Of course, we may not ask explicitly, and we may misconstrue the act, in which case the dialogue may take a meta-discursive detour to renegotiate its bases.

Examining the "lower-order" features of the interview (these are not linguistic features, but topoi), we may note that Ewart's tactics at the beginning are characteristic of the forensic use of interviewing. She goes over the material of the trial, and attacks her witness with a further accusation; he responds accordingly, protesting his innocence. Then she moves to deliberative territory with a question concerning Theophanous' future. Theophanous wants this deliberation to take place in private; Ewart treats him as a politician, fair game for public scrutiny. His position throughout is defensive as evinced by the moments when he repeats his answers: "That is not true. That is not true. ... that is not true;" "I want to take the weekend to reflect on that. I want to reflect on it and think about it and consider it. ... I really want to think about it over the weekend;" "This is an interview. It's an interview. ... It's an interview." He then reverts to the original context: this is a "celebration" of his acquittal in which his own intention has been to use the public forum afforded him by the interview: "I need to know that in this community, if you have gone through a trial like this and you've come out the other end and you've been declared innocent that people will then treat you with the respect that you deserve, or the same respect that you had prior to this happening." He wants his reputation to be restored. The contest of the interview is then repeated in a contest over two words, "fight" and "trial." For Theophanous, the "trial" refers not only to the judicial scene, but to the moral order, and "fight" is what he has done throughout his life as an immigrant. His moral fortitude is what he wants to assert. Ewart, however, restricts "fight" to his relations with his party, and it is clear that he will lose. The end of the interview brings a certain narrative to a close: Theophanous "goes down fighting." The interview allows the image of the brave little battler at the same time as effecting his defeat, pre-empting the public announcement of his resignation.

The interview makes striking use of the three traditional genres of ancient rhetoric: if the interviewer has mimicked the trial at first, then grilled her interviewee on his decisions for the future, she has moved from forensic to deliberative mode. Her interviewee, in turn, has invoked the third genre, the epideictic, the rhetoric of praise and blame, in which reputations are at stake. However, there remain significant differences: first, using Austin's (1962) criterion of "felicity conditions," we must say that the interviewer does not occupy an institutional role in which she can properly conduct questioning that would establish guilt or innocence under law. Second, the deliberative genre, also, is determined by a dynamic of roles or functions. It is typically the genre of the political domain or of moral conflict, but Ewart is not in a position to offer advice. Indeed, Theophanous claims the right to deliberate with his family, taking their advice in private: a television interview is not the place where he will do so. Thirdly, the epideictic speech—"I come to bury Caesar, not to praise him"—used in funeral orations or at formal farewells, is not given by its subject: Theophanous asks for it, but he cannot have it here. The interview is structured by questions and answers, in which interviewer and interviewee vie with one another about the control of what is said.

None of the three kinds of rhetoric defines the purpose of the interview, how it acts in and on its situation. This is a political interview; its relation with political institutions is to interact with the players not merely to narrate their play or analyze it. It is for this reason that it is possible for political interviews to intervene directly in the relationships of the players and to alter their dynamics. Here, the journalist intervenes in the power play between the party heavyweights and the individual party member; potentially, she could have lent her weight to either side. If Theophanous accepts the question concerning his contact with witnesses (see Freadman, 2012b for supplementary data online, 4-6) it is because it works for him as an opportunity to assert his innocence. This is consistent with his turning of the questions towards the "celebration" and the general issue of his good reputation. He wants at least a weekend, poor man, during which this is who he is. Rehearsing his achievements is also part of this desire, but Ewart takes that rehearsal as the sign that his career is effectively at an end. The more Theophanous continues to recount his struggles and his achievements, the more he plays into her hands. Is this an interview or is it a farewell? The binary form of this question is not helpful because it elicits an answer in terms of the intention of one or the other combatant. The appropriate question focuses on the act perpetrated by the interview as such:

what did the interview do by doing what it did? The answer is that it changed the situation in which it took place.

Implications

Discursive Event and Genre

It has become increasingly evident that no text or discursive event is merely the instantiation of a genre (see Coutinho & Miranda, 2009; Prior, 2009; Puschmann, 2009), but it is at the level of the specific event that social action can be observed. Without taking this fact into account, we risk giving very general, and sometimes, trivial accounts of the purpose or function of a genre.[19]

This has a bearing on the criteria for counting a grouping as a genre proposed by Miller (1994). I recall the point at which her account appears to slip: "The third way a genre claim may fail is if there is no pragmatic component, no way to understand the *genre* [emphasis added] as a social action" (p. 37). I have noted that genre is social action *ex hypothesi*, and that Miller clearly means that grouping texts under a name without regard for social action is not sufficient for sustaining a genre claim. This criterion runs counter to the conclusion I draw from my example, which is that the action is accomplished by the discursive event, and cannot be predicted from the genre of the interview. The interview, here, may provide the necessary conditions for this action, but by no means its sufficient conditions. However, if what Miller envisages is "a kind of social action," then the issue of typification extends from kinds of text through kinds of situation, to kinds of action, thus demonstrating one of the traps of genre theory, which is to resort to introducing new levels of classification whenever a new factor is introduced. It also tends to render Miller's criteria synchronic.

We need to ask whether the "pragmatic component" is a component of all the texts that instantiate a genre such that each fits the "recurrent rhetorical situation." If so, the pragmatic component must be a formal feature. If, on the other hand, a text acts differently when taken as a member of one group or of another, then the pragmatic component is an effect of the grouping, and the action of a given discursive event will depend upon what genre it is taken as (cf. Lotman, 1977).[20] In my example, Ewart's "that sounded like a farewell," makes the genre assignment and its function a matter of form; Theophanous' riposte "it's an interview" relies on the recurrent situation.[21]

Situation and Context

Genre is the context in which what is said has the force that it has. This context is made up of the speech situation and the historical occasion of the discursive event, and it is usual in genre theory to distinguish these two aspects as, respectively, the recurrent and typified, and the particular or contingent. However, no classification of speech situations is easier to achieve than a classification of genres, and for the same reason. This is shown in my example: the television current affairs show is defined as a recurrent situation by network programming decisions and identified by its time-slot, but it is also itself a genre. This recurrent situation conditions the structural relation of the political interview with the events of the day.

However, the conceptual basis for distinguishing the recurrent from the contingent is flawed. Following Derrida's (1980, 1988) argument concerning citation and recitation, or repetition and difference, the "same," repeated on different occasions, does not remain the same. Derrida makes this point in examining the effects of repeating the same string of signifiers, showing how they change their force in the process. It is for this reason *inter alia* that the distinction between text and context cannot be maintained.[22] Indeed, I suggest, it runs counter to what I take to be the central tenet of any theory of genre, that genre just is the nexus of text and context. Any formulation of this nexus that resolves it into "form" and "function," or "linguistic choices" and "surrounding context" has the effect of undermining the postulate of that nexus. Thus, for example, Flowerdew (2011) reduces Hyon's (1996) three paradigms to two, which he describes as "linguistic" and "contextual" (p. 121).

A homologous problem attends the requirement to delineate a recurrent, typified, speech situation in order to situate a genre. This recurrent situation would occur against a larger, more nebulous or undefined context. Yet, the wanted distinction between the speech situation and the context in which an instance of the genre is mobilized can only be drawn if we conceive of history as lying outside of the sociological or institutional determinants of speech. Since both the recurrent and the contingent are governed by time, the most we can say is that there may well be various temporal series and hence speeds involved (that of political events; that of the development and adaptation of television to its changing function in relation to new media; that of the training and recruitment of journalists, changes in programme scheduling and so on), but we cannot keep these watertight, uncontaminated from one another. This point goes to a poststructuralist critique of sociology, or ethnography, insofar as they rest on the presupposition of synchronic systems, and of new rhetorical work insofar as it rests on the social sciences.

In my analysis, the context that is affected as a result of this event is defined not only as a single "occasion" but as a sequence of events in time and across a variety of temporal sequences. Bakhtin calls this a responsive chain. The context goes back as far as we find it useful to take it (hence the "memory" of discursive events [see Freadman, 2002]); and its effects may not be apparent for some time in the future. The meaning, or force, of the text happens eventually: Theophanous did, in fact, take the weekend to announce his resignation, but the game was up by 8 p.m. on Friday night: as a result of the interview, there was no way he could decide not to resign. In my example, the relation between the judicial context and the political context makes no sense unless we understand the judicial context as providing an opportune moment for the party decision to play out. The interview brings the two together. The rhetorical term *kairos* names this opportunity, which is the pointy end of context.[23]

I insist on the need to take full account of time in our account of genre: the dynamics of the interchange itself, the temporal context of its action (whether this be instantaneous or over a period), and the temporal complexity of a larger conception of history. In my example, Bakhtin's notion of "responsive chains" shows not only that the generic nature of the interchange is modified by its own conduct, but also that the discursive event is responsive to what precedes it and has its effect after its close. Only on some basis such as this can we understand the action of discourse. Sometimes what we thought was "the" genre at the outset ceases to be the relevant description down the track. Theophanous started his interview with Ewart as an active member of parliament; he ended it as an ex-politician. The interview occasioned his eclipse from public life.[24]

Uptake

It is the topic of uptake that makes the crucial difference between "discursive event" and genre. Mastery of the genre may mean little more than the ability to avoid making egregious errors in controlled environments; skill, too, is needed. However, the exercise of skill is highly constrained by the interventions of our co-participants; this is the point of my analogy with the game of tennis (Freadman, 1987/1994). Hence we find that Quintilian (1920/1989) "consider[s] [the circumstances of the case] as much from [his] opponent's point of view as from [his] own" (VII, 4). This brings us back to pedagogy, and the importance of stressing "strategy" over "form." But the acquisition of a strategic rhetorical intelligence needs a lot more than the deductive or explicit teaching from models, because "the professor of rhetoric lays down rules, while the orator gives a practical demonstration" (Quintilian, X, I, 15). There are, writes Quintilian, general rules for "invention," the discovery of the issues raised by the subject matter of a speech, but there are no such rules for "arrangement," *dispositio*, composition (VII, 4). This is because "all imitation is artificial and moulded to a purpose which was not that of the original orator" (X, II, 11–12); he is concerned with the adaptation of good practice to a new purpose. The pairing of imitation and adaptation is key to understanding the pedagogical methods of the ancients, but beyond this, there is the acquisition of the art of eloquence. "Our present task," Quintilian writes at the beginning of Book X, "is to consider how our athlete who has learnt all the technique of his art from his trainer, is to be prepared by actual practice for the contests in which he will have to engage" (X, 4). For this the student must acquire "a certain store of resources, to be employed whenever they may be required" (X, i, 5); "we shall attain our aim by reading and listening to the best writers and orators" (X, i, 8), because "we need to do more than consider our own special task" (X, i, 9). Vast reading across the full range of rhetorical and poetic genres is what he recommends, reading with "the critical faculty" engaged (X, I, 17), and careful study of the ways and means of the masters (X, I, 19).

Calculating one's rhetoric in order to maximize the chances of securing a desirable uptake is one thing; "returning serve" in order to turn the play to one's advantage is another. They are complementary parts of the rhetorical enterprise, in whatever game we are playing. But it must be said that we never just serve: in our beginnings are our uptakes.

I hesitate to call this a "debate," but there can be found in the literature a disagreement concerning the uptake of my previous work. On the one hand, Bawarshi and Reiff (2010) write: "As Freadman is careful to note, uptake does not depend on causation but on *selection*" (p. 86). On the other, in a very thoughtful application, Emmons (2009) argues that my account minimizes the agency of real subjects (p. 152). Where Bawarshi and Reiff's reading points to the importance of skill, and hence invites pedagogical uptake, Emmons' critique leads her to distinguish discursive from generic uptake. This proposal preserves Miller's criterion, but at the cost of introducing a further level of classification. I doubt if we need the distinction. However "generic," any uptake is (part of) a discursive event intricated in unnumbered historical series. My concern has been to pursue the implications of uptake further into its effects and consequences for genre theory in general.

Uptake arises at every point—in the use of theory in teaching, in the exchanges that make up an interview, and in the long-term consequences of a discursive event. No genre can do more than predict the kind of uptake that would make it happy, and no speaker or writer can completely secure an uptake. This is partly because no discursive event is a pure example of any genre, and partly because of the unpredictable historical complexity of its moment and its ongoing action. We cannot, I think, reflect productively on uptake outside of discussions of genre, nor is it productive to theorize the action of genres without uptake. Genre is destabilized by uptake even as it asserts its powers. Trapped out as a theory that pins down language use, genre theory is like a rabbit trap, designed to catch its quarry. But nimble, fast-talking rabbits have been known to get away.

References

Aristotle. (2007). *Poetics*. Project Gutenberg. Retrieved from https://www.gutenberg.org/files/1974/1974-h/1974-h.htm.

Austin, J. L. 1962. *How to do things with words*. London: Oxford University Press.

Bakhtin, M. M. (1981). *The dialogic imagination* (C. Emerson & M. Holquist, Trans.). Austin, TX: University of Texas Press.

Bakhtin, M. M. (1986). *Speech genres and other late essays* (V. W. McGee, Trans.). Austin, TX: University of Texas Press.

Bawarshi, A. S. (2000). The genre function. *College English, 62*(3), 335–360.

Bawarshi, A. S. (2003). *Genre and the invention of the writer: Reconsidering the place of invention in composition*. Logan, UT: Utah State University Press.

Bawarshi, A., & Reiff, M. J. (2010). *Genre: An introduction to history, theory, research, and pedagogy*. Anderson, SC: Parlor Press.

Bazerman, C. (1988). *Shaping written knowledge: The genre and activity of the experimental article in science*. Madison, WI: University of Wisconsin Press.

Bazerman, C. (1994). Systems of genres and the enactment of social intentions. In A. Freedman & P. Medway (Eds.), *Genre and the new rhetoric* (pp. 67-86). London, UK: Taylor and Francis.

Bazerman, C. (2002). Genre and identity: Citizenship in the age of the internet and the age of global capitalism. In R. Coe, L. Lingard & T. Teslenko (Eds.), *The rhetoric and ideology of genre: Strategies for stability and change* (pp. 13-37). Creskill, NJ: Hampton Press.

Bazerman, C. (2004). Speech acts, genres, and activity systems: How texts organize activity and people. In C. Bazerman & P. Prior (Eds.), *What writing does and how it does it: An introduction to analyzing texts and textual practices* (pp. 309-339). Mahwah, NJ: Lawrence Erlbaum.

Bazerman, C., Bonini, A., & Figueiredo, D. (Eds.). (2009). *Genre in a changing world*. West Lafayette, IN: Parlor Press.

Berkenkotter, C. (2009). A case for historical "wide-angle" genre analysis: A personal retrospective. *Ibérica: Journal of the European Association of Language for Specific Purposes, 18*, 9–21.

de Certeau, M. (1984). *The practice of everyday life.* Berkeley, CA: University of California Press.

Clark, D. L. (1957). *Rhetoric in Greco-Roman education.* New York: Columbia University Press.

Coe, R. M., & Freedman, A. (1998). Genre theory: Australian and North American approaches. In M. L. Kennedy (Ed.), *Theorizing composition: A critical sourcebook of theory and scholarship in contemporary composition studies* (pp. 136-147). Westport, CT: Greenwood.

Coe, R., Lingard, L., & Teslenko, T. (Eds.). (2002). *The rhetoric and ideology of genre: Strategies for stability and change.* Creskill, NJ: Hampton Press.

Coutinho, M. A., & Miranda, F. (2009). To describe genres: Problems and strategies. In C. Bazerman, A. Bonini & D. Figueiredo (Eds.), *Genre in a changing world* (pp. 35-55). West Lafayette, IN: Parlor Press.

Derrida, J. (1980). The law of genre (A. Ronell, Trans.). *Critical Inquiry, 7*(1), 55–81.

Derrida, J. (1987). *The truth in painting* (G. Bennington & I. McLeod, Trans.). Chicago, IL: University of Chicago Press. (Original work published 1978.)

Derrida, J. (1988). *Limited Inc.* Evanston, IL: Northwestern University Press.

Devitt, A. (1993). Generalizing about genre: New conceptions of an old concept. *College Composition and Communication, 44,* 573–86.

Devitt, A. (2000). Integrating rhetorical and literary theories of genre. *College English, 62,* 696–718.

Devitt, A. (2004). *Writing genres.* Carbondale, IL: Southern Illinois University Press.

Devitt, A. (2009). Teaching critical genre awareness. In C. Bazerman, A. Bonini & D. Figueiredo (Eds.), *Genre in a changing world* (pp. 337-351). West Lafayette, IN: Parlor Press.

Eco, U. (2009). *The infinity of lists.* Bloomsbury, UK: MacLehose Press.

Emmons, K. (2009). Uptake and the biomedical subject. In C. Bazerman, A. Bonini & D. Figueiredo (Eds.), *Genre in a changing world* (pp. 134-157). West Lafayette, IN: Parlor Press.

Flowerdew, J. (2011). Reconciling approaches to genre analysis in ESP. In D. Belcher, A. M. Johns & B. Paltridge (Eds.), *New directions in*

English for specific purposes research (pp. 119-144). Ann Arbor, MI: University of Michigan Press.

Freadman, A. (1986). Le genre humain: A classification. In M. C. Spencer (Ed.), *Australian Journal of French Studies,* Special Number on prose fiction, *23*(3), 309-74.

Freadman, A. (1992). Ramus against Quintilian. *Southern Review,* 25(3), 252-267.

Freadman, A. (1994). Anyone for tennis? In A. Freedman & P. Medway (Eds.), *Genre and the new rhetoric* (pp. 43-66). London, UK: Taylor and Francis. (Original work published 1987.)

Freadman, A. (2002). Uptake. In R. Coe, L. Lingard & T. Teslenko (Eds.), *The rhetoric and ideology of genre: Strategies for stability and change* (pp. 39-53). Creskill, NJ: Hampton Press.

Freadman, A. (2004). *The machinery of talk: Charles Peirce and the sign hypothesis.* Redwood City, CA: Stanford University Press.

Freadman, A. (2012a). *The livres-souvenirs of Colette: Genre and the telling of time.* Oxford, UK: Legenda.

Freadman, A. (2012b). The traps and trappings of genre theory. *Applied Linguistics,* 33(5), 544- 563.

Freadman, A., & Macdonald, A. (1992). *What is this thing called "genre"? Four essays in the semiotics of genre.* Queensland, Australia: Boombana Publications.

Freedman, A., & Medway, P. (Eds.). (1994). *Genre and the new rhetoric.* London, UK: Taylor and Francis.

Giltrow, J., & Stein, D. (2009). *Genres in the internet.* Amsterdam: John Benjamins.

Hyland, K. (2007). Genre pedagogy: Language, literacy and L2 writing instruction. *Journal of Second Language Writing, 16,* 148-64.

Hyon, S. (1996). Genre in three traditions: Implications for ESL. *TESOL Quarterly, 30*(4), 693-722.

Johns, A. (2008). Genre awareness for the novice academic student: An ongoing quest. *Language Teaching, 41*(2), 237-252.

Kress, G. (1987). Genre in a social theory of language: A reply to John Dixon. In I. Reid (Ed.), *The place of genre in learning: Current debates* (pp. 25-45). Geelong, Australia: Deakin University Press.

Lotman, J. M. (1977). Problems in the typology of texts. In D. Lucid (Ed.), *Soviet semiotics: An anthology.* Baltimore, MD: Johns Hopkins University Press, ch. 12, 119-124.

Lyotard, J.F. 1983. *Le Differend.* Paris: Les editions de minuit. Translation: The Differend: Phrases in Dispute, trans. G. Van Den Abbeele. University of Minnesota Press, 1988.

Miller, C. 1994(1986). 'Genre as social action' in A. Freedman and P. Medway, ch. 2 (eds): *Genre and the New Rhetoric.* Taylor and Francis.

Miller, C., & Shepherd, D. (2004). Blogging as social action: A genre analysis of the weblog. In L. Gurak, S. Antonijevic, L. Johnson, C. Ratliff & J. Reyman (Eds.), *Into the blogosphere: Rhetoric, community, and culture of weblogs.* University of Minnesota Libraries. Retrieved from http://blog.lib.umn.edu/blogosphere/blogging_as_social_action.html.

Muecke, F. (2013). The invention of satire: A paradigmatic case? In T. D. Papanghelis, S. J. Harrison & S. Frangoulidis (Eds.), *Generic interfaces in Latin literature: Encounters, interactions and transformations* (pp. 283-295). Berlin: de Gruyter.

Platt, P. G. (1999). Shakespeare and rhetorical culture. In D. S. Kastan (Ed.), *A companion to Shakespeare* (pp. 277-296). Oxford, UK: Blackwell.

Prior, P. (2009). From speech genres to mediated multimodal genre systems: Bakhtin, Voloshinov, and the question of writing. In C. Bazerman, A. Bonini & D. Figueiredo (Eds.), *Genre in a changing world* (pp. 17-34). West Lafayette, IN: Parlor Press.

Puschmann, C. (2009). Lies at Wal-Mart: Style and the subversion of genre in the "Life at Wal-Mart" blog. In J. Giltrow & D. Stein (Eds.), *Genres in the internet* (pp. 49-84). Amsterdam: John Benjamins.

Quintilian. (1989). *Institutio oratoria* (H. E. Butler, Trans.). Cambridge, MA: Harvard University Press. (Original work published 1920)

Reid, I. (1987). A generic frame for debates about genre. In I. Reid (Ed.), *The place of genre in learning: Current debates* (pp. 1-8). Geelong, Australia: Deakin University Press.

Swales, J. (1990). *Genre analysis: English in academic and research settings.* Cambridge: Cambridge University Press.

Vickers, B. (1988). *In defence of rhetoric.* Oxford: Clarendon Press.

Wittgenstein, L. (1967). *Philosophical investigations* (G. E. M. Anscombe, Trans.). Oxford: Blackwell.

EndNotes

1   I am grateful to the organizers of the AAAL Atlanta 2010 for providing an opportunity to air an early version of this material, and to my colleagues at the University of Queensland, School of Languages and Comparative Cultural Studies for their helpful discussion on a second occasion. Most particularly, I thank Andrew Munro for his acute remarks. The analysis of the example was first shaped in a senior seminar on genre at the University of Melbourne, shortly after the broadcast in July 2009. The chapter originally appeared in *Applied Linguistics*, *33*(5), 544-563 (2012) by Oxford University Press. It is reproduced here by permission of Oxford University Press.

2   In ESP work, the starting point is more likely to be Swales 1990, e.g. Flowerdew (2011, p. 119). Other variants take a more personal view of the history, e.g., Johns (2008, p. 237).

3   Reid's collection is primarily concerned with the debate between the process writing movement and SFL accounts of genre, but the former is used as a springboard for other contestations of the latter.

4   http://www3.carleton.ca/genre2012.

5   I thank Rob McCormack for an illuminating conversation about epideictic rhetoric. See http://robmccormack. cgpublisher.com/.

6   The forgetting of the presupposition of genre in ancient rhetoric has an intricate and complex history (see Vickers, 1988), part of which can be attributed to the work of Ramus. I sought to delineate the shape of Ramus' excision of genre in Freadman (1992).

7   The fact that the tropes and figures could travel across generic domains does not deny the generic presupposition of rhetoric, but rather goes to confirm it.

8   Much of the philological tradition, including lexicography, continued to presuppose genre; however, the focus on discrete sound and morphological changes in historical linguistics did not.

9   Note that by using the term "discursive event," I am avoiding the pitfalls of the terms "utterance" and "text" discerned by Prior (2009). I return to this issue below.

10 My first foray into genre theory is a literary investigation into the class-name "prose fiction" (Freadman, 1986); my most recent is also a literary study (Freadman, 2012a). Within "genre circles" my work is usually associated with rhetorical theories (see Freedman & Medway, 1994; Coe et al., 2002; Bawarshi & Reiff, 2010).

11 Thus, with de Certeau (1984), he rejects the claim of linguistics, that even the fullest description of a linguistic system could predict use.

12 This point extrapolates from Lotman's (1977) view that "the social function

of a text determines its typological classification" and "a change in the function of a text gives it a new semantics and new syntax" (p.120).

13   Note that the last of these three criteria is apparently self-contradictory: if there is no pragmatic component, there is "no way to understand the genre as a social action." But genre is social action *ex hypothesi*. I shall return to this issue below.

14   For authorization of my assertion concerning the work done in collaboration between poetics and rhetoric, see Clark (1957, pp. 17–19), Muecke (2013), Platt (1999), and Quintilian (1989) on "style."

15   Clark (1957) points out that the tradition of locating rhetoric among the liberal arts goes back to Cicero (p. 12).

16   I recall Bakhtin's (1986) helpful observation that the simple genres can be integrated into the more complex genres.

17   These agendas are part of the "pre-writing" of the interview (see Prior, 2009, p. 28), another part being the preparatory planning by the production and camera staff.

18   The full transcript of the interview along with other supplementary material can be found at *Applied Linguistics* online.

19   I desist from singling out any example, preferring a pastiche: "when we characterize the function of the users' manual accompanying a piece of technology, it is obviously to teach the user how to use it."

20   Note, however, that Lotman's distinction between the writer's and the reader's grouping is restricted to literature.

21   See Freadman and Macdonald (1992) for an opposite example, where the question "is this a trial or a television interview?" posed by the interviewee, has the effect of disempowering the interviewer when he answers that it is an interview.

22   Derrida's (1978/1987) argument concerning the problematics of the frame is crucial in this regard.

23   "Kairos" refers to the timing either of a discursive event, or of any move that constitutes it. Miller and Shepherd (2002) use it also to refer to the time at which a new genre emerges.

24   Note that I do not write 'caused,' which would be an unsustainable claim.

Index

A

abstraction, conceptual categories and, 170f, 172

Academe magazine, 381

academic discourses

genre-based study of. *see* genre-based study of academic university discourse

university genres and, 116–120, 117f

Academic Literacies movement (New London School), 12, 96

action capacities, 409–410

activity theory, 85–86

Adam, J-M., 104

Adamzik, K., 255

Adequacy Program, 406

Affirm phase, 314t, 315, 324t–325t, 325

agents, bloggers as, 283

Alexander, R., 328

Almeida, M.C., 107

Altbach, Philip G., 381

Amabile, T.M., 343

American Sociological Review, 11

Analysing Genre: Language Use in Professional Contexts (Bhatia), 18–22

analysis

curriculum genre, 310–322, 313f, 314t, 316t, 318t–319t

familiar genre, 370–371

needs, 366–367

opinion editorial, 371–374, 379–381, 383–384

See also Critical Discourse Analysis (CDA); Critical Genre Analysis (CGA); Dialogic Discourse Analysis; genre analysis, discourse and

Anthology genre, 127

Applegarth, R., 192

Applied Linguistics, 96, 102, 106, 107

appropriation, of generic resources, 23–25, 24f

Araújo, A.D., 404

arbitration, colonization of, 20

Argumenty i fakty (Arguments and Facts) article, 288

Aristotle, 154, 162, 168, 429

Artemeva, N., 197, 198

Article of the Future project (Elsevier), 227, 236t, 237, 240–243, 241f

asymmetry, knowledge, 230–231, 244

attention, in Detailed Reading, 327f

Audiovisual Thinking journal, 226, 235, 236t, 238–240

Austin, J.L., 441

Australia, genre-based pedagogy in, 31–68

author-induced challenges, 238–240

autobiographical recounts, 58–66

B

background knowledge, 369
Baillie, J., 162
Bain, K., 364
Bakhtin, M.M.
contesting classifications, 434–435
on creativity, 57
genre and language, 403
influencing Brazilian genre studies, 99, 101
on responsive chain, 444
seminal works of, 426
social media and, 278–279, 281–282
on social speech, 87
use of repertoire, 256
Bakhtinian theory, Brazilian genre studies and, 101–103, 103t
Bakhtiniana—Revista de Estudos do Discurso, 102
Balak, B., 142
Basic Science disciplines, 130–133, 130f–132f
Bastian, Heather, 394–395
Bateman, J.A., 232
Bawarshi, A.S.
on beginnings, 425
on Brazilian model, 12, 95, 97, 404
on genre as actualizer, 281
on genre history, 33
on genre uptake, 186–201, 398, 446
on writing contexts, 367–368
Bazerman, Charles, 80–90, 187–188, 283, 409, 436
Beebee, T.O., 188
Benesch, S., 9–10
Bereiter, C., 230–231
Berkenkotter, C., 10, 156
Bernstein, B.
on culture as resource, 302–303
on curriculum, 277
on knowledge types, 304
on pedagogic practice, 310–312, 317, 321–322

Bhatia, Vijay K., 17–26, 118, 343, 366–367
biology, 157–160, 166–167, 167f
Biotechnology genres, 132–133, 132f
Bitzer, Lloyd F., 156, 175
The Blind Watchmaker (Dawkins), 173
block quotations, 8, 11
blog, Alexei Navalny's
adjusting genres to needs, 290–292
genre and identity in, 287–290
introduction to, 284–285
use of discourse in, 285–287
blogs
communication and, 277–278
development of, 275–276
dialogism and, 282–284
identity construction and, 279–281, 282
recontextualization in, 278–279
Blommaert, J., 359
Bolshevik political propaganda, 290–291
Bonini, A., 100
Bourdieu, P, 84, 344
Bowler, P.J., 159–160
Brazilian Conference on Genre Studies, 407
Brazilian genre studies
Bakhtinian influence on, 101–103, 103t
classifying, 100–101, 100t–101t
critical/complex/ecological views in, 103–107
emergence of, 97–98
four traditions of, 404–405
history of initiatives in, 405–408
introduction to, 95–96
notable research, 99
summary remarks, 107–108
synthesis in, 12, 96–97
Bronckart, J-P., 12, 97, 408–409, 410
Brooks, K., 390
Brunetière, Ferdinand, 164
Buffon, Comte de, 158–159
Burdiles, G., 138–139, 143
Burke, K., 175

recommendations for, 411–412, 412f
SDI and, 408–409
summary remarks, 419
teaching languages and, 412–419, 415t–418t
The Differend (Lyotard), 430
Direct phase, in Detailed Reading, 324t–325t, 325
direct quotes, 8, 11
disciplinary genres, 255
Disciplinary Text (DT) genre, 125–126, 126f, 127–129, 142, 143
discourse
function of, 276–277
genre analysis and, 18–22, 21f
in Navalny's blog, 285–287
discourse genre
research study of. *see* genre-based study of academic university discourse
three-dimensional, 118–119, 118f
discourse semantics
in modelling context of SFL, 35, 35f
register variables and, 315–316, 316t
discovery learning, 320–321
discursive event, 442–443
diversity continuum of genres, 141–142, 141f
Dolz, J., 102
domain, system theory of creativity and, 343, 343f, 356
downward classification, 166–167, 167f
DT (Disciplinary Text) genre, 125–126, 126f, 127–129, 142, 143
Dual Admissions Program at SDSU, 380
Dubrow, H., 162
Duff, D., 162, 163–164

E

ecological view of genre, 106–107
Economics genres, 138–139, 138f
Edelman, G., 315

education
Brazilian initiatives in, 405–408
students as genre scholars. *see* ESL/EFL classroom approach to genre
university. *see* genre-based study of academic university discourse
EFL. *See* English as a Foreign Language (EFL)
Eggins, S., 34
Ekho Moskvy (*The Echo of Moscow*) radio station, 285
Elaborate phase, 314t, 315, 324t–325t, 325
Eliot, T.S., 386
Emerging Genres in New Media Environments (Miller & Kelly), 277
Emmons, K.K., 196, 446
emotion, in Detailed Reading, 327f
The Encyclopedia of Urban Legends (Brunvand), 414
Engberg, Jan, 225–246
Engeström, Y., 85–86
English as a Foreign Language (EFL). *See* ESL/EFL classroom approach to genre
English as a Second Language (ESL)
classroom approach. *see* ESL/EFL classroom approach to genre
Genre in three traditions and, 3, 4–5
English for Specific Purposes (ESP), 2, 3
as accommodationist, 12
genre analysis and, 18, 21
goals/contributions of, 366–367
in three traditions overview, 66–68
English Text (Martin), 53
environmental science research course. *See Research Methods*
environmental science class
epideictic genre of rhetoric, 441
ESL. *See* English as a Second Language (ESL)
ESL/EFL classroom approach to genre

historical linguistics, 160–162, 166–167, 167f
historical materialism, 192
historical treaty genre, 214–220
History genres, 134–135, 134f
Hjelmslev, L., 39–43
Hobbs, P., 212–213
homely genres, 369–371
Horace, 162
horizontal identities, 280
Hughes, J., 232–233
Hull, D.L., 166
human sciences, evolutionary thought in, 160–166
Humboldt, W.v., 252
Hyland, K., 353–354, 366
Hyon, S., 32–34, 104, 403, 431, 437
1996 paper by, 2–13

I

Ibáñez, R., 123, 135, 143
Ibérica journal, 12
Identify phase, 314t, 315, 324t–325t, 325
identity in social media. *See* genre and identity in social media
Iedema, R., 54
illocutionary acts, 190
image-flow, 233, 236t, 238
immediate action context in language didactics, 410
independent construction stage, 304
indigenous people, genre writing pedagogy and, 58–65
indigenous people, genre writing pedagogy for, 58–65
individual, system theory of creativity and, 343, 343f, 356–357
Individual Rewriting genre, in *Reading to Learn* program, 330
inference
genre and, 220–221

in legal genres, 212–214
pragmatics and, 207–210
problem of, 210–212
treaty genre and, 214–220
innovation in genre. *See* genre innovation
institutional practices, 20–21, 21f
instructional practice, 311, 317
intentionalism, 212–213, 216–217
interactivity, new supplementary knowledge and, 241–242
interdiscursivity, 23–25, 24f
inter-modal realisation of genre, 39, 39f
internal activity theory, 86
Interpretation stage, 46–47, 54
intertextuality, 24, 87, 255, 262
interview genre, 438–442
investigative journalism, 288
invisible pedagogy, 321
irony, 285–286
Isocrates, 436

J

Jakubowicz, A., 225, 245–246
James, William, 431
Jarratt, S.C., 196
Jewitt, C., 228–229
Johns, A.M.
citational details and, 8–10
combining practice and theory, 386, 388, 392
genre for classrooms, 437
on students as genre scholars, 364–375, 379–384
Joint Construction genre, 61f, 65, 304, 331–332, 331t
Joint Rewriting genre, 61f, 65, 329–330
Journal of Visual Experiments, 226
journalistic culture, genre profiles and, 264–266

Soviet jargon, 286
Spain, genre-based pedagogy in, 13
special theory, 431
species, concept of, 168, 172
specimens, as prototypes, 171–172
Sperber, D., 207–208, 210
Spinuzzi, C., 85–86, 191, 196
Starfield, S., 366
statutory interpretation, 212–214
story genres, 48–49, 48t, 50f–51f
Strong Hypothesis, 393
structuralist revolution, 429
students as genre scholars
ESP/RGS contributions, 366–368
introduction to, 364–366
opinion editorial analysis, 371–374, 379–381, 383–384
utilizing familiar genres, 369–371
writing genre comparison, 374, 382
Stutz, L., 410
Sullivan, Ruth, 212–214, 218
summary quotations, 8
supervenient perspective on language, 37–42, 38f–39f
supplementary knowledge, 231, 241–242
Swales, John M.
on Brazilian approach, 95, 96, 97
categorization of, 169
communicative purpose, 174
on defining genre, 427
definition of genre, 118
on *Genre in three traditions*, 1–13
on occluded genres, 191
Sydney School
criticism of label, 9
history of, 31–68, 426
knowledge exchange and, 333–334
knowledge genre and. *see* knowledge genres, pedagogy and
See also Systemic Functional Linguistics (SFL)
symbols, communication and, 88–89
Symonds, John Addington, 164

Symposium on Genre Studies (*Simpósio sobre Gêneros Textuais*), 98
synchronic variation, 156, 159–160
Systema Naturae (Linnaeus), 158, 167
Systemic Functional Linguistics (SFL), 2
approach to genre in, 301
genealogy of term, 300
Genre in three traditions and, 3, 5, 9
history of, 31–34
modelling context, see *under* modelling
modelling genre in, 34–37, 35f–36f
in three traditions overview, 66–68
See also Sydney School
systems theory, genre innovation and, 343, 343f

T

"Tagesschau" (SwissTV news show)
genre frequencies of, 258–260, 259f
genre profile of, 255–256
genre repertoire, 256–258, 257t
journalistic culture of, 264–265
serial/sequential clusters in, 262–263
talking points genre, 372
Tardy, Christine M., 339–360
Tauber, Juan, 339–341, 340f
TB genre. *See* Textbook (TB) genre
teaching/learning cycles, 60, 61f, 304, 412–413
teleology, evolutionary thought and, 173–178, 175f–176f
televisual political interview, 438–442
tenor
in curriculum genre, 311–312
modelling context and, 36–37, 36f, 39–40
personal recounts and, 47, 54
as register variables, 300–301
Teslenko, T., 390
TESOL Quarterly, 2, 3

Printed in the United States
By Bookmasters